# The Settle and Carlisle Railway

Patrick Stephens Limited, a member of the Haynes Publishing Group, has published authoritative, quality books for enthusiasts for more than 25 years. During that time the company has established a reputation as one of the world's leading publishers of books on aviation, maritime, military, model-making, motor cycling, motoring, motor racing, railway and railway modelling subjects. Readers or authors with suggestions for books they would like to see published are invited to write to: The Editorial Director, Patrick Stephens Limited, Sparkford, Nr Yeovil, Somerset, BA22 7JJ.

# The Settle and Carlisle Railway

A personal story of Britain's most spectacular main line

## O. S. NOCK

Patrick Stephens Limited

First published 1992


British Library Cataloguing in Publication Data
A catalogue record for this book is available from the British Library

ISBN 1-85260-327-5

Patrick Stephens Limited is a member of the
Haynes Publishing Group plc, Sparkford, Nr Yeovil, Somerset, BA22 7JJ.

Typeset in Great Britain by BPCC Techset Ltd., Exeter, Devon.
Printed in Great Britain by Butler & Tanner Ltd., Frome, Somerset.

# Contents

# Preface

I suppose it was no more than natural that as a lifelong railway enthusiast, an Old Boy of Giggleswick School, and an engineer whose early training and professional contacts were with some of the men who were very much engaged in locomotive testing on the London, Midland & Scottish Railway in the mid-1920s I should, early in life, have developed a fixation so far as the Settle and Carlisle railway was concerned. I sought secluded footpaths leading to the line; I cycled beside it, and in later years lost no opportunity of travelling on its trains. In my early days as a journalist I wrote chatty articles about the runs I had timed, and as my literary work developed and my studies of the science and practice of locomotive testing extended, many of my earlier books contained long chapters about the 'Settle and Carlisle'. Then, to crown all, came the opportunity to write a major book about it. It was to be no ordinary book, but a weighty tome covering the inception and the cross-currents that surrounded the initial project, the constructional problems and hazards and a very full account of its operation from the early days down to the present time. But at the time of the preliminary discussions, as a result of which my kind publishers awarded me the contract to write it, for some time it did indeed seem that it would prove an obituary notice into the bargain! Happily this threat has now been removed, for a considerable time, at any rate.

At the same time I felt that my own story should end with the notice of the reprieve. The controversy over the introduction of 'Sprinter' trains, the references to the line in some correspondence as "a fun railway" and the piece in *The Daily Telegraph* of 23rd July 1990 about the stealing of the station nameplates only serve to show by how much matters have changed. One could hardly have imagined the signalman at Hawes Junction in the early hours of Christmas Eve 1910 thinking that he worked for a "fun railway", still less so the drivers and firemen and the testing staff in the dynamometer car trial runs of 1923–5! And so far as the purloining of station name boards the vandals would have needed a pantechnicon to remove the pre-Grouping Midland Railway station names!

In writing a book covering more than a hundred years of railway history an author has necessarily to consult previous works on the same or allied subjects, and I am glad to acknowledge my indebtedness to F. S. Williams' classic book on the Midland Railway, to the writings of E. L. Ahrons on locomotive engineering and history, and to C. Rous-Marten on train running. Neither of these two latter were known to me personally, but of later exponents of the art of train timing, R. E. Charlewood and Cecil J. Allen I have the liveliest recollections, over many years. As a professional engineer I became acquainted first with E. L. Diamond, who was a pupil of Sir Henry Fowler on the Midland Railway, and later I became personally and delightfully associated with another of Sir Henry's pupils, Roland C. Bond, who eventually rose to the heights of

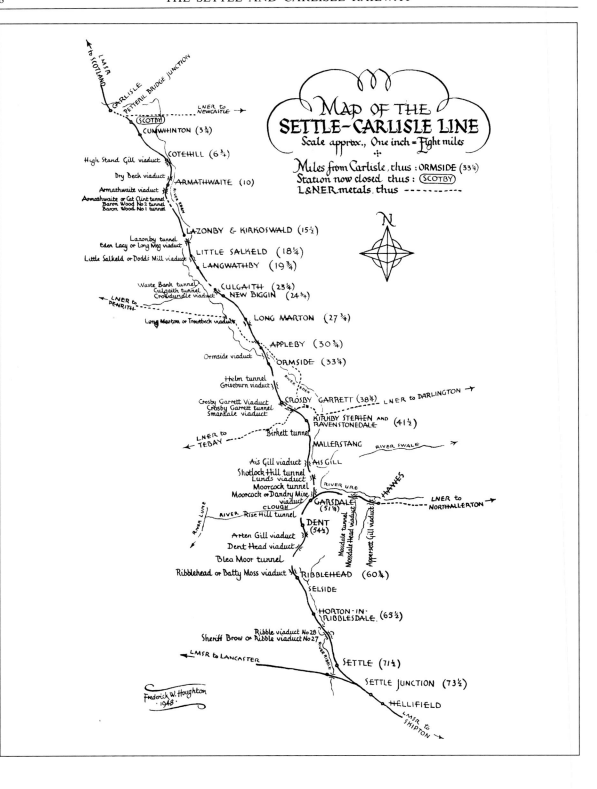

Deputy Chief Mechanical Engineer of the LMS, and still higher office under the Nationalised British Railways. Of those who furnished me with detailed logs of express train running over the line I am particularly indebted to the late Derek S. M. Barrie for a railway friendship lasting more than fifty years, and which, in his eventual eminent post of Chairman and General Manager of the Eastern and North Eastern Regions of British Railways, showed he had by no means lost the fascination of clocking the speed of trains by stop watch. Of the massive contribution to my pages by another high ranking railwayman Gerald J. Aston there is ample evidence in Chapter 13.

And what of the pictures? Norman Wilkinson is also an Old Boy of Giggleswick School, and as a skilled photographer he took many opportunities of driving from his home on Tyneside to his Alma Mater, and its district. During the Second World War I also had some correspondence with a photographer who then lived at Bingley; Hubert Foster by name. He took some pictures for me on my earliest post-war footplate trips, and also gave me some of his collection of lineside photographs on the Settle and Carlisle line, some of which I am proud to include in this book. After the war, with petrol rationing eventually waived, and the art of railway photography lifted at last from the traditional 'train-in-motion' technique to real pictures, the 'Settle and Carlisle' came into its own. Too late unfortunately to record the gargantuan dynamometer car trials carried out by British Railways in the 1950s.

Of the latter day master-hands some are no longer with us, but it is a privilege to be able to include in the book some superb examples of the work of Bishop Eric Treacy, Maurice Earley, Derek Cross and Ivo Peters, as well as many still very active and accomplished in their art. I am especially grateful to the Morrison's, Brian and Gavin, no relations, and living hundreds of miles apart, and David Eatwell for many beautiful pictures. But in a book of this kind many others have helped in a diversity of ways, and I should like to thank Paul Gribble and his wife Jenny for the part they have played, and lastly there is Linda Glyde. Her help in typing the manuscript, in transcribing the numerous tabulations from old and faded manuscripts, and not least for her frequent attendance at my home, since I am not nowadays able to drive myself is much appreciated.

O. S. Nock
Batheaston, 1992

# 1
# The Expanding Midland Railway

At its formation in 1844 The Midland Railway was essentially a provincial line, with its headquarters in Derby. Its longest constituent, the North Midland, extended to Leeds, while the Midland Counties ran southwards through Leicester to make a junction with the London & North Western at Rugby. The third of the three companies involved in the amalgamation of 1844 was the Birmingham & Derby. Years before then however the far-seeing men of Derby had begun to envisage their relatively local lines as the nucleus of a nationwide network, and with the opening of the York & North Midland Railway shortly before the completion of the North Midland itself, in 1840, it became possible to travel by train throughout from London to York, using the connection between the Midland Counties and the-then London & Birmingham Railway at Rugby. Indeed through carriages were being run from Euston to York from that very year.

The North Midlands of England had one staple product that was vital to the burgeoning prosperity of the entire British nation in mid- and later Victorian times — coal; and the Midland Railway was soon seeking every artery by which it could be conveyed to the centres of industry and commerce. It already had an outlet for

*The broad prospect of Ribblesdale, looking south from Giggleswick Scar. Settle Junction can be seen in the distance, with the 'little' North Western extending across the level ground to the right of the picture, Pendle Hill is on the sky-line.* (Norman Wilkinson)

*The original viaduct of the 'little' North Western line over the River Wenning in the approach to Clapham station, with Ingleborough towering up behind. (Engraving per F. S. Williams)*

the London traffic at Rugby, though relations with the London & North Western were at times a little less than friendly. To the south west the Birmingham & Gloucester Railway, since its opening in 1840, had been an ally of the Birmingham & Derby Junction, but at its southern end it had come up against the broad gauge bastion of the Bristol & Gloucester Railway, which the Great Western regarded as their protégée. Legend tells us that in no locality more than at Gloucester was the 'Battle of the Gauges' fought with greater physical inconvenience to passengers or greater damage to merchandise in the change between the gauges in the journey between Bristol and Birmingham. But in 1846 the Midland managed to secure control, and both the Bristol & Gloucester and the Birmingham & Gloucester were absorbed into the Midland Railway.

An outlet to the North West was provided by the opening of the first length of the Manchester, Buxton, Matlock & Midlands Junction Railway

in 1848 and completed in 1863. While this was not absorbed into the Midland Railway proper until 1871, Derby had been actively spreading its tentacles west of Manchester sometime before then by its acquiring a joint ownership in the Cheshire Lines Committee, which enabled its trains to run to Liverpool, and eventually, in 1884, to Southport. In the South, the construction of the short branch line from Mangotsfield to Bath in 1870 paved the way for the introduction of another interesting and profitable artery of traffic from the central nucleus to the South Coast. The arrival of the Midland Railway in Bath sparked off a very enterprising but financially calamitous venture by the Somerset & Dorset Railway of extending their hitherto wholly rural line over the crest of the Mendip hills from Evercreech Junction to Bath. Considering the nature of the intervening terrain the work was done with remarkable speed, but the Somerset & Dorset Railway went bankrupt as a result. Eventually, in 1875, the line was leased jointly to the

Midland and the London & South Western, with the working arrangement that the Midland should provide the locomotives and run the trains, while the LSWR maintained the track and provided the signalling. Thus the tentacles of Derby reached Bournemouth.

At an early date in Midland Railway history plans had been laid for a southward extension of the old Midland Counties line from a junction at Wigston running through Market Harborough, and Kettering to Bedford, and thence to make connection with the newly opened Great Northern Railway at Hitchin. This promised an alternative route to London, to that via Rugby and the London & North Western Railway. But financial strictures delayed this project, and it was not until 1857 that the line was opened and that Midland trains, exercising running powers over the Great Northern line from Hitchin, began working into King's Cross. It was far from a good workable arrangement. There was congestion on the line, and the primitive signalling arrangements of that time led to a monumental crash of three freight trains, two GN, one Midland, in the middle of Welwyn North Tunnel. The Midland had obviously to build their own line into London, and this was completed in 1868.

At the northern end of the original line the Leeds & Bradford Railway had been opened in 1846, and been extended to Skipton and Colne a year later. At the latter place, two years later, an end-on junction was made with a branch of the Lancashire & Yorkshire Railway running north eastwards from Burnley.

In the meantime another independent company, the North Western, had been incorporated to build a line northwards from Skipton, by way of Ingleton, to make a junction with the Lancaster & Carlisle, at Low Gill. Construction proceeded and in 1849 the line had reached Ingleton, but such appeared the costs of continuing through the mountainous regions ahead that the project was abandoned, and a continuation line built through easier country to Lancaster and Morecambe. The connection from the moorland Clapham Junction, on the slopes of Ingleborough, was completed in 1850, and at that time the Lancaster & Carlisle Railway was still independent, though working in general harmony with the London & North Western, as part of the West Coast route from London to Scotland. The Midland had taken over the working of the 'little'

North Western Railway in 1852, and regarding the Lancaster & Carlisle as an ally, began organising through carriage services to Kendal via Lancaster.

With Midland backing, and funds improving the 'little' North Western decided that the time had come to build their intended northward extension from Ingleton to Low Gill and then promoted a new Bill to secure the necessary Parliamentary powers. But the Lancaster & Carlisle, aware of this move, promoted their own Bill. The result of this was that the application of the 'little' North Western was defeated, and in 1857 the Lancaster & Carlisle obtained their Act. But before the line from Low Gill down to Ingleton was opened in October 1861, the owning company had been leased to the London & North Western, and so at Ingleton the Midland had to face a potential enemy. Moreover the branch line from Low Gill, 19 miles long, was double-tracked throughout and built up to main

*Sir James Allport, General Manager of the Midland Railway 1860–1880.* (British Railways)

*The Shambles, Settle, typical of the local architecture at the time the line was projected.*
(Norman Wilkinson)

line standards.

Although thus baulked at Ingleton, with conse-
quences to be related later, the Midland had
another interesting and eventually prosperous
enterprise in the North West. In 1863, jointly with
the Furness Railway, it sponsored the construction of the Furness & Midland Railway, a short
connecting line from the 'little' North Western, at
Wennington to Carnforth, a distance of $9\frac{1}{2}$ miles.
From the outset one of the three intermediate
stations, Arkholme, was prominently designated
as "For Kirkby Lonsdale". Although that pleasant town was over four miles to the north in the
Vale of Lune, and had a station of its own close
at hand on the newly constructed line between
Low Gill and Ingleton, it was not likely that the
expansionist tactics of the Midland management
of those days would acknowledge the existence
of a rival station, particularly as they had so
recently been "out-smarted" by the LNWR over
that very line. Moreover the Furness & Midland
was very far from a mere connecting line. It was
seen as a vital link to two further items of
business to which Derby was then giving serious
attention.

At Carnforth the intersection with the West
Coast Main Line was therefore no more than
incidental. The F&MR crossed it at high level,
making connection with the Furness freight yards
immediately to the west. But passenger trains
from the Midland, as Ahrons vividly explained it:
"described a partial logarithmic spiral — after the

manner of a descending aeroplane, to enter the
station from the opposite direction to that in
which it was travelling two minutes before". The
joint ownership of the line was the same arrangement as that subsequently established in the
South when the Midland and the London &
South Western assumed control of the Somerset
& Dorset. In the North the Furness manned the
stations and maintained the track while the
Midland provided the rolling stock and locomotives, and ran the trains. The Midland had their
own engine shed at Carnforth, and at one time
it housed no less than 25 engines, mostly 0-6-0
goods types.

From the opening of the Furness & Midland
Joint line Derby had their eyes on potential
tourist traffic to the Lake District, realising that
the Furness Railway branch, giving access to the
beautifully situated Windermere lakeside station
with the steamer quay immediately alongside,
provided a far more satisfying entrée to the region
than that of the London & North Western, with
its station high up at the back of the town at
Windermere. Nor was tourist traffic to the Lake
District itself the only passenger business that the
Midland management envisaged over the 'little'
North Western and its continuation to Carnforth.
At Piel Pier, south of Barrow, there was a jetty at
which small packet steamers could berth, and
it was not long before the Midland arranged
with the Furness for cross-channel services to
be organised, to the Isle of Man and to Belfast.

Later when dock facilities were established at Barrow itself the packet steamers sailed from Ramsden Dock, and the Midland boat trains lost their picturesque roof boards carrying the legend 'Barrow Piel Pier'.

I am afraid this has been something of a digression from the main subject matter of this book. But germane to the general theme of this first chapter is certainly a mention of the Midland Railway's forays into the Lake District and still more because of my personal associations with the 'little' North Western, and its offshoot to Carnforth. Between 1916 and 1921 when I was at Giggleswick School, and my parents lived in Barrow, I travelled on it regularly and became very familiar with its foibles, and the long times one often had to wait, sometimes at Wennington and more frequently at Carnforth for connecting trains. Long past were the days when the Midland boat trains, ran non-stop from Hellifield, and called at Carnforth East Junction, not the station, only for the purpose of changing engines. At that time however a conditional stop was provided at Giggleswick to take up passengers bound for stations beyond Carnforth.

After the completion of the London & North Western line from Ingleton to the junction with the West Coast Main Line at Low Gill the Midland found it was in a virtually impossible position with regard to traffic for Scotland. The connections with the main line trains at Ingleton and Tebay were virtually non existent. Passengers were turned out of Midland trains to find that eventually there was nothing to take them forward but a scruffy set of antiquated vehicles to which some goods trucks were also attached, and on arrival at Tebay, in due course there turned up one of the slowest of stopping trains to take them on to Carlisle. It was not surprising in these conditions that the Midland Railway over its newly found northern outlet carried not a single through passenger from important centres like Birmingham and Glasgow. Such became the deep concern of the very able General Manager, James Allport, who had some personal experience of the vagaries of travelling over the connecting link between Ingleton and Tebay. It should be explained that while the local trains entered upon the West Coast Main Line at Low Gill they continued to the junction at Tebay, where not only connection was made with the North Eastern line to Darlington but there was also a locomotive depot.

Allport then approached the London & North Western with a view to arranging running powers for Midland trains between Ingleton and Carlisle. Certainly the North Western would have been loath to see Midland trains in Carlisle, certainly as regards passengers, but even more so over freight, realising that south of Leeds there lay that vast industrial area that the Midland was tapping at its source. With existence of running powers north of Ingleton a new and heavy freight traffic would be directed towards Scotland. Allport's proposal led to a protracted argument over the rates the Midland could charge over the conveyance of freight. On their own line the practice was flexible, often to suit what potential customers were prepared to pay. As far as stations between Low Gill and Carlisle it was agreed that the rates could be subject to arbitration, but for traffic beyond Carlisle the Midland insisted that they must be free to make their own arrangements. Deputations from the Midland board and the LNWR board met to discuss details, but on hearing the Midland stipulation about rates for traffic beyond Carlisle, the North Western chairman simply said: "The negotiation is over". And that was that!

In 1866 the Midland board determined to have their own line to Carlisle, and the project aroused very little opposition. From Settle northwards, while it would run parallel to the valleys traversed by the 'little' North Western and the Lancaster & Carlisle, the terrain was actually quite separate, parted by a range of high hills. But it was at Carlisle itself that the main opposition centred, needless to say from the London & North West-

*Pen-y-Ghent, one of the mountains of North Ribblesdale past which the line would have to climb.* (Norman Wilkinson)

*Pennine fastnesses — the hamlet of Chapel-le-dale beneath the heights of Whernside, seen from the summit of Ingleborough.* (Norman Wilkinson)

ern Railway. They were joint owners with the Caledonian Railway of Citadel station, and they argued that there was not any more room to accommodate the Midland trains. It was a specious argument at any rate, seeing that they had been ready to provide room when running powers from Low Gill to Carlisle were being discussed. But whatever case the North Western had, or thought they had, was demolished, by reference to the terms on which the Caledonian and the Scottish North Eastern amalgamated in 1866, in which it was declared that, "whereas the railways of the Midland Railway Company form one of the lines of communication between the metropolis and Scotland, it is expedient that nothing shall be done which shall impede or obstruct the flow or transit of traffic of every description freely and expeditiously over the lines of the Midland Railway to and from Scotland". Thus it was that the North Western's Scottish ally sold the pass, and accordingly, running powers and use of the Caledonian part of the station were granted to the Midland Railway.

The Bill for construction of the Settle and Carlisle line passed through Parliament, but having surmounted the hurdle of opposition in Carlisle itself the Midland discovered that plans were fairly advanced for an amalgamation of the Caledonian Railway with the Glasgow & South Western. Hitherto the Midland had looked upon the 'Sou'West' as a potential ally and an artery over which Midland traffic could continue north into Scotland. But such an amalgamation would have effectively closed the door to any such prospects. Until now the two

Scottish companies had been in many respects competitors, and Allport realising the opposition that would be engendered if the project reached the stage of a Bill being presented to Parliament, countered the proposal by suggesting an amalgamation of the Midland with the Glasgow & South Western. This was taken very seriously in Scotland. There had always been a prominent faction on the 'Sou'West' that had an innate dislike, nay loathing of anything Caledonian, and they rejoiced at any alternative to the proposed amalgamation.

Nor was the Midland initiative welcomed solely on the Glasgow & South Western. From Scotland at that time the management of the North British Railway was 'empire-building' as vigorously as the men of Derby. They had absorbed the newly authorised line from Edinburgh to Hawick, even though it was not completed, and did not open for traffic throughout its length until some fifteen years later. Its continuation, the Border Union Railway, taking the line over the Cheviots and down to Carlisle, was completed in 1862. North British or not the company was not content with gaining an entry to Carlisle itself. It has a branch $21\frac{1}{2}$ miles long to Silloth on the Cumberland side of the Solway Firth, and another from Riccarton Junction, high up in the Cheviots down to Hexham. From this outlook one can well imagine that the Border Union line, running through rural and sparsely populated country, was regarded as no more than a 'probe' in North British strategy. At Carlisle, in the mid-1860s, the London & North Western, though accepting some goods traffic was in reality a no-go area, the prospect of the Midland building the Settle and Carlisle line opened up an attractive prospect for goods, regular passenger and summer tourist traffic.

The Bill for amalgamation of the Glasgow & South Western with the Midland had the warm approval of the North British management, because they foresaw that with the Settle and Carlisle line complete the Midland would not concentrate their Scottish efforts on Glasgow alone. They would expand their efforts to include Edinburgh and the eastern seaboard of Scotland north of the Firth of Forth. But the Bill for amalgamation was having a rough ride in the Parliamentary committee. Its opponents made much of the view that to be effective the Settle and Carlisle line would have to be built, and that not a thing had been done about that up to the minute. Counsel for the promotion of the Bill said: "The passing of this amalgamation bill will involve the completion of the Settle and Carlisle undoubtedly, as an indispensable condition. To say, therefore, that it is an argument against this amalgamation, that we have not made, and perhaps have not begun, and perhaps may not make, the Settle and Carlisle line, is an inconsistent argument. There is no doubt that the fear of the opponents is, not that it will not be made, but that it will be made, and that by its being made this amalgamation will be efficient. Can there be any better proof that we shall make the Settle and Carlisle line? Moreover, what harm will this amalgamation do to anybody if we cannot use it?"

While the Midland was eager to press ahead, London & North Western interests, fully cognisant of the fact that Authority to build the Settle and Carlisle line was already on the Statute Book, were deeply concerned with this further evidence of the Midland aims for aggrandisement, and they used every influence they could lay hands on to oppose the merger of the Glasgow & South Western Railway with the Midland. They were successful, and after the meeting at the House of Commons in 1867, it was announced that the Parliamentary committee were of the opinion it was not expedient to proceed further with the Bill for amalgamation. At first it seemed that the Midland management was undeterred by this, and the case was referred to a shareholders' meeting at Derby in June of that same year. In the meantime certain influen-

tial shareholders had begun to question the cost of building the Settle and Carlisle line, and whether the resulting traffic would justify the outlay. As a result the Midland Committee of the Railway Shareholders' Association, reopened negotiations with the London & North Western with a view to obtaining running powers between Ingleton and Carlisle.

While this could be seen as a rather inexplicable 'about turn' by the Midland management there is no doubt that the increasing difficulties of the proposed fusion with the Glasgow & South Western, not to mention the capital cost of building the Settle and Carlisle line were weighing heavily on Mr Allport. To his relief the LNWR at this juncture seemed to be ready to come forward with really liberal conditions for the use of the Lancaster & Carlisle line as far south as Low Gill and the Ingleton branch thereafter. Of course the principal factor was that the Midland relinquished their project to build the new line. Derby were in a weak position at that particular moment. Their counsels were divided, and that was not an ideal time to negotiate with a man of Richard Moon's calibre, and it was inevitable that there would much argument between representatives on both sides. Eventually the North

*Ais Ghyll Foss, on the side of Wild Boar Fell, a prospect not far from the ultimate summit of the line.* (Norman Wilkinson)

*The High Cross, Appleby, with the crenallated approaches to the Parish Church.* (O. S. Nock)

Western decided to refer the matter to the Board of Trade, all the time insisting that any such terms as might be agreed were subject to the Midland abandoning the Settle and Carlisle line.

In view of the relatively light traffic operated by the Midland Railway over the Settle and Carlisle, even in its pre-1914 heyday, one is bound to speculate upon what might have happened if the Act authorising its construction had been abandoned, and arrangements for regular running north of Ingleton been concluded with the LNWR. This thought occurred to me in 1963 when the RCTS organised the "Three Summits" tour one Sunday, starting from Leeds, going north via Ais Gill and Beattock, and returning via the G&SWR and Shap, via Ingleton to Hellifield. This was certainly a special occasion with Pacific haulage for all the main line running. But travelling on that train I recalled certain times when the Ingleton route has been used in emergency. One such was noted by Cecil J. Allen when he joined the 2.45 pm Scotch Express at Carlisle to travel to St Pancras and found he was being taken up the West Coast Main Line over Shap. A Midland compound with a moderate train load of 265 tons made a good run over the LNWR part of the journey, and then produced some exciting running down to Ingleton with a maximum speed of 75 mph near Sedburgh. They had to stop at the moorland Clapham Junction to exchange pilotmen, and after that the running was relatively quiet.

It was exactly the opposite on the "Three Summits" tour train. With a Gresley A4 Pacific and a load of 360 tons we did brilliantly up to Shap, but after exchanging pilotmen, on this occasion at Tebay, we ran very cautiously down the branch, not exceeding 53 mph until Ingleton had been passed, and it was only when we joined the 'little' North Western main line that we got a taste of 'A4' speed. But these two runs alone showed convincingly how the Ingleton route could have been used for regular traffic. The compound run on the 2.45 pm train reached Hellifield in a net time of 98 minutes from Carlisle, equivalent to the schedule operating over Ais Gill at that time, whereas if they had finished from Clapham in the same style as *Golden Eagle* on the "Three Summits" tour the time could have been cut by a further five minutes!

Now reverting to the year 1868, terms of agreement were drawn up by the London & North Western and the Midland Railway by which the latter was to have free and full access to Scotland over the Lancaster & Carlisle line, and whereby the Midland would abandon the authority it had already received from Parliament to build the Settle and Carlisle line. The North Western was to provide accommodation at intermediate stations for passenger and goods traffic, the Midland having power to place their own staff there, if desired. Both companies were to unite in applying to Parliament for the abandonment of the Settle and Carlisle line. This they did, and after a six day hearing the Commons Committee decided the evidence did not justify any such abandonment. It was the opposition of the North British and of the Lancashire & Yorkshire that turned the case against the LNWR and the Midland and so, at the end of 1868, the Midland was left 'holding the baby' — a baby that was a very tiresome offspring!

# 2
# Planning the Line

In his five-hundred page classic, *Midland Railway—its rise and progress*, F. S. Williams coming to the Settle and Carlisle tells how James Allport and his chief engineer John Crossley, finally committed to the actual building of the line, themselves went to North Ribblesdale to begin a personal inspection of the terrain. Williams tells in fifty vivid pages of his book what he himself and those who escorted him encountered when making a visit to the unfinished works on the line. He made a remarkably comprehensive tour, and illustrated his account with many attractive lithographic views. But it must not be forgotten that the first edition of his book was actually published before the line became in any way operational, and subsequent printings have done nothing to bring this feature of the book in any way up to date. On the other hand, to one who has made an in-depth study of the working of the line over many years it seems obvious that a degree of master-planning had taken place at Derby, even before Messrs Allport and Crossley went on their first reconnaissance.

What the High Command at Derby then appreciated was the profoundly altered status of the Midland Railway in the transportation system of Great Britain. No longer was it a railway of the Midland shires, reaching out from its central nucleus. Henceforth it would be a vital, possibly predominant partner in a third Anglo-Scottish train service network, prepared to run on equal terms with the already established West and East Coast routes, providing express connec-

tions and through carriages from London and the West Country, not only to Glasgow and

*John Sydney Crossley, Engineer-in-Chief of the Midland Railway in 1870. He retired in 1875 before the line was opened, and died in 1879 aged 67. (Borough Librarian, Derby)*

*Charles Stanley Sharland, Prospecting Engineer for the Settle and Carlisle Railway.* (Courtesy M. Sharland)

& Carlisle Railway, to make the preliminary surveys. Despite severe wintry weather conditions he is reported as walking the entire route in record time, being snowed up for several days in the process. But whether this experience affected his seemingly robust health is not related, but in fact he was not long on the line, developing tuberculosis, and dying in Torquay in 1871, at the early age of 26. His great wintry survey is mentioned in William's book, but nothing more, and at the time of the Settle-Carlisle Railway Centenary in 1975, having been co-opted as an honorary pro-tem member of the Settle and District Civic Society, I had the good fortune to become acquainted with a family of the name of Sharland, in Bristol. Contact being made it appeared that Roger was indeed a great nephew of the Settle and Carlisle Railway engineer. More important still, his father and mother, long resident in New Zealand, were coming to England on a visit that very summer. By some rapid fire organisation arrangements were made for Michael Sharland and his wife to visit Settle and meet the members of the local committee. They in their turn brought a family tree of the Sharland's, and a photograph of Charles, taken of him in October 1869, just after his memorable walk from Settle to Carlisle.

Now as to the masterplan for the line Upper Ribblesdale provided a natural route at the southern end. The course of the river, despite occasional rapids, presented a steady fall of about 13 miles from the sedgy wasteland at Ribblehead to where the new line was to join the 'little' North Western at what became Settle Junction. The natural inclination would have been a little less than 1 in 100 over this 13 miles, with little more than normal hazards on the way up; but Ribblehead presented a major problem. The moorland could have been traversed on a low embankment, in the style of a Ribblesdale Chat Moss, but immediately to the north the fells rose tier upon tier, and a long tunnel was inevitable. It was here that the planners showed rare foresight. North of the mountain mass through which the tunnel would have to go Dentdale would almost immediately have to be crossed at high level. But studying the gradient profile as it is now it might have seemed that the severity of the long incline from Settle Junction might have been considerably eased from Ribblehead onwards. The station there was originally called Batty Green, for

Edinburgh, but via the North British Railway to Aberdeen, Perth and Inverness. The West Highland line had not then been built, or one could have added Fort William as well. It was evident at the outset that the Settle and Carlisle line would have to be a fast express route providing all the facilities for speeding, as were already possessed by the Lancaster & Carlisle, and the East Coast Main Line north of Newcastle. In 1870 the London & North Western had no train timings north of Lancaster booked at more than 45 mph; but they could readily improve on that, and the Midland envisaged speeds ultimately of around 50 mph start-to-stop between Skipton and Carlisle. In such a countryside there could be no time lost through slowing down for speed restrictions over sharp curves, and so the route was planned for full speed throughout between Hellifield and the immediate approach to Carlisle.

After his first reconnaissance Crossley appointed a young Tasmanian engineer, C. S. Sharland, who had been lately on the Maryport

reasons to be told later, and if the line had been taken thence across the moorland, Chat Moss style, and dived into the flanks of Whernside, just beyond the track could have been taken on no more than a modestly rising gradient through the tunnel to arrive at a summit at the north end. From careful measurement I estimate that the gradient for the $3\frac{1}{4}$ miles from the present Ribblehead station to the north portal of Blea Moor Tunnel would be about 1 in 200.

While this would, in theory, ease the task of steam locomotives just when they seemed to be getting 'winded' by the toilsome job of surmounting 'The Long Drag', as the bank from Settle Junction became known to the enginemen, the continuance of the rising grade through the tunnel would have been a much greater hazard. Blea Moor Tunnel is habitually wet, and slipping on greasy rails would have been a very unpalatable climax to the heavy pounding up the bank from Settle Junction. So after a brief respite at 1 in 176 past Batty Green the 1 in 100 was continued over Ribblehead Viaduct, past Blea Moor sidings, and through the first dozen yards inside the tunnel itself. Then the planners made the gradient 1 in 440 down for the rest of the 2,629 yard bore. And a horrible place it proved to be to work in. Whatever the gradients that led up to it from the south, Crossley, Sharland and the men who made the more detailed surveys later, realised that the north portal of Blea Moor Tunnel was one of the nodal points in the entire strategic planning of the railway. Another lay a little over nine miles to the north at the watershed

of the rivers Ure and Eden on Ais Ghyll Moor. Even the most preliminary of the first surveys showed that these two nodal points were at roughly the same altitude above sea level, but between the two, in the High Pennines there was much wild tumbled countryside, anything but hospitable to the making of a fast express railway. The mountain road from Ingleton to Hawes having crossed the line of the railway at Ribblehead ascends to the end of Blea Moor itself and then at the 1,250 ft contour it throws off a side road to the left to descend very steeply into Dentdale. Photographers of our own times, who have climbed the road itself to record the passage of trains over the picturesque Dent Head Viaduct, may if they allow their thoughts to stray a little from immediate preoccupations appreciate some of the prospect that faced those pioneers of 1869–70. It was at the Gearstones Inn, two miles north-east of Ribblehead on the Hawes road that the intrepid Sharland and six of his men were snowed up for some days on the early surveys.

From Dent Head the range of high fells to the north presented much the same problems as were faced in later years by the men who built the West Highland Railway in Scotland. The countryside was just as forbidding. In Dentdale, where Rise Hill with its 1,800 ft contours lay immediately ahead of the direct line to the north, a circumvention on the lines of the Horseshoe Bend, near Tyndrum, would have involved a westerly detour on or around the 1,000 ft contour in a salient at least three miles deep, to attain the northern

*The Gearstones Inn, where Sharland was snowed up in the old building to left of picture.*
(W. Mitchell)

slopes of Rise Hill that overlook Garsdale. There would have been slow running on some of the curves, and an increase in the overall mileage of about eight. No; the only way to deal with Rise Hill was to drive clean through it, and this the Midland engineers did in a tunnel nearly a mile long. Before reaching it, however, the line which on a large scale ordnance map looks practically straight, has to cross some deep clefts in the fell sides. Immediately after emerging from Blea Moor Tunnel there is one between Wold Fell and the heights of Blea Moor itself, and another just over a mile to the north still deeper over the Arten Gill Beck. In Midland planning there was no question of making detours to reduce the constructional costs of viaducts over these ravines; the line must go straight across. Indeed in the exceedingly rugged country between the Blea Moor and Rise Hill tunnels the gradients are in the aggregate level throughout, with no inclination steeper than 1 in 264, and that for no more than a mile.

From Rise Hill Tunnel, which is level throughout its length of three quarters of a mile, the line emerges high up on the north-eastern flanks of Garsdale, down which the brawling little River Clough makes its way to its confluence with the

*Ways of communication before the railway — the pack-horse bridge across the River Ribble at Stainforth.* (Norman Wilkinson)

Lune. Above Garsdale the engineers had a fairly straight course for a few miles, generally level; indeed some years after the line was first built the Midland Railway laid down the highest ever set of water troughs on one of the lengths that was actually level. The road that struggles its way up Garsdale and attains the level of the railway about two miles beyond the northern end of Rise Hill Tunnel, goes on to make a junction with another lonely moorland track leading up from Wensleydale, to proceed northward over the watershed and down towards Carlisle. The road junction marked by the appropriately named Moorcock Inn became the site of a railway junction as well. The Midland management was aware that the North Eastern Railway was extending their line up Wensleydale. But at the time work on the Settle and Carlisle was begun in earnest the NER had not reached Askrigg, some ten miles down the valley from the Moorcock Inn, and the Midland received authority to build a branch line as far east as Hawes, a busy little market town, to block the approach of the North Eastern to the Settle and Carlisle main line. The branch was actually built and opened to traffic before the North Eastern reached Hawes.

If the Midland had been more poetically minded it might have named this moorland junction the Moorcock in keeping with the names of signal boxes farther south that took their titles from local pubs, like "Three Cocks", and "Bo Peep Junction". But the site on the moorland which was to give its name to one of the main line viaducts, Dandry Mire, and the neighbouring swamp, Mud Becks, was simply named Hawes Junction. On the one-inch Ordnance Survey map of 1914 one has to use a magnifying glass to locate 'Hawes Junction', and it would be hard to imagine what often went on at this Midland outpost at times of heavy traffic, even to the extent of one of the most important up Scotch expresses making its only passenger stop there between Carlisle and Leeds. Hawes Junction features prominently in several later chapters of this book. However, the pioneer engineers having worked their way on the level from Rise Hill, were soon in dead trouble when they came to cross the seemingly flat ground at the head of Garsdale to reach the slopes lying west of the higher reaches of the River Ure. I am not sure where the valley by which this beautiful river ceases in its moorland fastness to be Wensleydale,

*The bleak prospect looking south from Whernside over Ribblehead, with the hump of Pen-y-Ghent on the distant skyline, and the great railway viaduct almost lost in the tremendous landscape.*
(Norman Wilkinson)

I imagine around Hawes, for there is nothing dale-like in its scrambling over boulders coming down from the heights of Abbotside Common. To cross the flat ground in sight of the Moorcock Inn a low embankment was planned, but after tipping had gone on, *for two years*, without the slightest result a viaduct was decided upon. This was the last hazard before the summit of the whole line was reached at Ais Ghyll Moor. There were two short tunnels in the intervening distance from Hawes Junction, the Moorcock and the Shotlock Hill; and through these the gradients, although rising, were not enough to reduce the speed of a fast train much below 60 mph, or that was the hope of the planners.

Once over the watershed the course was now straight forward enough at first, beneath the ominous crags of Wild Boar Fell. The western side of the Upper Eden Valley is known as Mallerstang Common and this district gave its name to the first intermediate signal box on the Carlisle side of the summit, $3\frac{1}{2}$ miles north of Ais Gill and eventually provided with refuge loops on both sides of the line and a crossover road between the down and up main line. Had the Midland Railway been more romantically minded in naming its signal boxes, Mallerstang could well have been "Pendragon Castle". Little less than a mile to the north, on the west bank of the still-infant Eden river are the fragmentary ruins of the castle which legends tell us was originally built by King Uther Pendragon, and in later days it was owned by one of the ill-starred

Knights involved in the murder of Archbishop Becket in Canterbury Cathedral. After certain later vicissitudes the castle, as a fortress and residence was destroyed in 1685, but its site is still marked on the very latest of the Ordnance Survey maps. The railway engineers were to remember the site of Pendragon Castle in a very different way when it came to the actual construction

*Arten Gill, the immense height of the railway viaduct above the farm dwellings.* (Norman Wilkinson)

*Ais Gill Summit: a recent photograph, but one which emphasises the lonely scene beneath the slopes of Wild Boar Fell. (Brian Morrison)*

of the line, as will be told in a later chapter. When the restored 'King Arthur' class 4-6-0 No. 777 was sometimes working the "Cumbrian Mountain Express", and was indeed photographed near to the very site of Pendragon Castle, I wonder if any thought was given to a temporary change of name for the engine, substituting that originally borne by No. 737 *King Uther* for the actual name borne by No. 777, *Sir Lamiel*?

A little to the north of Pendragon Castle a rocky bluff rising to the 1,000 ft contour named Birkett Common lay ahead of the direct line of the railway. Studying the maps it would not have made much of a detour to skirt it on the river side, but Crossley and his men decided to go straight across, with a deep cutting through the shale formation and a tunnel 424 yards long. A detour eastwards would have brought the line nearer to the pleasant market town of Kirkby Stephen, but Crossley had other ideas, and the eventual station on the Settle and Carlisle railway was more than two miles from the town centre. Kirkby Stephen had a railway of its own from the year 1861, when the South Durham & Lancashire Union line was opened from Barnard Castle, over the very crest of the Pennines at Stainmore, and

thence via Kirkby Stephen and Ravenstonedale to Tebay, on the West Coast Main Line. It was not in any way a likely competitor to the Settle and Carlisle, because its principal traffic was a reciprocal mineral haulage in ore-iron from the Furness district and coal westwards from South Durham. West of Kirkby Stephen this line followed a wild moorland valley to the headwaters of the River Lune.

Meanwhile the track of the Settle and Carlisle railway was taken on what were no more than sweeping curves to the crossing of the Eden at Ormside. The only appreciable detour from a straight line was between Kirkby Stephen station and Crosby Garret, where the line makes a westward salient to cross the gorge in which the South Durham & Lancashire Union made its way to the west. Yet when the line came to be built the actual curves were laid in with such precision and the track itself so superbly maintained that sustained speeds of between 80 and 90 mph have been recorded between Birkett Tunnel and Ormside Viaduct in ordinary express passenger service. There is some lessening of the gradient around Crosby Garrett, but other than that the descent between Mallerstang and Orm-

*The ruin of Pendragon Castle in the foreground of an engraving of the Eden Valley, in which Wild Boar Fell is exaggerated to almost Alpine proportions.* (Engraving per F. S. Williams)

side is generally kept at about 1 in 100, never steeper. Almost exactly half way from Settle Junction and the end of the line in the approaches to Carlisle, near the hamlet of Griseburn, and where the Midland Railway later established some ballast sidings, the line of the new railway crossed a deep valley in which a brawling stream from a source high on Crosby Garrett Fell made its way. The local name, thereabouts, was apparently Potts Beck. But after meandering someway east of the line of the railway it drew nearer to the bluff which the Ordnance Survey names as Heights.

Local names apart, in that locality the so-called Potts Beck is rendered Helm Beck, and it is this latter name that the surveyors of the Midland Railway adopted when drawing the detailed plans for the construction of the line. It is probable that they had good reason for this choice of name, for the Helm Wind is sometimes a phenomenon in this district. A cloud cap on the ridge of the Pennines is usually a sign that the 'hurricane' is about to break. Cool winds from the North Sea sweeping over mile upon mile of gradually rising moorland suddenly meet on the crest of the Pennines, with the warm air of the western vales.

The outcome is the so-called Helm Wind, that sweeps down into the Eden Valley with the force of a miniature tornado. Not only the beck takes its name from this fearsome wind. There is a cluster of cottages which the present Ordnance Survey map names as Helm, and a farm on a by-road from Appleby to Kirkby Stephen named Helm Beck. When Crossley determined the actual route of the line and 'Heights' was in the way, as usual, he went through it, and the tunnel was naturally named Helm. Two miles beyond the northern end of Helm Tunnel the line crosses the River Eden, and at this point the long descent from Ais Gill summit ends.

Appleby, until recent years the County Town of Westmorland, is $2\frac{1}{2}$ miles from the foot of the bank. That very pleasant town had its first railway fourteen years before the Midland built the Settle and Carlisle line, when the Eden Valley Railway was opened. This new enterprise was an offshoot of the South Durham & Lancashire Union, branching from this latter at Kirkby Stephen and making its way down the Eden Valley in a wide sweep to the east, serving the villages of Great Musgrave and Warcop to come alongside the planned route of the Settle and

*Pendragon Castle, a recent picture.* (N. J. Mussett)

Carlisle at Appleby, though on a rather lower level. Proceeding farther north the Eden Valley Railway was carried westward across country to join the West Coast Main Line at Eden Valley Junction, between Clifton and Eamont Junction. While its main function, like that of the South Durham & Lancashire Union, was the conveyance of Cumbrian iron ore to Tees-side, local passenger business was not neglected though its activities in this respect seemed of no interest to the Midland. Connection between the two lines at Appleby appeared as more of an afterthought than anything else. Passenger connections between the two routes were non-existent even in the last years. I travelled by the evening train from Penrith to Darlington one Saturday in 1951, calling at all stations, and at Appleby itself the station stopping time was just 23 seconds!

Although Appleby was then a County Town then having no more than 1,500 inhabitants, and it is not much larger today, the Midland Railway regarded it as a much more important place than did the offshoots of the North Eastern, and as subsequent chapters of this book will tell, it became a stopping place for several of the Scotch Expresses. Even so the Midland planners took the higher way to the north-west rather than the route of the present A66 highway, and by-passed the large villages of Kirkby Thore and Temple Sowerby which were served on the North Eastern line to Penrith. The Settle and Carlisle had some unforeseen obstacles to contend with before the engineers were many miles north of Appleby. They were entering the region of wealthy landowners, the residences of whom are even today dotted on the large scale Ordnance Survey maps. Not all these individuals welcomed the advent of the new railway, and F. S. Williams in his classic work tells a good story of the owner of Newbiggin Hall.

From the heights of Cross Fell, the highest point of the northern ranges of the Pennines, the Crowdundle Beck cascades towards its eventual junction with the Eden. On the right bank opposite the village of Newbiggin there were fine woods, and an escarpment so steep as to cause the Ordnance Survey of today to mark the by-road approaching the river from the north as steeper than 1 in 7. Crossley planned to take the railway over the beck by a low-arched viaduct and through the woods by a deep cutting. The

*Aerial view of the Long Meg stone circle.* (Cambridge University Collection)

owner of Newbiggin Hall and most of the surrounding property was a clergyman, Richard Crackenthorpe by name, and Sharland encountered him on his first reconnaissance, in none too happy a frame of mind. Sensing that there might be difficulties Crossley, together with Allport himself, called on the Reverend Gentleman, and apparently pacified him. But when Sharland next met him, the following exchange, to quote Williams, took place:

"There is only one condition I have to make" said Mr Crackenthorpe. "It is that you spare me the largest and finest oak in my wood. Do you know what I want it for? It's to hang you and all the engineers of the Midland Railway upon it, for daring to come here at all!"

One of the charms of the countryside through which the line of the Settle and Carlisle railway was planned, lay in the constant variety of the terrain, albeit providing many a headache for the civil engineers. Here, once the forest lands north of the Crowdundle Valley have been passed, a wide open vista to the west is presented, extending far beyond Penrith to many well-recognised peaks of the Lake District. While near at hand the River Eamont, which gives its name to certain

features of the West Coast Main Line, comes to join the Eden just beyond where the proximity of the river caused some problems to Crossley and his men. A little to the north of the confluence of the Eamont and the Eden is Edenhall, the family seat of the Musgraves. Although the practice of engine naming hardly even touched the Midland one could dilate for folios on the philosophy, or apparent lack of it, which often seemed to guide those who chose the names for the express locomotives of the London & North Western Railway. Why on earth *Luck of Edenhall*? One can only think that the love of poetry must have animated some of the backroom boys of the Locomotive Department at Crewe charged with producing new engine names. Longfellow was in his mid-sixties when his ballad about the ancestral goblet cherished by the Musgrave family was published, and the little 2-4-0 engine of the LNWR named after it appeared soon afterwards.

Not many miles north of Edenhall, on the right bank of the river on the higher ground, is one of the 'lions' of North Country topography, not all that well known in its original association, but later the name became a household word in the railway operating sense — Long Meg. The quarries which later proved such a source of revenue to the London Midland Region take their name from a remarkable stone circle of prehistoric times — 'Long Meg and her daughters'. There are altogether 66 of them, arranged in a circle of about 350 feet diameter. It is actually a considerably more impressive array than the much better known circle near Keswick, but lying well away from the beaten track it is comparatively unknown. Its name however did not escape those seeking more engine names at Crewe, and at the same time as they used *Luck of Edenhall*, another 2-4-0 was named *Lang Meg*. It is interesting that they used the Scottish version, because on the Ordnance Survey maps the monument is noted as *Long Meg and her daughters*. Be this as it may, the LNWR *Lang Meg*, in the form of a superheater 4-4-0 of the 'George the Fifth' class ran express trains for many years after Grouping, but not on the Midland line!

Actually the first *Lang Meg* of the LNWR was a Leeds engine. Built at Crewe in 1878 she

*Long Meg herself, with a tall lady standing alongside.* (Norman Wilkinson)

was one of Webb's 'Precursor' class 2-4-0s with 5 ft 6 in coupled wheels designed to work over the North Country lines with heavy gradients. *Lang Meg* did not work over the Midland Railway but was based at the Farnley shed of the LNWR and ran over the steeply graded route westwards via Huddersfield to Manchester. The later *Lang Meg* was a powerful 4-4-0 of the second 'Precursor' series, built at Crewe in 1906, and at first took her run in the heavy and very busy duties allocated to those engines. Then, in the late autumn of 1909 the Great Western Railway was building a new cut-off line south-eastwards from a junction south of Banbury which would considerably reduce the distance between London and Birmingham, in fact making it several miles shorter than the historic route of the London & North Western Railway. At that time the fastest trains from Euston covered the 113 miles to Birmingham New Street in the level two hours, an average of $56\frac{1}{2}$ mph. Knowing the enterprising spirit of the 20th Century Great Western it was thought that it was more than likely that they would attempt to cash in on their lesser mileage between the two cities, and run some trains faster than the level two hours, which was until that time the fastest that the LNWR had scheduled between Euston and Birmingham New Street.

By way of preparation towards any eventualities in this direction on a quiet Sunday in November 1909 the North Western made a trial trip from Euston to Birmingham and back. A special six-coach train was made up, including the recently built Crewe dynamometer car, totalling about 210 tons behind the tender. The engine was the 4-4-0 'Precursor' No. 1387 *Lang Meg*. On the northbound run nothing much more than the ordinary two-hour schedule was attempted, and with a clear road the average speed from Euston to Birmingham was a little under 60 mph, but on the return run, also made non-stop, some considerably faster running was made. In fact the average speed was only a few decimal points short of the record average of 67 mph made by the 2-4-0 "Jumbo" *Hardwicke* from Crewe to Carlisle on the last night of the 1895 'Race to the North', in November 1909 — 113 miles in $102\frac{1}{4}$ minutes at $66\frac{1}{2}$ mph. On this later occasion the maximum speed of 83 mph was attained in the earlier part of the journey descending from Berkswell Tunnel towards Coventry. On the favourite racing stretches of the North Western main line, from Roade down to Castlethorpe troughs, and above all on the long descent from Tring Summit to Willesden, the speed did not exceed 80 mph, otherwise a considerably faster overall time could have been made.

Shortly after passing the breast of the hill on which Long Meg and her daughters are spread around, the line crosses the river at Eden Lacy Viaduct and thereafter it keeps on the western side for the rest of the way to Carlisle. Rather more than 55 years ago, in my energetic walking days, I spent an Easter weekend exploring the Lower Eden Valley, and from Lazonby I crossed the river and from Kirkoswald made my way by country lanes and field paths down stream towards Armathwaite. It was a Sunday and there were no trains, indeed there was no sight of the railway at all amid the tree-clad banks on the western side of the river. It occurred to me, in the seclusion that prevailed on that quiet April morning, that the scene I beheld must have looked just the same when Sharland and his men first tramped through on their historic walk from Settle to Carlisle. I took many photographs that day, not of railway subjects, but having processed them in the family home at Bushey, Hertfordshire, I was curious to look up a coloured plate that appeared in the July 1903 issue of *The Railway Magazine*, because it was to my recollection the first time there had been published any picture, coloured or otherwise, of a train on the Settle and Carlisle railway.

The 'build-up' to it in the previous issue of *The Railway Magazine* was terrific! "The subject chosen is the celebrated SCOTCH EXPRESS OF THE MIDLAND RAILWAY drawn by one of the new compound locomotives. The picture (which is painted in nine colours) faithfully portrays the famous train on its swift journey Northward; the spot selected for the picture being near Lazonby, on the romantic Settle and Carlisle section; the time chosen for the painting was a particularly happy one, as the train is thrown into relief by the vernal freshness of the delicate foliage. As a work of art applied to railways there can be no doubt that this picture

(which measures 20 in by $9\frac{1}{2}$ in) far and away surpasses anything ever before attempted in the application of the painter's craft to railways".

At that time the photogravure process was being used for colour illustrations of individual locomotives in *The Railway Magazine*, and many of these were conspicuously successful. The same however cannot be said of the Johnson compound No. 2632 featured in this prestigous plate, but the odd thing about the picture itself is the thought that the artist himself had probably never been near the railway. He had painted a very attractive background to the train, but nothing like any part of the Settle and Carlisle line, least of all in the lower Eden Valley.

In the confined river scenery that I found so charming on my Eastertide walks many hazards remained for those who were engineering the line, with the necessity of driving several tunnels, and dealing with some subsoil as treacherous as any encountered in the high Pennines. But once Cotehill was reached, the countryside opened out and permitted a straightforward downhill run towards Carlisle. The West Coast allies which had proved such obstacles to any Midland entry to the Border City were by no means the first to establish railway communications there. The Newcastle & Carlisle Railway was opened throughout in June 1838, and the Maryport & Carlisle Railway was opened in 1840. The Bill for construction of the Lancaster & Carlisle Railway received the Royal Assent in June 1844, and work began immediately afterwards. Both the smaller railways originally had their own passenger and goods stations in Carlisle, the Newcastle at London Road, and the Maryport at Crown Street. It was not until the Newcastle & Carlisle Railway was absorbed by the North Eastern in 1862 that a short double-line connection was put in from London Road Junction, to enable North Eastern trains to proceed to Citadel station. The Settle and Carlisle line ended at Petteril Junction whence Midland trains exercising running powers from the North Eastern railway made their way into Citadel.

# 3
# Constructional Work — the Mountain Section

The first turf was cut in November 1869 beside the Kendal road near Anley, about a mile to the north of the present Settle Junction signal box. The first structure of any size to be built was the viaduct beside the new church in the town of Settle itself, by which the line crosses the Kendal road. Incidentally, although an ancient town, Settle had no church of its own until 1838, prior to which the inhabitants had to cross the river and worship at the 14th Century parish church of Giggleswick, albeit no more than a mile away. The church viaduct

*Sheriff Brow bridge the lower, from an engraving when first built.* (Engraving per F. S. Williams)

at Settle was the scene of the only accident that has ever happened to a train on one of the major structures of the line. It occurred in 1894 when a wagon on a southbound freight became derailed farther north, and then hit the parapet of the viaduct and turned over, spilling the contents on to the ground below and leaving the wagon dangling on the brink. One did not have to go into the wilds to see the superb masonry work put into the structures of the Settle and Carlisle railway. One can enjoy it from the foot paths of the main road out of the town, towards Giggleswick.

Just beyond the Craven Lime Works, which has now cut so cruel a gash into the limestone hills of the line, there comes the first tunnel, Taitlands, only 120 yards it is true, but having a story about its origin. The road from Settle up the dale crossed the proposed line of the railway about half a mile above where the lime works came to be situated, and there in the direct line was the property of an old established landowner. Whether Sharland approached him personally I do not know, but whoever it was, met with an implacable refusal to facilitate the

progress of the railway and after much argument a short tunnel had to be built beneath the property. Taitlands, the house, is now a youth hostel. Far otherwise was the attitude of the property owner to the north of Taitlands Tunnel, whose estate extended northwards along the line proposed for the railway as far as Helwith Bridge. The owner, Thomas Foster-Knowles, had only recently inherited it from his aunt in 1870, and readily gave facilities to the Midland Railway engineers, himself making a path along the river bank from the old pack bridge as far as the first railway crossing. Williams in his book describes the bridge as Sheriff Brow; but locally it is known as Sherwood. Indeed Sherwood House nearby is marked on the one-inch Ordnance Survey map.

I have had the pleasure of meeting, and corresponding with Foster-Knowles's great nephew, Mr J. P. Koppel who owned the property in Stainforth for some years and was a Governor of Giggleswick School. His great-uncle had not only provided road access to the line of the proposed railway until the track was built, but also gave permission for the course of the river to be

*Sheriff Brow one hundred years later.* (W. Hubert Foster)

*Ribblehead Viaduct under construction — engraving showing some of the shanty town in the hillside beyond.* (Engraving per F. S. Williams)

diverted, between the lower and upper of the two Sherwood viaducts to help the construction. At the lower end of the gorge, though not seen from the railway is the picturesque cataract of Stainforth Force. It was in the middle of this awkward, though highly picturesque length, that the River Ribble by the cooperation of Thomas Foster-Knowles was induced to make a serpen-

*The old contractor's track above Blea Moor Tunnel with one of the ventilating shafts near at hand.* (Norman Wilkinson)

tine bend, and for the railway to maintain its fast running alignment to cross it twice in less than a mile, both on sharply inclined skew bridges. Both display the superb masonry characteristic of all other works on this line, but the odd thing is that there are rapids between the two bridges, and the arches on the lower one, hereabouts known as Sheriff Brow, are much taller than on the other one. The railway emerges from the glen at Helwith Bridge, and at once the prospect from the line opens out into the bleak countryside of Upper Ribblesdale with the peak of Pen-y-ghent towering up on the right. The mountain is seen at its finest from Helwith Bridge. Here there occurs the one break in the toilsome up grading of the 'Long Drag' which extends from Settle Junction to Blea Moor Tunnel, a little less than half a mile of dead level track past Helwith Bridge signal box and sidings.

Although the upward slopes on the western side of the dale are not precipitous or seared with the tracks of mountain torrents, the next seven miles almost entirely at 1 in 100, were built across ground covered with boulder clay, which in dry weather needed to be blasted with gunpowder and at other, turns into an awful gluey mess. When building the line it is important to record how careful the management of the Midland

*Top of Blea Moor Tunnel looking north into Dentdale with another of the vents in evidence.*
(Norman Wilkinson)

Railway were to provide permanent accommodation for the men and their families who would have to maintain the line. This was to be a fast express route, and by the lineside at Selside, two miles from Horton-in-Ribblesdale, a row of handsome cottages were built; no jerry-built workmens' shacks, but massive stone houses, an adornment to the wild upland landscape. Selside became an intermediate blockpost, with no more than a single crossover road, and I recall it from my train timing days as the approach to one of the slower spells on the upward journey, and to a part of the line when the drivers of southbound trains were often approaching 80 mph. And now the line is approaching Ribblehead. So much colourful prose has been written about the lifestyle of the men and their families who dwelt in this inhospitable region for some five or six years that one hesitates to try to add more. My own principal task is an appraisal of the work that was done.

On the first official gradient profile of the line, issued from the office of the Midland Railway's Chief Engineer at Derby in July 1875, the intermediate stations on the southern part of the line are marked as Settle, Horton and Batty Green. This last mentioned was changed to Ribblehead before long, but it is interesting to know how the

name Batty Green became used in railway parlance because it did not correspond with any of the local folk-lore as recalled by F. S. Williams. But whether Batty Moss, Batty's Wife, Batty Green, or Batty's Wife's Hole, it was an incredible place during the constructional period, having a far larger accumulation of human souls than any of the places on the route. At the height of the activity the Midland Railway was employing about two thousand men in this one area, and with all the ancillary activities, not to mention resident families, Batty Green, to use the railway name for it, must have mustered a population of well over three thousand. Why indeed were so many congregated in this one bleak, inhospitable area? Two of the most major works on the whole line were under construction near at hand, Ribblehead Viaduct, and the fearsome Blea Moor Tunnel, while the approaches to both involved prodigious amounts of pure digging and tipping.

To preserve the even upward slope of 1 in 100 from the Selside area to the very entrance to Blea Moor Tunnel involved a high level crossing of the marshy ground at the head waters of the Ribble and of the Greta, which makes its way north-eastwards from the Lune at Ingleton to this same watershed. The line had to be carried

*Ribblehead Viaduct in 1938, looking south from the outer sweep of the curve that used to see speeds of 70 mph and more, southbound.* (Norman Wilkinson)

more than one hundred feet above the ground. There was no waterway to cross and for the engineers there faced the problem of how far to extend the embankment on which the track was already on, at a considerable elevation in the region of Batty Green, where the station would eventually be, and how long a viaduct would follow. It would seem as though the strength of the available labour force settled the question. Originally the viaduct was planned to have 18 arches, but there was another factor in this locality apart from sheer man power. In the ordinary way, when settling the gradients of a line of railway, the engineers endeavoured to balance

*Ribblehead Viaduct, looking north.* (Norman Wilkinson)

the spill taken out of the cuttings by using it in the embankments; but there was no chance of doing this on the Settle and Carlisle line, least of all at Ribblehead. The situation there led to the engineers making the long viaduct of 24 arches, instead of 18.

It is a magnificent piece of constructional work. Such is the ground on which it was built that most of the piers are roughly the same height, some 105 ft from ground level; but they were carried down another 25 ft or so, to reach solid rock for the foundations. Throughout the length of the viaduct each sixth pier was made a 'King', 18 ft thick at the crown of the arch instead of the normal 6 ft, to provide a safeguard in case of unforeseen damage to the piers. In any untoward occurrence intermediately only the five piers between the 'Kings' would be liable to collapse. Ribblehead while by far the longest was not the tallest viaduct on the line. This latter distinction is carried by Smardale, north of Kirkby Stephen, referred to in the succeeding chapter of this book. Even at 130 ft above ground level the engineers of the Settle and Carlisle line did not have to resort to the technique used by Joseph Locke on the French line he built from Rennes to Brest in carrying the line over the valley at Morlaix, 190 ft above the town, and provided with a lower arcade of arches, about 50 ft above ground level.

Ribblehead Viaduct has arches of 45 ft span. The piers are most ruggedly built in limestone, quarried locally, while the arches themselves are of brick, with limestone voussoirs, or facing stones. Actually it is not until one gets underneath that one appreciates that the arches are built of brick. The renewal of them has provided a maintenance problem over the years. Not many years ago, a neighbour, a fellow enthusiast who had been visiting the district came back to present me with a very superannuated brick that had been removed from the viaduct, and it now rests on a table in my study! While the 24 towers arose from the moorland the incredible shanty town that supported the railway building activity prospered, in all its many sided guises. Equally, beneath the often-lowering slopes of Whernside, to the north-west of the railway route the lining up and embankments were being prepared for entry to the most hazardous work on the whole line — Blea Moor Tunnel. But before plunging into its depths one must give a last thought for Ribblehead, and its many thousand workers.

Brooding over all this great activity was the "muckle blue hill they ca' Ingleboro'", to quote Jeanie Deans, in *The Heart of Midlothian*. It seems however that Sir Walter Scott got rather mixed up in his geography here; for while his intrepid heroine far out-paced Sharland by tramping most of the way from Edinburgh to London, albeit not in the depths of winter, her author plots her route as passing Durham and York, and she would have to have made a wide and improbable westward detour, and climbed the wolds above Swaledale to get even a distant glimpse of the high mountains of Craven. One can hardly imagine that any of the thousands that were temporarily encamped in Batty Green, or its surroundings even took time off to climb to the flat top of Ingleborough, so flat indeed that a party of my school friends from Giggleswick once staged an impromptu game of 'stump cricket' on the summit.

Until comparatively recent years tunnel entrances were for the eyes of the engine crew, and occasionally for those privileged to ride on the footplate with them. There are, of course, exceptions like the western end of Box, and the near-distant view of Shakespeare's Cliff Tunnel from Dover, but prospects like the grim single-tracked bores of the original Woodhead, like Primrose Hill, and Kilsby, not to mention the great Alpine tunnel like the Lötschberg, and the Gothard with its spectacular spiral approaches, were for the driver's view only. It is all the more remarkable that so outstanding an engineering work as a Blea Moor Tunnel has so tame an entrance, at any rate on the south side where all the activity originally began. The line comes up from Selside, swings round the north-eastern flanks of Ingleborough and then heads seemingly, straight for the Greensett Craggs of Whernside. Then, when about to make a spectacular entry to the mountain side, it swings away to the north beside the Little Dale Beck, and enters the tunnel itself by what looks to be no more than a covered way. As originally surveyed the tunnel was to have been straight throughout and on a falling gradient of 1 in 440 towards the north, but because of the nature of the ground at this southern exit, it was decided to extend the tunnel over the crest of the bank, on a slight curve, and thus precluding, in these non-steam days, a sight through from end to end.

As an engineer myself I never cease to be fascinated by the story of the conception and building of Blea Moor Tunnel, back in the 1870s. Apart from the lurid tales of the primitive life of many of those who lived in the shanty towns at Ribblehead, discipline in the labour force was remarkably high; there were no wild-cat strikes, no appreciable absenteeism on Mondays after Bacchanalian junketings on Saturday nights, and over the weekends, indeed for many it was a seven-day week for much of the duration of the work. But backing up the efforts of the labour force the basic engineering was immaculate. Blea Moor Tunnel, as finally arranged, was 2,629 yards long, and despite its rather mild southern approach it passes later near to the 'Crag of Blea Moor', 1,753 ft high, beneath which slopes the railway at a maximum depth of some 500 ft below the surface of the ground. Using the tools and explosives then available a team of no more than four tunnellers could work at a single face at the same time. To maintain progress of the constructional work inside, roughly in unison with the building of the great Ribblehead Viaduct, it was determined that in the tunnel there would have to be fourteen working faces together with an additional one at each end.

Seven shafts had to be sunk on the line of the tunnel so spaced that from each there would be an approximately equal amount of tunnelling to perform on each side of the shaft itself, or so it was hoped. But before anything else could begin winding engines to take the workmen below, and lift the spoil out afterwards, had to be installed — no small job on a desolate moorland 1,500 ft above sea level. F. S. Williams has a vivid description of how the winding engines were hauled up, piece by piece, and then erected on site. Once the shafts were sunk tunnelling went on day and night. One can do nothing but applaud the work of the civil engineers who surveyed the route with such precision and determined the direction in which each heading should proceed from the bottom of each shaft. It is incredible to recall that on this work the tunnellers had no light but that of candles! Fortunately there were no other hazards. There were no subterranean streams that came bursting in and flooding the workings. The men became quite adept at the use of dynamite to blast the rocks, and when the tunnels broke through, one with another, all were gratified that the surveys had been accurate. In all the hazards of Blea Moor and its forbidding terrain this

*The southern approach to Blea Moor Tunnel — note retaining walls on the down side of the line, to guard against landslips.* (Norman Wilkinson)

was a remarkable railway civil engineering achievement. One thinks back to the case of a short tunnel in Scotland, bored from both ends, where the surveys were so much adrift that the two bores missed each other by the complete width!

At Blea Moor on its completion three of the seven shafts were retained as ventilation for the tunnel. The sites of these are marked on the one-inch Ordnance Survey map. Those spaced 0.44 and 0.63 miles from the south end were presumably intended to clear the exhausts of hard working locomotives, recovering slowly from their efforts up the 'Long Drag' from Settle Junction. The third, often seen smoking from the lineside at Dent Head, is 0.32 miles in from the north end. The engraving in Williams's book depicts a scene more dramatic than any of the Swiss Alpine tunnels, but of this same locality, while looking the opposite way, I have a personal tale to tell. In the early years of World War II, when the new periodical *Railways* was introducing some new writers to the railway scene I made the acquaintance, by post at first, of C. M. Doncaster, who was in the steel industry in Sheffield. I gathered he was a man much older than I was, because when he was at school at Reading he took photographs of the last broad gauge 8 ft singles at speed. Then late in 1941 business took me to Sheffield, a meeting was

quickly arranged and one evening he took me to his beautiful, though heavily blacked-out home in the village of Bradfield, high in the hills north-west of the city. As an active photographer of more than fifty years experience he had much to show me but one picture gripped my attention more than all others.

He had photographed a northbound freight train crossing Dent Head Viaduct. It was the first time I had ever seen that part of the line in a picture, although I had travelled over it many times by train; but I was enthralled by the breathtaking beauty of the scene, to which the railway, the viaduct and the freight train below were mere incidentals. The wide sweep of the Dee Valley to the west, the mass of Rise Hill beyond, and then the tremendous bulk of Baugh Fell with the clouds touching its highest ridges made a most majestic scene. In answer to my eulogies Doncaster gave me a print, and within a few months I had painted it in watercolours, but substituting for the northbound freight hauled by a humble Class 4 Midland 0-6-0 an up Scotch Express hauled by one of the two original Johnson compounds, with the double bogie tenders.

From the north end of Blea Moor Tunnel the line is carried on an almost level course along the 1,100 ft contour for about six miles, and the scenery from the left hand of the train is breath-

*The aqueduct carrying water from Force Gill, high up on Whernside, over the line, from which the photograph of the approach to the tunnel was taken.* (Norman Wilkinson)

taking. After crossing the minor road from which Charles Doncaster took the photograph which so excited my interest, comes Dent Head Viaduct. It originated at Newby Head Moss at an altitude of about 1,400 ft on the Ingleton to Hawes road, about three miles north of Gearstones, where Sharland was snowed up. This viaduct is of the usual handsome style used throughout the line, with ten arches, each of 45 ft span, and like Ribblehead has brick arched rings. The construction is in limestone, and the railway is carried 100 ft above the valley below. The road up to Newby Head Moss, passes under the railway in a fine stone bridge a short distance south of the viaduct itself. Only one pier out the nine was the specially strengthened construction used at Ribblehead. The viaduct marked the end of contract No. 1 let for the construction of the railway, and it was interesting that the very next one, a little over a mile to the north, over Arten Gill Beck, included a change in the method of construction. It also followed the graceful form displayed at Dent Head, with eleven spans, having a maximum height of 117 ft; but while the arches were also of 45 ft span, construction was in limestone throughout and no brickwork was used. The heavily strengthened piers, Nos 2 and 5 from the south end, were on each side of the narrow gully in which the Arten Gill Beck flows.

North of this viaduct the line follows the contour along the hillside with little in the way of earthworks until near Rise Hill Tunnel. This alignment no doubt proved a bonus for those building the railway, but on the eastern side of the valley, with the great fells piling up to eminences like Great Knoutberry Hill of 2,200 ft, no more than a mile abreast of the railway, it proved an almost overwhelming obstacle in wintry weather, such as the line experienced in the early months of 1946. In its earlier days the Midland Railway followed the practice of the Highland in building snow fences along the most exposed and valuable stretches of the Settle and Carlisle line, but these were useless in the face of such storms as hit the High Pennines in 1946. Dent station, opened in 1877, was high up the hill from the hamlet of Cowgill, itself some four miles from the picturesque village of Dent. In due course the station became far more than a mere block post, having refuge sidings of considerable length on both sides of the line, and from some recent photographs giving the impression that the route was quadrupled tracked in this location.

A mile beyond Dent station the line heads straight into Rise Hill Tunnel. Like Blea Moor it is not straight from end to end, and in this case the curve comes at the northern end where the line is already turning in a north-easterly direction to continue on the 1,100 ft contour to Hawes

Junction, as it was known for so many years. Rise Hill Tunnel, 1,213 yd long, has two ventilation shafts, although neither is as deep as those at Blea Moor. Emerging from the rock cutting from Rise Hill Tunnel, another charming prospect opens to the left of the line, with the Clough river, yet another of the tributaries of the Lune, coming up Garsdale with the tremendous mass of Baugh Fell as a background. The line continues level, indeed on one stretch the Midland Railway installed water troughs in 1907, to obviate the use of the huge bogie tenders fitted to the Johnson compounds and to many of the Class 3 Belpaire 4-4-0s working some of the long non-stop runs. Hawes Junction, lying at the very head of Garsdale, was at first purely a railway settlement. The Midland, first in the field, included in their authority to build the Settle and Carlisle the construction of a branch down the upper reaches of Wensleydale to meet the North Eastern branch from Northallerton, already under way. The Midland ownership would extend only to Hawes, just six miles down the dale, but instead of the embattled confrontation that existed between the LNWR and the Midland at Ingleton in Wensleydale the two companies arranged to reciprocal running powers, the North Eastern to work westwards to Hawes Junction and the Midland down the dale as far as Askrigg. It was an eminently practical arrangement, and

in due course the North Eastern branch trains continued to Hawes Junction. Any through passengers there might be were thus spared the inconvenience of alighting at Hawes and joining a Midland train for the last six miles of the journey.

Before construction on the branch line to Hawes had proceeded any way the engineers building the main line were in dire trouble within sight of the junction point. Garsdale Head like the headwaters of the Ribble and the Greta beneath the heights of Whernside and Ingleborough, is flanked by some marshy ground. The present Ordnance Survey map has some alluring names like Mud Becks, and Dandry Mire, and it was across this latter that the route to the north had been surveyed. As mentioned previously, the original intention had been to carry the line across the area on a low embankment, but tipping was of no avail. The bog then had to be drained and dug down deeply to find a rock formation on which to build the arches of a viaduct. It required a structure of twelve arches, 227 yd long, each of the spans being the usual 45 ft, but not so lofty as some of the more famous viaducts on the line. It was built in stone throughout of the very pleasing design characteristic of the line, with the fourth and eighth piers heavily strengthened. Williams names it Dandry Mire Viaduct, after the morass that led to its construction, but more

*Dent Head Viaduct, looking north-west.* (W. Hubert Foster)

recent works refer to it as the Moorcock after the inn at the road junction no more than about one-third of a mile away. Once over the viaduct the line heads round north again, through the two short tunnels of Moorcock and Shotlock Hill, on a rising gradient of 1 in 155 towards Ais Gill Summit with the crags of Wild Boar Fell filling the picture ahead of the line.

The Ais Gill Moor Cottages built by the Midland Railway for their signalmen and surfacemen mark the actual summit of the line, and no more than a brief walk across the moor to the east of the railway takes one to the headwaters of two rivers that flow respectively into the Solway Firth and the North Sea. Hell Gill Beck, which is the source of the River Eden, and the Ure, that flows down Wensleydale, are no more than half a mile apart on the side of Abbotside Common. From Ais Gill Summit the line is carried down on a 1 in 100 gradient on the slopes of Wild Boar Fell, and although the railway here is terribly exposed and subject to the wildest of wintry weather it is carried on the western side of the mountain range and thus not so liable to snow-blocks as that notorious stretch between Dent Head and Hawes Junction. There is only one break in the sustained climbing on 1 in 100 vouchsafed for the engines of southbound trains in this truly mountainous section of the line, in the three-quarters of a mile at 1 in 300 past

Mallerstang signal box, later an important block-post, and a point where freight trains could be berthed to clear the way for a succession of faster traffic. Although the steeper descent at 1 in 100 is resumed immediately afterwards, and continues unbrokenly for a further five miles, before getting down to what one may call hospitable regions the mountain country had one or two more quirks to play on the constructional engineers.

Going north, not far beyond Mallerstang signal box there is a high embankment and the broad prospect of the dale below makes one look out for a fleeting glimpse of the fragmentary ruin of Pendragon Castle. But the engineers who built the railway had thoughts far otherwise hereabouts, for the viewpoint from which the traveller can enjoy this particular prospect of the Eden Valley is the notorious Intake Embankment about 100 ft high. To quote Williams: "At this point an extraordinary circumstance occurred, the tipping proceeded for twelve months without this embankment advancing a yard. The tip rails, during that whole period, were unmoved, while the masses of slurry, as indicated in the engraving, rolled over one another in might convolutions persisting in anywhere and everywhere except where they were wanted". The reproduction of the engraving gives a vivid picture of the scene that daunted the engineers in construction days. Even so, they must have built strongly,

*Arten Gill Viaduct under construction — an engraving.* (Engraving per F. S. Williams)

*Moorcock Viaduct, just north of Hawes Junction. The engineers planned to cross the swampy Dandry Mire with an embankment, but the tipping proved impossible.* (W. Hubert Foster)

because in the 115 years since the railway was opened to traffic I have never heard of any mishap through subsidence at that particular location, which is more than can be said of certain far less potentially hazardous sections farther north.

While some of the workforce on No. 2 Contract, which extended from the north end of Dent Head Viaduct to north of Kirkby Stephen, were wrestling with the problems of the Intake Embankment, ahead, less than a mile away, were the heights of Wharton Fell and Birkett Common. The survey planned that the line should be taken straight through to maintain the fast-running alignment, and when Crossley and his men began to dig the rock cutting that was to lead to Birkett Tunnel they found geological features that surprised even the most erudite of them. Descending from Ais Gill Summit on the relatively uniform slopes below the crags of Wild Boar Fell they had not at first appreciated the underlying rock formation, or how the great outcrop of what is sometimes referred to as 'Mountain Limestone' fringes the New Red Sandstone of the Vale of

Eden in what the geologists call a 'fault-line valley'; but they soon had practical evidence of its features when they worked their way towards Birkett Tunnel.

As seen, the various components of the rocks include not only Mountain Limestone and shale, but the strata, rising from the ground well nigh vertically, reveal thin layers of slate, coal and lead ore. A study of the Ordnance Survey maps of the district show the frequency of worked-out lead mines, so it was not surprising to find evidences of it in the approach to Birkett Tunnel. Early pictures of the work give striking proof of the nature of the rock through which the cuttings were excavated. The tunnel itself, 424 yards in length, as might be expected from the terrain, gave considerable trouble, and at one stage there was a bad rock fall. Surprisingly, despite all the difficulties at Blea Moor and Rise Hill they do not seem to have been troubled with rock falls. And so, emerging from the north end of Birkett Tunnel, one can bid farewell to the mountain section of the Settle and Carlisle railway. Henceforth the countryside is more pastoral, even so definitely North Country.

# 4
# Constructional Work — North from Kirkby Stephen

Before leaving the mountain regions one cannot fail to note, despite the wild nature of the countryside, the beautiful buildings and comprehensive layouts of even the most remote wayside stations. I am thinking particularly of Horton, Ribblehead and Dent. At the outset there was no likelihood of any appreciable passenger traffic, but the stations were well equipped, and the goods yards ready to deal particularly well with cattle. At the height of Midland Railway business enterprise there were a considerably greater number of through express passenger trains on the line than there were locals. After the very first years when the timetables provided for conditional stops at many intermediate stations, with its rapid development as a major express route, Appleby was the only station serving an appreciable town that was regularly favoured. Settle was virtually ignored so far as through traffic was concerned. The remaining station in the High Pennines, Hawes Junction was, in Midland Railway days, something of a special case and references to its equipment, track layout, and operational facilities are dealt with at some length in Chapter 9, concerning the tragic happenings in the early hours of Christmas Eve 1910.

Studying a large-scale Ordnance Survey map of the country north and south of Appleby it seems strange at first that the new main line to the north did not follow the course of the River Eden through Kirkby Stephen itself, past the villages of Great Musgrave and Warcop, instead of striking out westwards. Of course in so doing it would have run alongside, or nearly so to the track of the North Eastern line from Darlington to Penrith, and involved some much less extensive civil engineering works. The Settle and Carlisle would have been robbed of four more of its picturesque viaducts, and two tunnels. One needs to have a walking pass to enjoy to the full the section between Kirkby Stephen and Crosby Garrett. The former station must have been a busy place in Midland days, with a capacious cattle dock adjacent to the up passenger platform, a big goods shed and two long sidings on the up side south of the station itself. As usual on the Settle and Carlisle line there was a terrace of substantially-built houses nearby for railway employees. They were about the only dwellings anywhere near the line, because the pleasant little town of Kirkby Stephen is more than two miles away.

North of the station the track begins swinging round until its direction becomes due westward for a short distance beside the hamlet of Smardale. Here the North Eastern line to Tebay approaches on the right, though when the Midland veers round northwards again to cross the deep ravine of the Scandal Beck, the other line is so deeply ensconced among the trees on its southern side, high up above the beck itself, that even a keen observer from a northbound Midland train could quite well miss spotting its track. Smardale Viaduct is the tallest on the Settle and Carlisle line at 130 ft above the level of the

*Birkett Tunnel — south end.* (Norman Wilkinson)

beck. Constructed entirely in grey limestone it has twelve arches each of 45 ft span and entirely conforming to the graceful design Crossley used in all the viaducts on the line. Northward of the viaduct the route follows the western side of the hills that bound the Eden Valley, bridging the gulleys in which further becks flow towards the river and tunnelling through any bluffs that intersect the direct line. The next tunnel comes soon after Smardale Viaduct, a short one, only 181 yards long, roughly a mile before Crosby Garrett station is reached.

This picturesque upland village lies in a trough of the hills crossed by another viaduct of no more than six arches, but all the same dominating the landscape. It is built in limestone, and like the more famous one at Ribblehead the arches have brick-lined rings. Crosby Garrett in its heyday must have been a busy place. The track layout included several goods sidings in addition to those giving access to the large goods shed and the six-bay cattle dock. There was also a lay-by for the berthing of goods trains on the down side of the line. The passenger accommodation consisted of the usual neat and handsome buildings characteristic of the whole line. Crosby Garrett is one of the few villages on the upland part of the Settle and Carlisle railway to be actually adjacent to the line, but before proceeding many miles farther north one comes to a location that could quite well have influenced Crossley and the top Midland management to take the line veering westwards from Kirkby Stephen, instead of following the actual course of the River Eden, as the North Eastern line

had done.

A little short of two miles north of Crosby Garrett, beside the hamlet of Griseburn, the Midland Railway purchased a tract of land adjacent to the line on a steep slope on the down side. Here was established a quarry to provide excellent ballast for the permanent way. The quarry was eventually extended to cover fully three-quarters of the land originally purchased, and its extent can be seen on the latest one-inch Ordnance Survey maps. The siting of the quarry at Griseburn, on the railway, undoubtedly facilitated the transport of permanent way material to many parts of the Midland Railway. Originally the connection was an unattended siding, but a signal box was erected in 1905, and Griseburn then became a main-line block post. South of this location there is another beautiful viaduct, notable because of its unusual decoration. The structure is of the usual Crossley design, six arches of 74 ft maximum height, of stone, although the facings of the arches and the parapets are in red sandstone, giving a distinctive decorative effect. The speed of northbound trains at this location is usually such that even the keenest sightseer would be unlikely to note the parapets as a Scotch Express sweeps across the pretty dell in which the Helm Beck rumbles towards the Eden.

Then comes Helm Tunnel, the associations with the wild natural phenomena of the district have been mentioned in an earlier chapter of this, and so to the crossing of the River Eden near Ormside station. The viaduct built in stone and having construction features in keeping with all

*Birkett Tunnel — north end.* (Norman Wilkinson)

the rest of the major works on the line, is distinct as crossing a broad open valley, with ten arches, one of which stands in mid-stream, and a maximum height of 90 ft. Less than three miles farther north comes the very pleasant north-country centre of Appleby, of which I have a personal confession to make, in that I first visited it not by train but road. When my father was still in business in Barrow-in-Furness we had as next-door neighbours a middle-aged couple who were keen motorists. The wife was a naturalist and expert gardener, and each weekend when the weather was fine they used to head off towards some of the less frequented areas of the Lake District. Very often my mother and father were invited to join them, and when I was at home for the occasional Bank Holiday weekend I was sometimes taken too.

Then came a memorable Sunday when our friends said they were going to explore towards the head waters of the River Lune. They were going straight to Kendal, over the hilly and unfrequented road direct from Newby Bridge at the foot of Windermere, and thence over the fells to the Lune Gorge, through which the West Coast Main Line makes its way to Tebay and the foot of the Shap Incline. It was fifty years or more before the M6 motorway was built through this wild country. At Tebay we were in our exploring region and we turned eastwards up the valley, alongside the one-time North Eastern line from Kirkby Stephen. We meandered along stopping to take photographs at Newbiggin-on-Lune and at Ravenstonedale, and then we turned north through Kirkby Stephen and made our way to

Appleby by tea-time. I was charmed with the place, with its wide main street leading up to the High Cross, with its ancient church, and its attractive entrance gate; but although I travelled in trains on the Settle and Carlisle line many times in after years I never had occasion to alight, until the very poignant day related near the end of this book. Appleby station, called at by some of the Scotch Expresses, is no more than a slightly larger and more elongated version of the wayside

*Smardale Viaduct — an engraving during the time of erection.* (Engraving per F. S. Williams)

stations on the line, and the connecting line to the North Eastern appears to have been very much of an afterthought.

North of Appleby the line traverses a broad belt of good farming country, overlooked nevertheless on the eastern side by some of the highest ridges of the Pennines. While the gradients are generally no more than gradual they favour northbound trains until the second crossing of the River Eden, before Lazonby. In the 15.4 miles between Appleby and the last mentioned place four intermediate stations were originally proposed; at Long Marton, 2.9 miles from Appleby, at Newbiggin — another one with no connection with the one in the Lune Valley — a further 3.2 miles, at Langwathby, and at Little Salkeld. The two last mentioned were no more than 1.3 miles apart, and Little Salkeld was 2.9 miles from Lazonby. When the plans for equipping the railway became known locally the village of Culgaith was aggrieved to find it had no station of its own. The four intermediate stations between Appleby and Lazonby were planned to have structures of the same general design as provided for the places farther south, and the Midland Railway evidently thought that a station at Newbiggin, 1.3 miles away would suffice also for Culgaith. But the

village, even by modern road maps, is a good three miles from Newbiggin station. That was not good enough for the local residents.

A strongly worded letter of protest was sent to Derby. When this plea for a station was summarily rejected the residents tried again, but this time, sensing that there might be something in it after all, the Board sent Crossley to interview the local vicar, who appeared to be the chief mouthpiece of the protestors. All was settled amicably and Culgaith got its station, curiously enough not one of the usual 'Settle and Carlisle' design, but of an attractive cottage style building, so far as I know, unique on the Midland Railway. Goods facilities were sparse however. No more than a single siding was provided on the down side of the line, this was thought to be adequate for the extensive traffic in potatoes which was handled in the appropriate season. While Culgaith was in some ways the 'odd-man out' in its equipment, reference to Chapter 8 will show that so far as Cecil J. Allen in his train timing activities were concerned, it is the only intermediate station featured in his many logs of train running that I myself have reproduced. Presumably, because it is almost half way in distance between Appleby and Lazonby prompted its

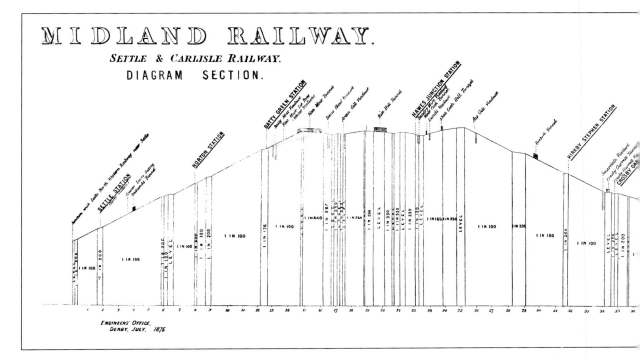

choice for inclusion in his logs.

Newbiggin, which the Midland Railway wanted the people of Culgaith to use, had a far more comprehensive layout with cattle pens, goods sidings and a loading dock in addition to the usual station buildings. It was the last point in the former County of Westmorland on the Settle and Carlisle line, because the county boundary came at the crossing of Crowdundle Beck, scene of the amusing contretemps between the engineers and the Rev. Crackenthorpe over his trees. Compared with the comparative absence of them on the West Coast Main Line one must remark upon the positive plethora of industrial sidings on the Settle and Carlisle, because in addition to the great quarries at Stainforth and Horton, there is a crop of them south of Newbiggin, all dealing with the valuable compound calcium sulphate, or to give it the commercial name, Gypsum. Several concerns quarried this material, one indeed, McGkie, set up an Alabaster Works beside the line about a quarter of a mile south of Newbiggin station. These industrial connections were equipped with ground frame control to be used as required.

Reverting to Culgaith, from the station platforms one can see through the 660 yard tunnel, which is straight, though in steam days I imagine there was some trouble with smoke as a ventilating shaft was provided, even in this short length. North of the tunnel the line comes immediately to the river bank, so near in fact that for a quarter of a mile Crossley instructed his contractor to tip spoil from the cuttings to reinforce the embankment, and incidentally to divert the course of the river in this locality. Just beyond, a short tunnel was cut through an intervening ridge, only 165 yards long, and as there was no village or other geographical feature nearby to give it a name the railway people called it 'Waste Bank Tunnel', and so it has remained ever since as a memorial to the artifice by which Crossley interfered with the 'environment'! No trouble was encountered with the nearness of the River Eden at this point though the dumping of the 'waste bank' was a wise precaution, against the likelihood of scour from flood water in storm times gouging out the railway bank. Forty years after the line had been built, and the works fully consolidated however, there was an alarming landslip not many miles to the north that completely wrecked a Scotch Express with many fatalities. Before we reach the site of this sad accident, and before even passing Langwathby, there is a charming vista

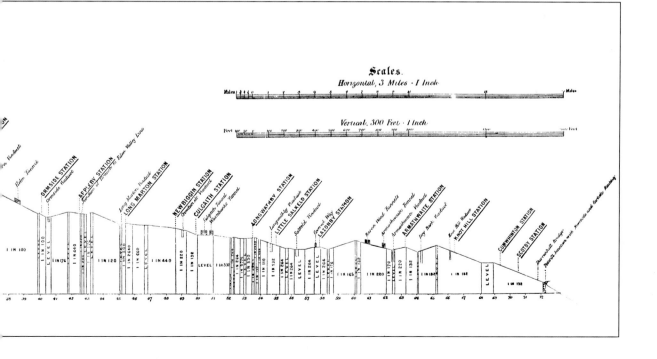

*Smardale Viaduct — the trees hide the line of the NER to Tebay.* (W. Hubert Foster)

to the west of the line over the confluence of the River Eamont, and the wooded policies of the Edenhall estates — shades of Crewe and its engine naming!

Langwathby had a very extensive station and yard layout. The station buildings and the stationmaster's house, while conforming to the style of architecture usual on the Settle and Carlisle line, were built in the local red sandstone, as was also the three-wagon goods shed. The yard had a six-bay cattle dock, and a crane beside one of the numerous sidings. In view of the relatively close proximity of another well-equipped station, Little Salkeld, only 1.3 miles to the north, one can well imagine the reluctance of the Midland Railway to build yet another at Culgaith. Between Langwathby and Little Salkeld there is a handsome viaduct in the customary style over the Briggle Beck. It has seven arches of 44 ft 7 in span and has a maximum height of 60 ft. Like Ribblehead it was built generally of stone while having brick arches. Little Salkeld station had an unusual provision of sidings on both sides of the line but no definitely specified cattle dock. In addition to the stationmaster's house there were the cottages for other railwaymen, and those working on the permanent way were able to give important evidence regarding the derailment of the 8.50 am from St Pancras to Glasgow, on the afternoon of 19th January 1918. I remember

*Smardale Viaduct — grey limestone with Millstone grit parapets.* (Norman Wilkinson)

*Crosby Garrett station in LMS days.* (W. Hubert Foster)

personally the climatic conditions on that particular weekend, though I did not hear about the accident until some time later.

On Friday, 18th January the Christmas holidays were ended and I was packed off to Giggleswick in very wintry weather. Snow fell heavily during the night and I remember how the gloom of being back at boarding school was relieved next morning by the enchanting sight of great trees near to the school bowed down by the snow. The thaw however was very rapid, and I should imagine this is what caused the landslip in the cutting north of Little Salkeld. The surfacemen were vigilant enough, and one man walked the length of the cutting both ways at 3.20 and

3.35 pm on the Saturday afternoon. The signals had been cleared for the passage of the Scotch Express, and moments only after the platelayer had passed the landslip occurred, blocking both down and up main lines. Within minutes the train came up at full speed, and the locomotive ploughing into the tumbled ground was brought to a violent halt. The two leading coaches telescoped on to the tender, and their timber framed bodies were completely smashed, while the rest of the eleven-coach train was derailed and ended up in various forms of disarray. It was a mercy that the train was running on its greatly decelerated wartime schedule and making a little under 60 mph on this favourable stretch of line, where

*Ormside Viaduct where the railway crosses the River Eden for the first time.* (W. Hubert Foster)

*An older crossing of the River Eden — the bridge at Appleby.* (Norman Wilkinson)

in pre-war days the speed of down Scotch Expresses was often around 80 mph. Fortunately also, there were fewer passengers travelling that day, otherwise the death toll in the leading coaches might have been much higher than the seven who were actually killed. The engine was the non-superheated compound No. 1010, though with an eleven-coach train it was almost certainly piloted up to Ais Gill, even on a war schedule.

L. T. C. Rolt in his fine book *Red for Danger* sites the foregoing accident as in the Long Meg cutting. At that time the signal box controlling entry to the siding serving the works of the Long Meg Plaster & Mineral Co. Ltd, installed in 1898, had been removed and movement to and from the sidings was controlled from a 3-lever ground frame, the operation of which was controlled by the station master at Little Salkeld. When the siding was first laid in Long Meg it was established as an ordinary block post and a crossover road put in on the main line. The works were situated on the right bank of the River Eden, within close sight of the railway when it crossed the handsome Eden Lacy Viaduct. Long Meg signal box was closed in 1915, and the modern equivalent of it, to cope with the vast anhydride traffic that developed, was opened in July 1955, as will be referred to in a later chapter. The ancient monument, 'Long Meg and her daughters', although relatively near at hand, is over the brow of the hill beside the River Eden and cannot be seen from the railway.

Eden Lacy Viaduct, which the Midland Railway engineers of constructional days at first called Long Meg, is unusual on the Settle and Carlisle line in being built of red sandstone throughout. It has seven arches of the usual 45 ft span, and four of the piers are set in the bed of the river. Coming at the foot of the long descending gradient from Long Marton, before the line rises beyond Lazonby to negotiate the hilly and marvellously picturesque stretch of the Eden Valley, it very often witnessed the highest maximum speed of the entire descent from Ais Gill Summit to Carlisle. Engines that had been unpiloted up the 'Long Drag' were often taken relatively easily down the steepest part of the ensuing descent, to give the fireman a rest and sometimes to restore the water level in the boiler, but from Appleby northwards they were away in earnest again, and sometimes exceeded 80 mph at the viaduct.

Lazonby, or 'Lazonby and Kirkoswald', to give it the full names emblazoned on those huge boards so characteristic of the Midland Railway, was a busy place in the old days. It had one of the usual goods sheds, large cattle pens, two loading docks, one equipped with a crane, and outside the station on the main road, there was even a 'Midland Hotel', though not of the size and appointments of those operated and run by the MR itself. Lazonby exists in a long chain of dwellings to west and east of the railway, while Kirkoswald lies rather over a mile away above the right bank of the Eden. Cattle traffic was intense

*The viaduct at Long Marton.* (W. Hubert Foster)

in Midland days, gathering in business from a wide area. The passenger accommodation was no more than that provided for the most rural of stations on the line. It was goods and cattle, not passengers, that counted at Lazonby.

I have never had the privilege of a walking pass on this part of the Settle and Carlisle line, but I feel that the stretch between Lazonby and Armathwaite is one of the most beautiful of all on the Midland Railway. Just where the line is opposite to the Nunnery Walks, which I found so delightful on one of my Eastertide explorations of the right bank of the river, there are immediately below the railway the remarkable rocks that rise some 100 ft above and form the entrance to what is known locally as Samson's Cave. F. S. Williams in his book on the Midland Railway quotes the name, so do the publishers of a sumptuous volume of coloured plates produced some eighty years ago, entitled *Rivers and Streams of England*. The artist of this latter work has an exquisite painting of the River Eden in the neighbourhood of Samson's Cave, and it would seem that he had set up his easel on, or near the Midland Railway line through the gorge, a location where many fine photographs of south-bound expresses have been taken in recent times. It is perhaps surprising that the latest one-inch Ordnance Survey map of the district does not include a reference to Samson's Cave, to pinpoint its location. North of the place where the train photographs have been taken are the two short Baron Wood tunnels, each no more than 200 to

250 yards long and separated by less than even that short distance between them. Such were the rocky bluffs lying across the line of the railway that had to be cleared by tunnelling.

From the second tunnel the line emerged into the extensive forest land of Baron Wood lying in the estates of the Ley family of Lazonby Hall. When the railway was first opened forestry traffic was dealt with at Lazonby goods yard, including the cartage of massive whole trees; but when the business in pit-props for colliery working developed, a private siding for the exclusive use of the Ley family was laid in north of the second Baron Wood Tunnel. The rail connection by a trailing crossover road was made only with the down main line and a covered three-lever ground frame was installed to operate it. Down goods trains attaching or detaching wagons for the siding obtained a releasing key from the signalman at Lazonby, and after use it was returned to the signalman at Armathwaite. Traffic from the Ley forest lands reached a peak of activity in the First World War, but with dwindling business afterwards the siding closed and the rail connection to the main line was removed in 1951. I have heard that the owner of the estate at that time was something of a locomotive enthusiast, and enjoyed travelling on the Settle and Carlisle line. The Baron Wood site extended almost to the next tunnel officially, the Armathwaite, but sometimes called Cat Clint. It is 325 yd long and precedes the long sweeping curve to the north east by which the railway follows the course of the River

Eden. From Lazonby, against northbound trains the gradients turn adverse for about two miles, at 1 in 165, and this usually pulled the speed down from the 70–75 mph dash from Appleby to under 60 abreast of Samson's Cave; but with the change after the Baron Wood tunnels the speed was usually in the high sixties again in crossing Armathwaite Viaduct.

Although the railway makes almost a right-angle to the north east in this locality the track alignment was good enough to permit the highest of speeds that steam locomotives could run. Armathwaite Viaduct is a characteristically pleasing structure of nine arches entirely on the curve, and there is another, about a further mile north of Armathwaite station, the Drybeck, preceded by an embankment that caused some concern to the engineers, not because of any local freaks of nature but by the sheer volume of soil that had got to be tipped in to build it. Williams quotes 400,000 cubic yards! Just beyond Drybeck Viaduct is Low House crossing, opened in 1890. The signal box and crossing gates were constructed to give access to some farmland property west of the railway, and it remained a block post on the main line until 1975. It had no points or sidings, only the level crossing gates. Located

near to the summit point of the toilsome bank, mostly on 1 in 132, out of Carlisle I found the signal box a convenient timing point, and many of my logs of trains running over this route include the time of passing Low House. Dry Beck, previously mentioned is the most northerly of the appreciable viaducts on the line, having seven arches, and a maximum height of 80 ft. In normal weather its name is justified, but in heavy storms, the dale it crosses does become somewhat water logged.

Even when reaching the final descent into Carlisle, the engineering difficulties were not ended. After passing Low House Crossing the railway, to follow the course of the river, turned north-westwards, and over the hills to the left of the line were, and still are, the woods of the extensive High Stand plantation, from which issued the High Stand Gill Beck, a tiny tributary of the River Eden. Approaching this wooded gulley through which this beck flowed a high embankment was necessary, and as soon as the engineers began to tip a landslip took place, and the whole ground began to move. Not only this, but the area between the line of the railway and the river seemed unable to resist the pressure of the embankment and the whole mass slid down

*Crowdondale — the viaduct in course of construction.* (Engraving per F. S. Williams)

towards the river. At one time it had been proposed to carry the line higher up the hillside, through the plantation, but the obvious difficulties of obtaining access to such a private area were enough deterrent to abandon this scheme, and despite the landslip troubles the line was eventually carried across the slip. Even more slipping occurred and carried some great trees with it. A level crossing was needed just north of the High Stand Gill Viaduct, and here another wayside station was sited. On the original Midland Railway drawings of the gradients of the line it is called Knot Hill, from the hamlet on the Carlisle road nearby, but it soon became Cotehill, after the large village some 1–2 miles to the west of the line.

After Cotehill on the continuing descent towards Carlisle there were two more intermediate stations, Cumwhinton and Scotby, and from the latter it was no more than a mile before the large freight and operational yards of Durran Hill were reached. The south sidings, access to and from which was controlled by Durran Hill South signal box, consisted of a nest of eighteen dead-end tracks ranged between the main line and the Newcastle & Carlisle line which swings alongside in this neighbourhood. The Midland's south sidings terminated before the road bridge that crosses the railway just before the $306\frac{1}{2}$ mile is reached. Adjoining this road, with suitable access from it, was the extensive establishment of the locomotive department on the west side of the main line, including two fitting shops, blacksmiths and joiners' shops and all the facilities for carrying out repairs to locomotives up to an intermediate stage. The running shed and all its adjoining equipment was built at the time of the original construction of the line, and while the Midland had several examples of the roundhouse type of shed, Durran Hill was built with dead-end tracks inside, except for the one road that led to the small turntables giving access to the fitting shops.

As originally laid out Durran Hill, with seven parallel tracks inside provided accommodation for at least one hundred main line locomotives. In addition to the many goods engines that were needed for the heavy through freight workings to and from Scotland the policy of the Midland Railway, in the early 1900s, in using nothing larger than 4-4-0 locomotives, and not large examples of these, made necessary the provision of a number of passenger engines to be used as pilots in case of heavy loading. Of Durran Hill

*The viaduct near Armathwaite.* (W. Hubert Foster)

shed there is a tale to be told, albeit of LMS times. The Midland Railway had always prided itself on the neat and tidy manner in which its main line engine sheds were kept, and after Grouping, with an ex-Midland man in charge of motive power arrangements for the entire railway, he had been appalled at slaphappy methods practiced at some of the ex-London & North Western sheds. In the late autumn of 1926 when arrangements were being made to test a Great Western 'Castle' class 4-6-0 between Crewe and Carlisle, and the diagrams needed a stop-over for the nights concerned, it was somewhat significant that the distinguished visiting engine was shedded at Durran Hill for the night, instead of at the LNWR shed at Upperby Bridge!

The freight traffic complex between Durran Hill Junction and Petteril Bridge Junction, where the Settle and Carlisle line ends with its joining the Newcastle & Carlisle branch of the North Eastern Railway, is worth some study because its layout and equipment reflects the position that the Midland Railway came to assume on its establishment in Carlisle. For terminating traffic a substantial goods shed was built adjacent to the main highway to the south, the London Road. The company had purchased a tract of land, triangular in shape, fanning out westwards of the main line to its base on the London Road. The River Petteril entered the property under the Harraby Bridge and to reach the goods shed and the large cattle dock bridges had to be provided. Cattle was one of the principal items of terminating traffic at Carlisle, and the company had its own set of slaughter houses beside the tracks leading to the goods shed. Alongside the wall of London Road were the stables for the many horses used for cartage of all kinds. A little further down stream from the bridges carrying the freight lines, respectively, to the goods shed and to the cattle dock, was the North Eastern Railway bridge over the River Petteril, over

which the Midland had running powers from the immediately adjacent Petteril Bridge Junction signal box, which was owned and worked by the North Eastern. The Newcastle & Carlisle was the first railway to enter the city, actually nearly forty years before the Settle and Carlisle was opened. The Maryport & Carlisle came next in 1843, and the establishment was to prove of vital significance to the Midland when they arrived on the scene in 1876.

The prime object of the top Midland Railway management in enterprising a line of their own to Carlisle was to muscle in upon the rapidly developing traffic between England and Scotland, particularly in freight, and the layout of the sidings between Petteril Bridge and Durran Hill Junction seems to bear this out. They were laid in for through traffic. Between the two junctions there are four running lines, two for passenger and two for goods trains, and for part of the way there are independent goods lines on each side. Other than that the whole complex consists of dead-end sidings, with little or no provision for marshalling up trains as on the modern concentration yards, such as those installed elsewhere on the Midland Railway. Other than with cattle the main outlet to and from the Settle and Carlisle line lay in its joint participation in the work of the Goods Traffic Committee (with the Caledonian, Glasgow & South Western and LNW railways,) and of the Dentonholme Joint Committee, in which the Midland were associated with the Glasgow & South Western and the North British. When the West Coast partners enterprised the building of the central passenger station, the Citadel, they were wise enough to keep their freight lines well clear, and so the line of the original joint committee (CR G&SWR and LNWR) was there for the Midland to join in, as well as having access to NER and Maryport & Carlisle lines. The passenger trains of course went into Citadel station.

# 5
# Operation — the First 25 Years

The track was completed and the permanent way laid throughout the line by mid-1875 and goods traffic inaugurated. A freight terminal a little south of the junction with the Newcastle & Carlisle section of the North Eastern Railway at Petteril Bridge, and between the River Petteril and the London Road there was a substation goods shed, equipped with hand cranes, a cattle dock, and extensive stabling for the many horses used for roadside deliveries and collecting traffic. The well-equipped locomotive running sheds had been built on the west side of the line, and entry to the locomotive yard was controlled by Durran Hill Junction signal box, about half a mile south of Petteril Bridge Junction. Extensive goods sidings were laid in on both sides of the main line, those on the up side eventually taking all the available space between the Midland and North Eastern lines. Although in later years the Settle and Carlisle featured in railway engineering literature almost entirely as a passenger, and engine testing route,

*Kirtley 0-6-0 No. 2707 on an up goods train at Settle station.* (J. M. Tomlinson)

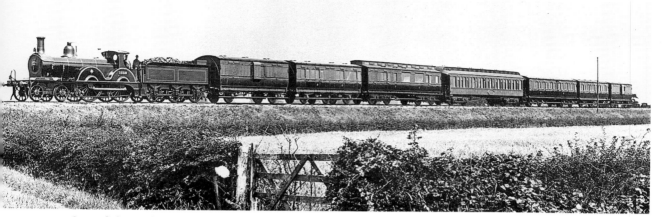

*One of the earliest Johnson 4-4-0s, No. 1338, in the green livery, posed with one of the Scottish Pullman trains.* (British Railways)

for the first fifty-odd years of its existence, certainly in pure Midland days it was an important freight artery.

S. W. Johnson had been appointed Locomotive Superintendent of the Midland Railway in 1873, following the death of Matthew Kirtley. When he came to Derby, from the Great Eastern Railway, all was agog with preparations for opening the Settle and Carlisle, and for the new traffic, and for the burgeoning farther south, orders were placed for no less than 120 new 0-6-0 goods engines of a more powerful design, with various builders. These fine engines, which remained the standard Midland class for about thirty years, were naturally distributed over the railway,

but Nos 1221 to 1251 were allocated to the Leeds–Carlisle route, fifteen engines each going to Leeds and Durran Hill sheds. These engines virtually 'opened the ball' on the Settle and Carlisle line and deserve special mention accordingly. They had $17\frac{1}{2}$ by 26 in cylinders, 4 ft 10 in coupled wheels, and a boiler pressure of 140 lb per sq in. The boilers and fireboxes were not even then large, but they steamed well and were firm favourites in the many-sided railway fraternity in the City of Carlisle. The Midland was the last company to become resident, and the fourth railway to have green engines. The previous shades of the colour varied from the bright, almost malachite of the Maryport, the dark

*Two engined snow-plough unit at Hellifield.* (British Railways)

myrtle of the G&SWR and the pale yellowish of Gateshead. The Midland were of a medium shade which Johnson changed to something considerably lighter — shown in a notable coloured postcard of a 2-4-0 by the Locomotive Publishing Company.

The passenger train service was inaugurated on 1st May 1876. Although most of the intermediate stations were completed and open for business from the very outset, the Settle and Carlisle took its place as a major express train route, though naturally speeds were not high at first. While the line itself continued to be considered as a separate entity, so far as through traffic was concerned locomotive operation had naturally to be originated farther south from Skipton, or in the case of freight services, usually at Leeds. In the early years while many train schedules at first included provision for conditional stops at intermediate stations Settle itself had no regular stops by the through Anglo-Scottish expresses. At this beginning one must designate these trains by the description used in the public timetables and those displayed on station time boards. Anything that ran north of Carlisle was labelled "Scotch Express", and this tradition lasted for some years after the Midland Railway had become a part of the LMS. A curious feature of railway history in the latter years of the 19th Century was the way in which the Midland Scotch services used to avoid Leeds. It is true that Wellington station, being a terminus, involved a change of direction for through trains, but seeing the extent the Midland prided itself on being a provincial rail-

way this attitude, which lasted for the first 25 years after the Settle and Carlisle line was opened for passenger traffic, was a little strange.

The morning Scottish expresses by the rival East and West Coast routes, both leaving their respective London terminus at 10 am, included luncheon stops in their schedules, at York and at Preston, a nominal half-hour. These stops were an acknowledged facility of the service, and of course the Midland had to do the same. It would have seemed that the obvious place to provide this facility would have been Leeds; but instead, at the junction where the Lancashire & Yorkshire line from Manchester joined the North Midland line, at Normanton, palatial dining rooms were installed. Not only that, but most of the Midland Scotch Expresses gave Leeds the 'go-by' altogether, and ran non-stop from the half-hour luncheon halt to Skipton, which was the next place where engines were changed. At first all passenger engine working on the Settle and Carlisle line was based on the sheds at Skipton and Durran Hill, and newly built Johnson 2-4-0s were allocated at the latter. At Skipton on the other hand, much of the most important express duties were at first performed by Kirtley 2-4-0s of the celebrated 800 class.

Leaving details of locomotives apart for the present, in May 1876 the down day Scotch Express was booked to run the $86\frac{3}{4}$ miles from Skipton to Carlisle in 125 minutes, an average speed of $41\frac{3}{4}$ mph. It is interesting to recall that the speed of its immediate rival, the 10 am West Coast express was almost identical over the

*The preserved Kirtley 2-4-0, No. 158A.* (British Railways)

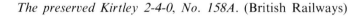

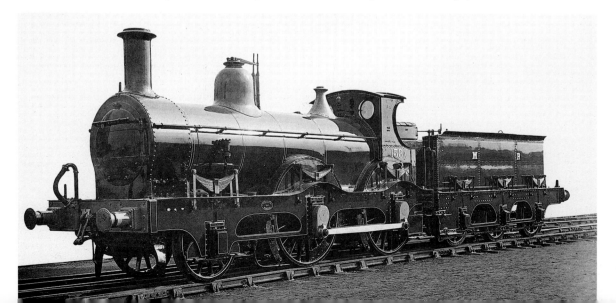

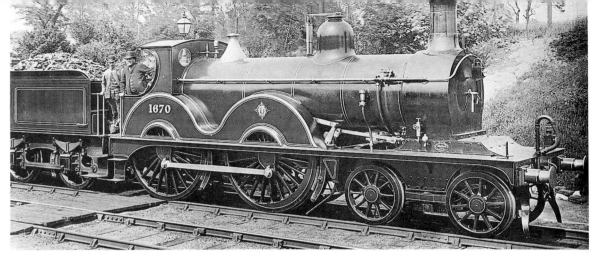

*A beautifully turned out Johnson 4-4-0, No. 1670, before the painting of the initials MR on tenders began and still in green livery.* (Author's Collection)

northern part of the LNWR — 90 miles from Preston to Carlisle in 130 minutes, $41\frac{1}{2}$ mph. But on the Midland acceleration came in no more than three months with the time for the non-stop train from Skipton to Carlisle reduced to 115 minutes, an average of $45\frac{3}{4}$ mph and this stayed the standard time until the first "Race to the North" in 1888, disturbed the peaceful existence of the London & North Western Railway and had the inevitable repercussions on the Midland timetables. Before then reference must be made to the introduction by both railways of express passenger engines with coupled wheels below the diameter usually reckoned as the usual for passenger service, of about 6 ft 6 in or even 7 ft. On the North Western Webb evidently considered that the 6 ft 7 in wheels of the Ramsbottom 'Newton' class were too large for working on a line with the gradients of the Lancaster & Carlisle, and he built the first 'Precursor' 2-4-0s with coupled wheels of no more than 5 ft 6 in diameter. On the Midland, for the Settle and Carlisle line, Johnson designed a class of 2-4-0s having 6 ft $2\frac{1}{2}$ in coupled wheels.

The curious thing about these designs of engines, specially for the mountain sections of these railways, was that they were both markedly unsuccessful. The North Western, virtually the same as the 'Precedent' class, with 6 ft 9 in wheels, reputedly knocked themselves to pieces in their downhill running and soon had to be taken off express work. The Midland 6 ft $2\frac{1}{2}$ in engines were unpopular from the very start because the Carlisle drivers, to whom most of them were allocated, said they "had no go in them". Recalling the speedworthiness of many recent

engines with smaller coupled wheels than Johnson's 'No. 1 Class' of 1876 their sluggishness, which was apparently never cured after they were moved away from the Carlisle road, was probably due to some defect in the valve setting, while Ahrons in his articles in *The Railway Magazine* reports that one or two of them 'blotted their copy books' by breaking their crank axles.

Of all the North-going railways of England the Midland, doubtless because of the competition that would be engendered by the building of the Settle and Carlisle line, had stepped out well away from the recognised standards of the day in passenger carriage building in the early 1870s. First of all, in 1872, the company began conveying third class passengers by all trains, regardless of whether they were slow, intermediate, or top class expresses. Then, from New Year's Day 1875 they abolished second class bookings throughout the railway and made all their second class carriages third class. In 1872 Allport had made a very extensive tour on American railways, and he was so impressed with the standards of comfort and smooth riding of the rolling stock, particularly the large bogie cars, that one of the designers, George M. Pullman, was invited to England, to meet the shareholders of the Midland Railway, at the half-yearly meeting at Derby in 1873. The proprietors were impressed, and the first American designed Pullman car to suit the British loading gauge took the road on the Midland Railway at the end of January 1874. Several more of them were put into traffic later, but they did not seem to be very popular for day-time travelling, although the smoothness of their riding impressed all who rode in them.

For the new Scotch Express services to be inaugurated in 1876 however Mr T. G. Clayton, the Carriage and Wagon Superintendent at Derby, designed something very different from the Pullmans for the ordinary first and third passengers, for those who did not wish to travel in the Pullman cars. In the winter of 1875 orders were given to two contractors to build composite bogie carriages, 54 ft long, carried on two six-wheeled bogies, and providing accommodation, in three first class compartments and four thirds. There was a compartment for luggage, but no toilet facilities. The bodies were handsomely styled, 8 ft 4 in inside, with clerestory roofs. The lighting was however primitive, with oil pots, and heating was by the time-honoured foot-warmers. The bogies were of the American equalised type, and made of Oak — the entire coach, indeed, was of timber construction. In those first years of the service over the Settle and Carlisle line the day Scotch Expresses would have presented an odd appearance, quite unlike the uniform look of a 20th Century Midland train, with eight-wheeled bogie carriages, some six-wheelers and even the odd horsebox or van to add to the twelve-wheeled 'Claytons' and one or two Pullman cars!

From the luncheon stop at Normanton the train ran non-stop to Skipton, where the rake brought in from the South had bogie coaches added from Liverpool and Manchester, conveyed there by the Lancashire & Yorkshire Railway; while the best that could be done for Leeds and Bradford was to attach one or two six-wheelers which had been brought to Skipton by a preced-ing stopping train. By that time the Scotch Express would have loaded to something like 300 tons, and from Skipton it was regularly divided into portions for Glasgow and Edinburgh. Even so, double-heading was needed with the motive power in use at that time. In the first 25 years of the service over the route it was the practice to stop and detach pilot engines, whether they had assisted from Skipton or from Carlisle, at Hawes Junction. This was a logical arrangement, seeing that a turntable had been installed near to the station; while for northbound trains there was a mile rising at 1 in 166 after passing over Moorcock Viaduct and this did not warrant the continuation of pilot assistance to Ais Gill Summit, which was three miles north of Hawes Junction. But at the turn of the century however the decree went forth that pilots of express passenger trains must be detached at Ais Gill Summit, and in consequence there were at times a remarkable number of light engine movements between the summit and Hawes Junction, by engines needing to turn before returning to their home stations.

Midland operating in the closing years of the 19th Century could be a little chaotic at times. Those who took detailed notes of train running, like A. C. W. Lowe, have reported the frequency with which express runs were spoiled by signal delays, and so far as the Settle and Carlisle line was concerned Ahrons has some interesting comments on the vagaries of some of the drivers of the through freight trains. "The Carlisle goods drivers were noted for the high speed at which they worked their trains, and with the 1222

*Kirtley 2-4-0 No. 76 in original condition.* (British Railways)

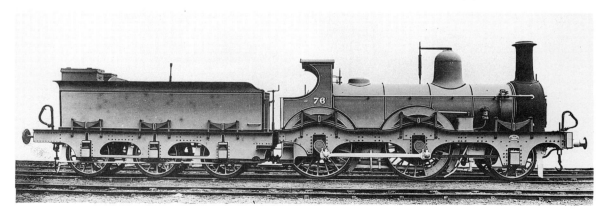

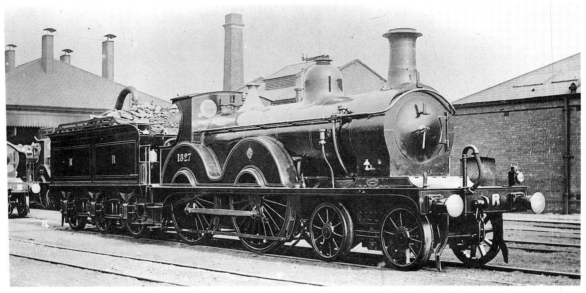

*Johnson 4-4-0 No. 1327 photographed in red livery, in 1904.* (W. J. Reynolds)

class they used to do some very fast running. The signalmen between Carlisle and Leeds would always give the Carlisle goods drivers 'the road', even when they were within measurable distance of a following passenger train, because the signalmen knew that the goods train would keep clear, but when the Leeds goods drivers came along they were promptly shunted into the nearest siding until the passenger train had passed." This happy-go-lucky way of operating was characteristic of many railways beside the Midland in those early days before telegraphic control methods were introduced.

I have not been able to trace details of any express train runs with 2-4-0 engines on the Settle and Carlisle line that were not piloted. One can think it was not the train loads alone that marked the limit of demarcation. The Midland had not installed water troughs on any part of the line in those years, and non-stop running over the $86\frac{3}{4}$ miles between Skipton and Carlisle was a feat not to be undertaken lightly with any appreciable load. Johnson provided his main line engines with six-wheeled tenders having a water-tank capacity considerably more than usual at that time, 3,250 gallons, against an average of about 2,800, but the coal space was less, $3\frac{1}{2}$ tons, against a general norm of 4 tons, or more. One gets the impression that on the longer non-stop runs the train-engine drivers left the pilot engines

to do most of the work from Settle Junction up to Blea Moor. The 'star' engines from the first years of the line were the 1288-1311 series of 2-4-0s built by Dubs & Co. in 1876. Only the last ten of them were allocated to Durran Hill shed, but there they became great favourites. They had 6 ft 6 in coupled wheels, $17\frac{1}{2}$ by 26 in cylinders and carried the then standard working of 140 lb per sq in. They were among the last Midland engines to have Johnson's original type of tender, with the springs inside the frames. One can imagine that this design did not last for very long, because photographs of this class of engine taken after painting had been changed to Derby red, show the tenders with the latter more-usual arrangement, with the springs outside.

The Midland was one of the first railways in Great Britain to use continuous brakes, and when the Settle and Carlisle line was opened all the Scotch Expresses were equipped with the Westinghouse type. The ten 2-4-0 engines nos 1302-11 were so fitted, as were also those working from the Skipton end. It is reported that at one time the Midland had more than sixty engines fitted, and of course all the coaching stock had to be treated likewise. It would seem however that the Westinghouse Brake Company were touchy about the way Derby moved their apparatus from engine to engine, consequent upon changing duties and shed allocations; but what really sent the Westinghouse 'balloon' up was when someone at Derby invented a sanding gear to obviate wheel-slip and used compressed air from the Westinghouse donkey-pump to actuate the device. In the meantime some of those at Derby, disliking anything that was not British, had been assiduously working on improvements to the Sanders & Bolitho Automatic Vacuum Brake and the row over the sanding gear was the last straw. All Westinghouse equipment was eventually taken off Midland engines and trains, and by 1889, the change to automatic vacuum was completed.

It was in 1876 that Johnson first introduced locomotives of the 4-4-0 type, but not originally for the Carlisle road. These ten engines, Nos 1312 to 1321, were sent to Liverpool, above all places, to work on the Cheshire Lines, and there they seemed to have remained for the rest of their not very eventful lives. But the second class, built by Dubs & Co. in 1877 had a much more varied existence. They, like the 1312–1321 class, were not originally intended to work north of Leeds, but in the general slaughter of all the smaller boilered Johnson 4-4-0s perpetuated at Derby in the early 1900s, they were the only ones left in their original condition, apart from the ten on the Cheshire Lines. Most of these, originally numbered 1327 to 1346, were congregated at Hellifield, for use as main line pilots on the Carlisle road and various duties westwards to Carnforth and Morecambe. It was then, from 1916 onwards, that they came within my sphere of observation. They were lovely engines, and

when one of my more general railway books *The Golden Age of Steam* had a chapter 'Midland in the North Country' I contrived to include a beautiful colour plate of one of them on a Morecambe-Leeds express.

The 4-4-0 engines numbered 1327–46, or 311–330, when most of them were allocated to Hellifield in the early 1900s had 7 ft coupled wheels. When the first 4-4-0s to be sent to Carlisle for regular express work on the line in 1882, the 1572–81 series, they had 6 ft 9 in coupled wheels, 18 in by 26 in cylinders, but rather smaller boilers than the Dubs 4-4-0s of 1877. They were fitted with the Westinghouse brake and did some fine work on the Scotch Expresses. They also were painted green at first, and at that time it was remarkable that Midland engines generally had no external marks of their ownership. Contractor-built engines like the Dubs 4-4-0s of 1877 had maker's plates on the splashers, but Derby's own jobs seemed to be entirely anonymous. Before the 1880s were out however there was to be a striking change. First Johnson experimented with a brick red colour, from all accounts not unlike the iron-ore red of the Furness Railway. But then there was developed the glorious crimson lake, which distinguished the Midland engines from all others. All the stock, passenger and goods alike were so treated at first, with the company initials suitably rendered on the tender panels. To enthusiasts whose sympathies lay elsewhere however the Midland colour was usually dismissed as "Derby red"!

*A composite dining car M.S.J.S. roof-boarded "London (St Pancras), and Glasgow St Enoch via Carlisle". (British Railways)*

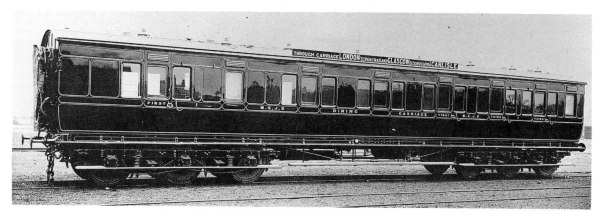

In the summer of 1888 the East and West Coast rivals for the day-time Anglo-Scottish traffic had become involved in the first 'Race to the North', and the Midland was forced to accelerate their morning express from St Pancras to keep in line with the others. The 10.30 am Scotch Express had always been a heavy train, and because of its accelerated timings throughout, the Edinburgh portion ran as a separate train from St Pancras, leaving there at 10.40 am. The Glasgow train ran non-stop from Leicester to Normanton, for the luncheon stop, and then, from Skipton, made a fast run to Carlisle in 109 minutes, a very good average of 47.8 mph. In the meantime the Edinburgh train was routed via Nottingham, ran through Normanton while the Glasgow passengers were lunching, and made its next stop at Leeds, also for lunch. The Edinburgh train called at Hellifield instead of Skipton and thereafter made an equally meritorious run to Carlisle, in 97 minutes. The times of these two trains, in 1888, are worth recalling between St Pancras and Carlisle.

### 10.30 am Glasgow Express

| Miles | | | | Speed mph |
|---|---|---|---|---|
| | St Pancras | dep | 10.20 am | 52.0 |
| $99\frac{1}{4}$ | Leicester | arr | 12.25 pm | |
| | | dep | 12.29 pm | 49.6 |
| $184\frac{1}{4}$ | Normanton | arr | 2.13 pm | |
| | | dep | 2.38 pm | 47.0 |
| $221\frac{1}{4}$ | Skipton | arr | 3.24 pm | |
| | | dep | 3.27 pm | 47.8 |
| 308 | Carlisle | arr | 5.16 pm | |

### 10.40 am Edinburgh Express

| Miles | | | | Speed mph |
|---|---|---|---|---|
| | St Pancras | dep | 10.40 am | |
| $123\frac{3}{4}$ | Nottingham | arr | 1.05 pm | 51.3 |
| | | dep | 1.09 pm | |
| 202 | Leeds | arr | 2.47 pm | 47.8 |
| | | dep | 3.12 pm | |
| $238\frac{1}{4}$ | Hellifield | arr | 4.06 pm | 40.3 |
| | | dep | 4.10 pm | |
| $314\frac{3}{4}$ | Carlisle | arr | 5.47 pm | 47.3 |

Note should be taken of the exiguous four minutes allowed for changing engines at Leicester, Nottingham and Hellifield, or of the even tighter three minutes for the 10.30 am at Skipton!

When Rous-Marten had a trip on the Glasgow train however, a few years after the accelerations, the train engine for the northern part of the journey was attached at Normanton and went through to Carlisle.

It was a very good run covering the Skipton-Carlisle length in 107 minutes. The load was reported as 15 coaches, about 180 tons, and the engine was a 6 ft 6 in 4-4-0 No. 86. Rous-Marten explained that the timidity of the descent from Ais Gill to Carlisle spoiled what would otherwise have been a good run, taking 53 minutes for the $48\frac{1}{4}$ downhill miles; but as they gained two minutes on the 109 minutes scheduled from Skipton there was really nothing to complain about. In any case the ascent to Blea Moor was first class. Rous-Marten clocked a length of 15 miles on the 'Long Drag' in 25 min 9 sec, an average speed of 35.7 mph with an absolute minimum of 32.7 mph. This was fine work for a 4-4-0 of this vintage, with a 180 ton load. The time from passing Hellifield to stopping in Carlisle was only 92 min 45 sec, an average of 50 mph despite the timid descent from Ais Gill. This run must have been made just before the introduction of third class dining cars on the morning Scotch trains and the abolition of the luncheon stop at Normanton.

The afternoon Scotch Express, which for many years left St Pancras at 2.10 pm, was unburdened with the necessity of making a prolonged luncheon halt, and ran between Leeds and Carlisle with no more than a three-minute stop at Hellifield. The time over the mountain section was 93 minutes start to stop, an excellent average of 49.2 mph. Ahrons quotes the working time of this train as passing Ais Gill Summit box at exactly 8 pm, and the running time allowed for the downhill length to Carlisle was no less than 55 minutes. One appreciates that the civil engineering department in those earlier days on the new route looked with disfavour at high maximum speeds while the structures and the earthworks were settling in. Equally one can note the hard work expected from the locomotives, seeing that the working time for the 28.5 miles from Hellifield to passing Ais Gill Summit was only 38 minutes. When I first made my timing journeys over the route more than thirty years later, the allowance was 41 minutes. In the 1890s and thereafter the train engines were more often than not piloted up to the summit, as the following details of running of the morning Scotch Express of 1895 bears out.

The introduction of third class dining cars on the 10.30 am Scotch Express in July 1894 was accompanied by an acceleration of the journey time from St Pancras to Carlisle of 35 minutes, bringing the train into Carlisle at 5 pm. In the autumn of that same year however the previous six minute stop at Normanton was changed to the much more practical stop at Chesterfield, and this remained in operation until the turn of the century.

In July 1895 when A. C. W. Lowe logged the running of this train a non-stop run was made from Chesterfield to Hellifield, having picked up two additional coaches, and the non-stop run of 85.1 miles, with a load of about 190 tons, was made in $110\frac{1}{2}$ minutes, by a Kirtley 2-4-0 of the 800 class, rebuilt by Johnson. These engines, twelve of which were shedded at Skipton for many years, were immensely popular with the running staff. It was a Skipton engine, No. 804, that hauled the train logged by A. C. W. Lowe and they were much in demand for piloting up to Ais Gill, and on the 'little' North Western line to Morecambe or Carnforth. On the occasion previously referred to three more coaches were added to the train at Hellifield, and with a total load of 240 tons piloting was essential.

The downhill gradients from Hellifield to Settle Junction always provided an excellent start to the climbing of the 'Long Drag', and comparing the time to passing Settle station with some of my own runs, to be discussed later in this book, it would seem that engines 83 and 197 attained at least 66 or 67 mph at Settle Junction, only 3.3 miles from the start. The climbing was very good, though surpassed by a run of my own, made in August 1930, when an ex-LNWR 'Claughton' class 4-6-0 piloted by a Midland Class 2 4-4-0 passed Ribblehead in $21\frac{1}{4}$ minutes, with a 375-ton train. On Mr Lowe's run the two Johnson 4-4-0s must have gone pretty hard from Blea Moor to average 48 mph from Ribblehead to the stop at Hawes Junction. Detaching pilots, whether at Ais Gill, or in earlier days at Hawes Junction, was a fine art. I have several records of up expresses being at rest for no more than 65 seconds at Ais Gill Summit, and Mr Lowe's run, made in 1895, with a stop of only 75 seconds at Hawes Junction shows the same tradition.

The log of this run shows very clearly the

Midland Railway: 10.30 am Scotch Express
Hellifield–Carlisle
Load: 3-12w, 4-8w, 5-6w, 240 tons
Engines: 6 ft 6 in 4-4-0s, Train 197,
Pilot to Hawes Junction 83

| Miles | | Time m | s | Av speed mph |
|---|---|---|---|---|
| 0.0 | Hellifield | 0 | 00 | — |
| 5.2 | Settle | 6 | 40 | 46.8 |
| 16.0 | Ribblehead | 23 | 10 | 39.2 |
| 25.4 | Hawes Junction | 34 | 55 | 48.0 |
| — | | 36 | 10 | — |
| 35.3 | Kirkby Stephen | 48 | 30 | 48.1 |
| 38.5 | Crosby Garrett | 52 | 20 | 50.0 |
| 43.5 | Ormside | 57 | 20 | 60.0 |
| 46.0 | Appleby | 60 | 10 | 52.9 |
| 57.0 | Langwathby | 72 | 10 | 55.0 |
| 62.3 | Lazonby | 76 | 25 | 60.7 |
| 66.8 | Armathwaite | 82 | 40 | 52.8 |
| 72.9 | Cumwhinton | 88 | 55 | 58.5 |
| 76.8 | Carlisle | 94 | 15 | 43.8 |

restraint that was imposed by the top management of the Midland Railway upon the attainment of any high downhill speeds over the Settle and Carlisle line in the first 25 years of its working. Here was the case of a top flight express leaving Hellifield five minutes late, and being worked up to Hawes Junction in brilliant style. Then, with 51 miles of easy road down to Carlisle the driver took 58 min 5 sec and still arrived nearly four minutes late. It was not as though there was a general embargo on high speed elsewhere on the Midland Railway. Indeed a maximum of no less than 90 mph had been recorded with one of the Johnson 7 ft 9 in 4-2-2s, the "Spinners", but that was south of Leicester.

*One of the famous 800 Class Kirtley 2-4-0s, as rebuilt and painted in Midland red by Johnson.*
(Author's Collection)

What the Leeds and Carlisle drivers could do in the way of speed once the restrictions were lifted will be told in subsequent chapters. In the meantime the changes in timetabling of the 10.30 am Scotch Express after the Normanton luncheon stop was cut out are tabulated herewith.

| Date | | July 1895 | July 1899 | October 1899 | July 1900 |
|---|---|---|---|---|---|
| Chesterfield | dep | 1.30 | 1.35 | 1.35 | 1.35 |
| Skipton | arr | — | 3.08 | — | 3.08 |
| Skipton | dep | — | 3.10 | — | 3.12 |
| Hellifield | arr | 3.20 | — | 3.20 | — |
| Hellifield | dep | 3.25 | — | 3.22 | — |
| Carlisle | arr | 5.00 | 5.00 | 5.00 | 5.00 |

From July 1900 the train was composed of corridor stock throughout.

*Midland 2-4-0, No. 44 later renumbered 188, as rebuilt at Derby in 1901.*
(F. Moore's Railway Photographs)

The turn of the century also saw the introduction of the last Johnson small-boilered 4-4-0s, the stately profile of which was so admired among locomotive enthusiasts. Ten of these beautiful engines were allocated to the Carlisle road, Nos 805 to 809 to Durran Hill, and Nos 2636 to 2640 to Leeds. Although looking no different from the original 4-4-0s of 1876 Johnson had made significant improvements over the years, in addition to increasing the boiler pressure from the original 140 to 170 lb per sq in. The fireboxes had been increased, as the grate area at first 110 sq ft, had been enlarged to 117 sq ft by increasing the coupled wheelbase of the engines to 9 ft, and then on the final batch to 9 ft 6 in, making possible a grate area of 128 sq ft. The cylinder diameter had been increased to 19 in on the last small boilered engines allocated to the Carlisle road, indeed on one batch drafted elsewhere the cylinders were $19\frac{1}{2}$ in. But on these Johnson seemed to have over-reached himself, because contemporary observers thought they seemed over-cylindered. The 19 in engines however did some very fine work during their short lives in their original condition. It is sad to think that all the 235 engines of the 4-4-0 type built between 1882 and 1899 were rebuilt out of all recognition within a few years of Johnson's retirement. Only the engines of the two earlier classes remained in their original condition.

To conclude these notes about the working on the line in its first 25 years, it may be added that the Edinburgh portion of the morning Scotch Express, leaving St Pancras at 10.40 am continued to call at Leeds after the third class restaurant cars were introduced. According to *The Railway Magazine* of December 1900 which included a fine lithographed colourplate of the train, it consisted of nine vehicles, three for Aberdeen and six for Edinburgh, but it also provided the first instance of a single-wheeler coming anywhere near to the Settle and Carlisle line. With the introduction of the huge bogie 4,000 gallon tenders on the final batch of "Spinners" through locomotive working between St Pancras and Leeds was instituted, via Nottingham, and according to *The Railway Magazine*, the addition of a three-coach Bradford portion between London and Leeds brought the total load up to 280 tons — a tough proposition for a 'single-wheeler'.

# 6
# 1901 Timetable Metamorphosis — High Speed at Last

It was in July 1901 that there came the radical changes in the Anglo-Scottish services of the Midland Railway that put the company in the forefront of express train speed in Great Britain. The Settle and Carlisle line featured prominently in the accelerations which made the overall time over the 308 miles between St Pancras and Carlisle via Leicester, the even six hours — an average of 51.2 mph, and this was achieved by three daytime expresses from London. While the 10.30 am of Victorian times still ran it was surpassed in speed by the new 9.30 am, 11.30 am and 1.30 pm departures from St Pancras, all of which called at Leeds. The first

of the three continued non-stop to Carlisle; the second made one intermediate stop at Appleby, while the third called at Hellifield. The night trains were nearly as fast, with the new 7.20 pm Highland express reaching Carlisle at 1.30 am. Water troughs had not yet been introduced on the Midland Railway but by use of the new "Belpaire" 4-4-0s with their huge bogie tenders, there was no difficulty in running the 113 miles between Leeds and Carlisle without a stop.

The "Belpaires", as they were always called, even down to LMS days, struck an entirely new note in the outward look of Midland engines. The large boiler, a plain dome bereft of the

*The first Johnson "Belpaire" 4-4-0, No. 2606, at Wellington station, Leeds. (W. Hubert Foster)*

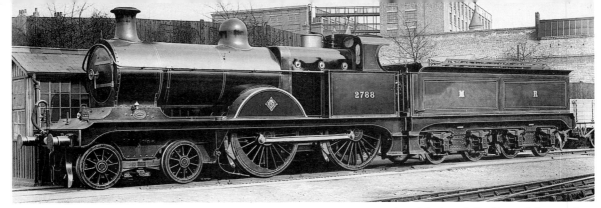

*A later example of a "Belpaire", No. 2788, still with bogie tender.* (National Railway Museum)

familiar safety valve mounted on it, the ugly cab, and the rectangular cab-side splashers for the rear pair of coupled wheels, seemed as if the new century had banished all the beauty of line that one had long-since regarded as everything that came from the Derby Drawing Office. Furthermore the first illustration of one of them, No. 2606, in *The Locomotive Magazine* of April 1901 appears to have been taken in very unpropitious conditions. The engine was in 'shop grey', and with a poor negative very clumsily touched up, the general effect was hideous! Technically the "Belpaires" were not all that more powerful than the 60 class, of which more were still being built in 1901. The larger engines had $19\frac{1}{2}$ in by 26 in cylinders, 6 ft 9 in coupled wheels and carried a boiler pressure of 180 lb per sq in. *The Locomotive Magazine* inadvertently added to the confusion with which these engines were first made known to enthusiasts by a misprint regarding the cylinder diameter. They printed it as $17\frac{1}{2}$ in. The first five of these engines, Nos

2606–2610, were allocated to Leeds, Whitehall Junction shed, for service on the Carlisle road. They had the same design of bogie tender, of 4,000 gallon capacity, as used on the final batch of "Spinners", but later examples of the "Belpaires" had an improved design carrying 4,500 gallons.

Despite the unfortunate start to their career, as portrayed in *The Locomotive Magazine* of April 1901 the "Belpaires" took the road with all the 'spit and polish' that Derby and the shed staff at Whitehall Junction could bestow on them, and it was not very long before we learned what they could do, for speed. In October 1902 one of Rous-Marten's train-timing friends, a Mr W. C. H. Church of Newcastle, decided to return home from Leeds via Carlisle instead of by the normal way, and he joined the 9.30 am from St Pancras. The load was an unusually heavy one for the Midland, 320 tons, and from the Hellifield stop, inserted in the winter schedule, even a "Belpaire" had to be piloted up to Ais Gill.

*One of the later Johnson 4-4-0s, No. 1668, with 7 ft coupled wheels.*
(F. Moore's Railway Photographs)

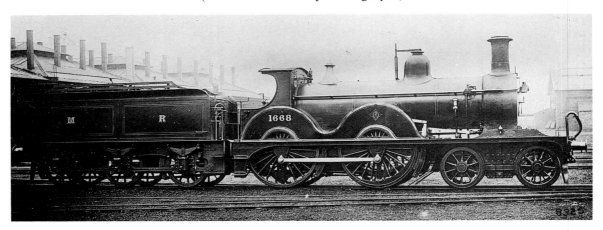

The engine was No. 2607, assisted by a Johnson 2-4-0. Having regard to the weight of the train the two engines and their crews did well to cover the 28.5 miles up from Hellifield in 37 min 47 sec, with the average speed up the 'Long Drag' only a fraction below 40 mph. Detaching the pilot took no more than 75 seconds, and then No. 2607 and her crew made an amazing run down to Carlisle — amazing that is compared to what used to be run on this line only a few years earlier. In brief, the 48.3 miles from the dead start at Ais Gill to the stop in Carlisle station were covered in 41 min 55 sec. The accompanying log shows the bare details of the point to point times, with the average speeds worked out but Mr Church was recording the times *at every milepost*, and some details of the run make exciting reading indeed.

The actual start was made from milepost $259\frac{1}{2}$, and the first mile and a half took no more than 3 min 6 sec. Subsequent miles took 62, 54, 50, 47, and 45 sec, so that the speed had reached 80 mph by the time Kirkby Stephen was passed. Down the continuing 1 in 100 grade acceleration continued until a full 90 mph was reached at Smardale Viaduct. Some slackening of the pace was registered on the easier gradients past Crosby Garrett, but on the resumption of the 1 in 100 descent, through Helm Tunnel and down to Ormside Viaduct, the maximum of 90 mph was repeated. The rising length at 1 in 176, a $\frac{1}{4}$ mile of it, was taken without the speed falling below 79 mph through Appleby, and on the easier

descending gradients that follow, a general average of 78 to 80 mph was maintained until, as usual, there was a spurt down the steeper pitch past Little Salkeld, where the speed rose to $86\frac{1}{2}$ mph. By the time Lazonby was passed the 27.3 miles from Kirkby Stephen had been covered in 19 min 25 sec, an average of 84.3 mph, a fitting 20th Century riposte to the timidity of the descents Rous-Marten complained of in earlier years. Of course this hurricane pace could not be maintained over the sharply undulating gradients in the beautiful stretch beside the gorge of the River Eden, past Armathwaite. The lowest speed here was 63 mph, while on the final descent towards Carlisle $76\frac{1}{2}$ mph was the maximum attained.

In 1902 further accelerations were made with a start-to-stop timing of 31 minutes for the 30.8 miles between Appleby and Carlisle, 59.5 mph average speed and the 9.30 am from St Pancras had a separate Edinburgh portion throughout from London to Carlisle. Among the up trains, the first morning express from Glasgow, leaving Carlisle at 12 noon, had its only intermediate stop before Leeds, at Hawes Junction above all places, from which it made a fast run over the remaining 61.5 miles in 69 minutes, an average of 53.4 mph. At this distance in time it is difficult to appreciate the reason for providing that remote Wensleydale branch with so auspicious a main line connection. I cannot trace that any of the Midland directors, or other high officials, had a country property nearby! In any case the stop at Hawes Junction

*A beautiful example of a Johnson 4-4-0 in the style of those which ran the Scotch Expresses over the line before 1900.* (Locomotive Publishing Co. Ltd)

lasted until the end of 1916, after which the drastic wartime reductions in train service altered everything. In the last months of the working Cecil J. Allen used the Hawes Junction stop. The train was a heavy one and had been double-headed up from Carlisle, but presumably the pilot was a Hellifield based engine, a Johnson 6 ft 6 in 2-4-0, and had not been detached at Ais Gill. By the war years an intermediate stop had been inserted at Hellifield, and with the train engine, a Class 2 4-4-0, the two locomotives made a fast run down from Blea Moor, sustaining speeds of 75 to 79 mph from Ribblehead to Settle Junction, and covering the $25\frac{1}{2}$ miles from Hawes Junction to Hellifield in 26 min 5 sec.

In 19th Century Britain the Midland Railway, for all its affluence, was never at the forefront of locomotive practice. While the London & North Western, the Caledonian, the Highland and the London & South Western were 'hitting the headlines' Johnson had chosen to play a less spectacular role, until he had produced his "Belpaires", and his friendship with W. M. Smith, Chief Locomotive Draughtsman at the North Eastern Railway engineering headquarters works, at Gateshead. Then, as few professional locomotive engineers, and in fact probably none at all, the erudite amateur enthusiasts appreciated the Settle and Carlisle line had become the stage on which one of the most momentous locomotive developments in British railway engineering history was taking place. The origin of the far-famed Midland compounds lay not at Derby, but at Gateshead, where Smith sought to make something more practical out of the Worsdell-Von Borries compounds, which were the acknowledged top class express locomotives then working on the North Eastern main line throughout between York and Edinburgh.

In Smith's three-cylinder compound 4-4-0 No. 1619 the engine was started very simply as a two-cylinder simple engine, with live steam from the boiler admitted only to the two low-pressure cylinders. Then, when the train was fairly on the move a so-called 'change-valve' was operated by the driver to initiate compound working. Then high-pressure steam from the boiler was admitted only to the high-pressure cylinder; direct admission of live steam to the low-pressure cylinders was cut off, and the latter were supplied from the intermediate receiver with steam exhausted from the one high-pressure

Midland Railway: 9.30 am Scotch Express
Load: 320 tons Engine:
"Belpaire" 4-4-0 No. 2607
Times from restart at Ais Gill after
detaching pilot

| Miles | | Time m s | Av speed mph |
|---|---|---|---|
| 0.0 | Ais Gill | 0 00 | — |
| 3.5 | Mallerstang Box | 5 18 | 39.6 |
| 6.8 | Kirkby Stephen | 7 57 | 74.0 |
| 10.0 | Crosby Garrett | 10 19 | 82.0 |
| 15.1 | Ormside | 13 55 | 85.1 |
| 17.5 | Appleby | 15 42 | 81.1 |
| 20.4 | Long Marton | 17 52 | 80.3 |
| 24.9 | Culgaith | 21 16 | 79.4 |
| 28.6 | Langwathby | 24 03 | 79.6 |
| 30.0 | Little Salkeld | 25 08 | 77.8 |
| 33.1 | Lazonby | 27 22 | 83.2 |
| 38.5 | Armathwaite | 32 13 | 65.2 |
| 44.4 | Cumwhinton | 37 30 | 70.0 |
| 48.3 | Carlisle | 41 55 | — |

cylinder. In proportioning the cylinders Smith was careful to avoid the mistakes that had been made in many earlier compound engines through restrictions in the flow of steam. In some cases the port areas through the valves were inadequate, and in others the low-pressure cylinders were not large enough.

One outstanding attribute of the steam loco-motive, that was not fully appreciated in many quarters until steam traction was in course of replacement by diesel in this country, is its capacity for making transitory outputs of power far beyond the maximum sustained capacity of the boiler. A skilful driver and fireman, by build-ing up the fire, and manipulating the injectors so as to have an absolutely full boiler, can then, for a brief period, steam the engine at a considerably higher rate than that which could be sustained indefinitely. It is an extremely useful source of reserve power, particularly when climb-ing a heavy bank. The boiler may be mortgaged in the process, with pressure dropped, water level reduced, or both. But as the heavy sections are likely to be followed immediately by downhill stretches there is normally no trouble in 'paying off the mortgage', restoring water level and steam pressure while the locomotive is coasting, or at any rate working under easy steam.

On the Settle and Carlisle line, with its long inclines, the opportunity of having a little 'extra' towards the conclusion of an ascent is worth

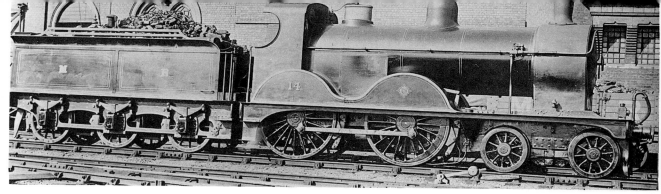

*A Deeley rebuild of a Johnson 6 ft 6 in 4-4-0 of 1891, No. 14, later No. 402.* (British Railways)

a good deal to a driver. On the North Eastern engine No. 1619 Smith provided the means of obtaining that 'extra' in an interesting way. An auxiliary valve was fitted that enabled the driver to admit a limited amount of live steam direct from the boiler to the low-pressure cylinders *while working compound*. In other words, while the low-pressure cylinders were taking steam from the intermediate receiver, which had been through the high-pressure cylinder, they received additional steam direct. The extra volume of steam passing through the low-pressure cylinders could, in certain circumstances, have a choking effect and by giving rise to excessive back pressure counteract and eliminate the very advantages that this method, in principle, provides. This difficulty Smith overcame by his arrangement of the valve gear.

The designer of a locomotive is apt to find himself in a cleft stick. In trying to produce a machine that shall be as simple as possible to manage, and shall at the same time have a high

overall efficiency, he is often faced with the problem that a feature that will increase the efficiency will add to the complication in handling. At the time the No. 1619 was built, complications in handling were not so serious as they became in later years. Locomotives engaged in top link express passenger work had regular crews. There were never more than two pairs of men allocated to an engine, and in working the same engine, week in week out, there was every chance to gain familiarity with every feature. In such circumstances any driver who persistently failed to take advantage of special items fitted to his engine was just put on another job.

Assured by the fact that engine No. 1619 would be skilfully handled, Smith fitted independently controlled reversing gears for the high and low-pressure cylinders. The driver had two reversers to operate when notching up, but there was no need to operate them uniformly. If the engine was being worked very hard, and some live steam was being admitted to the low-pressure cylinders,

*The first Smith-Johnson Midland compound, No. 2631, at Whitehall Junction shed, Leeds.*
(F. Moore's Railway Photographs)

*The second Midland compound, No. 2632.* (British Railways)

the driver could lengthen the cut-off in the low-pressure cylinders to avoid any choking effect there might be through the large volume of low-pressure steam trying to pass through. There were no hard and fast rules to go by in such circumstances. Successful working relied entirely on the good judgement of the driver. But a good engineman gaining complete familiarity with his machine — through driving no other! — would very quickly master the technique.

While the first two Midland compounds completed at Derby in January 1902 were design-wise little more than enlarged versions of the North Eastern 4-4-0 No. 1619, on the Midland they became at once as much part and parcel of the Settle and Carlisle line as the majestic scenery and the monumental civil engineering works. As soon as they were run in No. 2631 was allocated

*An up Scotch Express leaving Blea Moor Tunnel hauled by a "Belpaire".* (J. M. Tomlinson)

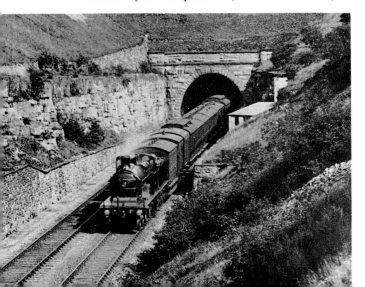

to Whitehall Junction shed, and No. 2632 to Durran Hill, each in the exclusive charge of a supremely competent driver. As on NER No. 1619 all three cylinders drove on the leading coupled axle. The outside cranks were at right angles, and the inside cranks bisected the obtuse angle between the other two.

Distribution of steam of the high-pressure cylinder was controlled by piston valves located directly beneath the cylinder, while the low-pressure cylinders were fed by slide valves, with vertical faces. The cylinder dimensions, 19 in diameter high pressure, 21 in low pressure, with a common stroke of 26 in, remained constant throughout the history of the class, except for a short period from 1923 to 1925 when a batch was built with cylinders having diameters of $19\frac{3}{4}$ in high pressure and $21\frac{3}{4}$ low pressure. The high-pressure cylinder exhausted direct to the steam chest common to the two low-pressure cylinders, without the intervention of any intermediate steam pipe.

As originally designed it was arranged that simultaneously with the admission of steam to the high-pressure steam chest, steam at a pre-determined pressure was automatically admitted also to the low-pressure steam chest by a specially constructed regulating valve on the right hand side of the smokebox, looking forward. The regulating valve was so arranged that when the maximum pressure allowed in the low-pressure steam chests was attained further supply of steam directly from the boiler was automatically cut off. The general distribution of power output from the three cylinders was so contrived, that although the boiler pressure was 195 lb per sq in,

*An up Scotch Express passing Ais Gill signal box, hauled by a "Belpaire".* (Author's Collection)

none of the pistons were ever subjected to pressure equal to that on the pistons in a simple engine working with a boiler pressure of 170 lb per sq in. In passing it would seem curious that this should have been included as a design feature, because it immediately threw away one of the great advantages of a compound engine — that is to increase the range of expansion of the steam.

When working compound the pressure in the low-pressure steam chests was found to vary between 40 and 60 lb per sq in according to the position of the reverser. But in working a heavy train up a steep gradient increased power could be obtained by admitting live steam from the boiler direct to the low-pressure steam chests for as long as might be necessary, or, of course, as long as the boiler would stand for it. The amount of steam that could be admitted in this way could be regulated by the driver between the maximum and minimum limits of pressure; he could, in fact, vary the low-pressure steam chest pressure to suit the work in hand. Independent reversing was provided for the high-pressure and low-pressure valve gears, though the mechanism was such that one handle would actuate both gears simultaneously if required. These controls certainly gave the driver a multiplicity of adjustments, that sound every bit as extensive as those then being provided on the De Glehn compounds in France. To prevent excessive forward or back pressure on the high-pressure pistons when starting, non-return valves were arranged so that steam could pass from the low-pressure steam chest into either end of the high-pressure cylinder.

All this not only sounds complicated; it was complicated, although the complications had

been contrived within a beautifully simple and handsome exterior. The new compounds, with their large boilers, outside cylinders, and huge bogie tenders, developed the new modern 'look' that was coming into Midland motive power; but why Johnson, with his previous attention to the aesthetics of locomotive design should have put on square splashers is difficult to understand. One can understand that Derby had not yet reached the stage of providing really adequate cabs, but those rear splashers, both on the "Belpaires" and on the compounds, rather defy all logical explanation. Nevertheless, the *ensemble* made up a highly original and distinctive design, and in the year 1902 they were, of course, finished with the gorgeous profusion of polished brass and ornate lining that characterised Midland locomotives of Johnson's day. The initials 'M.R.' on the tenders were painted and the number on the cab side sheets was rendered in raised brass figures.

From August until November 1902 engine No. 2631 was put through a remarkably comprehensive series of trials while working ordinary express passenger trains between Leeds and Carlisle. The loads were not augmented for test purposes, indeed on the southbound runs made on the 3.55 pm from Carlisle the tare load averaged no more than 153 tons on the seven occasions when indicator trials were conducted. At that time only the London & North Western Railway had a dynamometer car, and this was a very primitive type of 'measuring van'. Johnson sent a comprehensive report of the tests to *Engineering* and they were published in the fullest detail. For those of my friends who delight in the intricacies of locomotive performance

*Blea Moor signal box, as it was in 1938. Note the massive water tower opposite.*
(Norman Wilkinson)

the full details of the report are included in an appendix to this book. In the meantime some notes on the working of engine No. 2631 and of No. 2632 in ordinary and not test conditions are remarkable for the maximum speeds that were run.

First, to the pioneer engine, working the 1.30 pm Scotch Express from St Pancras recorded as leaving Hellifield $17\frac{1}{2}$ minutes late, with a

*Looking south towards Ribblehead viaduct; with Ingleborough in the background. The down distant signal for Blea Moor, and the up distant for Ribblehead are on the same post.* (Norman Wilkinson)

load reported as "equal to 13", and with the latest corridor stock throughout, this would have represented 229 tons tare behind the tender, or about 240 tons loaded. Getting away with characteristic vigour Settle Junction was passed at 63 mph, and then climbing to Blea Moor the speed had not fallen below 39 mph in the narrow glen above Stainforth and rose to 44 mph on the brief stretch of level past Helwith Bridge. The minimum speed on the climb was 35 mph near Ribblehead, but this had recovered to 37 mph at Blea Moor, which signal box was passed in the excellent time of $24\frac{3}{4}$ minutes from the start at Hellifield, $17\frac{1}{4}$ miles. Speed soon recovered from the heavy work on the 'Long Drag' to a maximum of 65 mph at Hawes Junction, and with the last upward slope taken at a minimum speed of 55 mph Ais Gill Summit, $28\frac{1}{2}$ miles from Hellifield, was passed in 37 minutes. This, although good work for the period, was of much the same standard as was registered with 300-ton trains by superheated Class 4 engines in the comparative trials of 1923–4, of which there will be much to comment on in a later chapter. What was not standard was the hurricane pace at which the driver of No. 2631 took the train down to Carlisle. The summary times show the 17.5 miles from Ais Gill covered in 15 minutes, and the 30.8 miles on to Carlisle completed in 27 minutes, but the speed details make exciting reading.

From Ais Gill this trip at first bade fair to give the "Belpaire" featured earlier in this chapter a "run for her money"; for the compound passed Kirkby Stephen at 81 mph and attained 86 mph at Smardale Viaduct. But the speed at Ormside was not more than 79 mph and the rise to Appleby was cleared at a minimum of 65. Even so the pace continued to be very hot with speeds of 75 to 79 mph to the crossing of the River Eden below Little Salkeld. The undulating stretch beside the river gorge was taken at speeds of between 55, 68 and 59 mph, and the final maximum, as was the case with the "Belpaire", was 76 mph. So the 48.3 miles from Ais Gill Summit to Carlisle took no more than 42 minutes pass to stop. This was not so spectacular as the 41 min 55 sec from a standing start at Ais Gill achieved by the crew of the "Belpaire", but it made possible a time of 79 minutes over the 76.7 miles, and a gain of 13 minutes on the schedule then operating. As regards downhill maximum speeds however Rous-Marten was soon to record some considerably higher speeds than the 86 mph at Smardale Viaduct registered on this trip with engine No. 2631.

The train this time was the 11.50 am up from Carlisle hauled by engine No. 2632, with a load also of 240 tons, and it would seem that the responsible men were determined to put on a show for the distinguished recorder who was travelling in the train. The details were published in *The Railway Magazine* for November 1903, which appropriately included a fine lithographed colour plate of No. 2632; but no mention of official collaboration is made in the text. In the early stages of the run Rous-Marten records no more detail than that a maximum speed of $72\frac{1}{2}$ mph occurred near Lazonby and the 30.8 miles from Carlisle start to passing Appleby took no more than 34 min 33 sec. In early LMS days when the comparative trials with various Class 4 engines were being made the standard time was 39 minutes. After Appleby was passed I quote Rous-Marten for the hillclimbing of No. 2632.

"Up to Crosby Garrett the speed never fell below 45 miles an hour — indeed only went so low as that for a single quarter mile, otherwise keeping to 47.4. After Crosby Garrett it rose steadily to 48, 50, 51.1 and even 53.6; then gradually sank to 51.1, 50 and 47.4 near Kirkby Stephen. Up the final length to Ais Gill Summit

our rate dropped to 45, and finally to 43 miles an hour, that being maintained as an absolute minimum mile after mile to the top of the bank. I had no previous experience of equal merit up that severe incline. The time for the 17.5 miles from Appleby to Ais Gill was only 23 min 5 sec. Thus the 48.3 mile climb of over 1,100 ft from Carlisle to Ais Gill was accomplished in 57 min 38 sec. Along the tableland which was a slightly downward grade from Ais Gill to Blea Moor, we were generally doing about 66 to 67 miles an hour".

But to my mind, having regard to the later history of the Midland compounds, and of my own extensive experience of their running, some of it on the footplate, it was the descent from Blea Moor that was the most significant performance of all. Rous-Marten recorded: "A rate of 75 miles an hour was soon reached; then 80 and 85. But still the speed rose steadily; quarter miles were done successively in 10.8, 10.6, 10.4, 10.2 and 10 seconds; 90 miles an hour had been reached, and my Midland's record with No. 117, a 7 ft 9 in single wheeler, had been equalled. It was immediately broken. The next quarter-mile was done in 9.8 seconds, and several successive quarter miles each in the same time. That represented a speed of 91.8 miles an hour." After discussing several other high maxima that he had recorded he continued: "It is my rule, as my readers are aware, never to publish any exceptional speeds noted by me until I shall first have received a written assurance that such publication will not be prejudicial to the interests of the driver, the engineer, or the railway concerned. Such assurance I have received in the case of Mr Johnson's engine, and therefore I am to publish the remarkable figures".

By that time the train had drawn so far ahead of schedule that some substantial easing down was essential. Even so they passed Hellifield in 83 min 12 sec from Carlisle, and Skipton in 93 min 18 sec. After that signal checks were inevitable, in fact they were twice brought to a dead stand, and severely checked by signal eleven times, but for all that arrived in Leeds $\frac{1}{4}$ minute early, in $136\frac{3}{4}$ minutes for the $112\frac{3}{4}$ miles from Carlisle. Rous-Marten estimates the net time as 119 minutes, despite the easing down before Settle, an overall average of 56.7 mph.

# 7
# Momentous Changes in Management

Johnson retired at the end of 1903 but before then he had built three more compound express 4-4-0s generally the same as Nos. 2631–2 but including a change which came to result in one significant feature of their performances, and indeed of all the several hundreds of these engines built in LMS days. The Johnson engines, Nos 2633–5 did not have independent control of the high pressure, and the low pressure valve gear. It was used on engines Nos 2631 and 2632 apparently so seldom as not to be worth the extra complication, and the facility for extra high speed running of the kind produced for Rous-Marten's benefit, as detailed in Chapter 6, was not in line with the capacity for regular hard work with the ordinary Midland express trains. In all my studies of the working of these very excellent engines I have never noted a higher maximum speed than 85 mph, and the general limit, both on the Midland line south of Nottingham and Leicester, and on the LNWR line south of Crewe, has been 80 to 82 mph. I had a maximum of 84 mph descending northbound from Ais Gill when one of the standard LMS compounds was piloting a Stanier "Black Five" 4-6-0 on the 86.8 mile non-stop run of the "Thames–Forth Express" from Skipton to Carlisle. I was travelling passenger at the time and so cannot say how either of the two engines was being worked. The Johnson compounds built in 1903 worked

*A Johnson 6 ft 9 in 4-4-0, built in 1882, as re-boiled by Deeley; No. 1563 before renumbering later as No. 329. (British Railways)*

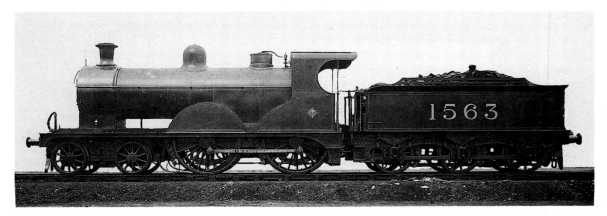

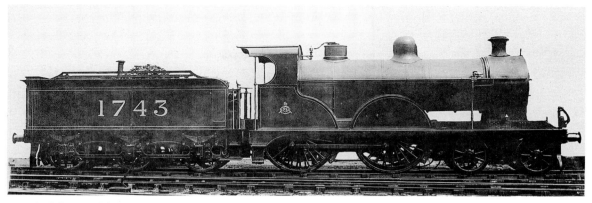

*A Johnson 7ft 4-4-0, as re-boilered by Deeley, before re-numbering; No. 1743 later No. 362.*
(British Railways)

south of Leeds.

When Johnson's coming retirement was announced in the late summer of 1903 there was considerable speculation as to the likely successor, both in the railway industry and in the technical press. At Derby at that time there was some strong and brilliant men rising in both status and influence. Johnson had never had a deputy, in fact as the origin of the compound engines made clear, his friendship with W. M. Smith at Gateshead bore some notable fruit. At Derby, in his last years, his Works Manager, R. M. Deeley, came to understudy Johnson, and it was said that the change in boiler design exemplified in the "Belpaires" was due to Deeley's influence. Alongside him was the Assistant Works Manager, Cecil W. Paget. As son and

heir of Sir Ernest Paget, Bart, it could be well imagined that he was already well up the ladder of Midland Railway management hierarchy, and irresponsibly perhaps, had been tipped as the likely successor to Johnson. While Cecil Paget came to prove himself a veritable colossus in any field of railway or industrial activity, in 1904 his turn had not yet come. Deeley got the job of Locomotive Superintendent and Paget moved up to become Works Manager at Derby.

Deeley had been in office a mere eighteen months when the Directors of the Midland Railway made an appointment of the utmost importance and significance in selecting Mr W. G. Granet to succeed E. W. Wells as Assistant General Manager. Up to that time Granet had not been a railwayman at all, but a barrister of

*No. 864, one of the later "Belpaires" introduced by Deeley with a six-wheeled tender, and simplified style of painting.* (Locomotive Publishing Co. Ltd)

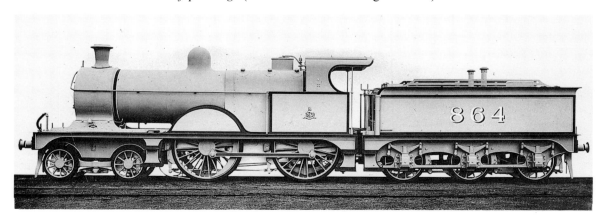

*Johnson 6 ft 6 in 4-4-0 No. 2587 in the original style of re-boilering by Deeley, with 'MR' on tender, and number on the cab side.* (F. Moore's Railway Photographs)

barely 38 years of age, who had been appointed to the secretaryship of the Railway Companies Association on the retirement of Sir Henry Oakley in October 1900. Within a year he had succeeded to the General Managership of the Midland Railway, and then all concerned, the staff, the customers, the press, and indeed the general public, were not slow in realising that there was a veritable lion at the helm. His years of service to the Railway Companies Association had given him a rare insight into railway management problems, and with the Midland in particular the glut of mineral traffic south of Leeds was

becoming a stranglehold upon the operation of the entire railway. But before Granet had arrived the newly appointed Locomotive Superintendent was making his influence felt in no uncertain way and much of it was soon to effect the Settle and Carlisle line.

While he was still Works Manager, and understudy to Johnson, Deeley it was generally understood, was the moving spirit in a large programme of boiler improvements. At first it concerned only the Johnson 0-6-0 goods engines, many of which could have benefited from larger boilers. But the shape of things to come

*The morning express from Glasgow to St Pancras stopping at Hawes Junction, then the only stop between Carlisle and Leeds — hauled by a "Belpaire".* (Author's Collection)

was revealed when Derby built three new 4-4-0 engines for the Somerset & Dorset Joint Railway at the end of 1903, under Johnson's supervision. Because of the severity of the gradients at the northern end of the line the coupled wheels were made no more than 6 ft 0 in diameter, but the boiler was considerably larger than Johnson had used hitherto for all his ordinary Midland 4-4-0s, excepting of course those of the "Belpaires" and of the compounds which were much larger. Once firmly in the saddle Deeley took the boiler design of the Somerset & Dorset 4-4-0 and readily adapted it to a programme of rebuilding the entire stud of 6 ft 6 in 4-4-0s, except the first ten, Nos 1312–21, which were ensconced on the Cheshire lines. By midsummer 1904, the first one to be so treated, No. 85, was back into traffic. This was one of the 1808 class built at Derby between 1888 and 1891, and by September six more of the class had been dealt with similarly.

By that time it was apparent that not only selected groups were being chosen, because with the September batch was one engine from the 2203 class built in 1893, and in December there were three more of them. By midsummer no fewer than 26 of the 6 ft 6 in 4-4-0s had been rebuilt. Many of these went to the Leeds–Carlisle line where they provided a useful increment of power. There were 80 of the engines with 6 ft 6 in coupled wheels and it was evident that Deeley

aimed at converting all of them as quickly as possible. Moreover, by the beginning of 1906 a start had been made in dealing with the 6 ft 9 in and the 7 ft coupled engines, and recalling that Derby Works was simultaneously building more "Belpaires" and many more compounds with Deeley's own methods of control one could well imagine the activity in the shops might well have rivalled Crewe in the days of the greatest productivity. At that time it must be remembered that Deeley, as Locomotive Superintendent was responsible for the running of all the trains, passenger and freight, as well as all the drivers, firemen and shed staff who reported to this department. At that time, *The Locomotive Magazine*, not always accurate in the information it published, told its readers that some of the new Deeley compounds were to be 'Atlantics'!

Not long after Deeley was appointed Locomotive Superintendent Paget was promoted to be Assistant; but Granet had already marked him out as the man to run the entire railway, young as he was, and at a Board Meeting on 5th April 1907, he was appointed to the new post of General Superintendent. *The Railway Magazine* had some very "Pertinent Paragraphs" in comment which I now quote: "The position has been created with the object of bringing the staff of the running section of the Locomotive Department and that of the Traffic Department more closely

*An up Scotch Express at Armathwaite hauled by two rebuilt 6 ft 6 in 4-4-0s with No. 444 leading.*
(British Railways)

together, and concentrating under one officer the whole of the arrangements connected with the movement of trains and the transportation of traffic. Although the department, of which Mr Paget is chief, is a new departure on the Midland Railway, the duties that will be performed by it formed the outstanding feature of early railway practice, and were then practically the work of a railway; the internal routine work being performed by a clerk or two.

"During recent years so much attention has been devoted to 'railway policy' and obscure 'railway politics', that head office staffs have been largely increased to attend to the mass of detail arising therefrom, whilst purely railway (traffic) matters (we are not referring to the Midland Railway in particular) have been somewhat neglected. Now, however, that the Midland Railway has made a movement in this direction, it is to be hoped that other railways will also give more attention to railway working, and let railway politics have a rest."

Almost as an after thought the commentary added that of course Mr. John Elliott retains his position as Superintendent of the line. In actual fact, with Paget's appointment, it became redundant, and he retired not long afterwards. It was very different in the Locomotive Department. The new organisation had left Deeley with nothing but the design of new locomotives, their construction, and their periodical overhaul in the main works at Derby. Paget had a senior officer designated Superintendent of Motive Power, and he was responsible for all the train running, and the management of staff at all the running sheds. Deeley's title was changed to that of Chief Mechanical Engineer. In his former far-reaching appointment he had been responsible for the introduction of water troughs on the Midland Railway, and his own compound engines, and those of the later batches of the "Belpaires" which had six-wheeled tenders, instead of the Johnson water-carts. All engines previously equipped with them, including the 'Princess of Wales' series of "Spinners" were subsequently fitted with high sided six-wheeled tenders.

A little before the time when the empire he had inherited from Johnson was about to be dissolved, Deeley had embarked on a project that profoundly affected the motive power situation on the Settle and Carlisle line for the next twenty years. Always of an inventive turn of mind, while he was still Works Manager at Derby he had given thought to the proliferation of the machinery between the frames of the traditional British inside cylinder locomotive, and it had occurred to him that the mechanical congestion could be greatly lessened by using the crosshead of one cylinder to provide the equivalent of the eccentric of the other. By so doing eccentrics of the usual kind were eliminated altogether. He had gone so far as designing a valve gear on these principles, but Johnson did not approve. But in the saddle himself and wishing to conduct some trials of compound versus simple locomotives of relatively equal tractive power, he revived his earlier plan for a two-cylinder simple 4-4-0 without the conventional valve gear, and applied for a patent in August 1905. Great was his surprise and indignation when in February 1906, before even his patent had been granted, Churchward's epoch-marking four-cylinder 'Atlantic', the *North Star*, was completed at Swindon, having precisely the same arrangement as Deeley was in the process of patenting! There were some strong words between Derby and Swindon on this situation, until Churchward explained that his drawing office had hit upon precisely the same idea as Deeley had put up to Johnson, in complete ignorance of any ideas from Derby.

The 'scissors gear', as it became known, was used on only one Great Western engine, the *North Star*, but Deeley used it on the ten 4-4-0s of the 999 class that he built in 1907 for comparative trials with the compounds. By the end of 1906 he had built thirty of his own version of these latter engines and the 999 class had the same boiler and firebox as the compounds, with a large grate of 28.4 sq ft and carrying a working pressure of 220 lb per sq in. They had cylinders of 19 in diameter by 26 in stroke, and coupled wheels of 6 ft 6 in, but although having a nominal tractive effort considerably greater than the Johnson "Belpaire" 4-4-0s, 22,750 lb against 18,845 lb, they were graded also as Class 3, against the Class 4 of the compounds, both while in their non-superheated condition. The 999 class were subjected to indicator trials between Derby and St Pancras, but afterwards all ten of them went north, with most of them shedded at Durran Hill. Evidently the results from them did not impress Deeley sufficiently to make him change his mind, because another ten compounds were

*An up Scotch Express leaving Carlisle, hauled by two rebuilt 6ft 6in 4-4-0s, Nos 432 and 446.*
(H. Gordon Tidey)

built at Derby, in 1908–9, after what would have been his *magnum opus* in locomotive design had been turned down by the top management of the Midland Railway.

After Johnson had retired relations remained very friendly between Derby and Gateshead, and even after Wilson Worsdell's visit to America, and his subsequent building of the huge V class 'Atlantics', it was evident that the North Eastern had not entirely finished with compounds. In 1906 W. M. Smith's two beautiful four-cylinder compound 'Atlantics', Nos 730 and 731 were built at Gateshead, and following on the production of the 999 class at Derby, Deeley had set his drawing office also onto the design of a four-cylinder compound. In the latter case this was a 4-6-0 using the 'scissors' type of valve gear to avoid any motion outside the frames. It would have been a mighty engine, with a nominal tractive effort of no less than 25,700 lb. It was designed in full detail, and in connection with a book I wrote some twenty-five years ago on the Midland compounds, the reigning superintendent at Derby sent me a copy of the general arrangement drawing. The drawing is dated November 1907 and by that time the clouds had begun to gather around Deeley's future career. It was not likely that a man of his intellect and disposition would take kindly to the fractionalisation of his former command, and there were tales of

increasing friction. Hamilton Ellis had a vivid, but probably slightly apocryphal account of the mechanics of his going in 1909.

While Paget's principal energies were at first concentrated towards improving the movement of the vast mineral traffic south of Leeds, the reorganising of passenger train operating over the whole line was dealt with, and the grouping of the locomotive power into no more than four classes was the predominating feature. In so doing the Midland Railway initiated what was virtually a new principle in the allocation of individual locomotives to the various duties. On all British railways the practice had been to keep the best units from a link to work the most important turns, often with picked drivers. The case of the first two Johnson compounds, at Leeds and Carlisle, each reserved for one crew only, was perhaps exceptional, but all over the country there were innumerable instances of picked engines and crews for picked jobs. The practice lasted virtually to the end of steam traction in some areas. But on the Midland, under Paget's systems of operation, all engines that were roadworthy were lumped together, good, bad, and indifferent alike, and the load limits fixed so that any engine that could turn a wheel could do the job — or so it was hoped.

Naturally the loads had to be calculated so that an engine in the poorest condition could time the train. For the slightest excess over the rostered load for the particular class engine the driver could claim a pilot, no matter how good, or otherwise his engine might be. On the heavy adverse gradients of the Settle and Carlisle line the maximum load that could be taken unpiloted was 230 tons, with a Class 4 engine. The grades for the various engines were as follows:

| Class of loading | Engine classes |
|---|---|
| 1 | All 2-4-0s, 4-2-2s and unrebuilt 4-4-0s. |
| 2 | Rebuilt 4-4-0s, 6 ft 6 in, 6 ft 9 in, 7 ft. |
| 3 | "Belpaire" 4-4-0s, 999 class 4-4-0s. |
| 4 | Three-cylinder compound 4-4-0s. |

On the fastest running main lines in the South and West of England the load limits for the four classes as first fixed were 150, 180, 200 and 240 tons, though I believe the Class 3 limit was increased to 205 tons after the "Belpaires" had been superheated.

While the loading limits were fixed, irrespective of the condition of engines, the standards of shed maintenance in the Paget regime, and thereafter, were high. I shall always remember the words of a celebrated son of Derby, who rose high in the realm of road-testing of locomotives, but who never lost his innate sense of humour in the process. In early LMS days at a meeting of the Institution of Locomotive Engineers he rocked the rafters by saying that while on the North Western they just did not care so long as their engines could rattle and bang their way along with a good paying load; on the Midland the nice little engines were made pets of. They were housed in nice clean sheds, and they were never over-loaded — indeed it seemed that there was a 'Society for Preventing Cruelty to Engines' presiding over all Midland locomotive running! At the risk of prolonging these premature references to early LMS I may quote an experience of November 1926 when it would seem that the 'SPCE' was still much in operation.

My family had some business in St Albans at the time, and I used to pay an occasional visit on Saturday afternoons, returning by an early evening train which ran non-stop to St Pancras. It was usually a light train, often less than 200 tons, and worked with Class 2 or Class 3 engines. On the November day in question it was very late.

There were no public address facilities in those days, and so I, and a score of other disgruntled passengers, just had to wait. When the train did eventually arrive it was double-headed, with a Kirtley 800 class 2-4-0, No. 53 piloting a Class 2 4-4-0. There was no time to check up on the load at St Albans, but we ran smartly enough down to St Pancras touching 71 mph at Hendon. Then, checking up on arrival I found we had 270 tons tare, and spoke to the driver of the Class 2. He said the load had been increased at Bedford to well over the limit, and he had demanded a pilot. Another engine was not immediately available, and he had refused to start, saying that such a load "would knock the engine all to pieces". And so the train sat in Bedford station while the old Kirtley 2-4-0 was prepared, and the 'SPCE' flourished. Had the driver, or "the system" had any sense of proportion, and worked the train engine as he would have done with a normal Class 2 load, the loss of time would have been minimal compared with the forty minutes or so we were kept waiting!

The establishment of the Paget operational organisation affected the Settle and Carlisle line in several different ways. Engine loadings were reduced north of Hellifield, so that in addition to the compound tonnage being 230, instead of 240 south of Leicester, the Class 2 limit was no more than 170 tons, with 200 from a Class 3 engine. Few, if any of the compounds were then stationed at Durran Hill, and with the original 999 class still in Class 3, it would seem that a great amount of piloting would be necessary. There was also the question of coal. At Leeds there was no trouble. Whitehall Junction shed was near enough to ample supplies of best hard Yorkshire coal, as good a locomotive fuel as any within easy reach of the Midland Railway; but conveying it up to Durran Hill was another matter. There were collieries in the Scottish Border country, and a contract had been placed with the Naworth Coal Company for supplies. Its best grades had an excellent calorific value, but that was unhappily not all, as the tragic events related in Chapter 9 bore witness.

Deeley's resignation in 1909 had left his two most senior assistants in embryo, as it were. They were J. E. Anderson the Works Assistant, and S. J. Symes, the Chief Locomotive Draughtsman. It was Symes' initials on the general arrangement drawing of the proposed four-cylinder compound

*Appleby station in Midland days showing the branch connections to the North Eastern line.*
(Norman Wilkinson)

4-6-0 which was not built. Granet did not choose either of these assistants to succeed Deeley as Chief Mechanical Engineer, instead he selected Henry Fowler, who after distinguished academic training in Birmingham, served his engineering apprenticeship on the Lancashire & Yorkshire Railway, becoming Chief of the Testing Department at Horwich Works, and then Gas Engineer. In 1900 he left the LYR to take up a similar position on the Midland, subsequently becoming Works Manager at Derby in 1907. Essentially of a scientific nature, he had also, unlike Deeley, an equable temperament and a natural ability to 'get on' well with colleagues of every estate. He was already a popular member of the Institutions of Civil and Mechanical Engineers, and delighted in reading scientific papers on various subjects. Anderson and Symes remained in their former posts, and all was then well for a continuation, on an even keel, of the Chief Mechanical Engineer's department at Derby.

Although the loading limits for the four categories of passenger engines had been fixed so relatively low, train loads were also low by the standards of some competitors of the Midland, and there seems to have been a tacit understanding from the top management that no more express passenger engines were to be built, for a long time ahead. Fowler's remit was to maintain the existing stock. Any improvements in design, to increase efficiency or to reduce coal consumption were to be made without any capital charges. Fowler revelled in the task. His first move was to test the effect of fitting one of the 999 class with a Schmidt superheater. To get quick results

it was essential to make the minimum of alterations to the existing locomotive. The cylinders were left unchanged while the boiler pressure was reduced from the original 220 lb per sq in to 200, and with the cylinders remaining at 19 in, diameter the nominal tractive effort was reduced to little more than that of the Johnson "Belpaires". Although the 999s were definitely Northern Division engines all the trials with No. 998 were made between Leeds and St Pancras.

It seems as if there had been a race between Crewe and Derby as to which works could get the first superheater engine into traffic. Certainly No. 998 had been run in, and the operating department had taken the measure of her in time for the first comprehensive trials on coal consumptions, when she was pitted against a standard Deeley compound, No. 1043 in mid-December 1910. The trials were made on the fastest trains then running on a double-home basis, up one day and down the next. On the six runs made by each engine the loads were relatively light, averaging 186.5 tons tare for the 999 and 187.6 tons for the compound. Neither engine was indicated, and in fact the runs were made on the same days. On 12th December for example, the compound took the 1.30 pm Scotch Express from St Pancras while No. 998 worked down to Leeds with the fast 6 pm train, non-stop from St Pancras to Trent. The latter engine came off considerably better than the compound in coal consumption, averaging 23 lb per mile on her six days, against 28.5 lb per mile. No. 1043 was of course non-superheated at that time.

A further series of runs were made in January

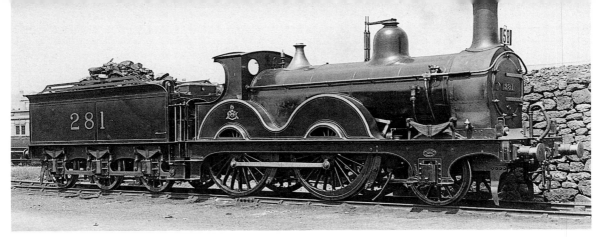

*Johnson 2-4-0 with 7 ft coupled wheels as built in 1881, but renumbered 281, from the original No. 1501.*
(British Railways)

and February 1911 between the superheated No. 998 and another engine of the class, No. 992, saturated, although oddly enough, with the boiler pressure also reduced from the original 220 lb per sq in, to 200. The compound on the 1910 test runs was working at her usual 220 lb per sq in. The second set of trials involved each engine in six return trips from Leeds to St Pancras on the same trains as previously and with much the same loads. On her twelve runs engine No. 992 had an average tare load of 184.5 tons, while No. 998 had 196.5 tons. As might be expected the superheater engine showed up to great advantage, using no more than 24.3 lb coal per mile, as against 31.4 lb per mile by the non-superheated No. 992. These results were published in a paper Fowler presented to the Institution of Civil Engineers in 1914, at which many of the leading figures in the railway world of that day were present, including Bowen Cooke, Churchward, Vincent Raven, Gresley, George Hughes and J. A. F. Aspinall. Reading the report of the lengthy discussion that took place afterwards one can be surprised that no mention was made of the surprisingly light loads hauled by the Midland engines tested.

With such convincing results as those with engine No. 998 to hand Fowler had no difficulty in getting authorisation for the conversion of the remaining nine engines of the class to superheating. However, it is to be feared that the use of Naworth coal at Durran Hill shed, where most of them were stationed, would not have given such favourable results as were obtained in the trials of 1910–11 when best quality hard Yorkshire coal was being used. But against the passenger train requirements of the Leeds–Carlisle line those ten were little more

than "a drop in the ocean". It seems also that Whitehall Junction shed could rarely spare a compound to go north, and with the "Belpaires" mostly moved south, the brunt of the working of the Scotch Expresses north of Leeds devolved upon the rebuilt Johnson 4-4-0s. By the time of Deeley's resignation all except the engines of the first two batches had been dealt with, the engines with 6 ft 6 in, 6 ft 9 in, and 7 ft coupled wheels retaining their original cylinders and frames, and being fitted with larger boilers and round topped fireboxes. As mentioned earlier in this chapter some of the earliest of the rebuilds retained their original cast brass numbers, while others succumbing to the new style of having the engine number painted in huge figures on the tender, were rebuilt before the general renumbering of the entire locomotive stock took place.

Even in the most carefully controlled Midland days however, tenders got mixed up occasionally as at least one photograph in *The Railway Magazine* has borne witness, while in early LMS days I was myself very nearly the victim of a similar transpositioning, on one of the finest runs I ever had over the Settle and Carlisle with Midland engines. I was travelling on the 12 noon from Edinburgh Waverley to St Pancras, and at Carlisle, after combining with the Glasgow portion, I noted that our fresh engines were a Class 2 rebuild and a new compound, No. 1108. I checked again the number of the pilot when it had coupled off at Ais Gill, and on arrival at Leeds I went forward to thank the driver of the train engine for such a splendid run. In so doing I happened to notice, painted in small black figures *inside the cab*, the number 1070, and hurrying forward to the front, because station times were notoriously short at Leeds in those

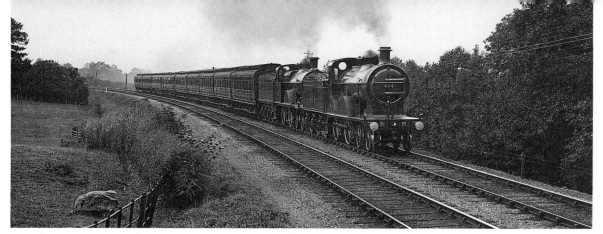

*Another up Scotch Express near Armathwaite, hauled by rebuilt 6 ft 6 in 4-4-0 No. 454 and an unidentified "Belpaire" with bogie tender.* (British Railways)

days, I saw that our engine from Carlisle had indeed been No. 1070. What she was doing with the tender from No. 1108 I had not time to enquire.

The Class 2 rebuilds, very many of which were regularly working north of Leeds, were renumbered as below, and it will be seen that the renumbering was carried out according to the dates when the engines were built originally, and that the wheel diameters were accordingly mixed up.

Midland Railway: Class 2 4-4-0s
As first rebuilt — non-superheated

| New running numbers | Date first built | Coupled wheel dia. | Total in group |
|---|---|---|---|
| 328–357 | 1882–1883 | 6′ 9″ | 30 |
| 358–377 | 1885–1887 | 7′ 0″ | 20 |
| 378–402 | 1888–1891 | 6′ 6″ | 25 |
| 403–427 | 1892–1896 | 7′ 0″ | 25 |
| 428–482 | 1893–1900 | 6′ 6″ | 55 |
| 483–562 | 1896–1901 | 7′ 0″ | 80 |

As a post-script to the pre-Paget days, when considerably larger loads were taken over Ais Gill without pilot assistance, I have tabulated two runs from the collection of R. E. Charlewood, who took over the authorship of 'British Locomotive Practice and Performance' in *The Railway Magazine* for a year following the sudden and lamented death of Charles Rous-Marten. He had no pretensions to any technical details of locomotives, indeed in the year of his authorship the 'Practice' side of the subject lay fallow. But as a recorder of train running he was immaculate. I came to know him personally just as he was on the point of retiring after a life-time's service on

the LNWR and the LMS. A lifelong bachelor, he lived in a cosy and charmingly-furnished flat in North-West London, where I and various kindred souls were always made very welcome. For nearly forty years of speed recording he always timed to exact mileposts rather than the easier way of timing to the centre of each station. The runs reproduced herewith were recorded in this way but I have worked the average speeds from point to point as Charlewood took no maximum and minimum speed readings, except a very few.

The southbound run, with a train of which the gross load behind the tender must have been at least 270 tons, was unchecked throughout, and they had made such good time up to Ais Gill that the driver ran at very moderate speed over the tableland to Blea Moor and did not exceed 75 mph down the bank. In comparing the net times of the two runs however it must be appreciated that the southbound run is considerably the harder gradient wise. Settle Junction stands a good 400 ft higher than the Carlisle end of the line at Petteril Bridge Junction, resulting in an average upward inclination of about 1 in 850 against southbound trains. The effect of this apparently slight gradient may be seen in the difference in speed between eastbound and westbound trains on the Great Western main line between Didcot and Swindon. So naturally the fastest Midland timings over over the Settle and Carlisle line have always been in the northbound direction, there being no location where permanent speed restrictions had to be enforced for curves.

Mr Charlewood's northbound journey got a bad start from a signal check at Settle Junction which he estimates cost $2\frac{1}{4}$ minutes. In spite of this hindrance the ascent of the 'Long Drag' was excellent, with an absolute minimum of 31 mph and a rapid recovery over Ribblehead Viaduct. A maximum of $80\frac{1}{2}$ mph was noted north of Kirkby Stephen and good time was made to Carlisle despite the checks. These runs do serve as a postscript to Midland running on the Settle and Carlisle line, because in the Paget era with loads of 240 and 255 tons tare, even Class 4 engines would have been piloted, and in the greatest

LMS days with the latest 6 ft 9 in superheater compounds the maximum load for an unpiloted engine was 270 tons.

Midland Railway: 1.13 pm Carlisle–Hellifield
Engine: Johnson "Belpaire" 4-4-0 No. 800
Load: 255 tons

| Miles | | Actual times m s | Average speed mph |
|---|---|---|---|
| 0.0 | Carlisle | 0 00 | — |
| 2.7 | Scotby | 5 55 | 27.4 |
| 8.0 | Milepost 300 | 14 14 | 37.8 |
| 9.9 | Armathwaite | 16 27 | 51.5 |
| 15.4 | Lazonby | 22 22 | 54.7 |
| 23.4 | Culgaith | 30 27 | 59.4 |
| 30.8 | Appleby | 39 10 | 50.7 |
| 33.0 | Milepost 275 | 41 34 | 56.0 |
| 41.4 | Kirkby Stephen | 54 05 | 41.2 |
| 48.3 | Ais Gill Box | 65 58 | 34.5 |
| 54.6 | Dent | 73 08 | 53.1 |
| 59.5 | Blea Moor Box | 78 28 | 55.0 |
| 65.5 | Horton | 83 51 | 68.5 |
| 71.6 | Settle | 88 57 | 71.8 |
| 76.0 | Milepost 232 | 93 14 | 62.3 |
| 76.8 | Hellifield | 94 39 | — |

Midland Railway: 2.17 pm Hellifield–Carlisle
Engine: Johnson "Belpaire" 4-4-0 No. 812
Load: 240 tons

| Miles | | Actual times m s | Average speed mph |
|---|---|---|---|
| 0.0 | Hellifield | 0 00 | — |
| 0.8 | Milepost 232 | 1 48 | — |
| — | | sig check | — |
| 5.2 | Settle | 8 12 | 41.4 |
| 11.3 | Horton | 19 05 | 33.7 |
| 16.0 | Ribblehead | 27 51 | 32.2 |
| 17.3 | Blea Moor Box | 30 06 | 34.6 |
| 22.2 | Dent | 36 44 | 44.3 |
| 25.4 | Hawes Junction | 40 05 | 57.7 |
| 28.5 | Ais Gill Box | 43 31 | 54.5 |
| 35.3 | Kirkby Stephen | 49 38 | 67.0 |
| 43.8 | Milepost 275 | 56 17 | 76.5 |
| 46.0 | Appleby | 58 43 | 53.1 |
| 53.4 | Culgaith | 64 36 | 75.0 |
| 61.6 | Lazonby | 71 43 | 69.1 |
| 66.8 | Armathwaite | 77 09 | 58.0 |
| 68.8 | Milepost 300 | 78 59 | 62.6 |
| 74.1 | Scotby | 83 58 | 63.5 |
| 75.8 | Milepost 307 | 85 40 | 60.0 |
| — | | sig check | |
| 76.8 | Carlisle | 87 50 | — |

Net time $85\frac{1}{4}$ minutes

# 8
# Express Train Running — 1910–1913

Not very long before the period which will be under review in this chapter Cecil J. Allen, who was described in the obituary notice published in *The Times* of 7th February 1973, as the "doyen of contemporary railway writers", had been appointed an inspector of permanent way materials on the staff of the Chief Engineer of the Great Eastern Railway. A railway enthusiast from the cradle he undertook with the utmost zest the many journeys to be made to the steel works of North-Eastern England and West Cumberland in connection with his professional duties and he logged the runs in detail.

Furthermore, from January 1911 he had been assigned the sole authorship of the monthly feature 'British Locomotives Practice and Performance' in *The Railway Magazine*, and details of his many trips from London to Carlisle, by both the London & North Western and by the Midland route were soon to intrigue the growing readership of those articles. The Midland instalments relating to the line north of Leeds came in the issues of August and September 1913, though the remarkable thing about the journeys detailed, as was also the case with a similar series dealing with the Crewe–Carlisle section of the LNWR earlier that same year, was no mention at all was made of any southbound journeys. The inference that could be made would be that the recorder returned to London by other means, perhaps using the "trusty Rudge Whitworth bicycle" that features in an earlier part of the author's

*The new Deeley 4-4-0, No. 999 classified '3', as originally built, non-superheated.* (British Railways)

*A Glasgow–St Pancras express leaving Carlisle, hauled by 4-4-0 No. 998.* (H. Gordon Tidey)

biography!

Levity apart however, the massive bank of data contained in those two articles has provided an invaluable insight into running conditions of that period, though of course from a single observer's viewpoint the variety of trains travelled upon was minimal. One would not like to appear greedy in view of the copious amount of information already provided, but one yearns for just a little about the very fast night train booked nominally non-stop from St Pancras to Carlisle! Actually it stopped on the curve outside Shipley station to change engines. It would have been inconvenient to do so on the crowded tracks beside Whitehall Junction engine sheds at Leeds. When rostered to this working the train ran from St Pancras to Carlisle in the level six hours, an average of $51\frac{1}{2}$ mph, but the load was usually no more than five coaches including two restaurant cars. Another six-hour train to Carlisle was the 7.30 pm Highland Express, which in its short life carried sleeping cars for Inverness and Fort William. The regular night trains were the 9.15 pm for Edinburgh, conveying also through carriages for Aberdeen, and the 9.30 pm for Glasgow. The midnight express from St Pancras was primarily a Glasgow train, but it carried a through portion for Edinburgh.

Turning now to the data provided in Cecil J. Allen's articles in *The Railway Magazine*, there are first of all five runs between Leeds and Hellifield, as preliminary to the hard work over the mountain section. With the reorganisation of the timetables the day-time expresses from St Pancras completely omitted the one-time regular stops at Skipton, and the train engine workings were in all cases from Leeds to Carlisle. Pilots, if they were needed, were attached at Hellifield, which was always a busy and important shed. It provided also for the Scotch services from the Lancashire & Yorkshire line, many of which were hauled by Midland engines southwards to Manchester. The line from Leeds to Hellifield is almost continuously adverse, and with the severe permanent speed restrictions on the curves at Shipley and Skipton the scheduled time of 47 minutes for the 36 miles does not leave much margin, even with loads so light as 200 tons. Allen does not give any speed details of the runs tabulated herewith, but referring to some of my own timings which will be discussed in some detail in later chapters, it is evident that to pass Shipley in the scheduled 15 minutes from Leeds required a speed of 53 to 54 mph up the rise from Kirkstall to Thackley Tunnel, and of 65 to 67 mph over the practically level stretch between Keighley and the approach to Skipton. I have clocked between $14\frac{1}{2}$ and $15\frac{1}{2}$ minutes start to stop between Skipton and Hellifield, with minimum speeds of 39 to 43 mph on the Bell Busk bank, the gradient profile of which is shown herewith.

The first run tabulated was made by one of the very few compounds to be stationed at Durran Hill, for some time I believe the only one, after

Midland Railway: Leeds–Hellifield

| Engine No. | | | 1010 | 998 | 995 | 1032 | 996 |
|---|---|---|---|---|---|---|---|
| Class | | | Compound | 999-s | 999-s | Compound | 999 |
| Load, axles | | | 28 | 28 | 32 | 34 | 39 |
| Tons | | | 185 | 185 | 215 | 235 | 270 |
| Distance | | Sch. | Actual | Actual | Actual | Actual | Actual |
| Miles | | min | m  s | m  s | m  s | m  s | m  s |
| 0.0 | Leeds | 0 | 0  00 | 0  00 | 0  00 | 0  00 | 0  00 |
| 4.5 | Newlay | — | 7  40 | 7  40 | 7  40 | 8  25 | 7  05 |
| — | | | — | — | p.w.s. | — | — |
| 10.9 | Shipley | 15 | 15  20 | 15  25 | 16  05 | 16  20 | 14  00 |
| 17.0 | Keighley | 22 | 23  05 | 23  15 | 24  30 | 23  30 | 21  30 |
| 26.2 | Skipton | 33 | 32  50 | 32  50 | 34  05 | 32  55 | 31  10 |
| 32.8 | Bell Busk | — | 41  50 | 42  15 | 43  10 | 41  40 | 40  40 |
| 36.2 | Hellifield | 47 | 47  05 | 47  30 | 47  55 | 46  40 | 45  20 |

-s, superheated

the Johnson No. 2632 had been transferred to Leeds. Little comment can be made on this run, with a light load, and also that of No. 998, even though the latter engine had already been superheated, and the power class stepped up from 3 to 4. Engine No. 995, also superheated was delayed by a permanent way check near Shipley, and was not unduly hurried thereafter, but compound No. 1032 with a heavier load, almost up to the Class 4 limit, ran well after a poor start to Shipley, with a maximum speed of 63 mph on the near-level after Keighley, and a reasonably good climb of the Bell Busk bank. Strangely enough it was the non-superheated '999', No. 996, that made by far the best run from Leeds to Hellifield, surprisingly in that she was well overloaded, as a Class 3 engine. It was the very vigorous start that made most of the difference, and before Newlay, the speed must have been almost if not quite 60 mph. The heavier load told on the Bell Busk bank, but even so it was first class work to reach Hellifield in $1\frac{3}{4}$ minutes less than the sharp booked time.

Now turning to the runs from Hellifield

*An up Scotch Express passing Hawes Junction in 1912, hauled by 7 ft rebuilt 4-4-0 No. 543. (R. J. Purves)*

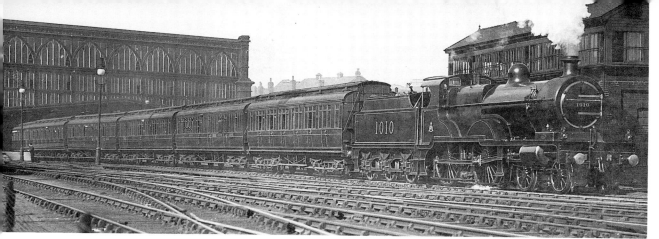

*A Glasgow–St Pancras express leaves Carlisle behind compound 4-4-0 No. 1010.* (F. E. Mackay)

to Carlisle I have segregated these into three groups, one being the non-stop runs on which no pilot was taken, secondly the runs which were piloted as far as Ais Gill Summit, and lastly four runs on the 1.30 pm from St Pancras which included an intermediate stop at Appleby and had three minutes extra time between Hellifield and Carlisle, and a sharp timing of 32 minutes start to stop over the 30.8 miles from Appleby. In the first group I have added one of my own runs, to include a specimen of night running. In pre-1916 Midland days the uphill schedules were severe, notably the booked average of 40 mph from Settle Junction to Blea Moor, followed by no more than 12 minutes for the tableland section of 11.2 miles from Blea Moor to Ais Gill. On the other hand the allowance of 49 minutes for the downhill run of 48.3 miles to Carlisle provided some margin for recovery, although in the Paget era high downhill speed was not encouraged. The first run in the table, with the 7 ft rebuilt 4-4-0 No. 522 was poor throughout. Even with no more than 190 tons the driver could have claimed a pilot up to Ais Gill, and probably did. By averaging less than 30 mph uphill between Horton and Blea Moor, and no more than 57 mph between Dent and Ais Gill he had lost $4\frac{1}{4}$ minutes on schedule to the summit, and regained only $\frac{1}{4}$ minute on the easy downhill timing.

The Compound No. 1010 which featured in several contemporary photographs of trains on the line, and also on one of the charming coloured picture postcards which the Locomotive Publishing Company used to sell for one penny each in my early boyhood, became a favourite of mine. In the accompanying table she was doing no more than 'pacing' the feeble '522' as far as

Settle, but she picked up afterwards, though not enough to avoid losing a minute on booked time to Blea Moor. Her average speed from Horton was 33 mph. It is not surprising that further time was lost on the very sharp booking of 12 minutes for the 11.3 miles from Blea Moor to Ais Gill, even though the maximum speed reached over 65 mph at Hawes Junction. There was however no difficulty in winning back the time that had been lost, with average speeds of 65 mph from Kirkby Stephen to Ormside and of 74 mph from Culgaith to Lazonby. The honours in this table however go to the then recently superheated 999 class 4-4-0, for although she had been upgraded to Class 4, the train load was considerably above the limit of 230 tons. Engine No. 995 had a driver who really meant business, whatever the official limitations of load may have been, though even he did not keep the 12 minute booking from Blea Moor to Ais Gill. But with a brilliantly smart start out of Hellifield and an average of all but 40 mph from Horton to Blea Moor he was $\frac{1}{2}$ minute ahead of the latter point and still 40 secs ahead of time at Ais Gill. Some fast running followed the signal check at Ormside, with a maximum speed of 85 mph at the crossing of the River Eden near Little Salkeld.

The fourth run is rather out of context so far as date is concerned, but it is the only run I have personally clocked behind a 999 class engine. It was made a few years after the monumental trials of 1923-4, and includes two new features. First of all, as a result from those trials, the official load limit for Class 4 engines had been increased to 270 tons, and secondly, because the compound building programme was expected to increase the stud to 300 engines, the 999s were renumbered. Actually compound building eventually stopped at No. 939. The night train by which I travelled had a schedule of 6 min to Settle Junction, 28 min to Blea Moor, 41 min to Ais Gill, 59 min to Appleby and 90 min to Carlisle. Up the 'Long Drag' with this 290 ton load the minimum speed was 29 mph, but we picked up well on the tableland, passed Hawes Junction at 65 mph and cleared Ais Gill at an excellent minimum of $57\frac{1}{2}$ mph. We were on time by Appleby, after a downhill maximum of 75 mph, but after Culgaith, the West of England train, which carried through carriages to both Edinburgh and Glasgow, and which was nominally booked non-stop from Leeds to Carlisle, was obviously not doing so well as we were, and we encountered adverse signals from her. We were all but stopped at Little Salkeld, normally one of the fastest stretches on the northbound run. We kept clear of her signals after that, but Carlisle was in a dreadful tangle that morning, and we

were held for 12 minutes outside before we could enter Citadel station. Our net time from Hellifield was no more than 87 minutes, only one minute more than the pre-1917 schedule, despite the considerably heavier load.

In turning to Table 3, which details the runs on which a pilot engine was taken from Hellifield to Ais Gill Summit, I must confess that in setting out the factual details of the journeys, made available to me in long past volumes of *The Railway Magazine*, I found myself wishing that more photographic records of those days had been preserved. My great friend of later signalling days at York made one isolated trip to Hawes Junction, but that was all; it was a pity because R. J. Purves was a superb photographer. The big names of the railway photographic world of those times, F. E. Mackay and H. Gordon Tidey, did not venture on to the Settle and Carlisle line beyond taking Midland trains as they entered and

Midland Railway: Hellifield–Carlisle

| Engine No. | | | 522* | | 1010 | | 955 | | 802 + | |
| Class | | | 4-4-0 '2' | | Compound | | 999-s | | 999-s | |
| Load, axles | | | 28 | | 28 | | 36 | | 38 | |
| Load, tons | | | 190 | | 190 | | 255 | | 290 | |
| Distance | | Sch. | Actual | | Actual | | Actual | | Actual | |
| Miles | | min | m | s | m | s | m | s | m | s |
| 0.0 | Hellifield | 0 | 0 | 00 | 0 | 00 | 0 | 00 | 0 | 00 |
| 3.3 | Settle Junction | +4 | 4 | 40 | 4 | 35 | 4 | 25 | 4 | 50 |
| 5.2 | Settle | | 6 | 45 | 6 | 45 | 6 | 20 | 7 | 00 |
| 11.3 | Horton | | 15 | 30 | 15 | 05 | 14 | 25 | 17 | 15 |
| 17.3 | Blea Moor Box | 25 | 27 | 40 | 26 | 00 | 23 | 30 | 28 | 55 |
| 22.2 | Dent | | 34 | 30 | 32 | 20 | 29 | 50 | 36 | 15 |
| 25.4 | Hawes Junction | | 37 | 55 | 35 | 35 | 33 | 15 | 39 | 35 |
| 28.5 | Ais Gill Box | 37 | 41 | 10 | 39 | 00 | 36 | 20 | 42 | 30 |
| 35.3 | Kirkby Stephen | | 47 | 25 | 45 | 05 | 43 | 15 | 48 | 35 |
| — | | | — | | — | | sigs | | — | |
| 43.6 | Ormside | | 55 | 20 | 52 | 40 | 51 | 40 | | |
| 46.0 | Appleby | 55 | 57 | 40 | 54 | 55 | 55 | 00 | 58 | 25 |
| 53.4 | Culgaith | | 64 | 45 | 61 | 25 | 61 | 45 | 65 | 05 |
| — | | | — | | — | | — | | sigs | |
| 61.6 | Lazonby | | 72 | 00 | 68 | 10 | 67 | 55 | 75 | 25 |
| 66.8 | Armathwaite | | 77 | 45 | 73 | 10 | 72 | 45 | 81 | 50 |
| 74.1 | Scotby | | 84 | 15 | 79 | 40 | 78 | 50 | 88 | 30 |
| — | | | — | | — | | — | | prolonged | |
| — | | | — | | — | | — | | stops | |
| 76.8 | Carlisle | 86 | 88 | 55 | 84 | 10 | 83 | 25 | 108 | 15 |
| | Net times | min | 89 | | $84\frac{1}{4}$ | | $81\frac{1}{2}$ | | 87 | |

*7 ft, non-superheater rebuild
+, engine renumbered
-s, superheated

*No. 995 heads an up three-coach slow train near Armathwaite.* (British Railways)

departed from the Citadel station. There was nothing on the 'Long Drag' and yet what a feast for the photographers even the six runs I have tabulated would have made! The locomotive combinations provided six different varieties, all different, and with the traditional cleanliness of Midland engines, what pictures would have been presented against the magnificent mountain scenery of Upper Ribblesdale and the high table-land between Dent Head and Hawes Junction.

The train engines on four of the six runs, Nos 1, 2, 3 and 6, were of the 6 ft 6 in rebuilt type that Deeley had fitted with the same boiler as he had used on the three engines he had built new at Derby for the Somerset & Dorset Joint line, not long after he had taken over from Johnson. The pilots on these four runs were all different classes. On No. 1 it was a Kirtley 6 ft 8 in 2-4-0 of the old 890 class, and on No. 2 the leader was of the same 6 ft 6 in rebuilt Class 2 4-4-0 as the train engine. On No. 3 the pilot was one of the beautiful unrebuilt 7 ft 0 in 4-4-0s of the original 1327 class of 1877 which were never rebuilt. While on the very heavily loaded No. 6 run the train engine had no more help than could be given by a Johnson 6 ft 9 in 2-4-0 — a lovely engine it is true, but not all that much help on a train that was considerably over the maximum for these two engines. On runs Nos 4 and 5 the pilots were in each case rebuilt 6 ft 6 in Class 2 4-4-0s, but of the variety that Deeley introduced in 1908 with Belpaire fireboxes and a very prominently extended smokebox, which some observers thought to include a superheater, but this was not so. The trains on runs 4 and 5 to make up the variety, were one of the last batch of 7 ft

compounds, and a non-superheated '999', then Class 3.

Continuing on the subject of pilot engine working I must draw attention to the extraordinary slickness of the process of detaching the assistant engines at Ais Gill. On only one of the six runs was the main train at rest for as much as 90 seconds, and in one instance it was away in a single minute. In *The Railway Magazine* of September 1913 Cecil J. Allen states that the actual point of trains detaching pilot engines was about a quarter of a mile south of Ais Gill box, but I think it cannot have been as far back as that. The trailing crossover road by which the pilot engines reversed on their way back to Hawes Junction to turn had its northern end almost opposite the signal box, and one would not imagine the train engine would be more than 250 to 300 yards in the rear when it stopped. Nevertheless I have not been on the footplate when a train has detached its pilot at Ais Gill, and I can well believe there were occasions so sharp was the working that the train engine driver actually re-started before the points were re-set after the crossover movement. This might account for the trains stopping a little distance short of the actual points. So far as detaching pilots in general, in my own travelling days the process lacked nothing in smartness from the time to which this chapter refers. Twice when travelling south from Carlisle the time, when we were actually at rest at Ais Gill was 65 seconds, and in one instance the driver of one of the new 6 ft 9 in compounds got away with such vigour, with a 415-ton load, as to cover the first 3.1 miles, to Hawes Junction, in 5 min 25 sec and be running at $58\frac{1}{2}$ mph in that relatively short distance.

Coming to the runs tabulated, the first one, even though two engines were concerned with no more than a moderate load, must have been an exhilarating experience to record. They fairly stormed up the 'Long Drag' averaging as much as 46.4 mph from Horton to Blea Moor, and made considerably the fastest time from Hellifield to the stop at Ais Gill Summit. The pilot engine was one of Kirtley's last series of 6 ft 8 in 2-4-0s, known originally as the 890 class, though at the time of this run rebuilt with standard Johnson boiler mountings. The train engine driver continued the earlier thrill of the journey, once he had observed a permanent way check near Mallerstang siding. The maximum speed was $83\frac{1}{2}$ mph at the crossing of the River Eden between Little Salkeld and Lazonby. The two 6 ft 6 in Class 2 4-4-0s also did well up the bank, but also ran in unusually fast over the tableland, attaining 67 mph at Hawes Junction. But No. 447 on her own was not particularly speedy downhill, and dropped nearly a minute between Appleby and Carlisle. On the other hand the sister engine, No. 448, which with the Johnson unrebuilt 4-4-0 as pilot, had lost time to Ais Gill made some amends with some fast running over the final stages of the descent north of Appleby. I am sorry, though, to present the Johnson 4-4-0 No. 312 in an unfavourable light, because they were most beautiful engines to behold.

On No. 4 run the compound and its Deeley Belpaire Class 2 pilot made a strangely bad start from Hellifield, indeed I wonder if there was some slight check that the recorder did not appreciate. Anyway the two engines were going well enough above Horton, and the compound was able to restart from the summit on time. A maximum of 75 mph was recorded at Ormside, but the driver adhered closely to schedule thereafter, and Carlisle was reached 50 sec ahead of time. On No. 5 run the non-superheated 999 class 4-4-0 No. 996 which, as referred to earlier in this chapter, had already done so well between Leeds and Hellifield, had another of the Deeley Belpaire Class 2 4-4-0s as pilot to Ais Gill and the two engines got away from Hellifield with customary smartness. With a good climb to Blea Moor and fast running thereafter the '999' had been able to re-start from Ais Gill slightly more than a minute ahead of the compound's time. More moderate downhill running however reduced the lead, until the two occasions were level in time on passing Armathwaite; but a dead stand for signals at Cumwhinton caused the arrival in Carlisle to be 4 minutes late. At that time there was some competition between the arrivals of Midland and LNWR trains at Carlisle because the 9.30 am from St Pancras, on most of which the tabulated runs were made, was booked into the Citadel station just ahead of the 10 am from Euston. Conflicting routes were avoided however by run-

*A period piece at Armathwaite, showing the large nameboards favoured by the Midland Railway. The up Scotch Express which is approaching, is hauled by the original Johnson compound, originally No. 2631 but by then renumbered 1000. It is seen in non-superheated form with the original square splashers to the trailing coupled wheels, but with 6-wheeled tender with water-pick-up gear. (British Railways)*

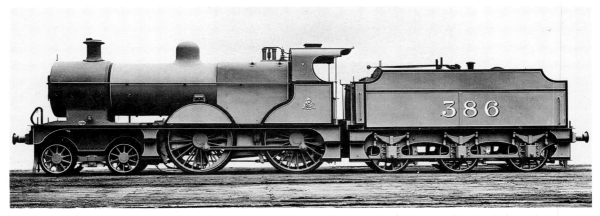

*Johnson 6 ft 6 in 4-4-0, No. 386, rebuilt a second time with Belpaire firebox and extended smokebox, but still not superheated.* (British Railways)

ning the Midland train into the central platform, indeed E. E. Mackay once photographed both trains simultaneously entering the station.

On the last run the load of 365 tons was considerably over the limit for a Class 1 and a Class 2 engine in combination. The train engine, No. 464, while having the very next number to that of the pilot engine on No. 5 run, was of the original Class 2 rebuilt series, with round-topped boiler. I judged the load to be divided in the proportion of 155 tons to the 2-4-0 and 210 tons to the train engine and on this basis I consider they made a good try at a sharply booked timing. I recall one of the 6 ft 9 in standard LMS compounds averaging no more than 30 mph with a 282-ton train from Horton to Blea Moor, and

taking 11 minutes to cover the ensuing 8.1 miles to Hawes Junction, whereas the two engines on No. 6 run averaged 34.6 mph and took 10 min 30 sec to cover the same 8.1 miles. For some reason detaching of the pilot was not done so speedily as on the other five runs, albeit it took no more than 90 sec, but the driver of No. 464 put in some robust downhill speed afterwards, attaining $77\frac{1}{2}$ mph after Kirkby Stephen, and some fast running after Lazonby. The sectional time of 49 minutes for the 48.3 miles from Ais Gill to Carlisle was practically kept. It was certainly a plucky effort with such a load as 365 tons.

The fourth tabulation relates to the running of the 1.30 pm express from St Pancras, which at the zenith of pre-1917 speed on the Midland had a

*Deeley 4-4-0 No. 994. Works an up Scotch Express near Armathwaite.* (British Railways)

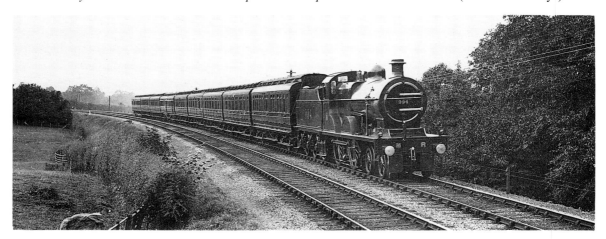

timing of no more than 31 minutes start-to-stop, over the 30.8 miles from Appleby to Carlisle. By the time the tabulated runs were made this timing had been eased to 32 minutes. In this case I have divided the tabulation relative to the work north and south of Appleby to include details of the average speeds run on the Appleby–Carlisle 32-minute sprint. In view of what was currently being done by superheater 4-4-0 engines on the West Coast route over Shap, one cannot be too enthusiastic over the performances of the 999s on the 1.30 pm Scotch Express from St Pancras as detailed in the adjoining tables. From a study of the figures it does seem to suggest that the drivers were not trying very hard with those light trains, and there was almost a suggestion that the shop stewards of that alleged society for the prevention of cruelty to Midland engines might have been looking over the shoulders of some of the drivers as they nursed their "nice little engines" gently up the 'Long Drag'.

On the other hand Cecil J. Allen, enthusiast and immaculate recorder as he had already become, had not long previously, at the age of no more than 22, been appointed a junior inspector of permanent way materials in the department of the Chief Civil Engineer of the Great Eastern Railway, and in spite of his inherent interest in locomotives, one could not have expected him to have acquired much information about the finer points of work on the footplate, least of all with the firing. And on the Midland Railway in these northern latitudes, in those years, things were sometimes not very happy on the left hand side of the footplate. At that time most, if not all the 999 class engines were stationed at Durran Hill, and although their big tenders, having a coal capacity of 7 tons, should have been ample for the return trip from Carlisle to Leeds and back, seeing that for any load above 230 tons a pilot could be claimed for the mountain sections, because of the physical nature of the coal usually supplied to the express engines at Durran Hill, there were sometimes difficulties. One could well imagine a harassed driver getting the coal-men at Whitehall Junction to put on one or two boxes of good 'hard Yorkshire' to help him on the return journey.

On the first run in the Hellifield–Appleby table all was evidently well, and engine No. 995 made light of the job, albeit with a light load, but on run No. 2, engine No. 998, which when newly

*A down Scotch Express near Helwith Bridge, double-headed by a Johnson 2-4-0 and a Deeley compound.* (J. M. Tomlinson)

superheated did so well on the indicator trials between Leeds and St Pancras in 1910-11, was in poor form and lost nearly three minutes to Appleby. On her second run the sectional time to Blea Moor was kept, and although as was most usual, a minute was lost over the tableland, and a brisk descent to Ormside put this right by Appleby. On the fourth run engine No. 993 was nominally overloaded, but her crew made good time up to Blea Moor. Some fast running followed, with a maximum speed of 67 mph at Hawes Junction, and a minimum of $55\frac{1}{2}$ mph at Ais Gill, and a descent involving a top speed of 77 mph below Kirkby Stephen. But below that station the speed was eased down as will be seen from the average of no more than 65.8 mph from there to Ormside. There was of course no particular need for hurry, as the train was a minute early at Appleby.

In the last table relating to the 32-minute runs from Appleby to Carlisle I have included a further run logged by Cecil J. Allen on the Edinburgh midday train from St Pancras. This had been checked by signal between Hellifield and Appleby and a late start, of no more than a few minutes, motivated the driver to the brilliant run tabulated. It certainly was the "exception that proves the rule" so far as the Appleby–Carlisle sprints were concerned. The maximum speed before Lazonby was $83\frac{1}{2}$ mph, and $2\frac{1}{4}$ minutes of the time lost earlier was regained. The first run of engine No. 998, which had shown up so poorly hitherto made some amends on the last

Midland Railway: Hellifield–Appleby
999 class superheater 4-4-0s

| Run No. | | | 1 | 2 | 3 | 4 |
|---|---|---|---|---|---|---|
| Engine No. | | | 995 | 998 | 998 | 993 |
| Load, tons | | | 175 | 175 | 190 | 245 |
| Distance | | Sch. | Actual | Actual | Actual | Actual |
| Miles | | min | m s | m s | m s | m s |
| 0.0 | Hellifield | 0 | 0 00 | 0 00 | 0 00 | 0 00 |
| 3.3 | Settle Jun | 4 | 4 30 | 4 50 | 4 55 | 5 00 |
| 5.3 | Settle | | 6 30 | 7 10 | 7 05 | 7 05 |
| 11.3 | Horton | | 14 45 | 17 10 | 15 50 | 16 00 |
| 17.3 | Blea Moor | 25 | 23 35 | 26 50 | 25 00 | 25 20 |
| 22.2 | Dent | | 29 30 | 33 15 | 31 15 | 31 35 |
| 25.4 | Hawes Junction | | 32 40 | 36 40 | 34 40 | 34 55 |
| 28.5 | Ais Gill | 37 | 35 35 | 40 05 | 37 55 | 38 05 |
| — | | | sigs | — | — | — |
| 35.3 | Kirkby Stephen | | 43 50 | 46 50 | 44 40 | 44 10 |
| 43.6 | Ormside | | 51 50 | 55 15 | 52 40 | 51 45 |
| 46.0 | Appleby | 56 | 54 40 | 58 40 | 55 45 | 54 45 |
| Average speed (mph): | | | | | | |
| Horton to Blea Moor | | | 40.8 | 37.2 | 39.3 | 38.6 |
| Dent to Ais Gill | | | 62.1 | 55.3 | 56.7 | 58.3 |
| Kirkby Stephen to Ormside | | | 62.2 | 58.8 | 62.2 | 65.8 |

stage, though not avoiding an arrival nearly three minutes late in Carlisle, but the last run of all, on which No. 993 had done so well up the bank with the 245-ton load, was disappointing. In connection with all these runs from Appleby to Carlisle it must not be forgotten that these

*A Glasgow–St Pancras express approaches Ais Gill Summit hauled by 6 ft 6 in rebuilt 4-4-0 No. 442 and Johnson 2-4-0 No. 253. (R. J. Purves)*

999 class engines, now superheated, had been upgraded from Class 3 to Class 4, and it is instructive to compare the work in the foregoing table with some that I personally recorded in the early 1930s on the Appleby–Carlisle run with Class 5 engines.

These were not new Stanier "Black Five" 4-6-0s, but ex-LNWR 'Claughtons', unrebuilt from the original design of 1913, except for having the original Schmidt trick-ported piston valves replaced by ones having six simple rings. In other respects these engines could be classed, almost, as contemporaries of the superheated '999s'. I had two runs with these engines, both heavily loaded and assisted up to Ais Gill by 4-4-0s shedded at Hellifield; but from Appleby the results were thus:

Load: 375 tons, to Lazonby 15 min 20 sec; to Scotby 26 mins 10 sec.
Load: 470 tons, to Lazonby 16 min 10 sec; to Scotby 28 min 10 sec.

Both trains were checked by signals in the approach to Carlisle, but the arrival times in Citadel station were 31 min 45 sec and 32 min 50 sec — no S.P.C.E. evident on these occasions! These splendid runs are described fully in a later chapter.

## Midland Railway: Appleby–Carlisle
### 999 class superheater 4-4-0s

| Run No. | | | 1 | | 2 | | 3 | | 4 | | 5 | |
|---------|---|---|---|---|---|---|---|---|---|---|---|---|
| Engine No. | | | 995 | | 995 | | 998 | | 998 | | 993 | |
| Load, tons | | | 160 | | 175 | | 175 | | 190 | | 254 | |
| | | | | Av | | Av | | Av | | Av | | Av |
| Distance | | Sch. | Actual | Speed | Actual | Speed | Actual | Speed | Actual | Speed | Actual | Speed |
| Miles | | min | m s | mph | m s | mph | m s | mph | m s | mph | m s | mph |
| 0.0 | Appleby | 0 | 0 00 | — | 0 00 | — | 0 00 | — | 0 00 | — | 0 00 | — |
| 7.4 | Culgaith | | 8 30 | 52.2 | 8 50 | 50.2 | 8 35 | 51.7 | 9 00 | 49.3 | 9 10 | 48.5 |
| 15.6 | Lazonby | | 14 40 | 79.8 | 15 25 | 74.8 | 15 20 | 72.9 | 16 15 | 68.2 | 16 25 | 68.2 |
| 20.8 | Armathwaite | | 19 30 | 64.5 | 20 25 | 62.5 | 20 25 | 61.5 | 21 35 | 58.6 | 22 05 | 58.6 |
| 28.1 | Scotby | | 25 50 | 69.0 | 26 45 | 69.0 | 26 50 | 68.3 | 28 20 | 64.9 | 28 50 | 64.9 |
| 30.8 | Carlisle | 32 | 29 45 | — | 31 20 | — | 31 30 | — | 32 15 | — | 32 35 | — |

## Midland Railway: Hellifield–Carlisle
### Double-headed runs as far as Ais Gill Summit

| Run No. | | | 1 | 2 | 3 | 4 | 5 | 6 |
|---------|---|---|---|---|---|---|---|---|
| Train Engine No. | | | 475 | 447 | 448 | 1032 | 996 | 464 |
| Engine type (4-4-0) | | | 6 ft 6 in reb | 6 ft 6 in reb | 6 ft 6 in | Compound | '999' 4-4-0 | 6 ft 6 in reb |
| Pilot Engine No. | | | 78 | 396 | 312 | 340 | 465 | 245 |
| Engine type | | | Kirtley 2-4-0 | 6 ft 6 in reb | Johnson | Belpaire reb 4-4-0 | Belpaire reb | Johnson 2-4-0 |
| Load, tons | | | 190 | 260 | 270 | 285 | 285 | 365 |
| Distance | | Sch | Actual | Actual | Actual | Actual | Actual | Actual |
| Miles | | min | m s | m s | m s | m s | m s | m s |
| 0.0 | Hellifield | 0 | 0 00 | 0 00 | 0 00 | 0 00 | 0 00 | 0 00 |
| 3.3 | Settle Junction | 4 | 4 30 | 4 30 | 4 45 | 5 15 | 4 25 | 4 50 |
| 5.2 | Settle | | 6 30 | 6 30 | 6 55 | 7 40 | 6 25 | 7 10 |
| 11.3 | Horton | | 13 45 | 14 30 | 15 55 | 16 25 | 14 30 | 17 10 |
| 17.3 | Blea Moor Box | 25 | 21 30 | 22 45 | 25 30 | 24 35 | 22 45 | 27 35 |
| 22.2 | Dent | | 26 55 | 28 00 | 31 40 | 29 45 | 28 30 | 34 25 |
| 25.4 | Hawes Junction | | 30 00 | 31 30 | 35 00 | 32 45 | 31 35 | 38 05 |
| 28.5 | Ais Gill Box | 37 | *33 15* | *34 35* | *38 20* | *35 50* | *34 45* | *41 45* |
| — | — | | 34 25 | 35 45 | 39 20 | 36 55 | 35 45 | 43 15 |
| | | | p.w.s | — | — | — | — | |
| 35.3 | Kirkby Stephen | | 43 25 | 44 05 | 47 40 | 44 55 | 44 00 | 51 50 |
| 43.6 | Ormside | | 50 45 | 51 05 | 54 45 | 52 35 | 51 30 | 58 55 |
| 46.0 | Appleby | 55 | 53 00 | 53 15 | 57 00 | 54 50 | 54 00 | 61 10 |
| 53.4 | Culgaith | | 59 20 | 60 05 | 64 00 | 61 35 | 60 55 | 68 45 |
| 61.6 | Lazonby | | 65 55 | 67 30 | 71 05 | 68 30 | 68 10 | 76 15 |
| 66.8 | Armathwaite | | 71 00 | 73 40 | 76 55 | 73 50 | 73 50 | 82 05 |
| 74.1 | Scotby | | 77 55 | 81 05 | 83 55 | 80 40 | sigs | 89 15 |
| 76.8 | Carlisle | 86 | 82 30 | 85 00 | 87 45 | 85 10 | 89 55 | 92 35 |
| | Net times | | $81\frac{1}{2}$ | 85 | $87\frac{3}{4}$ | $85\frac{1}{4}$ | $85\frac{1}{4}$ | $92\frac{1}{2}$ |
| Average speed (mph): | | | | | | | | |
| | Horton to Blea Moor | | 46.4 | 43.6 | 37.6 | 44.1 | 43.6 | 34.6 |
| | Kirkby Stephen to Lazonby | | 70.0 | 67.5 | 67.5 | 66.8 | 66.2 | 64.7 |

# 9
# Disaster in the High Pennines

It needs no more than a glance at the tabulations in the previous chapter to show that a high proportion of the trains were double-headed between Hellifield and Ais Gill Summit. The coupling-off of pilot engines, and the sending of them back to Hawes Junction where they could be turned, was a time-consuming business which had to be done in the intervals between the passage of other trains. The central control system had not yet been extended to the working of passenger trains, and while the signalmen came under the administrative jurisdiction of the station master at Hawes Junction, the one man in each of the boxes at Ais Gill Summit and at Hawes Junction were both on their own during the night hours. The trains concerned in the previous chapter were all running at normal times, mid-week when there were not many other trains about. But imagine the situation in the late evening of 23rd December 1910, when with extra workings and duplicate ordinary trains, no fewer than *seven* down expresses had been piloted up to

*The stockaded turntable at Hawes Junction, on which so many pilot engines were turned in the small hours of that tragic Christmas Eve of 1910.* (Norman Wilkinson)

Ais Gill and had detached their leading engines there, in the small hours of Christmas Eve. In addition to this, two southbound expresses had detached pilots at Ais Gill, and these had to be got back to Carlisle as soon as convenient.

The track layout at Ais Gill at that time, was as shown in the photograph from the overbridge just north of the signal box. At normal periods down expresses detaching pilots usually stopped just ahead of the home signal, to allow the pilot after coupling off to draw ahead of the cross-over road and then set back on to the up main line. Then, hopefully, it could be signalled away back to Hawes Junction. But if the up line was busy, and the crossover could not be used the pilot had to go ahead and set back into the down line siding, and wait. What the disposition was of the nine engines that were around Ais Gill between 3 and 4 am on that tragic Christmas Eve of 1910 cannot be said for certain, but the two Class 2 4-4-0s Nos. 548 and 448 were first to get away, and coupled together they arrived at Hawes Junction at 4.06 am. Another half hour passed before another cortege arrived, four engines coupled together; the 2-4-0s Nos 247 and 249, and the Johnson unrebuilt 4-4-0s Nos 313 and 314. By that time however the two Carlisle 4-4-0s Nos 548 and 448 had been turned, and parked in the branch platform line. Referring to the track plan it might at first be thought more logical to

have put them in the down siding, where they would have been conveniently sited to go north again, but the Hawes Junction signalman had got to get rid of the four engines that had just arrived on the up main line, and he crossed them, still coupled together, to the turntable road, as soon as a down express goods had passed at 4.41 am.

It was none too soon, because in no more than another five minutes three more engines arrived from Ais Gill, two Hellifield 4-4-0s, Nos 312 and 317 and a Kirtley 2-4-0, No. 42. These were crossed to the turntable at once to clear the up main line for an express goods, which according to the signal box records passed through at 4.49 am. It is surprising that the two Carlisle 4-4-0s, Nos 448 and 548, were not sent away after the passage of the down express goods, which had passed through at 4.41 am because there was then an interval of nearly three-quarters of an hour on the down line before a special express was expected. In the meantime the turntable road and the siding leading to the connection at its northern end to the down main line was well-nigh cluttered up with engines! How the crews of the seven ultimately parked there, sorted themselves out on a pitch-black night of high wind and heavy rain, is best left to the imagination. There was 500 ft of plain line between the points leading to the turntable itself and the

*A Metro-Cammell diesel multiple unit, No. C820, passes the scene where the collision of 1910 took place.*
(Brian Morrison)

*An up Scotch Express with a pair of engines the same as those on the down 'midnight' of 24th December 1910, with Kirtley 2-4-0 No. 50 leading.* (British Railways)

northern outlet to the main line, while the shunting neck of the southern one was barely long enough to take one engine. What transpired in that area was of no immediate concern to the Hawes Junction signalman except of course, that he was anxious to get rid of all those engines as soon as possible, when they had been turned. It is all the more surprising that he left the two Carlisle 4-4-0s lingering in the up branch line platform. Afterwards one gained the impression that the enginemen concerned were not in any hurry to get back to their home station!

After the passage of the down special express at 5.20 pm the two Carlisle engines were signalled out over the cross-over to the down main line with the intention of sending them away to Ais Gill as soon as the out-of section bell signal was received for the 5.20 am express. But it just happened that the Hawes Junction signalman, Alfred Sutton, was very busy when that signal came through. Three further engines were ready to depart, southward; another up express goods train had been signalled on the line from Ais Gill; one of the Leeds pilot enginemen required a message concerning his relief to be sent off, and there came a telephone enquiry about some Hellifield engines which were on the turntable road at that time. It will be appreciated that Sutton's attention was almost entirely taken up

with the various light engines and their movements and in his preoccupation he completely forgot the two Carlisle 4-4-0s which were standing some little distance short of the advanced starting signal. In the wind and rain that very dark December morning no one saw them, and not one of the four enginemen concerned seemed to realise that they were being kept there for a very long time. In their dilatory attitude neither of the drivers sent one of the firemen back, after five minutes, under the Rule 55 regulations, to remind the signalman they were there, and neither driver whistled, nor did anything else to attract attention.

There they sat until at 5.39 am Signalman Sutton was offered from Dent the most important train of the early morning, the 'midnight' from St Pancras to Glasgow St Enoch. He accepted it at once, and shortly afterwards offered it to Ais Gill, which accepted it at once. Immediately all the necessary signals were lowered, and at about 5.43 am having seen the advanced starting signal pulled off, the men on engines 448 and 548 started away for Carlisle, but in a very leisurely, unhurried fashion. In the meantime the 'midnight' running a little behind time and itself double-headed, was going like a bomb. It passed Hawes Junction at about 65 mph and at the speed those light engines were running the men on the

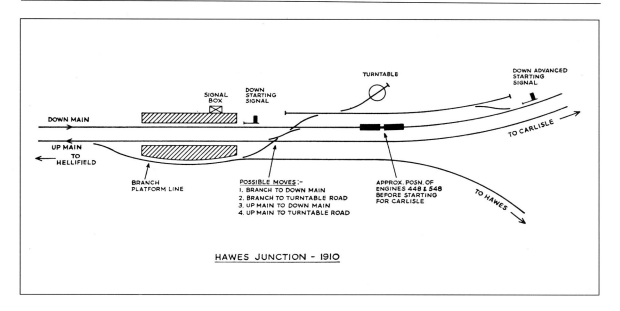

HAWES JUNCTION - 1910

express would soon have seen their tail lamp, but for the unfortunate intermission of Moorcock Tunnel, only a mile beyond Hawes Junction station. The imminence of disaster had been borne home to one of the pilot enginemen who had turned and was waiting for the signalman to move him across to the up main line. He had been aware of the two Carlisle 4-4-0s standing on the down main, and saw them slowly move away when the advance starting signal was cleared. He was concerned when that signal was not replaced to danger after they had gone, and horrified when the 'midnight' came through at full speed.

No sooner had the express gone than the ground signal cleared to allow the Hellifield engine to cross on to the up main line. Abreast of the signal box Sutton appears to have been rather testy with the driver saying that he had intended to couple him up to two other engines that were waiting to go south. But, he said, "you've been such a long time I have had to send the other two away". But this driver was not immediately concerned with his own movements and he shouted across to the signalmen asking what he had done with the two Carlisle pilots which had been standing on the main line for nearly a quarter of an hour. "They've gone to Carlisle" was the reply; but Sutton thought again, and rang the signalman at Ais Gill, and got the fatal reply that he had never been offered the two light engines, and where was the Glasgow

express, for which he had the 'train entering section' bell signal, fully eight minutes ago? When the day signalman came on duty at 6 am there was already a reflection on the low rain clouds that were scudding over the fells to the north, an ominous reflection that suggested a bad fire, and Sutton asked him to go to the stationmaster and say, "I am afraid I have wrecked the Scotch Express". He had indeed!

Those two light engines, strolling along at no more than 30 mph, were not half way between the Moorcock and the Shotlock Hill tunnels when the express emerged from the former, doing at least 65 mph, and the collision was a severe one. Although the train was made up to no more than eight vehicles its tare weight was above the 180-ton limit for all Class 2 locomotives, and the train engine, No. 549, a 7 ft non-superheater rebuilt, had been piloted from the start by Kirtley 2-4-0 No. 48. The impact drove the two light engines forward and the rearmost of them was derailed and the driver seriously injured. The Kirtley 2-4-0 took the full force of the collision and its exposed front end was badly smashed in, although remaining more or less upright. But the train engine fell on to its left side against the cutting and the coaches followed it crashing into the tender, with the first two being telescoped. The driver of the second light engine, although badly injured, made his way through Shotlock Hill Tunnel on over the mile to Ais Gill signal

*The engines of the 'midnight' after the accident, with the burnt-out remains of the leading coach just visible beyond the second tender.* (Courtesy A. W. H. Pearsall)

box to give the alarm, but before he got there the express was burning fiercely.

Midland express trains of those days were lit by compressed oil gas on the Pintsch system, and in the collision and subsequent telescoping of the two leading coaches some of the gas cylinders and their connections were damaged. The escaping gas ignited at once and with wooden bodied coaches the effect was disastrous. The telescoping of the two coaches rendered rescue work of the entrapped passengers exceedingly difficult, no less so by the paucity of suitable tools. One survivor of the disaster, a Canadian of extensive forestry experience, complained bitterly that large saws were not available, which he said he could readily have ripped open the panelling that was encasing the victims. Certainly one of the most distressing features of this accident was that some of the twelve persons who lost their lives were still conscious when the fire reached them. Owing to the locking of buffers and the derailment of wheels, it was not possible to uncouple more than the last two vehicles of the train, and so the remaining four coaches, in addition to the leading two which had been telescoped, were eventually completely destroyed by fire.

Although the immediate cause of the accident was the simple act of forgetfulness by Signalman Sutton in letting light engines Nos 548 and 448 pass from his mind, it was the plain fact that he had so many light engines to deal with, in addition to the handling of ordinary traffic, that undoubtedly led to his lapse. Great attention was subsequently paid to the means for safeguarding

against similar lapses, but it was a case of dealing with the effects rather than the true cause of the trouble. That cause was nothing more nor less than inadequate engine power. One of the crowning misfortunes of the whole affair was that in a matter of seconds the midnight express would have been slowing down to stop at Ais Gill and detach its own pilot. Had the Carlisle pilot engines left Hawes Junction more smartly they might have been sufficiently clear to have avoided the express as it drew in to stop at Ais Gill.

The inquiry was conducted by Lt Col. John Pringle and some of his recommendations were acted upon in so comprehensive a manner by the Midland Railway, as to influence subsequent practice in a way out of all proportion to the magnitude of the actual disaster, serious though it was. After reviewing all the circumstances that led to the two Carlisle light engines being forgotten by Signalman Sutton, and the failure of the enginemen concerned to carry out Rule 55 Col. Pringle recommended that, "in view of the turntable work at Hawes Junction, and the number of engine movements, this yard should be treated as a special case. The up and down lines between the advanced starting signals and the crossover roads in rear of them respectively should be track-circuited, and the levers working the starting signals thereby controlled. This block post can then be exempted from the operation of Rule 55."

To Guy Granet, who had set such store upon the efficient operation of the Midland Railway, the Hawes Junction accident was a great

*Johnson 6 ft 6 in rebuilt 4-4-0 No. 480, of the same class as that hauling the Edinburgh express in the 1913 collision.* (British Railways)

blow. On his recommendation the Board went much further in adopting safety measures than Col. Pringle had recommended. Track circuiting was installed at Hawes Junction, but in the light of it a survey of the whole Midland system was made, and it was decided that in over 2,000 places the traffic conditions were such as to require apparatus for guarding against possible failures of the human element. Upwards of 900 track circuits were installed, and this work constitutes one of the most extensive early examples of the use of track circuiting in mechanically-signalled territory. There is always a tendency to associate track circuiting primarily with power installation, either with large interlockings or with automatically signalled lines. At the time of the Hawes Junction accident track circuiting was still in its infancy.

The second disaster in the High Pennines came on 2nd September 1913 at a place about three-quarters of a mile north of Ais Gill Summit. This involved two southbound night expresses, the first from Glasgow booked to leave Carlisle at 1.35 am and including a portion from Stranraer, and the second including coaches from Edinburgh and Inverness, due out of Carlisle at 1.49 am. Once again the cause of the troubles was inadequate engine power, although this time not involving pilot engine working. However, it was the inability at Durran Hill to provide a pilot for one of the trains concerned that was a major factor in the troubles that developed afterwards. The Glasgow train was allocated a superheated 999 class 4-4-0 engine, then Class 4, and allowed

to take a maximum tare load of 230 tons from Carlisle up to Ais Gill. But when the Stranraer portion was attached to the main part of the train in Citadel station the load was given to the driver as 243 tons. No top link man of lengthy experience, with as good an engine as a superheated 999 would think twice in the ordinary way of taking an excess of no more than 13 tons over the stipulated maximum, but on the night in question circumstances were not normal and the driver of engine No. 993 asked for a pilot, only to be told there was not one available.

With the evident intention of reducing the cost of transporting locomotive coal the Midland Railway had placed a contract with a Cumberland firm, the Naworth Coal Co. for supplying Durran Hill shed. This fuel had an excellent calorific value, but the express drivers did not like it as a substitute for the hard Yorkshire grades on which Midland engines used to thrive. The driver of No. 993, on taking over at the shed, saw that the tender had been loaded with what seemed to be a pretty poor consignment; it had not been screened, and included a high proportion of smalls and slack. The driver allocated to the second of the two expresses, on 6 ft 6 in Class 2 non-superheater rebuilt 4-4-0 No. 446, was scathing on the quality of the coal provided remarking, "If she'll steam on this she'll steam on anything". Moreover he had got a load of only 157 tons, 23 tons inside his limit with a Class 2 engine, despite which he immediately lost four minutes on the initial timing of 38 minutes to passing Appleby, 30.8 miles from Carlisle.

The driver of engine No. 993 with the Glasgow train did far better than this over the first stage of the run, passing Appleby in a little over 39 minutes, which latter was the regular working time of "The Thames–Clyde Express" in early LMS days. Then, when they got on to the really severe lengths of the Ais Gill ascent the steaming deteriorated rapidly, and the driver of No. 993 told in subsequent evidence how he took the shovel for a time to try to 'pull the boiler round'. Above Kirkby Stephen they were not making more than 20 mph, and out of Birkett Tunnel and past Mallerstang box they had less than 100 lb per sq in in the boiler. But even with pressure down to 80 or 90 lb/sq in it would have been possible to surmount the final stage of the climb had not the vacuum in the train pipe been partially destroyed, and the brakes leaked on in consequence. While most types of ejector will operate satisfactorily over a considerable range of steam pressure, on reaching the lower critical point the efficiency drops abruptly, and this evidently happened on engine No. 993 south of Mallerstang. Driver Nicholson said that the vacuum had fallen from the normal 20 in to 15 in before they stalled, with the engine only about half a mile from the level road at the summit.

In the meantime the second express, having taken 45 minutes from Carlisle to Ormside, a loss of four minutes, was making considerably better speed than the first express had done between Ormside and Mallerstang, although to a lesser extent her steaming was also suffering from the effects of small coal. This engine was not then fitted with a superheater; mechanical lubrication had not been applied, and the driver followed the prevailing custom of going round the engine, while running, to replenish the auxiliary oil boxes. In doing so, enginemen would naturally choose a stretch of line where the speed was not high, and on this occasion the driver went out as they were approaching Birkett Tunnel. Before this the steaming had given some trouble, and he admitted feeling anxious on that account. He was out on the running plate when they passed through the tunnel. Subsequently he said, "I remember when we came out of Birkett Tunnel I looked ahead and could see the Mallerstang distant signal, and got the impression it was in the clear position". When, however, he returned to the cab there was no water showing in the gauge glass; the right-hand injector had failed and the left-hand injector was not functioning properly on account of low steam pressure — 140 lb/sq in instead of the normal 175 lb/sq in. Although he had taken so perfunctory a look at the Mallerstang distant signal, the driver so busied himself in getting the right-hand injector to work, that he ran past the remaining Mallerstang signals at about 30 mph without observing them at all.

Even so, the Mallerstang signalman himself may have contributed in one degree towards the accident, although the men on the second-express did not claim that his action in any way influenced their subsequent action. Having had his distant signal on, and the home likewise, when he saw the train approaching, his first impression was that it was going to stop all right, and he lowered his home signal to allow, as he thought, the train to draw up to the starting signal. But as the train neared his box he saw to his horror that it was steaming hard, and it ran past all his signals without the slightest sign of having taken any warning. If the driver had seen the home signal change from red to green it might have misled him. But he never made the point in evidence. All his subsequent actions were based on that quick perfunctory look at the Mallerstang distant, seen when he was out on the front of his engine passing through Birkett Tunnel. The train is recorded as having passed Mallerstang at 2.57 am, the precise moment that the first express stalled north of Ais Gill.

Although the circumstances in which Caudle passed Mallerstang without properly observing the signals can be appreciated, it is difficult to understand his subsequent negligence. It would seem that he was so worried about maintaining steam pressure as to let this one point override every other consideration. According to his evidence, they were continually losing pressure, although he quoted no actual figures, so that he, too, may have foreseen a possible loss of vacuum in the train pipe. In any event he maintained his previous regulator and reverse positions, thus continuing to steam the engine hard, and watched the fireman at his work to see that the coal was put on to the best advantage. Although he was proceeding thus blindly towards the standing train, there was still a chance that a collision might be averted. The crew of the first express saw in the distance the glare from the open fire-door as the second express climbed the bank, and later heard the heavy exhaust beat. One of the guards went back to give warning, but the enginemen of the second express were so pre-occupied that when they did at last sight the tail lamps, and the hand lamp carried by this guard, there was scarcely time to apply the brake before the engine crashed into the first train. It is sad to reflect that up to the very last minute the second express might have been stopped.

As it was, the affair ended in a tragic repetition of Christmas Eve, 1910. The engine ploughed through the last vehicle of the standing train, which was fortunately a van, and buried itself in the passenger coach immediately in front. Fire broke out, but in this instance the 14 passengers whom it was not possible to extricate from the wreckage, were all so severely injured in the actual collision that it is fairly certain that they were either dead or unconscious when the fire reached them. Two other passengers died later. To the Midland Railway management, the occurrence of a second accident in the same neighbourhood less than three years later was a crushing misfortune. Granet took the unusual step of asking to be permitted to make a special statement during the inquiry into the Ais Gill collision. He recalled the Inspecting Officer's comments upon the 1910 accident, and described in detail the steps that had been taken in particular to implement his recommendation about track circuiting at Hawes Junction. About the gas lighting of the carriages his statement was not so reassuring.

Three years before I went to Giggleswick school I had become intensely aware of the Settle and Carlisle line. I was on holiday with my parents, at Weymouth, when news came of the tragic collision of two night expresses at Ais Gill. Artist correspondents of the newspapers of the day fairly let themselves go in giving lurid impressions of the burning train, with engine No. 446 standing like some black and evil monster in the midst of the conflagration. Descriptions of the lonely moorland countryside where it all happened had impressed themselves upon my boyish imagination, so much so that I had not been very long at Giggleswick before I mentioned the accident to my housemaster when a crowd of us boys were on a long country walk. At the time I remember how amazed I was that he scarcely remembered Ais Gill at all, let alone

*The tragic aftermath: removing bodies of some of the victims in a North Eastern Railway brake coach.* (Norman Wilkinson Collection)

what had happened there. He was not to know that on my 'one track' mind of those days Ais Gill had made a far deeper impression than the sinking of the *Titanic*!

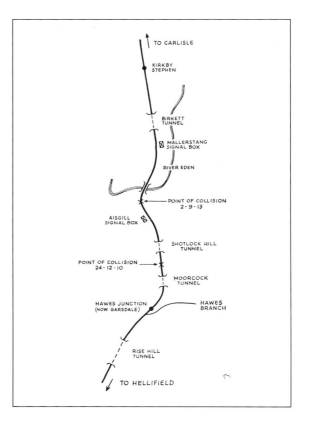

# 10
# Midland in the North Country — Personal Entrée

In the spring of the 1916 the United Counties Bank, of which my father was Manager of the branch in Reading, was taken over by Barclay's. Because there was already a much larger and more established branch of the latter in Reading another post had to be found for my father, and he was sent to Barrow-in-Furness. At the beginning of June we went north, and as a railway enthusiast from my cradle I was all agog to see new lines. Arrived in the North, and comfortably settled temporarily in the Furness Abbey Hotel, my mother was immediately exercised as to where she could park us children while she got our new house ready. The furniture had

been consigned by rail from Reading and was expected any minute, in the meanwhile my aunt and uncle, having left their large house in central Bradford and gone to live at Harrogate, had expressed a wish to see us. The problem then was of getting there. At the tender age of eight I had become a railway season ticket holder, first on the Great Western from Reading to Mortimer, and then on the South Eastern & Chatham, from Reading to Wokingham. But a cross-country journey on strange lines was another matter. My uncle had recently taken up motoring and it was arranged that he would meet us at Skipton, to which he drove over the wild Blubberhouses

*Johnson 2-4-0 No. 260 was used for piloting and working on the 'little' North Western line.*
(F. Moore's Railway Photographs)

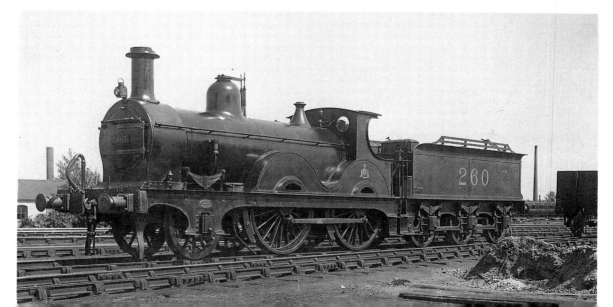

Moor and thence via Bolton Abbey.

I shall always remember my first impressions of travel on the Midland Railway, of the spacious clerestory-roofed non-corridor carriage that we entered at Carnforth, and the gleaming red 4-4-0 engine that was to haul one train. I believe it was one of the non-Belpaire 6 ft 6 in type. I don't remember much of the journey, except for the many red trains I saw, but on arrival at Skipton, where my uncle was waiting, we enjoyed an alfresco lunch on the station until the time when my mother's return train was due. When it came it was a brilliant sight rounding the curve of the station, drawn by two immaculate 2-4-0s. I cannot remember how we ourselves returned from Harrogate to our new home in Barrow, but by the end of that summer I was becoming steeped in Midland Railway lore, with my parents having decided to send me as a boarder to Giggleswick School. The station there was a little short of the main line to Scotland, but it was near enough for some exciting observation. Boys of my tender age were not permitted to go into Settle unattended, but one of the principal sports fields had a bank some 150 ft high on the western side. This provided an excellent grand stand for the junior boys who were not allowed to mingle with the rest on the touch line when a Rugger match was in progress. Up there I, and one or two other kindred spirits, used to look forward to seeing, across the valley, the 9.30 am Scotch Express from St Pancras, pounding up the bank through Settle, almost always hauled by a 999

class 4-4-0.

Within my first year at Giggleswick I had occasion to visit Harrogate again, this time on my own. When the Easter holiday time came both my mother and sister were recovering from 'flu' and I was best out of the way. On term-end day the only compulsory school engagement was early morning Chapel, at about 7 am, and while breakfast was available in school, many of the boys ignored this and made their way immediately to Giggleswick station whence Midland trains, both westbound and eastbound departed around 8 am. The last mentioned was the Morecambe-Bradford "Residential" which carried a first class club carriage for those wealthy season ticket holders who could afford the extra privacy and refreshment facilities that the 'club' subscriptions provided. The Midland had introduced this facility between Bradford and Morecambe in the early 1900s, seeing what success the Lancashire & Yorkshire had made of the so-called 'club trains' running between Manchester and Southport and Manchester and Blackpool. The journey time on the Midland however was considerably longer. On that occasion, not anywhere near the club car(!), I was travelling with a contingent of Leeds boys and we had to change at Shipley to avoid being taken into Bradford. Very soon a luxurious corridor express for St Pancras came in, and I finished this part of the journey in some style.

In post-war years the "Residential" became a real express. It conveyed portions for both Bradford and Leeds, and ran non-stop from

*Giggleswick station, built in 1848 to serve the town of Settle, before the line to Carlisle was built. Originally named 'Settle', which was 1½ miles away. (Norman Wilkinson)*

*The second 'Settle' station, built in 1870 at the site where the new line branched off from the 'little' North Western.* (Norman Wilkinson)

Lancaster (Green Ayre) to Skipton, where it was divided. The Bradford portion continued first, non-stop to Forster Square, and the Leeds followed eight minutes later, calling only at Keighley to provide an arrival in Leeds at 9.25 am. The Bradford arrival was at 9.15 am from a departure at 7.42 am from Morecambe Promenade. In LMS days the return trains left Leeds at 4.55 pm and Bradford at 5.10 pm combined at Skipton, and then ran non-stop to Lancaster (Green Ayre). The distance between Skipton and Lancaster was $38\frac{3}{4}$ miles, and to cover it in 50 minutes in the westbound direction, and 53 minutes in the considerably harder morning up run must have involved some fine locomotive work. From near Hornby about eight miles east of Lancaster there was a continuous ascent of more than eleven miles, nothing easier than 1 in 180 and some of it at 1 in 100. After passing the moorland Clapham Junction, where the Ingleton line is joined, at greatly reduced speed there was some respite, and a sharp descent to the Ribble Valley past Giggleswick. It was uphill again on the main line from Settle Junction, through Hellifield to the summit point above Bell Busk. No-one seems to have logged the running of that train. For some years until the compounds began to be displaced from top-link main line duties the Class 2 superheater rebuild 4-4-0s were the largest engines used on the Carnforth and Morecambe lines. After the post-war acceleration there was an eastbound train from Giggleswick at 7.44 am from which home-

ward bound boys for Bradford and Leeds changed into the appropriate sections of the Morecambe "Residential" at Skipton.

Reverting to my earliest days on the Midland in the North Country, it was in November 1916 that the Railway Executive Committee which, from the outbreak of war in August 1914, had managed all the British railways under Government control, ordered a big cut in passenger train services. There had been a previous reduction in 1915 which the Midland had made in passenger train mileage, largely to offset the increased demands made on its motive power for wartime specials leave trains, and the transfer of certain passenger engines to help in the working of freight trains. One important cut in service, effected in February 1915, was the cancellation of the 1.30 pm Scotch Express from St Pancras, and the corresponding southbound train from St Enoch. These afternoon trains by the Midland route were never restored after the war. It is important to recall however that while the 1915 cuts, amounting to a weekly mileage of 28,000, were in some ways drastic, and reflected upon the growing anxieties of the war situation, none of the express train timings were decelerated and with increased loading and no relaxation of the tonnage limits that were to be taken by each individual engine class, an increased amount of piloting was inevitable.

In the last year of the pre-war standard of running Cecil J. Allen had a journey on the 11.30 am Scotch Express from St Pancras the details of which are tabulated herewith. It is of interest in that the engine was No. 998, which figured so prominently in the dynamometer car trials conducted after Grouping, in January 1924. At that time the engine had been modified from the condition in which it had been superheated, with enlarged cylinders and a reduced boiler pressure. What state it was in on Allen's run of 1916, I cannot say. Compared to the loads taken in the 1924 trials the engine certainly had an easy task, although rough weather in the fells pulled the speed down from the steady 40 mph at which much of the 'Long Drag' had been climbed to 37 mph over Ribblehead Viaduct.

Allen had a run in the late summer of 1916 when he joined the 9.20 am from Glasgow St Enoch on making its stop at Hawes junction. The train was a very heavy one of 359 tons tare and 385 tons full. It had been hauled up from Carlisle

Midland Railway: Hellifield–Carlisle
Load: 36 axles, 210 tons tare 220 tons full
Engine: 4-4-0 No. 998

| Distance Miles | | Sch min | Actual m s | Speeds mph |
|---|---|---|---|---|
| 0.0 | Hellifield | 0 | 0 00 | — |
| 3.3 | Settle Junction | 4 | 4 40 | 64½ |
| 5.2 | Settle | | 6 55 | — |
| 11.3 | Horton | | 15 40 | 40 |
| 17.3 | Blea Moor Box | 25 | 25 25 | 37 |
| 25.4 | Hawes Junction | | 34 40 | 60 |
| 28.5 | Ais Gill Box | 37 | 37 55 | — |
| 35.3 | Kirkby Stephen | | 44 00 | 75 |
| 46.0 | Appleby | 55 | 54 20 | — |
| 61.6 | Lazonby | | 69 15 | 69 |
| 68.4 | Armathwaite | | 75 05 | 49½ |
| 74.1 | Scotby | | 82 00 | — |
| — | | | sigs | |
| 76.8 | Carlisle | 86 | 86 35 | — |

by a superheater rebuilt Class 2 4-4-0 piloted by No. 182, one of the 6 ft 6 in series which, as No. 1307, was a member of the class which went new to the Settle and Carlisle line on its first opening in 1876. She had not been set down at Ais Gill on Allen's run in 1916, and continued to head the train. The load was considerably more than the maximum stipulated for a combination of these two types of locomotive, but they set off in gallant style and covered the virtually level 8.1 miles to Blea Moor Box in 10 min 35 sec and then ran fast down to Settle Junction. Speed

reached 77½ mph below Ribblehead, and though there were several intermediate slowings, there followed a maximum of 79 mph before Settle Junction. This latter point, 22.1 miles from Hawes Junction was passed in 22¼ minutes, and with the last 3.3 miles into Hellifield covered in 3 min 50 sec it made up the smart start-to-stop time of 25 min 5 sec from Hawes Junction.

Now turning to the drastic restrictions in passenger train service that were imposed by the Railway Executive Committee it is important to refer briefly to some of the factors in the war situation that undoubtedly influenced their decisions. First of all, although the Royal Navy in the Battle of Jutland, albeit at the cost of grievous losses in ships and men, had driven the German High Seas Fleet back to its bases from which it never again ventured out, the submarine warfare was taking an increasingly heavy toll of the merchant shipping, on which Britain as an island race depended so much in those years. Worst of all to the British people, on the Western Front the grand assault by our new armies on the German lines in the great and sustained Battle of the Somme had produced no more than minimal gains in territory with appalling loss of life. On the home railways the reorganising of much of the workshop capacity to war production was resulting in much reduced time and facilities being available for the routine repairing of loco- motives, but rather than forego a lower standard

*Johnson goods 0-6-0 No. 2931, of the type used for express freight traffic on the Settle and Carlisle line.* (British Railways)

of maintenance other restrictions had to be adopted. The Midland Railway and its staff, like all others, had responded to the national emergency. Many hundreds of the men of all grades in service had joined the armed services, and for most of the war the company was without the service of three of its most important chief officers.

Cecil Paget, the General Superintendent, whose reforms had transformed the operation of the mineral traffic of the company, was in command of the Railway Operating Division (ROD) of the Royal Engineers on the Western Front. When Lloyd George had been appointed Minister of Munitions, in H. H. Asquith's early War Cabinet, he selected Henry Fowler and David Bain, the Carriage and Wagon Engineer, to be his chief technical assistants, and both of them went into Whitehall for the rest of the war. Paget left his chief assistant, J. H. Follows who eventually succeeded him and later became a Vice-President of the LMS, as head of the operating department on the Midland Railway, and J. E. Anderson acted as Chief Mechanical Engineer in Fowler's absence. Follows, as will be

*The great water tower at Settle station.* (Norman Wilkinson)

told later, instituted a change in passenger train operating which had some repercussions, not only on the wartime Midland Railway but later. Fowler eventually returned from his wartime labours with a knighthood and the KBE.

Reverting now to January 1917 the big cut in passenger train services that the R.E.C. ordered virtually abolished the pre-war character of the Midland timetables. A further weekly saving of 126,000 miles was made, and an attempt was made to book all trains at the same speed. Though not affecting the lines north of Leeds, all slip-coach services were cancelled and many through carriage workings with other railways abandoned. Only one day Scotch Express remained in each direction, and the new 9.15 am from St Pancras did not at first reach Glasgow St Enoch until 7 pm. It was, to be still slower before the war ended. On R.E.C. instructions the maximum speed of passenger trains was not to exceed 60 mph anywhere on Britain's railways, this being in a joint endeavour to reduce running costs of locomotives and rolling stock, to lessen coal and oil consumption, and reduce maintenance work on the track. For those who compiled records of train running it ushered in a most depressing era. Worse than that, on the Midland Railway, even though the schedules were much slower than previously, the existing regulations regarding the load limits for the different classes of passenger engines prevailed and there was much piloting.

There was a definite allocation by order of the Railway Executive Committee of the day Anglo-Scottish traffic from London. With the morning departures all passengers bound for Glasgow had to go from St Pancras, and those for Edinburgh from King's Cross. The morning express from Euston picked up Scottish traffic en-route, London passengers for Scotland being restricted to those bound for stations on the Caledonian line north of Coatbridge. Although the 9.15 am. Scotch Express from St Pancras thus catered for a much wider clientele than previously it, and all other Midland expresses on this greatly attenuated service, were rarely loaded up to as much as 300 tons, and were still provided with pilots when the load exceeded 240 tons with Class 4 engines. In December 1917, when the departure time from St Pancras had been altered to 9.10 am Cecil J. Allen joined the train at Leeds, and had to be content with a stand in the corridor, even though he was travelling first class. The train was made up to twelve coaches, which the usual Midland stock of that period registered a tare weight of no more than 317 tons, but from the passenger loading he judged that the gross weight was 345 tons.

From Leeds the train was unpiloted with a Class 4 superheater 4-4-0, No. 991, for this initial run to Skipton. The pre-war allowance for this 26.2 miles had been 33 minutes but in 1917 it had increased to 37 minutes, and on this timing almost a minute was lost, 37 min 55 sec. Here a pilot was coupled on ahead for the non-stop run to Carlisle, booked in 113 minutes for the 86.8 miles. The total scheduled running time from Leeds to Carlisle was thus 150 minutes compared with 133 minutes previous to the decelerations. The pilot on this occasion was a newly-rebuilt and superheated Class 2 4-4-0, No. 470. The two engines with their 345-ton load made something like pre-war speed on the long bank, attaining a maximum speed of $64\frac{1}{2}$ mph at Settle Junction, and not falling below 31 mph afterwards. A stop was made to couple-off the pilot engine at Ais Gill Summit, and then after no more than

60 seconds standing engine No. 991 covered the $48\frac{1}{4}$ miles down to Carlisle in 54 min 5 sec, or 51 minutes net allowing for delays at the finish, after hardly ever having exceeded the statutory 60 mph. The total time for the 86.8 miles from Skipton was 109 min 25 sec — more than $3\frac{1}{2}$ minutes inside the scheduled allowance.

This is the only run over the Settle and Carlisle line made in the latter part of the war of which I have seen detailed particulars, and those details cause one to think deeply. The comparative ease with which the overall running time was improved upon seems to call in question some of the operating methods displayed, particularly in view of a pilot engine for the 'Long Drag'. I am writing with the advantage of hind-sight in this respect, for I have before me the details of the series of dynamometer car trials made with engine No. 998 in January 1924. The nominal load of the 4.7 pm express from Leeds to Carlisle was usually 300 tons tare, but as it was a regular service train one would expect the gross load behind the tender to be about 320 tons with passengers and luggage. The data I have shows the minimum speed on the 'Long Drag' on four occasions: when the actual

*The derailment of the Scotch Express which ran into a landslip that had only just occurred at Little Salkeld, in January 1918. (Author's Collection)*

*Another view of the Little Salkeld derailment. The engine, compound No. 1010, seems little damaged, but the leading coaches, telescoped at about 60 mph, were completely shattered.* (Author's Collection)

tare load was 298.6 tons, 29 mph, with 298.6 tons, 26 mph, with 301.6 tons, 27.7 mph, and 295.6, 30.5 mph. On another, when a detailed log was published, a gross load of 310 tons was taken from Settle Junction to Blea Moor in 19¾ minutes, three minutes *less* than that of the piloted train of 1917, and if the latter had been taken up unassisted, fully three minutes would have been saved by the avoidance of the stop to detach the pilot at Ais Gill. There would also have been the saving in coal used by the leading engine, and its returning light to Hellifield. The piloting of the 9.10 am Scotch Express on this occasion thus did not seem a very economical proposition!

There was another important change in Midland Railway passenger train working initiated, indirectly, as a result of the drastic cuts in service from January 1917 onwards. When Cecil Paget launched his epoch-marking scheme for centralised train control working over the entire system, it applied only to freight and the enormous traffic in coal, which was in many ways the life-blood of the railway. In 1917 however, J. H. Follows, acting as General Superintendent, applied the control system to passenger trains, taking advantage of the greatly reduced service to initiate this change. By this system authority was removed from local stations to headquarters, this applying to the addition of extra coaches to meet sudden demands. From then onwards authority for such "strengthening" could only be obtained from Derby. This did not go down at all well when such additions were often a last moment's necessity at important provincial stations. I have often wondered since how term-

end was dealt with at Giggleswick when more than fifty high-spirited boys presented themselves, and most of their luggage for the wartime Morecambe-Bradford "Residential" before eight o'clock in the morning! I was usually one of a mere handful going in the opposite direction. Having initiated "control" the Midland Railway assumed rather autocratic methods in dealing with the general public.

At this stage in the story of the Settle and Carlisle line and its approaches much more than a passing mention must be made of those important medium power express passenger engines, the superheater Class 2 4-4-0s. On many other British railways they would have been classed as 'light' rather of medium power; but on the Midland in pre-Grouping days they were certainly 'intermediate', although remaining in the No. 2 Class. Deeley had hardly taken over the job of Locomotive Superintendent before he had started fitting the Johnson 4-4-0s with larger boilers. Those with 6 ft 6 in coupled wheels were the first to be treated, but while the rebuilds were comely engines to behold it is to be doubted whether Johnson himself, in his old age, would have recognised them. Deeley produced similar rebuilds of the 6 ft 9 in and 7 ft 4-4-0s and it was with a batch of these last mentioned that Fowler undertook a second and still more extensive rebuilding. Eventually the majority of the Johnson 4-4-0s were altered to correspond, the 6 ft 6 in and 6 ft 9 in engines even having new 7 ft coupled wheels. In all else but name the Fowler superheater Class 2 were virtually new rather than rebuild engines, although no doubt care would be taken to register their previous existence accountancy-wise.

The first engine to emerge from Derby Works in its new guise was No. 483, the precursor of forty engines of this so-called "150 class". While they became Nos 483 to 522 in the 1907 renumbering, the first ten engines were originally numbered 1667 to 1676. Some at first had 19 in cylinders and others $18\frac{1}{2}$ in, all with piston valves, and working with a boiler pressure of 160 lb per sq in. In their renewal form the dimensional particulars published on various occasions in 1913 reveal a number of wide discrepancies. Fowler himself in his paper on 'Superheating in Locomotives' read before the Institution of Civil Engineers quotes the cylinder diameter of engine No. 489, which was subjected to indicator trials between Derby and St Pancras, as $19\frac{1}{2}$ in by 26 in stroke, and the boiler pressure as 175 lb per sq in. However, the apparently 'official' description of engine No. 483, illustrated in *The Locomotive Magazine* of February 1913 quotes the dimensions as $20\frac{1}{2}$ dia by 26 in stroke, working at 160 lb per sq in. Subsequent information, including the brochure issued by the LMS in the late 1920s, confirm the latter dimensions and pressure but those quoted for No. 489 are curious coming from Fowler himself. His trials with superheater engines had begun late in 1910 when the first of the 999 class had been so treated. No. 998, was run against a standard compound, No. 1043, and on three return trips between St Pancras and Leeds by each engine, No. 998 averaged a coal consumption of 0.050 lb ton-mile, against 0.094 by the compound.

One can sense that in these early tests of superheater-equipped engines the aim was to have working conditions as equal as practicable, because early in 1911, when a still more exhaustive set of trials were run between engine No. 998 and a non-superheated engine of the same class, No. 992, both engines had cylinders 19 in by 26 in stroke, and worked at a pressure of 200 lb per sq in. On the other hand, on the British railways before Grouping it was a fairly general practice, exceptionally not on the Great Western, to use superheating as a means to reduce boiler pressure, or as on the London & North Western, to increase cylinder proportions supplied by the same general dimensions as the existing boilers. With the Midland 4-4-0s the accompanying table makes clear the differences between the varieties

of Class 2 and the '999' series. A curious point in the latter case is that the last mentioned class were advanced from Class 3 to Class 4 after superheating. In the table it is shown that, except for the reduction in pressure from the original 220 lb per sq in on the 999 class, there was little in it for either class when superheating was applied.

The results so far as consumption are concerned have been taken from the data published in Fowler's paper to the Institution of Civil Engineers in 1913.

Midland Railway: Coal Consumption Test

| | Train tons tare | Ton-miles | Coal per ton-mile lb | Water per ton-mile lb |
|---|---|---|---|---|
| January–February 1911: St Pancras–Leeds — average six days | | | | |
| Engine No. 992 (saturated) | 182 | 57,480 | 0.109 | 0.94 |
| 998 (superheated) | 187 | 58,769 | 0.083 | 0.73 |
| June–July 1913: Derby–St Pancras — average five days | | | | |
| Engine No. 484 (saturated) | 158 | 62,662 | 0.1643 | 1.337 |
| 489 | 160 | 65,087 | 0.115 | 0.882 |

The figures for ton-miles quoted need some explanation because those for the 999 class engines relate to a single run from St Pancras to Leeds or vice-versa, whereas those for the Class 2 engines cover a return trip from Derby

*No. 367, a rebuilt 7 ft 4-4-0 heads an up stopping train near Armathwaite.* (British Railways)

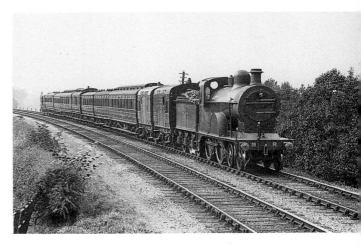

Midland Railways: Non-compound 4-4-0 locomotives

| Engine No. | 484 | 489 | 483 | 999 | 992 | 998 | 998 |
|---|---|---|---|---|---|---|---|
| Engine Class | 2 | 2 | 2 | 3 | ? | 4 | 4 |
| Cylinders dia × stroke in | $19\frac{1}{2}$ × 26 | $19\frac{1}{2}$ × 26 | $20\frac{1}{2}$ × 26 | 19 × 26 | 19 × 26 | 19 × 26 | $20\frac{1}{2}$ × 26 |
| Coupled wheel dia ft-in | 7-0 | 7-0 | 7-0 | 6-6 | 6-6 | 6-6 | 6-6 |
| Boiler pressure psi | 175 | 175 | 160 | 220 | 200 | 200 | 180 |
| Superheated yes or no | non | yes | yes | non | non | yes | yes |
| Nom. tractive effort lb | 17470 | 17470 | 17630 | 22350 | 20550 | 20350 | 21350 |
| Data, based on: | 1913 Trials Derby– St Pancras | 1913 Trials Derby– St Pancras | Standard engine | Original built in 1907 | 1911 Trials Leeds– St Pancras | 1911 Trials Leeds– St Pancras | Standard engine used in 1924 trials |

to St Pancras on the same day. Working out the coal consumption per train mile, which is the figure most readily appreciated for comparative purposes, the averages are 31.3 lbs and 24.3 lbs for the 999 class engines and 39.3 lbs and 28 lbs for the Class 2 engines. Having regard to the lightness of the loads hauled consistently on those tests they cannot be regarded as altogether complimentary to Midland engines, although the improvement effected by superheating was very marked.

To conclude this chapter I would like to add one or two personal recollections of the years just prior to Grouping. Because of intensive school engagements at Giggleswick I had no opportunities for much in the way of lineside observation,

not that there were very many trains at all, until the first post-war reconstruction timetables in the summer of 1920; but some occasions I well remember are worth recalling. The only train on which a compound was seen was the one up day Scotch Express which passed Settle at about three o'clock. I have good reason to remember this train, because early in 1919 with my mother I joined it at Hellifield to Leeds, where I was going into a nursing home to have my appendix removed! The engine was the first compound I had ever seen, No. 1004, one of the original Johnsons, but by that time rebuilt and superheated. Once or twice in my last summer at Giggleswick I attempted to photograph compounds on this train, but inexperience in the art gave me poor results.

*Settle, showing the main line and the viaduct.* (Courtesy Norman Wilkinson)

*Ribblehead station in Midland days, showing Whernside in the background.* (Norman Wilkinson)

One day in that same summer a free half-holiday was granted at short notice to certain senior boys, so suddenly that it caught me without a film in my camera. It was a lovely afternoon, so two friends and I cycled westwards along the highway that led eventually to Kendal, turning north when we were about four miles on our way to Austwick and then making our way eastward through country lanes back into Ribblesdale, at Helwith Bridge, just as the signals were pulled off for an up train. We had not long to wait, for an up Scotch Express, "on the wings of the wind", as the saying goes, came tearing down hauled by one of the Johnson Class 3 4-4-0s, always known on the Midland as the "Belpaires", although most of the 4-4-0s eventually had that type of firebox.

In my school days the Class 2 superheated 4-4-0s were not much in evidence on the main line, although after one of our family holidays on the East Coast we joined a St Pancras-Edinburgh express at Leeds, for the run to Hellifield, which was hauled by one of these

engines. Some of them were to be seen on the Morecambe trains. When I was on training runs for the annual Scar-Rigg cross-country race at the end of the spring term, we used to make a circuit crossing the 'little' North Western line at an overbridge a mile or so west of Giggleswick station. There several times I saw a train from Morecambe hauled by a superheated Class 2 4-4-0 coming chugging purposefully up the bank from Clapham in the immaculate splendour in which most Midland passenger engines of that era used to go about their work. But the most memorable railway cameo of my school days was when I was travelling with my parents from Barrow to Leeds, bound for some resort on the East Coast, and our train was stopped by a signal on the approach to Settle Junction. Soon, going all-out at the start of the 'Long Drag', was the morning Scotch Express from Leeds to Glasgow hauled by one of the beautiful un-rebuilt Johnson 4-4-0s piloting a 999 — a very satisfying sight!

# 11
# The LMS:
# The Settle and Carlisle as a
# Major Test Route

In coming to the epoch-making January of 1923 when the Grouping of all the main line railways of Great Britain was inaugurated it is important to digress from the main subject of this book for a few paragraphs to explain how the engineers of the Midland Railway became the driving and controlling factor in locomotive testing on the LMS for many years after Grouping. The two other major English constituents of the group, the London & North Western and the Lancashire & Yorkshire, both had well-equipped dynamometer cars, which in the LNW case had, in 1913, registered the highest indicated horsepower to be recorded with any British locomotive until post-Grouping days — considerably higher than anything noted in the Great Western dynamometer car at the same period. Of course after the amalgamation of the Lancashire & Yorkshire Railway with the London & North Western, Crewe, presided over by a new Chief Mechanical Engineer much younger in years and professional status than the veteran George Hughes of the LYR, had to play second fiddle to Horwich in the greater London & North Western Railway. But this was no more than an interim stage, prior to the Grouping proper, which took effect from January 1923. Then, the Midland virtually took control of the entire LMS.

While Sir Guy Granet had retired from the General Managership of the Midland at the end of 1918 he had been honoured by a seat on the Board, and as such he was still a mighty power in the land. When Parliament had authorised the plan for Grouping the main line railways he

*Competitors in 1923: 1 — a standard superheater Midland compound, No. 1000.* (British Railways)

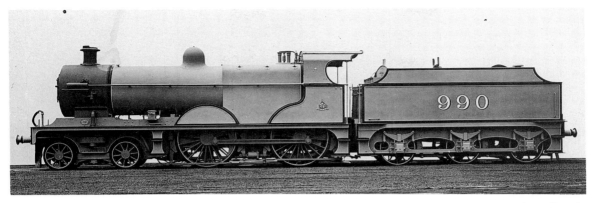

*Competitors in 1923: 2 — one of the 999 class 4-4-0s, an official view, showing class '4' on the cab side.*
(British Railways)

was in the thick of the negotiations and virtually dictated the terms of amalgamation between the individual companies forming the LMS group. Still proving himself by far the strongest personality in the field he made sure that the Midland precepts of management were adopted for the whole of the LMS, and what was more vital still, that the Midland organisation for traffic and train running control was introduced generally. J. H. Follows was appointed Chief General Superintendent, and J. E. Anderson, who had been Deputy CME of the Midland, and who had carried on the work of the department during Fowler's wartime absence at the Ministry of Munitions, was appointed Superintendent of Motive Power. Thus, for the entire LMS system, responsibility for the locomotive running was separated from the Chief Mechanical Engineer, as had been done on the Midland from 1907. Fowler had returned from his wartime service with a knighthood and a KBE, and he became Deputy CME until Hughes retired, two years later. But generally from the outset, the mechanical engineering influence was from the ex-Midland officers, and nowhere more so than in locomotive running.

Follows and Anderson were at once thinking of an all-line timetable reorganisation, running a swarm of relatively light express trains in the Midland style, rather than the intermittent heavyweights characteristic of the West Coast Main Line. For such a service Anderson considered the Midland compound ideal. He had quickly taken a poor view of all engines in the other constituent companies' stocks, and with the ready co-operation of his former colleagues in the locomotive department at Derby, he set out to prove that for future traffic requirements the former Midland types were the only ones worth considering! Follows regarded Class 4 as adequate to run the express passenger trains he contemplated for the entire LMS service, even though they had to be double-headed on the Midland main line south of Leeds when the tare load was more than 240 tons. On the North Western such a load as 240 tons would have been hardly worth pulling, seeing that the 'Prince of Wales' class 4-6-0s, which came with the LMS classification as '4' used to take 400 tons on the 55 mph bookings between Euston and Crewe. Actually, in pre-war days the 'George the Fifth' 4-4-0s were reckoned equal to the 'Princes' in haulage capacity, both classes coming within the general classification, "superheater engines" so far as load limits were concerned. And yet under LMS jurisdiction the 'George the Fifth's' were Class 3!

At the time of Grouping the Midland had 55 express passenger engines in Class 4, 45 compounds, not all of them superheated, and the ten 999 class simples. Against this the North Western had 245 superheater 4-6-0s of the 'Prince of Wales' class, about which Anderson was not long in forming a poor opinion. Of course such a stud could not be disregarded, however partisan feelings intruded. There was only one way to convince the top management, and that was by running comparative trials. In the last years of the Midland Railway as an independent company some important indicator trials had been carried out between Derby and Manchester under

*One of the original Johnson compounds, rebuilt and superheated, and numbered 1003.* (British Railways)

supervision of that very able engineer Frank Sutherland. For the trials between rival Class 4 engines the LMS had two dynamometer cars from which that of the former Lancashire & Yorkshire Railway was of course chosen, seeing that George Hughes was Chief Mechanical Engineer. With North Western engines likely to be involved the Settle and Carlisle line seemed an obvious testing ground with engines based at the northern end; and although the ex-LYR dynamometer car was used it seemed that the Derby faction took charge of the entire exercise from the very outset.

The trials, which began on 10th December 1923 lasted until 17th January 1924 and were made on the 12.10 pm up from Carlisle, and the 4.7 pm down from Leeds, both trains then running non-stop in both directions. The booked average speeds over the 113.0 miles were 47.2 mph southbound and 50.2 mph northbound. Both trains came within the 'limited load' category for timing and in normal working the maximum unpiloted load for a Class 4 engine was 260 tons. But maybe because of the North Western plea that such a load was not worth pulling the loads for the test trains were made up to 300 and 350 tons. In pre-war days the load of the down West Coast "Corridor", booked to average 52 mph from Preston to Carlisle, over Shap, was frequently worked by 'George the Fifth' and 'Prince of

Wales' class engines with tare loads of 350 tons, unpiloted. In 1923 the first engine was the 'Prince' No. 388 (unnamed). The crew, normally based at Upperby Bridge shed, had learned the road beforehand and gave a very competent display, with both ranges of load, although from the outset the Midland people thought she was burning a lot of coal. Then it was the turn of a Midland compound. This was not one of those working over the Carlisle road, but one, to quote the official report, which "had just worked into condition after general repairs in Derby Shops". A friend of mine who was a pupil of Sir Henry Fowler at the time once referred to No. 1008 as "the flower of the whole flock". Derby undoubtedly saw to it that an outstanding example of a Midland compound represented them in those trials.

With the '999' it seems as if someone high up in authority was not entirely convinced with the compound principle as such, for while five days sufficed to put the 'Prince' through its paces, and six days for the compound, on two of which the load on the northbound run was very much below the stipulated tonnage, no less than eleven days were spent in testing No. 998, of these only two were with 350-ton loads, with which she did not do too well on the banks, and seven were with 300-ton trains. It was emphasised that particular attention should be paid to the maintenance of the working book times uphill. For the test period the three competing engines were based at Durran Hill shed although they did not use the coal normally supplied to Midland express locomotives working from that depot, which was Tyneside. Instead, the test engines were fired with one of the very best South Yorkshire 'hards' Grimesthorpe, which was a grade normally used by engines working from Leeds Whitehall Junction shed. Grimesthorpe would have been an unfamiliar coal to the North Western driver of the 'Prince of Wales' class 4-6-0 No. 388. This driver and engine had been working regularly between Carlisle and Leeds for sometime prior to the tests. The driver was quite familiar with the road, but not with Grimesthorpe coal, and so for a week prior to the tests engine No. 388 was supplied with Grimesthorpe 'hards' for its ordinary work. The driver thus entered upon the test period familiar with the road, and needing no pilotman, and reasonably familiar with the coal.

It can be said, without any exaggeration, that never before had there been such running on the Midland Railway. The enginemen entered into the spirit of it with tremendous gusto; partisanship for the Midland on the one hand, and for the North Western on the other, rose to fever heat, so that quite apart from the scientific aspects of the tests some magnificent individual feats were achieved with each of the competing locomotives. The bare details of performance are given in the Tables I and II.

The first table gives the passing times at Lazonby, Ais Gill and Blea Moor, together with the overall times from Carlisle to Leeds, and it

Table I
Carlisle–Leeds: Passing Times

| Miles from Carlisle Station etc | | Lazonby | | Ais Gill | | Blea Moor | | Leeds | |
|---|---|---|---|---|---|---|---|---|---|
| Schedule (min) | | 21 | | 68 | | 80 | | 143 | |
| Engine No. | Load tons | Actual m s | | Actual m s | | Actual m s | | Actual m s | |
| 388 | $305\frac{1}{2}$ | 24 | 24 | 68 | 46 | 81 | 12 | 141 | 51 |
| | $302\frac{1}{2}$ | 23 | 13 | 68 | 53 | 81 | 24 | 142 | 14 |
| | $305\frac{1}{2}$ | 23 | 37 | 66 | 58 | 79 | 36 | 143 | 28 |
| 1008 | $305\frac{1}{2}$ | 23 | 18 | 63 | 01 | 75 | 18 | 140 | 23 |
| | $209\frac{1}{2}$ | 23 | 16 | 66 | 09 | 79 | 09 | 141 | 07 |
| 998 | $309\frac{1}{2}$ | 23 | 05 | 64 | 28 | 76 | 30 | 140 | 47 |
| | $293\frac{1}{2}$ | 24 | 11 | 67 | 18 | 78 | 46 | 140 | 10 |
| | $303\frac{1}{2}$ | 24 | 05 | 69 | 29 | 81 | 54 | 139 | 18 |
| | $302\frac{1}{2}$ | 24 | 15 | 70 | 33 | 83 | 00 | 142 | 08 |
| | $304\frac{1}{2}$ | 23 | 48 | 68 | 08 | 80 | 16 | 136 | 56 |
| | $313\frac{1}{2}$ | 23 | 23 | 68 | 56 | 80 | 55 | 144 | 25 |
| 388 | $352\frac{1}{2}$ | 23 | 20 | 66 | 09 | 78 | 17 | 143 | 06 |
| | $354\frac{1}{2}$ | 25 | 08 | 72 | 34 | 85 | 15 | 143 | 41 |
| 1008 | $354\frac{1}{2}$ | 22 | 51 | 64 | 31 | 76 | 54 | 139 | 40 |
| | $355\frac{1}{2}$ | 23 | 46 | 65 | 39 | 78 | 59 | 142 | 18 |
| | $349\frac{1}{2}$ | 23 | 16 | 67 | 32 | 79 | 36 | 137 | 40 |
| | $352\frac{1}{2}$ | 24 | 22 | 67 | 19 | 79 | 54 | 143 | 04 |
| 998 | $356\frac{1}{2}$ | 25 | 07 | 83 | 59 | 96 | 28 | 150 | 54 |
| | $353\frac{1}{2}$ | 23 | 57 | 71 | 59 | 85 | 03 | 150 | 01 |

will be seen that except on those runs when signal checks were experienced, good time was kept from end to end, though there was some variation in the sectional timings. Nevertheless, the idea

*No. 995, one of the 999 class, as superheated, in MR livery.* (British Railways)

of a Midland compound consistently taking a tare load of 350 tons past Ais Gill Summit in less than 68 min from the start at Carlisle was so revolutionary that prior to the winter of 1923–34 the most ardent of Midland supporters would have stoutly resisted any suggestion that such a thing was possible.

Although there is no specific information on this point in the official report, one can draw the conclusion that the weather was tolerably good for most of the trial period. The equality of performance between the three engines in the heaviest working conditions is most clearly illustrated in Table II, in the climbing from Settle Junction to Blea Moor with 350-ton trains. Here all three engines lost time on the sharp allowance of 22 min, and the variation between one engine and another, and between trip and trip were a matter of seconds rather than minutes.

All the same, when minimum speeds on the bank are studied the 999 class engine made the poorest showing. It was common practice with these engines to run very hard on the initial stretch downhill from Hellifield to Settle Junction, and by passing the latter point at well over 70 mph to gain some useful impetus for the climb. On the two runs with the 350-ton trains it seems fairly clear that engine No. 998 was short of steam at Blea Moor, and the slow recovery to Ais Gill on the last run of the series provides corroborative evidence. It is sometimes said that

Table II
Leeds–Carlisle

| Engine No. | Load tons tare | Settle Jc Blea Moor Actual m  s | Blea Moor Ais Gill Actual m  s | Min. speed on bank mph |
|---|---|---|---|---|
| Schedule (min) | | 22 | 13 | |
| 388 | 290½ | 21  59 | 12  56 | 33.8 |
| | 300½ | 22  50 | 13  27 | 29.0 |
| | 294½ | 21  54 | 11  53 | 30.0 |
| 1008 | 293½ | 20  43 | 13  06 | 33.1 |
| 998 | 298½ | 21  53 | 13  17 | 29.0 |
| | 302½ | 24  59 | 13  21 | not |
| | 281½ | 21  21 | 12  56 | quoted |
| | 298½ | 24  02 | 15  26 | 26.8 |
| | 301½ | 22  02 | 13  45 | 27.7 |
| | 295½ | 21  28 | 13  13 | 30.5 |
| 388 | 345½ | 24  29 | 13  38 | 28.5 |
| | 342½ | 25  28 | 13  57 | 26.2 |
| 1008 | 343½ | 25  21 | 14  10 | 26.0 |
| | 342½ | 25  15 | 12  53 | 25.0 |
| 998 | 353½ | 24  56 | 14  48 | 22.0 |
| | 344½ | 25  45 | 16  12 | 19.5 |

the capacity of a locomotive can be gauged from its grate area. On this basis, and on the exact similarity of their boilers, the compound and the

*A LNWR 'Prince of Wales' class 4-6-0, No. 86* Mark Twain *in original LNWR livery, working a southbound freight train from the Caledonian line at Carlisle.* (Author's Collection)

'999' should have put up identical performances. But it does not require any examination of the dynamometer car records to appreciate that in the most severe conditions of working, the compound had a very definite advantage over her rival. A practiced observer, travelling as a passenger in those Scottish expresses and recording the times, mile by mile, could tell quite clearly when the 999s effort began to flag.

All the same it was a hard task to set for any engine of Class 4 capacity. Fourteen miles of almost continuous 1 in 100 ascent: past the old-world town of Settle, beneath the limestone cliffs of Stainforth, and then through the dramatic gorge of the Ribble, crossing that brawling mountain stream on massive stone bridges, the piers of which are clearly designed to withstand a torrent of flood water. Then out into the bleak wastes of moorland, with the mountains of upper Ribblesdale and the vastness of the landscape making the trains look like the tiniest models when seen from any distance away. It was certainly a majestic arena in which to stage a trial of strength, just as the drag from Ormside Viaduct up to Ais Gill, on the northern side of the summit can be a 'killer' to the engines of southbound trains. In many ways, however, the northbound climb is more severe, for it is followed by the sharply-timed run of 11.2 miles on the level and slightly rising gradients from Blea Moor to Ais Gill; it was here that

No. 998 on her last trip was limping to such an extent as to lose $3\frac{1}{4}$ min in this relatively short distance.

The work of the compound, No. 1008, was consistently superb, and from Table I it will be seen that she made considerably the fastest times between Carlisle and Ais Gill Summit in both the 300-ton and the 350-ton series of tests. These two runs, made on 17th and 18th December 1923, probably represent the finest all-round performances ever achieved with the true Midland compounds, considered apart from those of later variants of the design standardised by the LMSR. It is perhaps significant of the absolute mastery over the job shown by No. 1008 and her crew that after no more than one round trip with a 300-ton train the test authorities gave the engine 355 tons on the very next day! The North Western 'Prince' had three days of 300-ton running before she was given 350. The logs of the runs made by No. 1008 in her first two southbound trips are detailed in Table III.

There is a gruelling start out of Carlisle, with six miles out of the first 8.4 inclined at 1 in 133, and in such conditions it was astonishing work by previous Midland standards, to pass Low House box in $15\frac{3}{4}$ min with a load not far short of 400 tons gross behind the tender. Then came the sharply undulating length on the wooded hillsides above the River Eden, where it makes so picturesque a course deep in the rocky gorges of

*A 'Prince of Wales' class 4-6-0, still in original condition except renumbering as LMS No. 25752.* (British Railways)

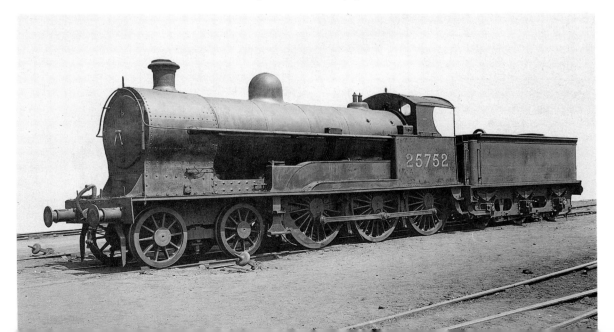

Table III
LMSR 12.01 pm Carlisle–Leeds
Engine: 4-4-0 Compound No. 1008

| Date | | | | 17.12.23 | | 18.12.23 | |
| Loads, tons E/F | | | | 306/320 | | 355/370 | |
| Dist.<br>Miles | | Sch.<br>min. | Actual<br>m  s | Speeds<br>mph | Actual<br>m  s | Speeds<br>mph |
|---|---|---|---|---|---|---|
| 0.0 | CARLISLE | 0 | 0 00 | — | 0 00 | — |
| 2.7 | Scotby | | 6 23 | 32¼ | 6 15 | 31 |
| — | | | — | 41½ | — | 42 |
| 8.4 | *Low House* | | 15 42 | 34 | 15 40 | 37½ |
| 13.5 | *Summit* | | 21 19 | 50 | 21 08 | 53 |
| 15.4 | Lazonby | 21 | 23 19 | 66 | 22 51 | 69½ |
| 19.8 | Langwathby | | 27 36 | 51 | 26 47 | 56½ |
| 23.4 | Culgaith | | 30 53 | 59½ | 30 38 | 64½ |
| 27.9 | Long Marton | | 36 05 | 64¼ | 34 51 | 63½ |
| 30.8 | APPLEBY | 39 | 39 00 | 55½ | 37 51 | 52½ |
| 33.2 | Ormside | | 41 19 | 69½ | 40 20 | 64½ |
| 36.5 | *Top of 1 in 100* | | 45 12 | 42½ | 44 39 | 37 |
| 38.3 | Crosby Garrett | | 47 30 | 50 | 47 13 | 47 |
| 41.5 | Kirkby Stephen | | 51 46 | 38 | 51 45 | 35 |
| 44.8 | *Mallerstang* | | 57 23 | 32 | 58 03 | 27 |
| — | | | — | 41 | — | 37½ |
| 48.3 | Ais Gill | 68 | 63 03 | 32 | 64 35 | 27 |
| 51.4 | Hawes Jc | | 66 47 | 61 | 68 21 | 62½ |
| 59.5 | *Blea Moor* | 80 | 75 20 | 55 | 76 58 | 53 |
| 73.5 | *Settle Jc* | 93 | 86 58<br>sigs. | 78* | 89 14<br>sigs. | 76* |
| 76.8 | HELLIFIELD | 97 | 90 13 | — | 92 21 | — |
| — | | | — | 63½ | — | 61 |
| 86.8 | SKIPTON | 109 | 102 48<br>sigs. | — | 105 48<br>sigs. | — |
| 102.1 | Shipley<br>(Bingley Jc) | 129 | 126 55 | — | 126 19 | — |
| — | | | — | 63½ | — | 65 |
| 113.0 | LEEDS | 143 | 140 24 | — | 139 40 | — |

Armathwaite and Baron Wood. Even with such hammering as was meted out to No. 1008 she could not, even with the 300-ton load, keep the sectional time to Lazonby, but on the downhill stretch to Lazonby itself, and on the gradual rise to Long Marton the initial loss of time was recovered — in fact, on the second trip, with the heavier train, the crew of No. 1008 were substantially improving on their efforts of the previous day.

Then, after the welcome respite afforded by the falling gradients from Appleby to Ormside Viaduct, there comes the main ascent. There is 15 miles of it, though it certainly does include two appreciable breaks in the climbing. From a point near Griseburn signal box the 1 in 100 eases to 1 in 162, and this further eases to the crossing of Smardale Viaduct, near Crosby Garrett. Then comes the worst pitch, a solid five miles of 1 in 100 through the wildest of moorland and mountain country, until Mallerstang box is neared. The speed usually falls to its lowest

figure anywhere on the ascent from Carlisle at the south end of Birkett Tunnel, and at this point there is the welcome ¾ mile at 1 in 302 past Mallerstang before entering upon the final three miles at 1 in 100 up to Ais Gill Summit.

Magnificent though the work of No. 1008 was on her second trip, one could hardly expect her to maintain the lead over the 300-ton run in arduous mountain conditions, and the 350-ton trip had dropped down to level going at Kirkby Stephen, and fell behind to the extent of ½ min at Ais Gill Summit. Even so, on a schedule planned for a 260-ton maximum load they were 3½ min early passing the summit, with a 370-ton train. There was some brisk running down to Settle Junction on both trips, but by that time the train was close on the tail of the preceding express from Glasgow to St Pancras, and signal checks prevented the making of any further fast time.

By the summer of 1924 those in command of the Locomotive Department had developed such a superiority complex where the compounds were concerned that they seemed ready to back them against all comers. Use of them in Scotland was already envisaged, and in the late autumn of 1924 a further series of trials over the Settle and Carlisle line was organised, in which compounds would be tested against Caledonian Railway 4-4-0s and North Western 4-6-0s. Although in the earlier trials the going had been fairly close, so far as power output was con-

Table IV
Performance of Engine No. 1008

| Date<br>Load, tons E/F | 17.12.23<br>306/320 | 18.12.23<br>355/370 |
|---|---|---|
| Average drawbar pull | 2.44 | 2.73 |
| Max db pull on bank, tons | 4.25 | 4.55 |
| Max drawbar hp | 954 | 1025 |
| Locality of max, dbhp | one mile<br>north of<br>Appleby | near<br>Langwathby |
| Speed at max dbhp, mph | 57 | 59 |
| Coal consumption | | |
| per train mile lb | 42.4 | 46.2 |
| per dbhp hr lb | 3.93 | 3.83 |
| per sq ft of grate area<br>per hr lb | 71.8 | 78.7 |
| Water consumption | | |
| gallons per mile | 29.9 | 29.4 |
| pounds per lb of coal | 7.05 | 6.37 |

cerned, between the compound and the LNWR 'Prince of Wales' 4-6-0, Derby were evidently convinced of the overwhelming superiority of their own engine. In November 1924 they decided to challenge one of the much larger and heavier 'Claughton' class 4-6-0s of the LNWR on equal terms — equal, that is, so far as haulage tasks set to the competing locomotives were concerned.

On paper the trials seemed unequal from the start, for whereas in the earlier series, in 1923–4, the engines engaged were all Class 4, in the November and December trials of 1924 the compounds were matched against a Class 5 4-6-0 and a Class 3 4-4-0 simple from the Caledonian. Events contrived to make the trials unequal in other respects too.

As in the previous trials the trains concerned were to be the 12.10 pm from Carlisle to Leeds and the 4.3 pm down. Since the time of the first series the latter train had been retimed to include a stop at Hellifield. The engines and men concerned were based on Durran Hill shed, Carlisle, and this introduced a factor that, in November 1924, considerably affected the results and led to a lot of wrong conclusions being drawn. The West Coast Main Line, despite the introduction of a number of new Lancashire & Yorkshire four-cylinder 4-6-0s, was very short of engine power. The LMSR authorities had reduced drastically the maximum tonnages that could be taken unassisted, not only over Shap, but throughout between Euston and Carlisle. The result was an enormous amount of double-heading and a shortage of engines in consequence. The North

Western shed at Carlisle could not spare a 'Claughton' for trials over the Midland line to Leeds, and so Edge Hill shed was instructed to transfer one of its own stud. Whether the shed master was told why, I cannot say, though from subsequent events I very much doubt it.

When one shed is instructed to part with one of its engines to another depot, it is no more than human nature to send the worst that will comply with the instructions, and on 19th November Edge Hill transferred No. 2221 *Sir Francis Dent*. This engine had been out-shopped at Crewe in July 1924 after a general repair. It was then worked hard for those days, averaging 6,000 miles a month, before it was sent to Carlisle. The driver and fireman who were to work it in the trials made two return trips with it from Carlisle to Leeds in the following week, and then on 2nd December came the first of the dynamometer car trials.

The Caledonian engine was completely outclassed and apparently one return trip was enough to show that she was not up to the haulage of 300-ton trains, let alone anything heavier. The 'Claughton' steamed badly throughout, and although the engine had sufficient reserve of power for the driver to work these trains to time, the record of coal consumption suffered in consequence, and the results were not representative of the class as a whole. It will be seen, however, that three different compounds were used at different times, two being of the new short-chimneyed series, and one a standard Derby 7 ft superheater engine.

*The 'Claughton' 4-6-0 that took part in the trials of 1924; No. 2221* Sir Francis Dent.
(British Railways)

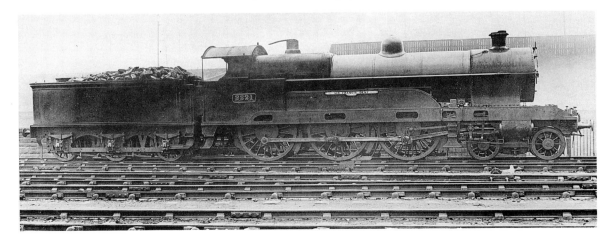

It is the work of the compounds, however, that is of the greatest interest, particularly when compared with the results achieved with No. 1008 roughly a year earlier. These engines were gaining a reputation for being the most economical on the entire LMSR system, and in discussing the results of November–December 1924 it is, from the outset, worth looking at the bald results tabulated in terms of coal consumption per drawbar horsepower hour, and nothing else. The three engines in these later trials showed very consistent results on this basis alone, all considerably above the best results recorded with No. 1008 a year earlier. It is a rather sobering reflection to compare the consistent results from three different Midland compounds with those from the North Western 'Prince of Wales' No. 388, in 1923, for it was on the basis of the superiority of No. 1008 over No. 388 that the Midland case for the multiplication of the compounds was based.

The North Western figures in December 1923 were far more consistent than those obtained with No. 1008, and on the five return trips the values of coal consumption per dhp hour, in pounds were: 4.43, 4.77, 4.52, 4.62, 4.31, 5.12, 4.31, 5.12, 4.31, 4.97, 4.39 and 4.67. The average works out at 4.60 against the average of eight Midland compound trips in November and December 1924 of 4.45. To anyone familiar with the variations in coal consumption inherent in road trials with the dynamometer car on service trains, the

| | | Load | Coal | |
|---|---|---|---|---|
| | Engine | (nominal | (lb per dhp hr) | |
| Date | No. | tare tons) | Up | Down |
| 17.12.23 | 1008 | 300 | 3.93 | 3.64 |
| 18.12.23 | 1008 | 350 | 3.83 | 3.73 |
| 19.12.23 | 1008 | 350 | 4.02 | — |
| 19.12.23 | 1008 | 221 | — | 4.22 |
| 20.12.23 | 1008 | 300 | 4.02 | — |
| 20.12.23 | 1008 | 227 | — | 4.5 |
| 31.12.23 | 1008 | 350 | | — |
| 31.12.23 | 1008 | 249 | — | 3.94 |
| 15. 1.24 | 1008 | 350 | 3.7 | 3.9 |
| 18.11.24 | 1065 | 300 | 4.46 | |
| 19.11 24 | 1065 | 300 | 4.39 | |
| 20.11.24 | 1065 | 350 | 4.33 | |
| 21.11.24 | 1065 | 350 | 4.45 | |
| 27.11.24 | 1023 | 350 | 4.45 | |
| 28.11.24 | 1023 | 350 | 4.42 | |
| 9.12.24 | 1066 | 300 | 4.68 | |
| 10.12.24 | 1066 | 350 | 4.43 | |

Midland Compound Tests: Leeds–Carlisle

difference between the 'Prince of Wales' and the Midland compounds would be negligible. But when official comparison between the two classes was made it was with the very exceptional No. 1008 that the 'Prince' was contrasted.

Moreover, the coal consumption figures alone do not tell anything like the full story of the November and December tests of 1924. Engines Nos 1065 and 1066 were both relatively new; they had the larger cylinders and 6 ft 9 in coupled wheels of the post-Grouping engines of the 1045–1084 series, whereas No. 1023 was a standard 7 ft superheated example of the Midland Railway Deeley series, by all ordinary reckonings identical to No. 1008. All three compounds had run roughly 14,000 miles since leaving the shops; in the case of No. 1023 this was, of course, from the last general repair. The new engines, Nos 1065 and 1066, both did well, and their uphill running will be discussed in more detail later; but No. 1023 put up a consistently shocking performance on the banks. Against a schedule of 67 min from Carlisle to Ais Gill she took 76 min 49 sec on her first trip with 350 tons, and 74 min 55 sec on the second. These efforts were followed up by losses of roughly another minute in each case from Ais Gill to Blea Moor, thus totalling losses of 11 min and 9 min from Carlisle to Blea Moor. Against these totals by No. 1023 of 89 min 47 sec and 87 min 53 sec

*One of the Caledonian Railway Pickersgill 4-4-0s, No. 114, another of the classes that took part in the trials of 1924–5.* (British Railways)

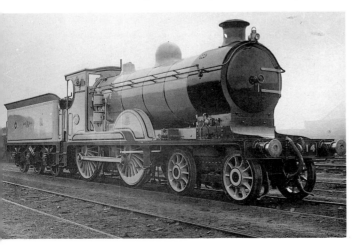

| Date | Engine No. | Actual load (tare tons) | Running times Settle Blea Moor m s | | Blea Moor Ais Gill m s | | Min sp (mph) | Max dp (tons) | Max edhp |
|---|---|---|---|---|---|---|---|---|---|
| 18.11.24 | 1065 | 311 | 25 | 00 | 13 | 33 | 26 | 3.93 | 769 |
| 19.11.24 | 1065 | 324 | 23 | 35 | 13 | 45 | 28 | 4.08 | 857 |
| 20.11.24 | 1065 | 361 | 25 | 47 | 14 | 29 | 25 | 4.5 | 829 |
| 21.11.24 | 1065 | 353 | 28 | 28 | 14 | 27 | 22½ | 4.6 | 758 |
| 9.12.24 | 1066 | 305 | 23 | 05 | 15 | 59 | 30 | 3.75 | 870 |
| 10.12.24 | 1066 | 347 | 23 | 58 | 14 | 15 | 28½ | 4.26 | 906 |

engine No. 1008, a year earlier, had made times of 76 min 54 sec, 78 min 59 sec, 79 min 36 sec and 79 min 54 sec on the four runs she made with 350-ton trains.

The work of the new compounds Nos 1065 and 1066 can best be exemplified from the climbing from Settle Junction to Blea Moor, and on the tableland section onwards to Ais Gill. As previously mentioned, the scheduled times over the mountain section were 22 and 13 min respectively so that on no occasion did either engine maintain strict time. On the other hand, the timings were laid down for a load of 260 tons tare, and on 20th November for example, with 361 tons behind the tender the gross trailing load would probably have been 380 or even 385 tons — a tremendous load for a 4-4-0 engine in such conditions.

By the end of 1924, the run of 10th December by No. 1066 stands out as the best ever, and this is reflected in the figure for the equivalent drawbar horsepower.

I cannot say if any relaxing of the statutory load limit for Class 4 engines, below the previous figure of 260 tons, had taken place in view of the performances recorded in the trials of 1923-5, but certainly I myself had a fine trip with one of the 999 class engines on the night express to Edinburgh when we took a load of 273 tons without a pilot. One of Cecil J. Allen's regular correspondents, himself a locomotive engineer, had an outstanding run, with the same train on which all the dynamometer tests had been made, the morning express from Edinburgh Waverley, leaving Carlisle at 12.10 pm and hauled by the same 6 ft 9 in compound, No. 1066, which had done so well in the tests. On the 'ordinary' run

LMSR 12.10 pm Carlisle–Hellifield
Load: 301 tons tare, 320 tons full
Engine: 6 ft 9 in Compound 4-4-0 No. 1066

| Distance Miles | | Sch min | Actual m s | Speed mph |
|---|---|---|---|---|
| 0.0 | Carlisle | 0 | 0 00 | — |
| 2.7 | Scotby | | 6 15 | 34 |
| 3.9 | Cumwhinton | | 8 18 | 36 |
| — | | | — | 44½ |
| 6.8 | Cotehill | | 12 25 | 39½ |
| 10.0 | Armathwaite | | 16 30 | 61 |
| — | | | | 53 |
| 15.5 | Lazonby | 21 | 22 06 | 70 |
| 18.4 | Little Salkeld | | 24 40 | 64 |
| 19.8 | Langwathby | | 26 04 | 57½ |
| 23.4 | Culgaith | | 29 34 | 62 |
| 24.7 | New Biggin | | 31 00 | 56 |
| 27.9 | Long Marton | | 34 20 | 62 |
| 30.8 | Appleby | 39 | 37 25 | 52 |
| 33.3 | Ormside | | 39 56 | 64½ |
| — | Helm Tunnel | | — | 39 |
| 38.3 | Crosby Garrett | | 46 35 | 49 |
| 41.5 | Kirkby Stephen | | 51 00 | 36 |
| — | Birkett Tunnel | | — | 30 |
| 44.8 | Mallerstang Box | | — | 39 |
| 48.4 | Ais Gill | 67 | 63 19 | 27 |
| 51.4 | Hawes Junction | | 67 10 | 61 |
| 54.7 | Dent | | 70 38 | 56 |
| — | | | — | 64 |
| 59.5 | Blea Moor Box | 79 | 75 34 | 53 |
| 71.6 | Settle | | 85 35 | — |
| 73.5 | Settle Junction | 92 | 87 02 | 82 |
| 76.8 | Hellifield | 96 | 90 21 | — |

not only was a tare load of 301 tons taken unpiloted up to Ais Gill, but the summit was passed just over 3½ minutes early. The log of this excellent run forms a fitting conclusion to this chapter.

# 12
# Major Management Changes — Effects on the Settle and Carlisle

The significance of the later series of dynamometer car trials between Leeds and Carlisle, and particularly the details of coal consumption, was not lost on J. E. Anderson and those of his staff with North Western sentiments. They did not share the compound building enthusiasm that then prevailed at CME headquarters at Derby; neither apparently did Sir Guy Granet. After four years of the LMS his pre-Grouping all-Midland precepts had changed considerably and he was quite ready to listen to the

urgent objections of the Motive Power Department to the large four-cylinder compound Pacific of which the construction of two had already begun. Granet was so impressed by the arguments stressed that Fowler was ordered to stop work on the two new engines. Anderson had found ready allies in his anti-compound campaign in the former LNWR drawing office at Crewe, and they apparently looked out the drawings of the boiler originally proposed for the 'Claughton' class 4-6-0s, but not used owing to

*No. 1102, a standard LMS compound with left-hand drive.* (British Railways)

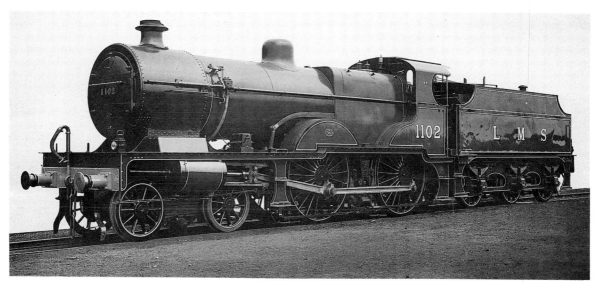

the weight restrictions imposed by the Chief Engineer of those pre-war days. The proposal that a new larger-boilered 'Claughton' would take the place of the Fowler compound Pacific gained credence to the extent of its mention in the railway press of the day.

The project, which indirectly led to an important new motive power development for the Settle and Carlisle line, was shelved temporarily by the experimental working of a Great Western 'Castle' class 4-6-0 between Euston and Carlisle and the subsequent introduction of the 'Royal Scot' class three-cylinder 4-6-0s. In the meantime, on the top management side of the LMS the appointment of Sir Josiah Stamp as President of the Executive, in January 1926, had been followed a year later by four Vice-Presidents, one of whom was J. H. Follows. His place as Chief General Superintendent was significantly taken by a former LNWR Officer, C. R. Byrom. The Vice-President for Works and Ancillary Undertakings, to whom, in the new organisation the Chief Mechanical Engineer reported, was R. W. Reid, who before the Grouping was Carriage and Wagon Superintendent of the Midland Railway. A comparatively young man it seemed as though he had a brilliant career ahead of him. The introduction of no less than 50 of the 'Royal Scot' class locomotives from the early autumn of 1927 made a number of the 'Claughton' class 4-6-0s surplus to

requirements on the West Coast Main Line, and in due course some of these were transferred to the Midland Division. Between Leeds and Carlisle, on the steep rising gradients their load was fixed at 340 tons before a pilot could be claimed.

In the euphoria surrounding the introduction of the new 4-6-0s on the West Coast route and the naming of the historic 10 am departures from Euston and Glasgow Central as "The Royal Scot", even before the new locomotives were available to haul them, a number of other LMS expresses were named, including the morning Scotch Expresses by the Midland route the "Thames–Forth Express" for Edinburgh Waverley, and "The Thames–Clyde Express", for Glasgow St Enoch. My personal recollections of those years however is the negligible publicity given to those Midland Scotch trains. At first nothing more powerful than the compounds were available for haulage and on my first trip with the up "Thames–Forth Express", when I was travelling through from Edinburgh to St Pancras, the best the Midland Division could provide for a tare load of 240 tons was a couple of Class 2 superheater 4-4-0s. They made short work of it up to Ais Gill, and after detaching the pilot the second engine, No. 337, ran merrily enough down to Hellifield, where, believe it or not, engines were changed and a Class 3 "Belpaire" 4-4-0, No. 735

*Class 4 Midland 0-6-0 No. 3944 at Blea Moor.* (Norman Wilkinson)

*The up "Thames-Clyde Express" leaving Carlisle in 1931 with a Class 2 4-4-0, No. 436 piloting ex-LNWR 4-6-0 No. 5900* Sir Gilbert Claughton. (Rail Archive Stephenson — F. R. Hebron)

came on for the run to Leeds.

After the 'Royal Scots' had been launched into traffic on the West Coast Main Line Crewe Works received an order to build a number of the enlarged 'Claughton' boilers, not for new engines but for reboilering some of the older ones, and because of the higher pressure used, 200 lb per sq in instead of 175, advancing their tractive effort to a figure mid-way between that of the original 'Claughtons' and that of the 'Royal Scots'. The latter had been classified '6P' in the

motive power stud, and the larger boilered 'Claughtons' became '5XP'. These latter 4-6-0s were always confined to the Western Division of the LMS, but a three-cylinder variation of Class 5XP was to come to the Midland Division, and more particularly the Settle and Carlisle line in another two years. In the meantime the popular acclaim with which the 'Royal Scot' class locomotives had 'hit the headlines' in 1927 was wearing distinctly thin by the summer service of 1928. The marvellously low coal consumptions of the first few engines of the class, with which Sir Henry Fowler had regaled members of the Institution of Mechanical Engineers in January 1928, were showing an alarming increase, in some cases to nearly 80 per cent. The cause was ultimately traced to the use on the new engines of the Schmidt type of piston valve with one broad ring of packing. This was standard at Derby for all superheater engines, and these, traditionally worked lightly, suffered no appreciable loss through piston valve leakage. But it was another matter with hard worked 'Royal Scots'! The solution was to use piston valves with six narrow rings, and it worked like a charm.

This digression on the early vicissitudes of the 'Royal Scots' is equally pertinent to an account of the motive power developments on the Settle and Carlisle line. Crewe Works lost no time in fitting the improved piston valves to the 'Claughtons', and the Leeds and Durran Hill men working the Scotch Expresses soon appreciated the greatly reduced coal consumption on which they were able to work their hardest turns. The impressions

*Class 3 goods 0-6-0 No. 3231 on up goods train near Baron Wood.* (Norman Wilkinson)

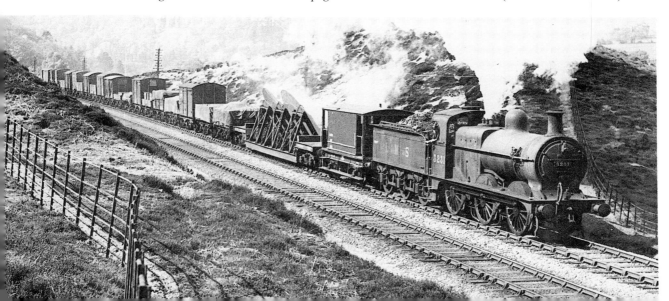

*A poor photograph, but a very rare scene, showing the down midday Scotch Express from St Pancras with LNER coaches for Edinburgh Waverley, in very dull Pennine weather at Ribblehead. Hauled by ex-LNWR 'Claughton' class engine No. 6005.* (Author's Collection)

of individual enginemen and the running inspectors at Whitehall Junction were amply confirmed by a set of dynamometer test runs made in May and June 1930. They were made to determine the improvement in steaming and evaporation and the consequent saving in fuel to be obtained by fitting the Kylälä blast pipe. The small boilered 'Claughtons' were tested, both having hollow type piston valves with six narrow rings, No. 6001 with the Kylälä blast pipe and No. 5973 with the standard blast pipe and chimney. The trains on which the tests were made were the up "Thames–Clyde Express" leaving Carlisle at 12.5 pm and the 4.3 pm down from Leeds, both made up to a nominal tare load of 300 tons. Engine No. 6001 was used first, making return trips on 12th and 13th May 1930. She showed a great improvement on previous 'Claughton' coal consumption figures, returning 4.08 and 3.79 lb per drawbar horsepower hour.

At this stage it is very important to note the change in attitude of those conducting indicator trials on the Settle and Carlisle line. In 1923-4 the results obtained with the 7 ft compound engine No. 1008 were so much superior to all those recorded with later engines of the type, including the exceptional No. 1066, as to raise certain suspicions, particularly as it was the results with this one engine that gave the signal for extensive building of many more 4-4-0 compounds. Had

the results from those excellent 6 ft 9 in compounds Nos 1065 and 1066 been available the management might have had second thoughts when comparing their coal consumption per drawbar horsepower with that of the North Western 'Prince of Wales' class 4-6-0 No. 388, which did not show up so well against the quite exceptional No. 1008, in the first series of trials. In 1930 it did not take the invigilating engineers long to realise that the standard 'Claughton', No. 5973 was not in the best of condition, even though her coal consumption per drawbar horsepower hour was almost the same as that of the compounds Nos 1065 and 1066. Since the 'Kylälä' engine was in very good condition it was felt that the comparison on the basis of two return trips from Carlisle to Leeds and back by each engine was not entirely fair. So the interesting step was taken of removing the Kylälä apparatus and restoring the standard blast pipe and chimney, and running two more return trips, on 3rd and 4th June 1930. As thus altered No. 6001 with the same driver and fireman who had worked her in the 'Kylälä' condition, did considerably better, and in fact yielded a superb performance on both days.

Later in that same summer I travelled by the 10.18 am from Leeds, the morning Glasgow express, and was interested to find engine No. 6001 at the head of a substantial load of 298 tons.

*Class 2, superheated 4-4-0 No. 434 on a down goods train near Baron Wood.* (Norman Wilkinson)

From the outset the running was absolutely first class, though when we reached Hellifield and found the Manchester portion of three more coaches to be attached to our rear end, the tare load was increased to 352 tons, and this being the Midland Division we had to take a pilot up to Ais Gill, the 'Claughton' load being 340 tons. Of course we romped up to Blea Moor passing the box four minutes early, and even after we had spent a leisurely two minutes detaching the pilot at Ais Gill we were still $3\frac{1}{2}$ minutes early at Appleby. The engine ran freely downhill reaching a maximum of 79 mph at Ormside, though not as fast as another of the class which gave me a maximum speed of 88 mph descending from Blea Moor towards Settle.

On the relatively sharp timing of 33 minutes for the concluding 30.8 miles from Appleby to Carlisle the engine ran well, with the 375 ton load, particularly in the opening stages where the gradients are not steep, maintaining speeds of 74 to 79 mph continuously from before Culgaith to Lazonby, and averaging 77 mph for 8.2 miles. The average speed over the 25.2 miles from Long Marton to Scotby, including the sharply undulating stretch beside the gorge of the River Eden from Lazonby northwards was 71.6 mph. On this form it seems as if the driver of No. 6001 could well have dispensed with pilot assistance from Hellifield to Ais Gill, as one would have readily

LMS Midland Division
10.18 am Leeds–Carlisle: 30th Aug. 1930

Load: 298 tons tare 320 tons full
Engine: 'Claughton' class 4-6-0 No. 6001

| Distance Miles | | Sch min | Actual m | s | Speed mph |
|---|---|---|---|---|---|
| 0.0 | Leeds | 0 | 0 | 00 | — |
| 3.1 | Kirkstall | | 6 | 20 | 54 |
| 5.8 | Calverley | | 9 | 20 | $54\frac{1}{2}$ |
| 7.5 | Apperley Bridge | | 11 | 15 | $51\frac{7}{10}$ |
| 10.9 | Shipley (Bingley Jc) | | 15 | 10 | 35 |
| 13.8 | Bingley | | 19 | 10 | $52\frac{1}{2}$ |
| 17.0 | Keighley | | 22 | 40 | $55\frac{1}{2}$ |
| 20.1 | Steeton | | 25 | 35 | $66\frac{1}{2}$ |
| 23.2 | Cononley | | 28 | 27 | $66\frac{1}{2}$ |
| 25.4 | Milepost $220\frac{1}{2}$ | | 30 | 30 | $67\frac{1}{2}$ |
| 26.2 | Skipton | 33 | 31 | 55 | |
| 0.5 | Skipton Jc | | 1 | 40 | 50 |
| 3.7 | Gargrave | | 5 | 50 | $47\frac{1}{2}$ |
| 6.6 | Bell Busk | | 9 | 30 | $48\frac{1}{2}$ |
| 8.7 | Milepost 230 | | 12 | 20 | 44 |
| — | | | sigs | | — |
| 10.0 | Hellifield | 16 | 15 | 45 | — |

Load: 352 tons tare 375 tons full
Pilot to Ais Gill: Class 2 4-4-0 No. 472

| | | | | | |
|---|---|---|---|---|---|
| 0.0 | Hellifield | 0 | 0 | 00 | — |
| 3.3 | Settle Junction | 5 | 4 | 35 | 68 |
| 5.2 | Settle | | 6 | 25 | 58 |
| 9.6 | Helwith Bridge Box | | 11 | 50 | 43/45 |
| 11.3 | Horton | | 14 | 15 | 39 |
| 13.6 | Selside Box | | 17 | 40 | 41 |
| 16.0 | Ribblehead | | 21 | 15 | $39\frac{1}{2}$ |
| 17.3 | Blea Moor Box | 27 | 23 | 05 | 41 |
| — | Tunnel South End | | — | | 40 |
| 22.2 | Dent | | 28 | 50 | 60 |
| 25.4 | Hawes Junction | | 31 | 50 | $72\frac{1}{2}$ |
| 28.5 | Ais Gill Box | 40 | 34 | 35 | |
| — | | | 36 | 55 | Pilot detached |
| 32.0 | Mallerstang | | 42 | 05 | 65 |
| 35.3 | Kirkby Stephen | | 45 | 05 | $71\frac{1}{2}$ |
| 38.5 | Crosby Garrett | | 47 | 40 | 78 |
| 40.5 | Griseburn Box | | 49 | 20 | 72 |
| 43.6 | Ormside | | 51 | 45 | 79 |
| 46.0 | Appleby | 58 | 54 | 25 | — |
| 2.9 | Long Marton | | 4 | 55 | $62\frac{1}{2}$ |
| 6.1 | New Biggin | | 7 | 50 | 69 |
| 7.4 | Culgaith | | 8 | 55 | 75 |
| 11.1 | Langwathby | | 11 | 50 | 74 |
| 12.5 | Little Salkeld | | 12 | 55 | 79 |
| 15.6 | Lazonby | | 15 | 20 | — |
| 17.7 | Milepost 295 | | 17 | 17 | 61 |
| 20.8 | Armathwaite | | 20 | 02 | $72\frac{1}{2}$ |
| 22.4 | Low House Box | | 21 | 25 | 63 |
| 24.0 | Cotehill | | 22 | 50 | 75 |
| 26.9 | Cumwhinton | | 25 | 10 | 69 |
| 28.1 | Scotby | | 26 | 10 | 74 |
| 29.9 | Petteril Bridge Jc | 30 | 28 | 10 | — |
| — | | | sigs | | |
| 30.8 | Carlisle | 33 | 31 | 45 | — |

imagined a London & North Western driver doing with such a small access as 12 tons over the stipulated maximum, with a first class engine and fine weather conditions.

In the autumn of that same year Derby Works was preparing its own version of a 5XP express passenger 4-6-0. The enlarged 'Claughton' boiler, combined with the improved type of piston valves had produced a remarkably successful engine of a tractive power a little lower than that of the 'Royal Scots'. The new project was also a rebuild, but applying a three-cylinder engine to the 'Claughton' chassis. The original frames were used, and the existing bogie, and the cylinders and motion were the same as those of the 'Royal Scots'. The enlarged 'Claughton' boiler was used, working at 200 lb per sq in, and the nominal tractive effort of this rebuild was 26,520 lb. This compared with the 33,150 lb of the 'Royal Scots' and 27,150 lb on the large-boilered 'Claughtons', and like the latter, they were classified '5X'. At first they were given the rather ponderous official name of 'Three-cylinder Converted Claughton', but the enginemen soon found a much better name — "Baby Scot" which suited their looks perfectly.

In 1930 two engines were rebuilt at Derby, Nos 5902 and 5971. They included quite a number of parts of the original engines, but they were fitted with the standard Midland 3,500-gallon tender. No. 5902 retained its original name, *Sir Frank Ree*, though rendered in 'Royal Scot', rather than traditional Crewe style, but No. 5971 at first was nameless. Soon after her first construction as

LNWR No. 2511, in 1920, she had been named *Croxteth*, taken from the 6 ft "Jumbo", No. 731 which had been scrapped not long previously. The last named had been the fourth Crewe engine to have borne it, its predecessors being an Allan 2-4-0 goods engine, from 1852; then a DX Ramsbottom goods and then a 'Samson' 2-4-0 from 1864. The 6 ft Jumbo that was scrapped just after the end of the First World War dated from 1889. *Croxteth* as a 'Claughton', carrying the post-Grouping number 5971, was the first ex-LNWR engine to be painted in the new red livery and the Locomotive Publishing Company produced one of their handsome coloured post cards by 'F. Moore'. On the West Coast route itself however it seems that this engine, far from being the flag-ship of the new era, was a source of annoyance to all Crewe men. The renumbering went on very slowly indeed in the early summer of 1926. I travelled in 'Claughton' hauled trains behind engines still carrying their old LNWR number plates, and when indeed the change was made the majority of the top line express engines remained black at first.

Nameless or not, when early in 1931 I went to Carlisle for a journey to Leeds I found the "Baby Scot" standing in Citadel station ready to take over the "Thames–Clyde Express" on its arrival from Glasgow. The load proved to be disappointingly light, only 270 tons tare, on the same schedule that Class 4 engines had been loaded up to 350 tons in the dynamometer car runs of 1923-5; and apart from a vigorous start to Lazonby the performance was of little

*The first of the rebuilt 3-cylinder 'Claughtons', originally known as "Baby Scots", No. 5902* Sir Frank Ree. *(British Railways)*

interest. But I determined to go again at the first opportunity, and a few weeks later, after an exhilarating weekend of mountain climbing and photography in the Lake District, I took the local train from Penrith to Carlisle once more. In Citadel station, in due course there backed down ready to take the up Scotch Express, not No. 5971, but, of all engines *Sir Gilbert Claughton*, certainly in red and magnificently burnished up, fit to work on a Royal Train! On the occasion the "Thames–Clyde Express" was heavier than previously, only one coach short of the Class 5 maximum of 340 tons on the 'limited load' timing, though the allowance from Carlisle to Leeds had been reduced by five minutes since I travelled behind No. 5971 on the same train.

On the second journey the running times of which are tabulated herewith, *Sir Gilbert Claughton* was very comfortably master of the job. The accelerated scheduled times were 21 minutes to Lazonby, 40 to Appleby, 69 to Ais Gill and 95 to Settle Junction, and apart from not being pressed at the start to keep the sharp initial timing to Lazonby, the work was excellent, and very quietly done even on the heaviest ascents. The fitting of the improved type of piston valves had been most advantageous. On the dynamometer car test runs with engine No. 6001 with the standard blast pipe, when the booked schedule time from Carlisle to Leeds was 144 minutes, the uphill times with trains loaded to almost exactly the same tare tonnage as hauled by No. 5900 on

*The second "Baby Scot", No. 5971, eventually named* Croxteth, *but nameless at first when rebuilt — here seen leaving Carlisle with the "Thames–Clyde Express", in 1931.* (Rail Archive Stephenson — F. R. Hebron)

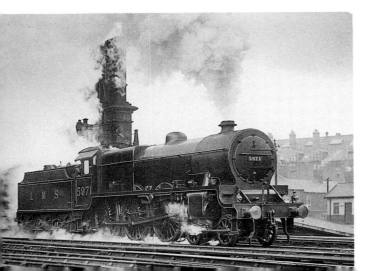

my own trip were:

|         | m  | s  | m  | s  |
|---------|----|----|----|----|
| Lazonby | 22 | 10 | 23 | 00 |
| Appleby | 38 | 07 | 39 | 42 |
| Ais Gill| 64 | 47 | 65 | 02 |

Against a booked passing time of 70 minutes at the summit, I have little doubt that the performance of No. 5900 on 8th August 1931 would have yielded a coal consumption of around 35 lb per mile. As to downhill speeds with the 'Claughtons' in contrast to the relatively moderate descents in the adjoining table, I have a record of the 2.42 pm up from Carlisle, when we had been delayed on the ascent to Ais Gill, when engine No. 5960 with a 330-ton load covered the 14 miles from Blea Moor down to Settle Junction in 11 min 17 sec, an average of 75 mph with a maximum of 88 mph near Horton.

Carlisle–Leeds: "The Thames–Clyde Express"

| Loads, tons/tare full: | | 270/290 | | 313/335 | |
|---|---|---|---|---|---|
| Engine No.: | | 5971 | | 5900 | |
| Engine Class: | | "Baby Scot" | | 'Claughton' | |
| Distance | | Actual | Speed | Actual | Speed |
| Miles | | m  s | mph | m  s | mph |
| 0.0 | Carlisle | 0  00 | — | 0  00 | — |
| 3.9 | Cumwhinton | 7  35 | 49½ | 8  20 | 44½ |
| 8.4 | Low House Box | 13  35 | 43½ | 14  55 | 39 |
| 10.0 | Armathwaite | 15  15 | 62½ | 16  45 | 58½ |
| — | Milepost 295 | — | 54½ | — | 52½ |
| 15.2 | Lazonby | 20  35 | 70½ | 22  30 | 68 |
| 19.7 | Langwathby | 24  37 | 57 | 26  42 | 55½ |
| 23.4 | Culgaith | 28  25 | 60 | 30  32 | 61 |
| 27.9 | Long Marton | 33  40 | 50 | 35  45 | 57 |
| 30.8 | Appleby | 37  25 | 41 | 39  05 | 48 |
| 33.2 | Ormside | 40  25 | 56 | 41  45 | 63½ |
| — | | p.w.s | 22 | — | — |
| 36.1 | Griseburn Box | 45  40 | — | 45  40 | 35½ |
| 38.3 | Crosby Garrett | 51  30 | 41 | 49  10 | 46 |
| 41.5 | Kirkby Stephen | 55  50 | — | 54  10 | 34½ |
| 44.8 | Mallerstang Box | 61  50 | 31 | 60  10 | 31/39 |
| 48.3 | Ais Gill Box | 68  40 | 27 | 66  02 | 34 |
| 51.4 | Hawes Junction | 72  35 | 59 | 69  45 | 61½ |
| 59.5 | Blea Moor Box | 81  25 | 53 | 78  27 | 54 |
| 65.5 | Horton | 87  15 | 66½ | 84  05 | 72 |
| | | | | | (max) |
| 73.5 | Settle Junction | 95  00 | easy | 91  20 | 70 |
| 76.8 | Hellifield | 99  50 | — | 94  35 | 52/46 |
| 83.1 | Gargrave | 107  50 | — | 101  15 | 66 |
| 86.8 | Skipton | 111  45 | — | 105  30 | — |
| — | | — | 67 | sigs | — |
| 96.0 | Keighley | 121  50 | 47 | 116  45 | — |
| — | | — | — | sigs | — |
| 102.0 | Shipley (Bingley Jc) | 128  55 | — | 125  45 | — |
| — | | — | — | sigs | — |
| 109.9 | Kirkstall | 139  25 | 66 | 135  10 | — |
| 113.0 | Leeds | 144  20 | — | 140  00 | — |
| | Net times min | 139½ | | 136 | |

# 13
# The Nineteen-Thirties

This chapter goes some way towards presenting a comprehensive review of working on the day-time expresses over the Settle and Carlisle in the 1930s. The new non-Midland locomotives were coming into use and with the Stanier 4-6-0's double-home workings were being introduced between Leeds and Glasgow. Indeed it was not confined to the new engines in some cases. In 1936 I travelled from Leeds when an unassisted 3-cylinder compound 4-4-0 worked through to Glasgow St Enoch. That my review is so comprehensive is due in large measure to the good offices of my friend Gerald Aston, who as a senior operating officer in the department of the Chief General Superintendent of the LMS, and then stationed at Derby, lost no

opportunity for a trip over the Settle and Carlisle line, always taking notes of the running in the fullest detail expected in the "British Locomotive Practice and Performance" articles in *The Railway Magazine*. He also accompanied the important trial runs made in October 1937 to test the feasibility of generally accelerated schedules on the Midland and G&SW routes. Mr Aston's runs, together with a few more of my own, have been grouped into three tables, relating to the "Thames–Forth Express" from Skipton, and to the 10.20 am and 4.30 pm departures from Leeds, in the last two cases covering the running from Hellifield northwards.

The "Thames–Forth Express", having a running average speed from Skipton to Carlisle

*An up express goods train leaving Rise Hill Tunnel, between Garsdale and Dent, with Class 4 0-6-0 No. 4190. (W. Hubert Foster)*

*An up Scotch Express near Long Marton with "Black Five" 4-6-0 No. 4847.* (W. Hubert Foster)

of 55.3 mph was considerably the fastest train over the route, though for most of the year it carried a relatively light load. It had the sharp uphill timing of 30 minutes for the 25.2 miles from Settle Junction to Ais Gill, compared with the 35 minutes allowed the afternoon Scotch Express and the 10.20 am from Leeds. In 1938 the "Thames–Forth" was further accelerated to a 90-minute run from Skipton to Carlisle, a remarkable average over such a route as 58 mph, but it was interesting to see that the quickening of the working times took place only north of Ais Gill, with the passing time at Appleby being 62 minutes and only 28 minutes for the last 30.8

miles into Carlisle. On the first run in the table with a compound, a load of less than 200 tons, and obviously a keen driver, the train was run virtually to the accelerated timing although the journey took place in June 1936. Nor should the first ten miles of the run from Skipton be forgotten because this initial stage includes eight miles of continuous climbing to Milepost $229\frac{3}{4}$, finishing at 1 in 132. The downhill length through Hellifield to Settle Junction was restricted as to maximum speed, and as the table shows the "Thames–Forth Express" seldom entered upon the 'Long Drag' at more than about 60 mph.

The compound, No. 1086, gave a very sound display. Beginning the climb at 62 mph the speed no more than briefly fell below 40 mph, although nearly a minute was dropped on the sharp uphill timing of 18 minutes for the 14 miles from Settle Junction to Blea Moor. A smart recovery followed on the tableland stretch to Garsdale, and Ais Gill was passed almost exactly on time at 60 mph. In column 2 of the table the 'Jubilee', No. 5636 *Uganda* was leaving Skipton five minutes late, but it would seem that the driver was not of a temperament to bestir himself and after a brisk start up the bank past Bell Busk, although having an almost superfluity of engine power as compared with the first run, he lost nearly two minutes between Settle Junction and Ais Gill. The third run was made in 1938 after the accelerations, but the "Black Five" still having a gross load of less than 200 tons did little better than the compound up the main bank. This train

*Pennine weather again: an ex-LNWR G2 class goods 0-8-0 on the water-troughs south of Garsdale, in pouring rain, 1938.* (Norman Wilkinson)

had left Skipton on time. The honours, so far as climbing the 'Long Drag', most fairly go to the compound, No. 931, in column 4. She was leaving Skipton two minutes late, and yet passed Blea Moor practically on time. The start uphill past Gargrave and Bell Busk was vigorous, and it was followed by a full-blooded charge at the 'Long Drag' with a maximum speed of 72 mph at Settle Junction. At no time on the ascent did speed fall below 41 mph and with a bracing recovery over the tableland section and a minimum of 62 mph over the summit, Ais Gill box was passed in the notable time of $44\frac{3}{4}$ minutes from Skipton.

In column 5 the same compound, with a somewhat heavier load was not so energetic, while leaving Skipton $5\frac{1}{2}$ minutes late. Nevertheless the performance was sound enough, keeping the fast uphill running time to Blea Moor and passing Ais Gill at 60 mph. The sixth run in the table was of my own timing, in the summer of 1938. I was bound for Inverness in a week's note-taking and railway photography, and from London I took the Midland route to Carlisle to clock the running of the accelerated "Thames–Forth Express" north of Leeds. To my disappointment, we were double-headed, presumably a pilot working home, because one could not imagine a "Black Five" needing assistance on this schedule with a tare load of less than 300 tons. After a signal check at Hellifield the two engines made merry up the bank, at no time falling below 45 mph and then gaining nearly a further minute between Blea Moor and Ais Gill, with a maximum speed of 69 mph at Lunds Viaduct just north of Garsdale station. The last run must have been disappointing to record. It was made on a Saturday in July 1937 with a heavy load, though not above the maximum tonnage for a compound piloted by a Class 2 superheater 4-4-0. Leaving Skipton 14 minutes late they were 19 minutes late on leaving Ais Gill after a rather leisurely stop of more than two minutes detaching the pilot at the summit.

On the downhill run to Carlisle, compound No. 1086 was taken on easy steam at first, not much exceeding 70 mph until Ormside was passed; but then there came a fine spurt down the lower Eden Valley, with sustained speeds of $77\frac{1}{2}$ mph towards Culgaith. But for the pronounced easing after Armathwaite the train would have been four minutes early into Carlisle. The 'Jubilee' by contrast gave a poor showing. If the driver had been so inclined the five minutes of lateness with which Skipton had been left could easily have been recovered, but instead the train was still three minutes late into Carlisle, without any checks on the way. The "Black Five" in column 3 was equally disappointing. They had come smartly down from Ais Gill and passed Appleby slightly ahead of the accelerated timing of the train from 1938, but then after Culgaith the effort was relaxed too much and Carlisle was reached nearly a minute late. The fourth run must have been an exhilarating experience to record. Having recovered the initial lateness on passing Ais Gill the men on No. 931 continued in tremen-

*An up Scotch Express arrives at Ais Gill Summit to detach its pilot, compound No. 1137.*
(W. Hubert Foster)

*Detaching the pilot. The fireman of the train engine, Class 5XP, 'Jubilee' 4-6-0 No. 5594* Bhopal, *secures the headlamps.* (W. Hubert Foster)

dous style and reached Carlisle three minutes early, having the notable average speed of 58.6 mph from Skipton. The same engine with a slightly heavier train was not so vigorously driven in the fifth run, though weather conditions were not so favourable this October day.

My own run with the double-headed train, column 6, began with a perfect riot of high speed, with 79 mph before Mallerstang, and 84 mph at Smardale Viaduct. Things were eased a little after Appleby, and the faircopy book, in which the rough notes I took on the actual journey were carefully transcribed, contains no record of the time of passing Lazonby. After a lapse of fifty years it is not surprising that the pocket book in which I made my immediate notes has disappeared and therefore there is no clue as to whether the passage of some ravishing blonde down the corridor, or some other distraction caused my momentary inattention from the job in hand! It seems that I was quickly on the ball again, because my fair-copy log records the passage, in 74 min 33 sec from Skipton of Milepost 295, at $54\frac{1}{2}$ mph! At this stage we were

*The 9.40 am Bamfurlong–Carlisle goods approaches Blea Moor, showing the curving line southwards to Ribblehead. Power is provided by No. 45451, a "Black Five" 4-6-0.* (I. S. Pearsall)

less than half a minute ahead of the times of that fire-eating compound; but having regard to the vigour with the two engines on my run, recovered from the ensuing signal check I have credited them with a net time of 87 minutes from Skipton and a net time of 'under even' to passing Scotby. On the last run the driver of engine No. 1149 having got rid of his ineffective Class 2 pilot did some good work with his heavy train and but for the relaying slack at Crosby Garrett no more time would have been lost — note 30 min 11 sec for the final 30.8 miles from Appleby into Carlisle.

The second tabulation relates to the 4.3 pm ex-Leeds from Hellifield onwards. The first run, with compound No. 1072 was recorded by Cecil J. Allen on a wintry day when Upper Ribblesdale was scourged in a blizzard of sleet and snow. It was not surprising that some time was lost to Ais Gill, but with the weather clearing afterwards some fast running was made down to Appleby, including a maximum speed of 85 mph at Ormside, and the last 30.8 miles into Carlisle took no more than 29 minutes, pass to stop. The second run, at the end of November 1932, was with one of the earliest "Baby Scots" to be converted at Crewe. By the time the train left Hellifield it was dark and Mr Aston took no maximum speeds except at Horton and Blea Moor. The running was good, and despite a permanent way caution near Lazonby they clocked into Carlisle $3\frac{1}{2}$ minutes early. The third run with one of the original 'Claughtons' was undelayed until the immediate approach to Carlisle, and the driver took things easily up the 'Long Drag' knowing that the free running capacity of his engine could make up the two minutes with which he had passed Ais Gill quite easily by Appleby. Speed twice attained 78 mph on the descent, and the running afterwards was of no particular note.

It is the 'Jubilee', No. 5598 *Basutoland* that claims the principal honours in this table, in column 4. They were leaving Hellifield seven minutes late, and were checked slightly by signals at Long Preston. But the ascent to Blea Moor was first class, gaining $2\frac{1}{2}$ minutes on this stretch alone, while this was followed by some fast running over the tableland attaining 71 mph beyond Garsdale and topping Ais Gill Summit at 62 mph. This driver went under easy steam to Appleby, falling as low as 50 mph through the

*The up "Thames–Clyde Express" approaching Ais Gill, with '5XP' 4-6-0 No. 5568.* (M. W. Earley)

station, but there were no half measures about the continuation with its maximum of 80 mph at Eden Lacy Viaduct. The net time on this fine run was no more than 81 minutes. The 'Claughton', No. 6005 in column 5 made one of the fastest overall times in the table, with an entire absence of delays, a good climb to Blea Moor and fast running below Mallerstang. The arrival in Carlisle was nearly four minutes early. I am sorry to finish with a failure. Run No. 6 in the table was made just after Christmas 1934, and the less said about it the better! It started 30 minutes late from Hellifield, and although not carrying the 'Claughton' load of 340 tons tare, five minutes were lost on schedule between Settle Junction and Blea Moor and a further minute was dropped on to Ais Gill. Some amends were made on the descent, but the train arrived in Carlisle 34 minutes late — a black mark for "Baby Scots" on that occasion.

Coming now to the morning express from Leeds, the first run was made in September 1938, after the schedule had been markedly accelerated from the actual times tabulated for the rest of the runs. The later working times were 23 min to Blea Moor, 35 min to Ais Gill, and 52 min to Appleby, and these, the "Baby Scot" with no more than a moderate load, observed easily. The engine in question was actually the same as featuring in column 2 of the table. The latter run

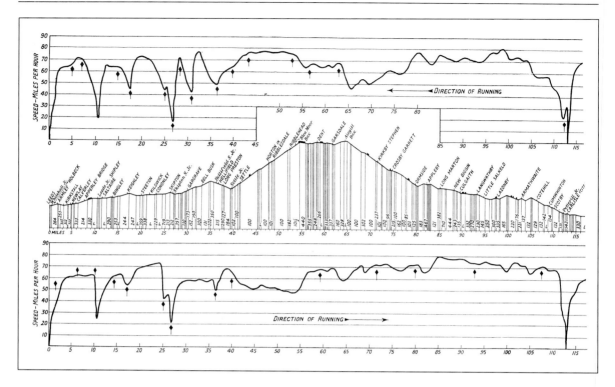

was made in 1933 not long after the engine had been converted from the original 'Claughton', in this particular case at Derby. At the time of Mr Aston's run the renumbered engine, 5535 was carrying the name of *Sir Herbert Walker KCB*. This name was originally allotted to one of the third batch of 'Claughtons' built at Crewe in 1916, in honour of he, who was not only the distinguished General Manager of the London & South Western Railway, and himself a former LNWR officer, but in the war years he was Chairman of the Railway Executive Committee. The engine named after him became No. 5926 in the LMS list, and it was converted to a "Baby Scot" bearing the same number. Later, when this engine was renamed *Stephenson*, the name *Sir Herbert Walker KCB* was transferred to No. 5535 previously No. 5997 and unnamed in the LNWR list.

Named or not, engine No. 5535 made short work of the 'Long Drag', doing well over 40 mph all the way up until just before entering Blea Moor Tunnel, when no doubt the steaming was eased. They romped their way across the table-land, and with a smart descent clocked into Appleby two minutes early, having achieved

the notable start-to-stop average from Hellifield of 55.2 mph. The same engine, when numbered 5997, was running 22 minutes late from the start, but in wintry November weather made a good run. Speed tailed off to 32 mph at Ribblehead, but some fast running was made across to Ais Gill, and by Appleby five minutes of the late start had been regained. The third run was one of my own timing. At Leeds I was interested to learn that by then in the summer of 1937 through engine workings between Leeds and Glasgow had been instituted, though in the present case with the engine remanned at Carlisle. The particular engine, compound No. 1066, had covered itself with glory at the time of the dynamometer trials of 1925, but I gathered from the driver she was not too good and at Hellifield finding that the increased load by attachment of the Manchester portion was 282 tons, he had asked for a pilot. The compound load for this booking was then 270 tons, but no pilot was available.

On this occasion my wife and I were travelling to the West Highland for a week on the steamers in Hebridean seas, but as we headed into North Ribblesdale the weather became terrible. For some reason we were stopped briefly at Settle, and we left in torrents of thundery rain, which continued until we were some way north of Blea Moor Tunnel. In such conditions with an engine then not reputedly in the best of condition the driver did very well. From the dead start at Settle on the 1 in 100 gradient speed slowly mounted to 28 mph and at Helwith Bridge it increased smartly to 35 mph before Horton, and then in the teeth of the storm fell back to $27\frac{1}{2}$ mph before Ribblehead. The average speed of 30.8 mph between Helwith Bridge and Blea Moor was very credible in such conditions. Once past Ais Gill some fast running was made down to Appleby, with a maximum speed of $80\frac{1}{2}$ mph at Ormside. The last two runs were worked by unrebuilt 'Claughtons' with the normal rake of coaches heavily reinforced to provide for pre-Bank Holiday traffic and piloted in each case by ex-Midland Class 2 superheater 4-4-0s. On run No. 5 I was travelling from Manchester, and arriving at Victoria station to find the 9.20 am express made up entirely of coaches for Scottish destinations and totalling up to a tare load of 262 tons I realised that the Manchester portion of the main train, usually not more than two coaches, would have to be run as a separate train from Hellifield. So it proved, and I alighted and waited for the train from Leeds.

Mr Aston's run in column 4 was his first ever on the Settle and Carlisle line, and he did not make many notes of speed on the ascent to Blea Moor. Judging from a comparison with the times of my own run, column 5, it would seem as though they got away from Hellifield pretty smartly, attaining 66 to 67 mph at Settle Junction, and not going below 50 at Settle itself. The gain in time to Blea Moor was advantageous to offset the effects of the permanent way check near Garsdale which cost about $2\frac{1}{2}$ minutes. On my own run, when we had a very heavy and crowded train, with many passengers standing in the corridors, the two engines made a full blooded ascent of the 'Long Drag', never falling below $34\frac{1}{2}$ mph and going on over the tableland to pass Ais Gill two minutes inside schedule time at 60 mph. Neither Mr Aston's train nor mine stopped to detach their bank engines. The first of these ran fairly easily after Kirkby Stephen but *Sir Thomas Williams* and his pilot ran harder, and cut $5\frac{1}{2}$ minutes off the working time from Hellifield to Appleby. The Class 2 4-4-0 continued to Carlisle on run No. 4, but on my run the 'Claughton' continued on its own with the 470-ton load.

The 30.8 mile run from Appleby to Carlisle usually provided some fast running, especially on the first run in the table, on the accelerated timing of 30 minutes start to stop, averaging 61.6 mph. Engine No. 5535 *Sir Herbert Walker KCB* ran appropriately hard, reaching even time from the start as early as Langwathby, a maximum of $86\frac{1}{2}$ mph at Eden Lacy Viaduct, and passing Scotby in good time to make an early arrival in Carlisle by $1\frac{1}{2}$ minutes at least, a net average of 65 mph start to stop. But the engine in her original numbered state, and nameless, was

*'Patriot' Class 4-6-0 No. 5538* Giggleswick. *(See following chapter for further notes on this locomotive.)*
(British Railways)

*Amid the High Pennines: The 10.18 am express from Leeds to Glasgow St Enoch just after leaving Rise Hill Tunnel and approaching Garsdale water-troughs, hauled by ex-LNWR 'Claughton' class 4-6-0 No. 5932* Sir Thomas Williams. *(From a water colour by Paul Gribble)*

almost as fast in column 2, though running on a schedule of 32 minutes. Compound No. 1066, having drawn away from the dreadful thundery weather centred on North Ribblesdale and the High Pennines, ran smartly enough down to Carlisle, and but for the seemingly inevitable signal check at the finish would have gained nearly one minute on schedule. I may add that the fresh driver who took the engine over at Carlisle

did not do so well on the run to St Enoch.

On the fourth run in the table 'Claughton' No. 5984 and her pilot set off from Appleby as though they were going to make a 30-minute run to Carlisle, with a maximum of 79 mph at Eden Lacy Viaduct, and even time before Lazonby. Mr Aston did not record any speeds north of the latter station, but by comparison with the time of the other runs, I judge that the

*The "Thames–Forth Express" crossing the Lunds embankment after passing Garsdale, with compound No. 931. (From a water colour by Paul Gribble)*

minimum at Milepost 295 cannot have been less than 60 mph, and the maximum at Armathwaite at least 70. In column 5 *Sir Thomas Williams*, now with 470 tons unaided, did very well. The 17.9 miles of no more than easy descent from Long Marton to Armathwaite were covered in 16 min 20 sec at an average speed of 66.7 mph, and with a smart finish down from Low House the driver should have been able to maintain the 32-minutes booked time, despite the 470-ton load, but for the final signal check.

The preliminaries to the accelerated timings worked on run 6 in the "Thames–Forth" table,

Experimental Run, 13th October 1937: Leeds–Carlisle
Engine: Class 5XP 4-6-0 No. 5660 Rooke
Load: 9 coaches (including dynamometer car)
302 tons tare, 305 tons full

| Distance Miles | | Sch min | Actual m  s | Speeds mph |
|---|---|---|---|---|
| 0.0 | Leeds | 0 | 0  00 | — |
| 4.6 | Newlay | | 7  24 | 61 |
| 10.7 | Shipley (Leeds Jc) | 14 | 13  44 | 22* |
| 17.0 | Keighley | 21 | 21  11 | — |
| 23.1 | Cononley | | 26  45 | 72 |
| — | | | p.w.s. | |
| 26.2 | Skipton | 30 | 30  22 | 18 |
| — | | | p.w.s. | |
| 29.9 | Gargrave | | 35  09 | 58 |
| 34.7 | Milepost $229\frac{3}{4}$ | | 40  12 | 54 |
| 36.2 | Hellifield | 42 | 41  49 | 46* |
| 39.5 | Settle Jc | 45 | 45  00 | 63 |
| 41.4 | Settle | | 47  00 | 55/50 |
| 47.4 | Horton | | 54  00 | 53/51 |
| 52.2 | Ribblehead | | 59  43 | 47/49 |
| 53.4 | Blea Moor Box | 63 | 61  20 | 46 |
| 58.3 | Dent | | 66  35 | 63 |
| 61.6 | Garsdale | | 69  34 | 68 |
| 64.6 | Ais Gill Box | 75 | 72  34 | 55 |
| 71.5 | Kirkby Stephen | | 78  51 | 71 |
| 74.7 | Crosby Garrett | | 81  34 | 66 |
| 79.7 | Ormside | | 86  03 | 71 |
| 82.2 | Appleby | 90 | 88  15 | 63 |
| 85.1 | Long Marton | | 90  42 | 79 |
| 88.3 | New Biggin | | 93  11 | 75 |
| 93.2 | Langwathby | | 97  12 | 70 |
| 97.5 | Lazonby | | 100  48 | 72 |
| 99.9 | Milepost 295 | | — | 64 |
| 103.0 | Armathwaite | | 105  30 | 75 |
| 104.6 | Low House Box | | 106  51 | 62 |
| 106.2 | Cotehill | | 108  19 | 71 |
| 110.3 | Scotby | | 111  53 | 66 |
| 112.1 | Petteril Bridge Jc | 115 | 113  58 | 20* |
| 113.0 | Carlisle | 117 | 117  00 | — |

*Speed restrictions

Experimental Run, 14th October 1937: Carlisle–Leeds
Engine: Class 5XP No. 5660 Rooke
Load: 9 coaches (including dynamometer car)
302 tons tare, 305 tons full

| Distance Miles | | Sch min | Actual m  s | Speeds mph |
|---|---|---|---|---|
| 0.0 | Carlisle | 0 | 0  00 | — |
| 0.9 | Petteril Bridge Jc | 3 | 2  21 | — |
| 2.7 | Scotby | | 5  10 | 46 |
| 6.8 | Cotehill | | 9  51 | 56 |
| 8.4 | Low House Box | | 11  31 | 55 |
| 10.0 | Armathwaite | | 12  55 | 74 |
| 13.1 | Milepost 295 | | 15  32 | 69 |
| 15.5 | Lazonby | 19 | 17  26 | $80\frac{1}{2}$ |
| 19.8 | Langwathby | | 20  59 | 62/72 |
| 24.7 | New Biggin | | 25  10 | 69 |
| 27.9 | Long Marton | | 27  48 | 75 |
| 30.8 | Appleby | 35 | 30  20 | 67 |
| 33.3 | Ormside | | 32  21 | $77\frac{1}{2}$ |
| 38.3 | Crosby Garrett | | 37  10 | 58 |
| 41.5 | Kirkby Stephen | | 40  25 | 54 |
| 44.9 | Mallerstang Box | | 44  18 | 48/53 |
| 48.4 | Ais Gill Box | 59 | 48  36 | $46\frac{1}{2}$ |
| 51.4 | Garsdale | | 51  33 | 69 |
| 54.7 | Dent | | 54  41 | 67 |
| 59.6 | Blea Moor Box | 70 | 59  14 | 71 |
| 65.6 | Horton | | 64  04 | $76\frac{1}{2}$ (max) |
| 73.5 | Settle Jc | 82 | 70  44 | — |
| 76.8 | Hellifield | 85 | 74  08 | — |
| — | | | p.w.s. | — |
| 86.8 | Skipton | 96 | 85  13 | — |
| 102.3 | Shipley Leeds Jc | 112 | 101  56 | — |
| — | | | — | |
| 113.0 | Leeds | 125 | 115  38 | — |

and No. 1 in relating to the 10.20 am from Leeds took the form of a very strenuous four days of running in October 1937 with one '5XP' 'Jubilee' class 4-6-0, No. 5660 *Rooke*, from Bristol to Glasgow and back via the Midland and G&SW route. The special train which carried no ordinary passengers included the Horwich dynamometer car, but no indicator diagrams were taken. Mr Aston clocked the running on all four days, and the official logs, of which the sections between Leeds and Carlisle are tabulated herewith were prepared as a result of his observations. It is important to emphasise that while some very hard running was made on certain parts of the route no attempt was made to establish record times, and indeed the most scrupulous attention was paid to observance of the permanent speed restrictions on the route, and there were many

Details of uphill performance

| Section of Route | Settle–Blea Moor | Ormside–Ais Gill |
|---|---|---|
| Length of ascent | 14.0 miles | 14.9 miles |
| Av Drawbar Horsepower | 1129 | 1054 |
| Max Drawbar Horsepower | 1240 | 1133 |
| Max Indicated Horsepower (calculated) | 1844 | 1773 |
| Av speed of ascent (mph) | 53.6 | 56.0 |
| Cut-off range (per cent) | 35 | 35–40 |
| Boiler pressure (psi) | 225 | 225 |

Coal and water consumption

| Date | 13th October | 14th October |
|---|---|---|
| Journey | Leeds to Glasgow | Glasgow to Leeds |
| Distance, miles | 228.5 | 228.5 |
| Actual running times (min) | 243.6 | 241.3 |
| Average speed (mph) | 56.3 | 56.8 |
| Schedule time (min) | 243.0 | 253.0 |
| Fastest time then booked (min) | 262.0 | 270.0 |
| Coal consumption (excluding shed duties) | | |
| lb per mile | 42.7 | 43.6 |
| lb per dhp hour | 3.93 | 3.87 |
| lb per sq ft of grate | 77.7 | 80.2 |
| Water consumption (excluding shed duties) | | |
| gal per mile | 29.7 | 28.8 |
| lb per dhp hour | 27.3 | 25.8 |
| Evaporation | | |
| lb of water per lb coal | 6.94 | 6.58 |

of those between Leeds and Settle Junction. The outstanding feature of these runs was the hill climbing between Settle Junction and Blea Moor on the down journey, and the phenomenally sustained effort from Scotby throughout to Ais Gill on the following day, by which the summit was passed in no more than a few seconds over 'even time' from the dead start! The logs are worthy of the closest study. See speed chart on page 134.

Naturally such working involved some very hard work on the footplate, and the official report published in *The Railway Gazette* a month after the trials concerning the actual engine working, and details covering the running between Leeds and Carlisle are tabulated herewith.

The coal consumption figures published related to the full days running on each of the four days, so that it is not possible to isolate those for the Leeds-Carlisle section, but in relation to the work done the coal consumption seems not to have

*The "Thames–Clyde Express" passing Arten Gill Viaduct, hauled by "Baby Scot" 4-6-0 then numbered 5982. (From a water colour by Paul Gribble)*

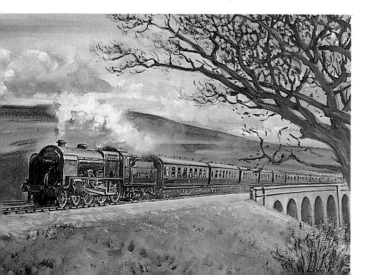

been inordinately high.

In the Locomotive Department at Derby Headquarters much satisfaction was felt that one of the 5XP 4-6-0s could, if pressed, surpass the maximum horsepower figures published for the Great Western 'Castle' class, with which Stanier had been closely associated before he came to the LMS. In the 1924 trials of *Caldicot Castle*, between leaving Taunton and the approach to Whiteball Tunnel, with full regulator and 30 per cent cut-off the maximum indicated horsepower was a little under 1,600, compared with *Rooke*'s 1,773 and 1,844 on the Settle and Carlisle ascents, at much the same speeds. Of course the latter could be regarded as a 'one-off job', much the same as with the 'Claughton' *Ralph Brocklebank* in 1913, which registered a little under 1,700 indicated horsepower going up Shap. One-offs apart, in 1937 the crew of *Rooke*, Driver North and Fireman George of Leeds, and their Bristol colleagues who worked the test train in both directions south of Leeds set up a classic of locomotive performance that was not surpassed in steam days. Although there is no mention of it in the official report, there would undoubtedly have been a locomotive running inspector on the footplate, and probably also Frank Sutherland, the Chief Testing Engineer in the Locomotive Department, who rode on the most important trials in those pre-war days.

Skipton–Carlisle: The "Thames–Forth Express"

| Run No. | | | 1 | | | 2 | | | 3 | | | 4 | | | 5 | | | 6 | | | 7 | | |
|---|---|---|---|---|---|---|---|---|---|---|---|---|---|---|---|---|---|---|---|---|---|---|---|
| Engine No. | | | 1086 | | | 5636 | | | 5067 | | | 931 | | | 931 | | | 5155 | | | | | |
| Engine Class | | | 4P | | | "Jubilee" | | | 5P5F | | | 4P | | | 4P | | | 5P5F | | | 1149 | | |
| Pilot Engine No. | | | — | | | — | | | — | | | — | | | — | | | 1098 | | | 484* | | |
| Pilot Engine Class | | | — | | | — | | | — | | | — | | | — | | | 4P | | | 2P | | |
| Load tons tare | | | 166 | | | 168 | | | 178 | | | 199 | | | 212 | | | 291 | | | 354 | | |
| Load tons full | | | 175 | | | 175 | | | 195 | | | 210 | | | 225 | | | 315 | | | 375 | | |
| Distance Miles | | Sch min | m | s | mph | m | s | mph | m | s | mph | m | s | mph | m | s | mph | m | s | mph | m | s | mph |
| 0.0 | Skipton | 0 | 0 | 00 | — | 0 | 00 | — | 0 | 00 | — | 0 | 00 | — | 0 | 00 | — | 0 | 00 | — | 0 | 00 | — |
| 3.7 | Gargrave | | 5 | 42 | 51 | 5 | 33 | 53½ | 5 | 33 | 50 | 5 | 25 | 53 | 5 | 25 | — | 5 | 11 | 54½ | 6 | 07 | 44 |
| 6.6 | Bell Busk | | 9 | 09 | | 8 | 41 | 55 | 9 | 00 | 52 | 8 | 45 | — | 9 | 25 | 51 | 8 | 14 | 60 | 9 | 56 | 48 |
| — | | | — | | 48½ | — | | 49 | — | | 46 | — | | 50 | — | | 50 | sigs | | — | — | | 44 |
| 10.0 | Hellifield | 14 | 13 | 08 | 58 | 12 | 36 | 60 | 13 | 03 | 59 | 12 | 37 | 60 | 13 | 21 | 62 | 12 | 42 | — | 14 | 15 | 56 |
| 13.3 | Settle Junction | 17 | 16 | 27 | 62 | 15 | 46 | 62 | 16 | 09 | 66 | 15 | 31 | 72 | 16 | 22 | 66½ | 16 | 15 | 67 | 17 | 26 | 65 |
| 15.2 | Settle | | 18 | 33 | 53 | 17 | 55 | 49 | 18 | 20 | 48 | 17 | 26 | 56 | 18 | 21 | 54½ | 18 | 12 | 55 | 19 | 38 | 48 |
| 19.6 | Helwith Bridge | | 24 | 25 | 42 | 24 | 03 | 39½ | 24 | 17 | 43 | 22 | 56 | 45 | 23 | 59 | 43 | 23 | 46 | 45 | 26 | 27 | 36 |
| 21.3 | Horton | | 26 | 38 | 45 | 26 | 18 | 45 | 26 | 26 | 47 | 25 | 02 | 47 | 26 | 06 | 47 | 25 | 56 | 49 | 28 | 47 | 43 |
| 26.0 | Ribblehead | | 33 | 32 | 39½ | 33 | 14 | 39 | 33 | 04 | 41 | 31 | 31 | 41 | 32 | 46 | — | 32 | 06 | 45 | 35 | 42 | 40 |
| — | | | — | | 43½ | — | | 41½ | — | | 46 | — | | 43 | — | | 40 | — | | 47 | — | | 42 |
| 27.3 | Blea Moor Box | 35 | 35 | 20 | 42 | 35 | 08 | 39½ | 34 | 51 | 43 | 33 | 19 | 41 | 34 | 41 | 39 | 33 | 44 | 45½ | 37 | 34 | 41 |
| 32.2 | Dent | | 40 | 58 | 62 | 41 | 05 | 58 | 40 | 16 | 65 | 38 | 56 | 64 | 40 | 51 | — | 39 | 05 | 64½ | 43 | 23 | 58 |
| 35.4 | Garsdale | | 44 | 03 | 63 | 44 | 21 | 61 | 43 | 27 | 66 | 41 | 59 | 66½ | 44 | 11 | 64 | 42 | 09 | 69 | 46 | 39 | 67 |
| 38.5 | Ais Gill Box | 47 | 46 | 57 | 60 | 47 | 29 | 55 | 46 | 26 | 58 | 44 | 45 | 62 | 47 | 06 | 60 | 44 | 55 | 62 | 50 | 07 | |
| | | | | | | | | | | | | | | | | | | | | | 52 | 13 | |
| 42.0 | Mallerstang Box | | 50 | 06 | 72 | 50 | 54 | 66 | 49 | 30 | 75 | 47 | 46 | 75 | 50 | 20 | 72 | 47 | 59 | 79 | 57 | 35 | 66½ |
| 45.3 | Kirkby Stephen | | 52 | 58 | 71 | 53 | 44 | 73 | 52 | 13 | 74 | 50 | 26 | 78 | 53 | 08 | 75 | 50 | 29 | 75 | 60 | 25 | 76½ |
| — | | | — | | | — | | | — | | | — | | | — | | | — | | 84 | p.w.s. | | 32 |
| 48.5 | Crosby Garrett | | 55 | 41 | 70 | 56 | 25 | 66 | 54 | 56 | 66 | 52 | 59 | 75 | 55 | 44 | 65 | 52 | 52 | 75½ | 63 | 41 | — |
| 53.6 | Ormside | | 60 | 11 | 73 | 60 | 58 | 73 | 59 | 19 | 76½ | 57 | 19 | 72 | 60 | 08 | 72 | 56 | 52 | 82 | 69 | 20 | 72 |
| 56.0 | Appleby | 64 | 62 | 22 | 64 | 63 | 10 | 62 | 61 | 29 | 62 | 59 | 37 | 60 | 62 | 27 | 58 | 58 | 55 | 65 | 71 | 39 | 58 |
| 58.9 | Long Marton | | 64 | 50 | 77 | 65 | 55 | 68 | 64 | 22 | 65 | 62 | 09 | 75 | 65 | 19 | 66½ | 61 | 30 | 75 | 74 | 31 | 69 |
| 63.4 | Culgaith | | 68 | 24 | 77½ | 69 | 58 | 68 | 68 | 13 | 77½ | 65 | 47 | 75 | 69 | 28 | 69 | 65 | 20 | 69 | 78 | 43 | 67 |
| 67.1 | Langwathby | | 71 | 17 | 72 | 73 | 08 | 66 | 71 | 11 | 66 | 68 | 45 | 69 | 72 | 40 | 75 | 68 | 29 | 67 | 81 | 58 | 64 |
| — | | | — | | 71½ | — | | 76½ | — | | 69 | — | | 72 | — | | | — | | 74½ | — | | 70 |
| 71.4 | Lazonby | | 74 | 44 | 73 | 76 | 44 | 68 | 75 | 01 | 68 | 72 | 25 | 69 | 76 | 23 | 69 | — | | 66 | 85 | 51 | 64 |
| — | | | — | | 65 | — | | 54 | — | | 60 | — | | 54½ | — | | 56 | — | | 54½ | — | | 54 |
| 76.8 | Armathwaite | | 79 | 30 | 72 | 82 | 04 | 65 | 79 | 59 | 73 | 77 | 51 | 64 | 81 | 36 | 69 | 77 | 29 | 69 | 91 | 25 | 64 |
| 78.4 | Low House Box | | 80 | 52 | 61 | 83 | 29 | 62 | 81 | 26 | 58 | 79 | 22 | 56 | 83 | 01 | 64 | sigs | | 25 | 92 | 55 | 55 |
| — | | | easy | | | — | | 72 | — | | 75 | — | | | — | | | — | | — | — | | — |
| 84.1 | Scotby | | 86 | 23 | 58 | 88 | 28 | 69 | 86 | 30 | 69 | 84 | 35 | 69 | 87 | 56 | 69 | 85 | 39 | 72 | 98 | 00 | 73 |
| — | | | — | | | — | | | — | | | — | | | sigs | | | sigs | | | — | | |
| 86.8 | Carlisle | 94 | 91 | 02 | | 92 | 14 | | 90 | 50 | | 89 | 04 | | 93 | 42 | | 94 | 47 | | 101 | 50 | |
| Net times (min) | | | 91 | | | 92¼ | | | 90¾ | | | 89 | | | 92½ | | | 87 | | | 99¾ | | |

*Pilot to Ais Gill only

Hellifield–Carlisle: the 4.3 pm ex-Leeds

| Run No. | 1 | 2 | 3 | 4 | 5 | 6 |
|---|---|---|---|---|---|---|
| Engine No. | 1072 | 5992 | 6012 | 5598 | 6005 | 5534 |
| Engine Class | 4P | "Baby Scot" | "Claughton" | "Jubilee" | "Claughton" | "Baby Scot" |
| Load tons tare | 247 | 266 | 296 | 298 | 304 | 332 |
| Load tons full | 260 | 280 | 315 | 315 | 320 | 350 |

| Distance Miles | | Sch min | 1 m | s | mph | 2 m | s | mph | 3 m | s | mph | 4 m | s | mph | 5 m | s | mph | 6 m | s | mph |
|---|---|---|---|---|---|---|---|---|---|---|---|---|---|---|---|---|---|---|---|---|
| 0.0 | Hellifield | 0 | 0 | 00 | | 0 | 00 | | 0 | 00 | | 0 | 00 | | 0 | 00 | | 0 | 00 | |
| 1.2 | Long Preston | | 4 | 45 | 62½ | 2 | 40 | | 2 | 40 | 60 | 2 | 51 | 51 | 2 | 35 | 64 | 2 | 52 | |
| 3.3 | Settle Junction | | 6 | 50 | 45 | 4 | 50 | | 4 | 55 | 45 | 5 | 24 | 53 | 4 | 45 | 45 | 5 | 04 | |
| 5.2 | Settle | 5 | | | | 7 | 05 | | 7 | 10 | 32 | 7 | 30 | 39 | 6 | 55 | 30 | 7 | 21 | |
| 9.6 | Helwith Bridge Box | | | | 31½ | 14 | 00 | 41 | 14 | 40 | 37½ | 13 | 38 | 45 | 14 | 40 | 37½ | 15 | 38 | 28 |
| 11.3 | Horton | | 16 | 45 | 37½ | 16 | 25 | | 17 | 30 | 31 | 15 | 54 | 38 | 17 | 20 | 36 | 18 | 42 | 31 |
| 16.0 | Ribblehead | | 25 | 30 | 33 | 23 | 30 | | 26 | 05 | 31½ | 22 | 49 | 40 | 25 | 20 | 39 | 29 | 12 | 26½ |
| — | | | | | 37½ | | | 33 | | | | | | 36 | | | | | | |
| 17.3 | Blea Moor Box | 27 | 27 | 35 | 34½ | 25 | 32 | | 28 | 20 | | 24 | 50 | | 27 | 30 | 34 | 32 | 00 | 30 |
| 22.2 | Dent | | 34 (p.w.s.) | 29 | | 32 | 25 | | 35 | 45 | | 30 | 54 | 61 | 34 | 00 | 54½ | 39 | 38 | |
| 25.4 | Garsdale | | 38 | 10 | 57 | 35 | 40 | | 38 | 40 | | 33 | 54 | 71 | 37 | 25 | 60 | 43 | 10 | |
| 28.5 | Ais Gill Box | 40 | 41 | 50 | 43½ | 38 | 40 | | 42 | 05 | | 36 | 54 | 62 | 41 | 00 | 45 | 46 | 14 | 56 |
| 32.0 | Mallerstang Box | | | | | 41 (p.w.s.) | 50 | | 45 | 30 | 66½ | 41 (p.w.s.) | 29 | 28 | 44 | 25 | 69 | 49 | 32 | |
| 35.3 | Kirkby Stephen | | 48 | 35 | | 44 | 40 | | 48 | 25 | 78 | 44 | 44 | 59 | 47 | 10 | 72 | 52 | 20 | 74 |
| 38.5 | Crosby Garrett | | 51 | 15 | 82 | 47 | 25 | | 51 | 00 | 69 | 47 | 36 | 68 | 49 | 45 | | 55 | 57 | 71 |
| 43.6 | Ormside | | 54 | 55 | 85 | 51 | 55 | | 55 | 10 | 78 | 52 | 20 | 64 | 53 | 55 | 78 | 59 | 25 | |
| 46.0 | Appleby | 57 | 57 | 00 | 65 | 54 | 30 | | 57 | 15 | 64 | 54 | 46 | 50 | 56 | 05 | | 62 (p.w.s.) | 27 | |
| 48.9 | Long Marton | | 59 | 35 | 76½ | 57 | 45 | | 59 | 55 | 69 | 57 | 38 | 71 | 58 | 40 | 75 | 66 | 13 | |
| 53.4 | Culgaith | | 63 | 20 | 74 | 62 | 00 | | 64 | 05 | 66½ | 61 | 33 | 70 | 62 | 35 | 69 | 70 | 16 | 73 |
| 57.1 | Langwathby | | 66 | 25 | 67 | 64 | 55 | | 67 | 25 | 60 | 64 | 28 | 75 | 65 | 45 | 69 | 73 | 11 | 70 |
| — | | | | | | | | | | | 69 | | | 80 | | | 59½ | | | |
| 61.4 | Lazonby | | 70 | 00 | 75 | 69 (p.w.s.) | 40 | | 71 | 25 | 60 | 67 | 50 | 75 | 69 | 20 | 69 | 76 | 37 | 77 |
| 66.8 | Armathwaite | | 75 | 30 | 67 | 75 | 00 | | 76 | 55 | 62 | 72 | 36 | 64 | 74 | 40 | 66½ | 81 | 32 | 72 |
| 68.4 | Low House Box | | | | 55 | 76 | 00 | | 78 | 25 | 56 | 73 | 55 | 73 | 76 | 05 | 60 | 82 | 54 | 67 |
| — | | | | | 72 | | | | sigs | | | sigs | | | | | 75 | | | |
| 74.1 | Scotby | | 82 | 10 | 70 | 81 | 00 | | 83 | 50 | 64 | 78 | 50 | 66 | 81 | 10 | | 88 | 04 | |
| 76.8 | Carlisle | 89 | 86 | 00 | | 85 | 30 | | 88 | 40 | | 84 | 24 | | 85 | 10 | | 93 | 07 | |
| | Net times | | | 85 | | | 83¾ | | | 88 | | | 81 | | | 85¼ | | | 91 | |

## Hellifield–Carlisle: the 10.20 am ex-Leeds

| Run No. | 1 | 2 | 3 | 4 | 5 |
|---|---|---|---|---|---|
| Engine No. | 5535 | 5997 | 1066 | 5984 | 5932 |
| Engine Class | "Baby Scot" | "Baby Scot" | 4P | "Claughton" | "Claughton" |
| Pilot Engine | — | — | — | 471 | 458* |
| Pilot Class | — | — | — | 2P | 2P |
| Load tons tare | 239 | 251 | 282 | 415 | 433 |
| Load tons full | 255 | 265 | 300 | 435 | 470 |

| Distance Miles | | Sch min | 1 m s | 1 mph | 2 m s | 2 mph | 3 m s | 3 mph | 4 m s | 4 mph | 5 m s | 5 mph |
|---|---|---|---|---|---|---|---|---|---|---|---|---|
| 0.0 | Hellifield | 0 | 0 00 | — | 0 00 | — | 0 00 | — | 0 00 | — | 0 00 | — |
| 1.2 | Long Preston | | 2 28 | 52½ | 2 29 | — | 3 03 | 46 | 2 40 | — | 2 35 | — |
| 3.3 | Settle Junction | 5 | 4 27 | 68 | 4 38 | 64 | 5 28 | 61 | 4 45 | — | 4 45 | 66 |
| 5.2 | Settle | | 6 21 | 57 | 6 44 | 50 | 8 08 | — | 6 45 | — | 6 50 | 51 |
| — | | | | | | | 8 41 | | | | | |
| 9.6 | Helwith Bridge | | 12 02 | 44 | 13 34 | 36 | 20 31 | 28 | 13 00 | — | 13 35 | 35 |
| 11.3 | Horton | | 14 07 | 48 | 16 05 | 41 | 23 39 | 35 | 15 40 | 38 | 16 05 | 41 |
| 16.0 | Ribblehead | | 20 37 | 41 | 24 13 | 32 | 33 03 | 27½ | 23 15 | 36 | 23 45 | 34½ |
| — | | | | 44 | | | | 33½ | | | | 37½ |
| 17.3 | Blea Moor Box | 27 | 22 28 | 37½ | 26 25 | 33 | 35 31 | 30 | 25 20 | — | 25 50 | 36 |
| 20.2 | Dent | | 28 28 | 58 | 32 46 | 60 | 42 53 | 50 | 31 35 | 58 | 31 55 | 60 |
| — | | | | | | | | | | p.w.r. | | |
| 25.4 | Garsdale | | 31 36 | 70 | 35 46 | 69 | 46 33 | 61 | 36 25 | — | 35 05 | 69 |
| 28.5 | Ais Gill Box | 40 | 34 26 | 61 | 38 33 | 60 | 49 55 | 51½ | 40 00 | — | 37 55 | 60 |
| 32.0 | Mallerstang Box | | 37 35 | 72 | 41 44 | 75 | 53 16 | 72½ | 43 25 | 75 | 41 10 | 72 |
| 35.3 | Kirkby Stephen | | 40 21 | 75 | 44 33 | 75 | 56 00 | 76½ | 46 20 | 68 | 44 00 | 69 |
| 38.5 | Crosby Garrett | | 42 59 | 69 | 47 29 | — | 58 34 | 72½ | 49 20 | — | 46 40 | 75 |
| — | | | | | | | | 69 | | | | 67 |
| 43.6 | Ormside | | 47 19 | 75 | 52 14 | 75 | 62 45 | 80½ | 54 05 | — | 51 15 | easy |
| 46.0 | Appleby | 60 | 49 59 | — | 54 58 | — | 65 16 | — | 56 55 | — | 54 30 | — |
| 2.9 | Long Marton | | 4 33 | 65 | 4 29 | 64 | 5 00 | 61 | 4 25 | 64 | 5 00 | 60 |
| 7.4 | Culgaith | | 8 22 | 78 | 8 22 | 78 | 9 16 | 69 | 8 40 | 70 | 9 15 | 70½ |
| 11.0 | Langwathby | | 11 04 | 80 | 11 08 | 75 | 12 30 | 67 | 11 35 | 70 | 12 25 | 67 |
| — | | | | 86½ | | 84 | | 75 | | 79 | | 75 |
| 15.4 | Lazonby | | 14 14 | 77½ | 14 24 | 75 | 16 09 | 67½ | 15 05 | 66 | 16 10 | 68½ |
| — | | | | 68 | | 64 | | 54 | | | | 56 |
| 20.8 | Armathwaite | | 18 42 | 79 | 19 06 | 76 | 21 23 | 68½ | 19 55 | — | 21 20 | 65½ |
| 22.4 | Low House Box | | 19 59 | 70 | 20 25 | 64/82 | 22 55 | 60 | 21 25 | — | — | 54 |
| — | | | | 74½ | sigs | | | 72 | | | | |
| 28.1 | Scotby | | 24 39 | 71 | 26 21 | — | 27 56 | 74 | 26 50 | — | 28 10 | 69 |
| | | | sigs | | | | sigs | | sigs | | sigs | |
| 30.8 | Carlisle | 32 | 30 03 | — | 31 28 | — | 32 30 | — | 32 15 | — | 32 50 | — |

*Pilot only to Ais Gill

# 14
# The War Years,
# and Just After

Before coming to tell how the Settle and Carlisle line fared in the global tragedy in which most civilised countries of the world were ultimately involved from September 1939 onwards, there is a postscript to be added to the last chapter on the subject of engine naming. In 1935 the last of the original LNWR 'Claughtons' were withdrawn. One of these was the special War Memorial engine *Patriot*, originally No. 1914, and since Grouping LMS No. 5964, and eventually painted in Midland red. As such the engine had largely lost its original deep significance, but someone in high authority decided that the name must be perpetuated on a new engine. Since conversion the first of the "Baby Scots", No. 5971, had been nameless, and with the renumbering, following the introduction of the 'Jubilees' it became the class-leader of all the

*The naming ceremony for 'Patriot' 4-6-0 No. 5538: the headmaster, Mr E. H. Partridge with academic robes, on the dais with dignitaries of the School and the LMSR. (Author's Collection)*

'5Xs', numbered 5500. The name *Patriot* was allocated to the first of the "Baby Scots" in 1937, but I was never very happy with the subsequent classifying all the "Baby Scots" as the 'Patriot' class, however official the name might have been deemed so, in high LMS circles. In all my journeyings I never saw the engine again after my run behind her described in Chapter 12. While several engines of the class were featured in naming ceremonies I cannot trace that *Patriot* herself, as LMS No. 5500, was so honoured.

It was far otherwise with No. 5538, a later engine of the same class. In the summer of 1938 Sir Harold Hartley, a Vice-President of the LMS was the guest of honour on Speech Day at Giggleswick School, and distributed the prizes. On that occasion someone fairly high up in the School's hierarchy mentioned that the Southern Railway had some top line express locomotives named after public schools. Sir Harold took the hint, and when the School reassembled for the Michaelmas term all concerned were delighted to learn that one of the "Baby Scot" 4-6-0s, stationed at Leeds and regularly working over the Settle and Carlisle line, No. 5538, was to be named *Giggleswick*. The ceremony took place with full scholastic honours at Settle station, with the whole school, and much of the resident population of Giggleswick and Settle present to see the redoubtable Head Master, Edward Partridge, in full academic robes, break the traditional bottle of champagne over the nameplate of the engine.

Now, to turn to less happier circumstances, within weeks of the declaration of war with Nazi Germany the express passenger train service over the whole of Great Britain, both in frequency and speed, was reduced to a mere shadow. Even then when the fear of immediate vicious aerial attack had considerably lessened the service improvements were few and acceleration of running times virtually nil. On the Settle and Carlisle line there was only one day service from St Pancras to Scotland and north of Leeds this was booked to call at Skipton, Hellifield and Appleby. From Leeds there was a stopping train following the Scotch Express calling at all stations, and this provided connection at Carlisle for stations in Scotland. Often however when the London train was running very late, as not infrequently it was during the war years, the local, to maintain its connections at Carlisle, was despatched at its regular time, and the London train if carrying passengers for any intermediate stations north of Hellifield would have to make special stops to set them down. The lateness leaving Leeds was

*Giggleswick was a Leeds engine, and so she worked north to Carlisle and southwards to London. Seen here on the "Thames–Clyde Express" near Radlett, Hertfordshire. (E. D. Bruton)*

*On the only day Scotch Express by the Midland route in 1945: a converted 'Royal Scot', No. 6117* Welsh Guardsman, *near Bell Busk with the author on the footplate.* (W. Hubert Foster)

thus increased considerably. Cecil J. Allen had a few runs on this train when travelling to West Cumberland on his usual inspection duties, and he took a poor view of it.

War or no war however there were some interesting developments in LMS locomotive headquarters at Derby. Maintenance statistics were showing that the Swindon inspired taper boilers on the '5X' 'Jubilees' and the "Black Fives" were proving somewhat cheaper in repair costs than the Crewe-designed boilers of the "Baby Scots", and indeed those of the 'Royal Scots'. A taper-boilered Class 6 had been built on the chassis of Sir Henry Fowler's ill-starred super-high pressure compound 4-6-0, *Fury*, and this, the handsome No. 6170, *British Legion*, had already made the impression that it was as good, if not better, than the best of the existing 'Royal Scots'. But *British Legion*, like the ordinary 'Scots', was too heavy for the Midland line and after some experiments with 'Kylchap' blast pipes on some of the 'Jubilees', design work at Derby settled on a modified *British Legion* boiler which could be used on 'Royal Scots', "Baby Scots", or 'Jubilees'. The first mentioned, having been introduced in 1927 were approaching the time when their boilers would require renewing, and the logical thing to do was to replace them with new ones which would permit of their use on the Midland Division. The new boilers compared to

that of *British Legion* are shown in the table below.

| Taper Boiler class used on | 2 No. 6170 | 2A 5X conversions and rebuilt "Royal Scots" |
|---|---|---|
| Heating surfaces, tubes: | | |
| Small, number | 180 | 198 |
| Small, outside dia (in) | $1\frac{7}{8}$ | $1\frac{3}{4}$ |
| Flues, number | 28 | 28 |
| Flues, outside dia (in) | $5\frac{1}{8}$ | $5\frac{1}{8}$ |
| Superheater elements (in) | $1\frac{1}{4}$ | $1\frac{1}{4}$ |
| Distance between tube plate (ft-in) | 14.3 | 13.0 |
| Tube heating surface (sq ft) | 1793 | 1667 |
| Firebox heating surface (sq ft) | 195 | 195 |
| Total evaporative (sq ft) | 1988 | 1862 |
| Superheater (sq ft) | 348 | 348 |
| Grate area (sq ft) | 31.25 | 31.25 |

It was not until the late autumn of 1942 that the first engine with the 2A boiler took the road, and it was a 'Jubilee', No. 5736 *Phoenix*. As shown in the accompanying diagram it retained the original size of cylinders, and remained at first classified '5XP'. A second engine of the class, No. 5735 *Comet* was reboilered at the same time, and both engines were sent to Whitehall Junction shed at Leeds to partake in the double-home workings of engines and men between Leeds and Glasgow St Enoch. In the middle years of the war there had been some deplorably bad running over the route. It was not only late arrivals from the south that exacerbated the trouble. Cases were quoted in the railway press of 'Jubilees' coming on fresh at Leeds and stalling through shortage of steam half way up between Settle Junction and Blea Moor. Seeing that their tenders would have been freshly coaled up at Whitehall Junction for the run to Glasgow one does indeed wonder what sort of stuff was put on, knowing that Leeds usually got reasonably good hard Yorkshire coal for its express passenger jobs. The two '5XP' engines with 2A boilers soon earned an excellent reputation, and when the order was given to Crewe Works for the conversion of twenty 'Royal Scots', three of the first to be done, Nos 6103, 6108 and 6109, were sent to Leeds for the Midland Division as soon as they were run in.

No. 6103 *Royal Scots Fusilier*, was the first, and
finished in the dull unlined black of wartime was
the subject of the official photographs issued to
the Press in July 1943.

From various sources the news of what the new
engines were was interesting, though not enough
to tempt me to go and see for myself. I was
then far too involved down in Wessex with the
multiple activities of wartime. But from the early
days of the War I had been contributing to
*The Engineer* the occasional meaty article on
current railway engineering subjects, and then in
1944 that great and wholly charming Editor,
Loughnan Pendred, himself a distinguished
Past-President of the Institution of Mechanical
Engineers, asked whether I would consider doing
a series of articles on 'British Locomotive Working in Wartime'. He knew that I was no stranger
to footplate conditions, but in wartime with the
flying bomb attacks at their worst, to ask for
facilities of that kind did not at first seem likely
that they would be granted. But Pendred was
nothing if he was not persistent, and to meet
his requests some journeys over routes then un-
affected by the flying bombs were planned. The
double-home turns worked by the "Converted
Scots" seemed an ideal choice, running through
between Leeds and Glasgow St Enoch, if I could
get the time. In another connection I had been in
correspondence with H. G. Ivatt, then principal

*The up day Scotch Express in 1945, near Bingley,
hauled by '5XP' 4-6-0 No. 5565* Victoria, *on
which the author rode through from Glasgow.*
(W. Hubert Foster)

assistant to the Chief Mechanical Engineer, and
he had sent me a complete set of the indicator
diagrams taken off engine No. 6138 *London Irish
Rifleman* in July 1944.

I do not know the circumstances in which the
various indicator cards reproduced were obtained
but in 1944 it would have been in very severe
wartime conditions, and there is no instance of

*Garsdale water-troughs; a summer prospect.* (W. Hubert Foster)

a card taken at a higher speed than 62 mph. A locomotive that can give a fat enough card to yield 925 ihp in 5 per cent cut-off at 62 mph and 1,070 ihp in 10 per cent at 60 mph has a very excellent valve gear. In view of the investigations at Crewe prior to the building of the first taper-boiler 'Scot', No. 6170 *British Legion* in 1935, it is interesting to see that no instance of 2,000 ihp was recorded with No. 6138, though the ascending values of ihp with increasing cut-off and decreasing speed are impressive:

| Speed (mph) | Cut-off (per cent) | ihp |
| --- | --- | --- |
| 62 | 18 | 1,670 |
| 56 | 22 | 1,700 |
| 52 | 26 | 1,820 |
| 44 | 32 | 1,840 |

These diagrams, with the engine working hard, all show a good deal of throttling of the steam at admission, the effect of which can be seen when the theoretical shape is super-imposed upon the actual shape for one of the cards taken at 22 per cent cut-off.

Mr Ivatt very kindly arranged for me to make some footplate runs on the rebuilt engines on the double-home turns between Leeds and Glasgow but at the turn of the year 1944 it was easier said than done, so far as I personally was concerned. However, early in 1945 I managed to get mortgaged a day of my exiguous annual leave for the forthcoming year to supplement one of my pre-

*Garsdale troughs — what it was like in February 1947, with soldiers trying to clear the line of snow.*
(W. Hubert Foster)

cious few free weekends and so was able to make the journey to Glasgow and back. On the Saturday I travelled up the Scotch Express was loaded to 416 tons tare, and about 450 tons full, with the fourth of the converted engines to arrive at Leeds, No. 6117 *Welsh Guardsman*. Fortunately the train had not been unduly delayed south of Leeds so that we were ready to start only 16 minutes late, and this gave opportunity for some regaining of lost time. The engine was reputedly in good condition, and with a keen crew and excellent hard Yorkshire coal all seemed set fair for a good trip. From the very outset I was interested to see that the driver used an absolutely full regulator opening for all the hard steaming, and very short cut-offs, thus verifying the working of engine No. 6138 as shown on the indicator diagrams sent to me by Mr Ivatt. From Hellifield the driver started very gently, linking up to 15 per cent cut-off as we passed the platform end at Hellifield, with the regulator one-half open. This took us up to 62 mph at Settle Junction, and there the regulator was opened to the full. Recalling that the indicator cards taken on No. 6138 had given 1,520 indicated horsepower in 15 per cent at 60 mph, it was evident that for all this apparently modest working No. 6117 was producing the power.

The ascent to Blea Moor proved to be quite impressive. When at a point four miles above Settle speed had fallen to 33 mph the cut-off was increased to 22 per cent and we sustained 28 mph on the continuing 1 in 100 to Helwith Bridge; but at Horton the cut-off was increased to 30 per cent. Speed had by then begun to fall again from the 34 mph attained on the brief easing of the 1 in 100 gradient past Helwith Bridge, but that further opening-out produced a marked acceleration to a sustained 36 mph. On the footplate, I was able to see that this fine effort, requiring about 1,420 equivalent drawbar horsepower, was easily sustained by the boiler performance in steady maintenance of pressure and water level. I judged the indicated horsepower to be about 1,750. Cut-off was reduced to 22 per cent at Ribblehead, 15 once we were into Blea Moor Tunnel, and 10 per cent at Dent Head. This took us up to 58 mph at Garsdale without any further opening-out, and over Ais Gill Summit at 45 mph. The regulator had remained full open throughout.

The accompanying tabulation shows the running times and the speeds concerned from

Hellifield to Appleby. The schedule times were considerably slower than those being worked before the war but although the descent from Ais Gill was made entirely without steam, with regulator closed and with valves set in 54 per cent cut-off, to provide cushioning and preventing the speed from rising too high, we gained $7\frac{1}{2}$ minutes on this schedule from Hellifield. Continuing from Appleby we passed Lazonby, 15.3 miles in $16\frac{3}{4}$ minutes but adverse signals delayed the approach to Carlisle and prevented our keeping of the wartime schedule of 35 minutes for the 30.8 miles from Appleby. But *Welsh Guardsman* and her crew continued to do good work in Scotland and they brought the train into St Enoch exactly on time.

*Dent station in February 1947.*
(W. Hubert Foster)

LMS — Midland: Hellifield–Appleby
Load: 416 tons tare 450 tons full
Engine: "Converted Scot" No. 6117 *Welsh Guardsman*

| Distance Miles | | Sch min | Actual m s | Speeds mph |
|---|---|---|---|---|
| 0.0 | Hellifield | 0 | 0 00 | — |
| 3.3 | Settle Junction | 5 | 5 15 | 62 |
| 5.2 | Settle | | 7 29 | — |
| 9.6 | Helwith Bridge Box | | 15 30 | 28 |
| 11.2 | Horton | | 18 49 | 35 |
| 13.5 | Selside Box | | 22 49 | 36 |
| 16.0 | Ribblehead | | 26 53 | 36 |
| 17.3 | Blea Moor Box | 33 | 28 57 | 33 |
| 22.2 | Dent | | 36 30 | — |
| 25.4 | Garsdale | | 40 31 | 58 |
| 28.4 | Ais Gill Box | 49 | 44 09 | 45 |
| 35.3 | Kirkby Stephen | | 50 49 | easy |
| 43.5 | Ormside | | 58 27 | easy |
| 46.0 | Appleby | 69 | 61 27 | |

her worth on the run down from Glasgow, and the driver now pounded her with a vengeance. We roared up past Scotby with the regulator wide open and 47 per cent cut-off, and the speed rose rapidly to $40\frac{1}{2}$ mph on the 1 in 132 gradient. To avoid quoting a large number of figures, I have prepared a diagram which shows the speed, the gradients, and the cut-offs used, so that the whole of the working on this superb piece of hill-climbing can be carefully studied.

The boiler was steaming well, and the driver had no difficulty in keeping pressure nicely above the 200 mark. The drawbar horsepower rose at times to nearly 1,500 on this ascent, and the

*Snow clearing near Arten Gill Viaduct, 1947.*
(W. Hubert Foster)

On the Monday morning I found a 'Jubilee' at the head of the 10 am to St Pancras, with a 13-coach train of 364 tons tare, but by the time we left Dumfries on the way south the coaches and luggage compartment were literally packed with passengers, and I estimated that the gross load behind the tender of No. 5565 *Victoria* was not less than 410 tons. In one of my earliest railway books, written in 1946, I wrote that *Victoria* would have cut a shabby figure. Indeed, my heart sank when I saw her come backing down at St Enoch in place of the expected 'Scot'; but her grime was deceptive, and we had not travelled far out of Glasgow before I realised she was in first-rate condition. *Victoria* had proved

engine generally appeared to be game for anything; so, at 44 mph we thundered over the first summit from Carlisle, at Milepost 300, and dipped down towards Armathwaite. High on the hillside, through woods newly in leaf, we looked down on one of the loveliest stretches of river scenery in all England; in the bright spring sunshine the delicate greens of new foliage, the warm russet of the surrounding hills, and the River Eden winding like a sparkling thread far below made so exquisite a picture that I found my attention straying more than once from the pulsating cab of *Victoria*. We attained a full 60 mph before Armathwaite, took the 1 in 220 grade through Baron Wood Tunnel at a minimum of 53, and then, with a brief spell on the first valve of the regulator, raced up to 66 mph at Lazonby. But the lever was soon hard over once more, and with cut-offs varying between 15 and 20 per cent, as shown in the diagram we went magnificently up the rising grades towards Appleby; through the red cuttings of Langwathby, then on to the open hillside with a broad view westward to the Lakeland mountains. Thus we reached Appleby (30.8 miles) in $38\frac{1}{4}$ min from Carlisle, a gain of nearly five minutes on scheduled time.

The final stage of the climb to Ais Gill can be very trying. The railway is carried high on the range of hills forming the western flank of the Eden Valley; it is bleak in the extreme, and when the Helm wind is roaring across the valley the 15-mile stretch from Ormside Viaduct to the summit can be a holy terror. But today all was fair. The mile of 1 in 183 descent from Appleby makes possible a flying attack on the bank, and we crossed the viaduct at $52\frac{1}{2}$ mph; then, on to the 1 in 100, 41 mph through Helm Tunnel, heavier going; cut-off advanced from 25 to 37 per cent and No. 5565 was roaring in earnest. Above Griseburn the grade eases somewhat; the cut-off was shortened a little from 37 to 32 per cent, but already the speed was romping up, and it was certainly in full cry that we swung through the moorland station of Crosby Garrett. Over Smardale Viaduct where the track is level for a brief space we reached 50 mph and then fairly dug into the next long stretch of 1 in 100. Cut-off was advanced to 37 per cent, again as we neared Kirkby Stephen, and speed settled down to a steady 38 mph. This was great work, and the engine seemed to revel in it; the pressure gauge needle was hovering around 210 to 215 lb per sq in, the fireman's task was by no means exhausting, and by the time we passed Mallerstang signal box it was evident we were getting well ahead of schedule. So as we drove under the bold escarpments of Wild Boar Fell, and the surfacemen's cottages on Ais Gill Moor came into view the driver eased his engine right back to 22 per cent. Even so we passed the summit

*An abandoned brake van near Dent, February 1947.* (W. Hubert Foster)

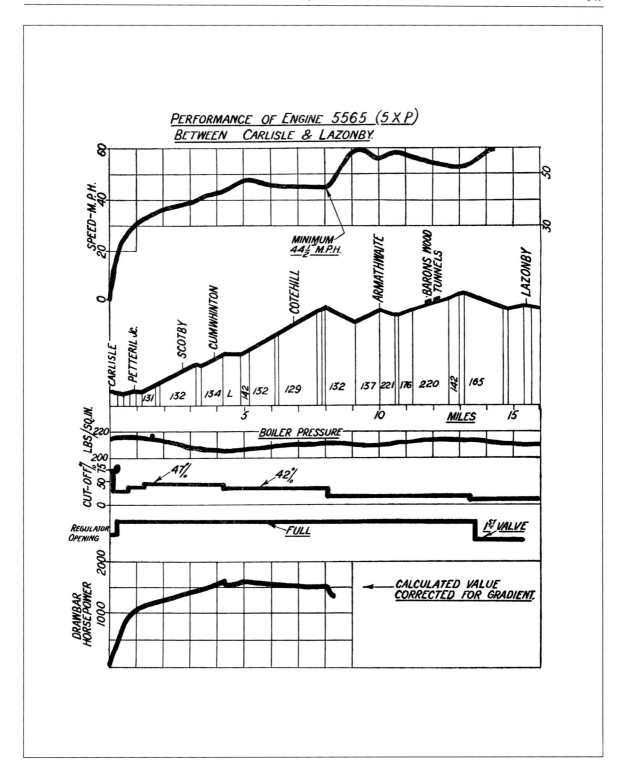

PERFORMANCE OF ENGINE 5565 (5 X P)
BETWEEN CARLISLE & LAZONBY.

box in 30½ min from Appleby (17.5 miles) — 4½ minutes early!

It was a great day to be in the fell country. The air was like wine, and the bright sunshine made brilliant play from our own course over the general watershed of Northern England, to the far horizons. We were running under very easy steam now: downhill through Shotlock Hill and Moorcock Tunnels to the moorland station of Garsdale — still perhaps known best by its old name of Hawes Junction; on over the water-troughs, with Garsdale itself falling steeply away to the west. We were ourselves continuing level, high on the hillside, soon to plunge through the mile-long tunnel under Rise Hill; then out again, with the wide prospect of Dentdale spread below, and a glimpse of the little mountain station of Dent, so neat, so characteristic of the Midland Railway. We bowled on at 60 mph towards the mountain cul de sac of Denthead: high on the slope of Pikes Moss; the line protected by a double row of snow fences, and swinging in a long right-hand curve towards the dale head, where the white ribbon of a road goes scrambling up the mountain side to the lonely waste of Gayle Moor. The railway crossing the infant River Dee on a high viaduct then plunges straight under the loftiest of the surrounding heights. Such is the northern approach to Blea Moor Tunnel. The setting could scarcely be more dramatic, yet today a down goods had recently passed through the tunnel and white smoke was slowly belching from the entrance; far up the mountainside a second plume showed the whereabouts of the first ventilating shaft.

We emerged two minutes later into the moorland wastes of Ribblehead, to a scene encompassed by some of the finest mountains of the Pennines. Whernside was behind us, Ingleborough — that "muckle blue hill" — directly ahead, and away to the south-east rising abruptly was the truncated cone of Pen-y-Ghent. On the long 1 in 100 descent we were soon into the 'seventies'; the scene was changing swiftly, and with the engine now coasting the driver made numerous slight applications of the brake to prevent the speed from rising too high. Our maximum was 72 mph, and so beneath the beetling crags of Settle, and past the limestone scars of Giggleswick we came to Settle Junction and the end of this incomparable piece of railway. The 25.2 miles from Ais Gill had been covered in a shade under the 27 minutes allowed, and with a quick finish up the last 3.3 miles we stopped at Hellifield in 62¼ min from Appleby (46 miles), nearly five minutes early. The rest of the run to

*On Ribblehead Viaduct, a Glasgow to St Pancras express in June 1961, hauled by 'Jubilee' class 4-6-0 No. 5725* Repulse. *(Derek Cross)*

Leeds is mostly downhill and easily timed, and I spent it in the train scraping off the grime I had collected in $4\frac{1}{2}$ hours on the footplate. It was a great run, and one could scarcely wish for a more willing or hard-working engine than this '5X'.

A great day to be in the fell country, yet, but I do not think I should have been so lyrically minded had I been there two years later, when blizzard conditions, the worst in living memory, swept the district and blocked the Settle and Carlisle line completely for three weeks! My good friend the late W. Hubert Foster of Bingley, a professional photographer, has told how he came to be invited to go up to the High Pennines and see for himself. Apparently the Cabinet, of the recently elected Labour government of Great Britain had no conception of the difficulties the northern railways were facing in such weather, and why, for several weeks, all traffic normally routed over the Settle and Carlisle line had to be diverted via Ingleton, Low Gill, and Shap. The only way was to show them some photographs of what the line north of Blea Moor Tunnel looked like! So one icy evening, 13th February to be exact, Foster was rung up by the District Engineer of the LMS at Leeds asking if he could join a small party going up 'into the wilderness' next morning, and bring his camera. So soon after ten o'clock next morning he joined them at Skipton in the inspection saloon. He has written:

"Soon settled in an armchair commanding a fine view through the large rear windows; which were kept free from snow by massive windscreen wipers, I had my first sight of big drifts overhanging a cutting just south of Bell Busk. A big drift had been cut through at Hellifield also. On past Settle, and climbing rapidly up the 1-100 ruling grade towards Blea Moor, the views were magnificent; the snow which had been falling at Skipton had now ceased; field, fell and mountain standing out clear and sharp in the clean, crisp air.

At Ribblehead, two engines stood tender to tender, each mounting a snow plough on its buffer beam. I was interested to see that one of these engines was one of the new 2-6-0s, No. 6408. On passing over the Ingleton road, we could just see the roof of an abandoned car, well and truly fast in a drift. Passing over Ribblehead Viaduct we were soon running into Blea Moor Tunnel, our speed being now gently reduced; leaving the tunnel and passing over Dent Head Viaduct, we came to a stand just beyond Dent Head signal box."

Further progress with the saloon was not possible, because the running lines were occupied by trains with their engines, mainly those which had brought railway workers to help clear the line, also trains of open wagons for removing the snow. Beyond these trains it was seen that only the down line was clear of snow, and the up line was covered up to about eight or nine feet. A brake van hauled by a 2-8-0 was on hand and the party climbed aboard and they were taken northwards toward Dent station. All along these two miles the up line was buried under great drifts. Many, which had been cut through to clear the down line, stood as high as the brake van in which the party were then travelling. Dent station up platform and waiting room were almost buried under snow. The photographs taken by Mr Foster tell more than words. The stationmaster told them that at times the blizzard was so bad that work had to be abandoned and men were forced to shelter, crawling on hands and knees to prevent themselves being blown over the viaducts. Even when conditions were not so bad, men quickly became coated with ice, icicles hanging from their eyebrows and eyelids; several collapsed and had to receive aid.

Many of the men worked night and day and later naval search-lights manned by Fleet Air Arm personnel, provided ample illumination during hours of darkness. A number of ingenious methods to counter the icy blasts were tried by the men, one of the most successful being to cover head and shoulders with a sack having two holes cut in for seeing through.

I have always thought it to be a freak of geography in these Pennine regions that the Settle and Carlisle line should be so affected by snow — and the early months of 1947 were by no means the only instance — whereas Shap, for all its exposed situation remained largely immune. And what about the line between the moorland Clapham Junction and Low Gill? The Midland and the LNWR must have been mighty glad that the section north of Ingleton was engineered and maintained as a double-track railway. Now thanks to the Beeching 'Axe' it is no more!

# 15
# 1948: Nationalisation —
# First Developments

From January 1948 the Midland Division of the LMS, apart from those lines west of Hereford, remained at first territorially intact in the London Midland Region of British Railways. The double-home working between Leeds and Glasgow also continued, by mutual arrangement of the LM and Scottish Regions. In setting up the Railway Executive, in its headquarters at 222 Marylebone Road, London, in the former Great Central Hotel, engineers from the former LMS preponderated on the mechanical engineering branches. R. A. Riddles, who had returned to the LMS from his wartime duties, had been made a Vice-President, and in 1948 he was appointed Member of the Railway Executive for Mechanical and Electrical Engineering. He selected R. C. Bond, previously deputy CME of the LMS, as his Chief Officer for Locomotive Works, and E. S. Cox to look after locomotive design. Although the new triumvirate

*The "Thames–Clyde Express" passing Marley Junction near Keighley, with converted 'Royal Scot' 4-6-0 No. 6103 Royal Scots Fusilier. (Millbrook House Ltd — Bishop Eric Treacy)*

*The "Flying Scotsman", diverted because of flood damage north of Berwick, in 1947, with LNER Class A4 4-6-2 No. 25* Falcon, *passing Marley Junction.* (Millbrook House Ltd —Bishop Eric Treacy)

had all been LMS men before the Grouping, they had been on the LNWR, the Midland and the Lancashire & Yorkshire Railways.

There can be little doubt that these men of the LMS, basking in the success of the Stanier regime, and the selection of the '8F' 2-8-0 for extensive wartime service, entered British Railways service — be it whispered — with a feeling of a complete superiority complex. Within weeks of vesting day arrangements were being made for a comprehensive series of Interchange Trials with express passenger, mixed traffic and heavy freight locomotives with representative classes from all four of the previous independent companies. From this it was hoped that those of the LMS would emerge supreme on all counts. Unfortunately for the boffins of No. 222 Marylebone Road, 'The Kremlin' as its detractors nicknamed it, did not work out that way at all. Largely due to the personality of some of the enginemen allocated to the job, the Stanier "Black Five" 4-6-0s gave generally disappointing results, while the Camden driver working the 'Duchess' class Pacifics assumed such a superiority complex of his own, by ignoring the guidance of some of the pilotmen who rode with him on the foreign routes, sometimes endangered his train in the observance of speed restrictions, or not so. His colleague from Camden, who I personally knew

to be a man of outstanding ability, and who had engines of the "Converted Scot" class, was handicapped by the rough riding of these engines on some of the routes worked, a legacy partly due to arrears of track maintenance following the fearful weather of the early months of 1947.

But while the Interchange Trials of 1948 have been called, somewhat unkindly in certain quarters, as a "monument of wasted effort" they created an intense interest in the railway fraternity, whether professional or amateur, and the report of the proceedings when The Railway Executive published it a year later was a comprehensive document of 130 pages. In time the 'rough and ready' methods of the road testing of locomotives, necessarily used on all the routes in the Interchange Trials of 1948, was subject to a new examination by the men at No. 222. Those trials had originally been organised by a subcommittee of engineers from all four of the original main line companies, and the cross-breeding, as it may be called, was to prove advantageous beyond all measure, particularly in the way the Settle and Carlisle line came to play in the process of testing locomotives of very varied origin. The time for that was not to begin until several years had elapsed after the Interchange Trials had ended. A little before Nationalisation the LMS had taken delivery of a

Mobile Testing Plant, the very elaborate electrical equipment of which enabled locomotives to be tested at constant speed on the open road regardless of the gradients, or any other factors of testing the speed of running. On the LMS and the LNER the maintenance of constant speed on a road trial was at one time thought to be the only logical 'outdoor' equivalent to provide corroborative data to that obtained on a stationary testing plant, like that recently brought into commission, through the joint auspices of the LMS and the LNER at Rugby.

The Mobile Testing Plant of the LMS was described in a learned paper to the Institution of Mechanical Engineers in April 1948 by one of the men who had largely been responsible for its conception and design. As one member of the audience on that occasion said in the subsequent discussion, the possession of it at the time of railway unification was a great asset, and had put Great Britain in the lead in the art and science of railway rolling stock testing. The paper at the Institution of Mechanical Engineers was presented however, only a few weeks before the beginning of the 1948 Interchange Trials, and all thoughts of such scientific investigations as those envisaged with the Mobile Testing Plant had to be set on one side for several months.

The representative of the Western Region on the British Railways sub-committee for locomo-tive testing was S. O. Ell, who was engineer in charge of testing under the assistant Chief Draughtsman for locomotives. Ell had been associated with Charles Roberts and A. W. J. Dymond in the modernisation of the Swindon Stationary Plant and dynamometer car testing on the Great Western Railway in the later 1930s, and in 1948 he was becoming a practiced exponent of the technique of Controlled Road Testing of locomotives. This was a development of the latest Swindon Test Plant procedure, and in contrast to previous practice on locomotives and the lines the engineers of the LMS and LNER had been taking prior to Nationalisation. The maintenance of constant speed had been the basis, but the Swindon method had its basis on constant rates of combustion and evaporation over relatively long periods, and the measurement of coal and water rates during such tests was by what was termed the 'summation of increments' method. The procedure was first to establish the combustion rate during a period of constant speed, after which a series of tests were made over the whole range of working speeds, maintaining a constant rate of evaporation with the aid of a special instrument which gave an indication of the rate of steam exhausting.

Coal was placed at the disposal of the fireman in equal increments, the weight of such increments being chosen so that it required about five

*Passing Pen-y-Ghent: one of the last batch of "Black Fives" with double chimney, electric lighting and Caprotti valve gear, No. 44755, on the 1.55 pm Leeds to Edinburgh Waverley.*
(Millbrook House Ltd — Bishop Eric Treacy)

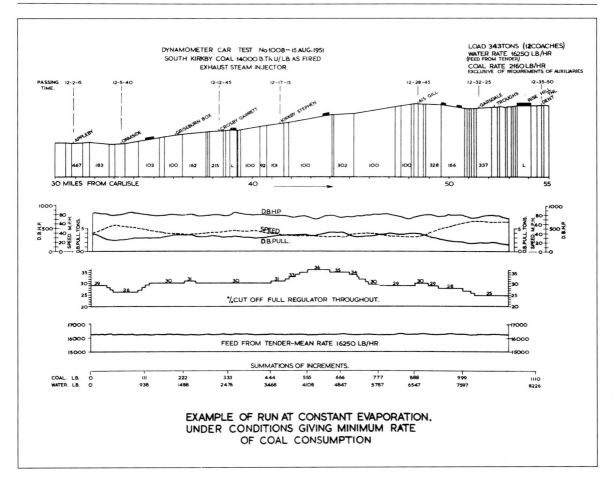

DYNAMOMETER CAR TEST No 1008 — 15 AUG. 1951
SOUTH KIRKBY COAL 14000 B.Th.U/LB. AS FIRED
EXHAUST STEAM INJECTOR.

LOAD 343 TONS (12 COACHES)
WATER RATE 16250 LB/HR
(FEED FROM TENDER)
COAL RATE 2160 LB/HR
EXCLUSIVE OF REQUIREMENTS OF AUXILIARIES

**EXAMPLE OF RUN AT CONSTANT EVAPORATION.
UNDER CONDITIONS GIVING MINIMUM RATE
OF COAL CONSUMPTION**

to seven minutes for its consumption. The time was taken at the moment the fireman finished one increment and was given another, and the water injected up to that moment was also measured, so that as the test progressed a graph could be plotted of coal fired and water injected against the time elapsed. The validity of the test was shown when it was possible to draw fair straight lines through the points on this graph, covering at least the stipulated test period. The slopes of these lines established the coal and water rates, and as a check the water/coal ratio, reckoned at the end of each increment was also plotted.

When the water and coal rates appeared firmly established the mean value of the exhaust flow indication could be ascertained for guidance during the variable speed trials, and a movable pointer on the scale of this instrument was set at this value. This instrument, for indication of

the rate of steam exhausting, employed the blast pipe orifice as a metering device by measuring the pressure differential across it, though in actual practice it was necessary to measure only the pressure below the orifice. This was done by balancing the pressure below the orifice with air pressure, and measuring the air pressure by sensitive manometers, one of which was located on the control table. With the movable pointer of this instrument set to indicate the mean value of the flow indication the speed of the locomotive could then be varied, by altering the cut-off, in steps of about 5 mph. The cut-off was noted at each step, and several indicator cards were taken. Great care was, of course, necessary to observe that cards were taken only when the exhaust steam flow indication was exactly opposite to the preset pointer. It will thus be realised that, in a few steps of speed, a wide range of working

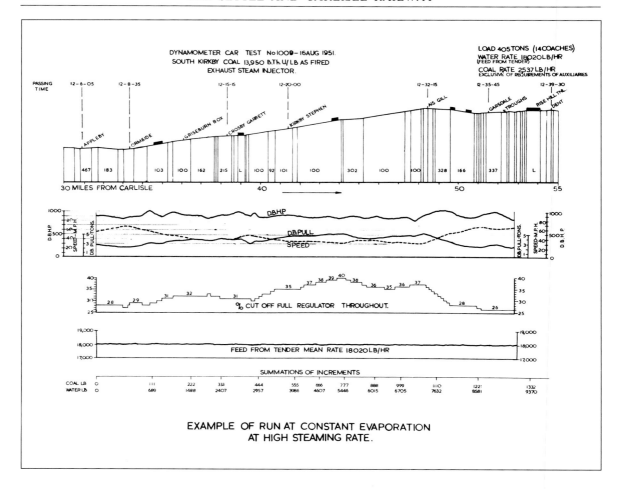

DYNAMOMETER CAR TEST No.1009—16 AUG 1951.
SOUTH KIRKBY COAL 13,950 B.Th.U/LB AS FIRED
EXHAUST STEAM INJECTOR.

LOAD 405 TONS (14 COACHES)
WATER RATE 18020 LB/HR (FEED FROM TENDER)
COAL RATE 2537 LB/HR EXCLUSIVE OF REQUIREMENTS OF AUXILIARIES

EXAMPLE OF RUN AT CONSTANT EVAPORATION
AT HIGH STEAMING RATE.

conditions could be covered. In the meantime, the 'summation of increments' graphs were continued, and these had to be shown to follow straight line extensions of the graphs made in the first stages of the test, when the coal and water rates were established at constant speed. A very interesting and important fact determined during these tests at Swindon was that the combustion-steam-air cycle of the boiler was found to function irrespective of engine working conditions.

By this method, in one variable speed test, the dual relationship of coal and steam, steam and power can be established over a wide working range, and by repeating the procedure at other rates of evaporation the whole of the working range of the locomotive may be covered. With the 'Hall' class engine, for example, tests were made at rates varying between 8,000 lb and 23,000 lb of steam per hour; on the stationary testing plant the test period proper was approximately 90 minutes on an average, and it was not less than 60 minutes at the highest rates of evaporation. The arrangements at Rugby, under which the B1 class 4-6-0 locomotive was tested, were similar, except that the engine was not at any time indicated. This latter part of the testing of this engine was to be done later.

The system of controlled road testing, as developed at Swindon, provided a means of verifying and amplifying tests obtained on the stationary testing plant. Again the rate of evaporation was maintained constantly during any particular test, and data covering variations in speed were provided by the fluctuations in speed due to the rise and fall of the road.

The tests with the Western Region dynamometer car were conducted between Wantage Road and Filton Junction, while those of the B1 engine were conducted with the London Midland No. 1 dynamometer car over that favourite northern testing route, the Settle and Carlisle line. The coal and water rates were established by the 'summation of increments' method suitably adapted to road testing, and the steam flow indicator equipment was also used. For road testing one special manometer was fitted in the cab for the driver; there were visual and recording manometers in the dynamometer car. On the Western Region tests, on which the engines concerned were indicated, an additional manometer was fitted in the indicator shelter on the front of the locomotive. Control was left entirely in the hands of the driver who, with full or partial opening of the regulator as would have been decided upon previously, adjusted the cut-off so that whatever the speed the steam flow indication was kept at a preset mark on the manometer. This working was under constant surveillance from the dynamometer car, and as usual there was telephonic communication between the car and its observer in the locomotive cab.

The rate of coal consumption was recorded in a similar manner to that used in the stationary tests. During the actual test run the fireman took coal from a partitioned section of the shovelling plate of the tender into which the coal increments were tipped as required from previously weighed bags. The observer in the cab signalled this operation to the dynamometer car, where the time was noted and the feed water injected up to that moment was read from a water meter. The graphs representing coal and water were drawn as the test progressed, and the straight lines through the points established the validity of the test and provided the basis upon which the whole run was considered. As on the stationary tests indicator diagrams were taken only when the flow indications on the manometer were exactly level with the preset mark.

On Friday 18th May 1951 I was one of a party of technical journalists invited to see a test on the new Locomotive Testing Station at Rugby. From Euston the party was conveyed in two extra coaches attached to the regular 10.30 am express to which the Horwich dynamometer car was coupled next to the tender. It was a day for the new 'Britannia' class 4-6-2s, and on the way down to Rugby I was interested to learn from Mr E. S. Cox, Design and Testing Engineer of The Railway Executive, that the Controlled Road Testing System, as developed by the Great Western Railway prior to 1948, had been adopted as standard for British Railways. Furthermore,

*The up "Thames–Clyde Express", with two 'Jubilees'; No. 45729* Furious *leading, near Armathwaite.*
(Millbrook House Ltd — Bishop Eric Treacy)

Leading Dimensions of Locomotives Tested

| Engine class | 'Hall' | LM 2-6-0 | B1 |
|---|---|---|---|
| Cylinders, diameter and stroke (in) | $18\frac{1}{2} \times 30$ | $17\frac{1}{2} \times 26$ | $20 \times 26$ |
| Coupled wheel dia | 6 ft | 5 ft 3 in | 6 ft 2 in |
| Total heating surface (sq ft) | 2032.5 | 1452 | 2005 |
| Grate area (sq ft) | 27.07 | 23 | 27.9 |
| Boiler pressure (lb per sq in) | 225 | 225 | 225 |
| Adhesion weight (tons) | $57\frac{1}{2}$ | $48\frac{1}{2}$ | $52\frac{1}{2}$ |
| Total weight, engine only (tons) | $76\frac{3}{4}$ | 59 | 71 |

while engines tested on the existing plant in Swindon Works would continue to have the corroborative running trials on the usual Western Region routes, those tested on the new plant at Rugby would have their road trials on the Settle and Carlisle line. Geographically of course it would be some distance from Rugby, and I understood that a separate set of engineers would do the testing. However, the relative infrequency of the regular passenger train service over the

Settle and Carlisle line made it a great deal easier to provide paths for the special test trains.

It is important to emphasis the difference between the test trains that began to run over the line from 1951 onwards and those that were run in the early days of the LMS. The latter were all conducted on regular service trains, in most cases with the coaches for ordinary passenger augmented to make up the loads specified in the tests. In 1923-4 the midday departure from Carlisle was made by the Edinburgh, rather than by the Glasgow service, because in the latter case the loads might in any case have exceeded the stipulated tonnage and normally required pilot assistance. The BR trials were made with empty stock, apart from the staff manning the dynamometer car and they started from the sidings adjacent to Durran Hill Junction and ran as far as Skipton. The first locomotive tested under the Controlled Road System was a Class B1 mixed traffic 4-6-0 from the Eastern Region, one of the class that Edward Thompson introduced on the LNER soon after he had been appointed Chief Mechanical Engineer, after the death of Sir Nigel Gresley. Engines of this class

*The up "Thames–Clyde Express" in Carlisle Citadel station, hauled by rebuilt 'Royal Scot' No. 46108 Seaforth Highlander. (British Railways)*

*The up "Waverley" at Durran Hill Junction, hauled by 'Jubilee' No. 45728 Defiance.*
(Millbrook House Ltd — Bishop Eric Treacy)

gave a good account of themselves during the Interchange Trials of 1948, and with a stud of more than 400 of them in British Railways' ownership there was every reason why their performance should be analysed precisely.

On the other hand the basis of their design lay so much apart from the Stanier type so firmly planted on the LMS from 1933 onwards, and with which the reigning hierarchy on the Nationalised Railway Executive, seemed so thoroughly

*The "Waverley" leaving Leeds with 'Jubilee' class 4-6-0 No. 45694 Bellerophon in charge.*
(Millbrook House Ltd — Bishop Eric Treacy)

*The up "Thames–Clyde Express" near Armath-
waite hauled by converted 'Royal Scot' No. 46133
The Green Howards.*
(Millbrook House Ltd — Bishop Eric Treacy)

convinced, at first, that it was the only way. The multiplicity of the B1 class, of which more new ones were being delivered even when the trials of engine No. 61353 on the Rugby Testing Plant and on the Settle and Carlisle line had begun, was principally due to the acute shortage of medium powered locomotives with which the LNER had been faced immediately after the war. Because of the financial stringencies of the early 1930s the railway had not been able to adopt the 'scrap and build' policy in locomotive construction followed by the LMS under Sir Josiah Stamp's leadership. The end of the war had thus found the LNER saddled with a swarm of outdated and poorly maintained Atlantic express engines, honorable though the previous careers of all their several varieties had been. The Thompson B1 4-6-0, in its useful synthesis of the well-tried 'Sandringham' boiler and the machinery of the Gresley K2 class Mogul, provided the ideal type for reproduction in bulk. Even so, one can imagine Riddles and his former LMS assistants looking askance at a locomotive with a parallel boiler and a round-topped firebox.

Although Thompson had been at pains to explain to me personally his reasons for designing the B1, instead of continuing the three-cylinder traditions of Sir Nigel Gresley, and arranged for me to make some footplate runs on his new engines, I cannot personally say I found the B1

class particularly exhilarating. In the Doncaster tradition of the Gresley era they were built with generous clearances in the working parts and the driving wheel bearings, and in no time at all they became rough. I rode one of the first of the class, then stationed at Ipswich, northwards to March, and in a letter just afterwards, and of which I have still kept a copy, I stigmatised the engine as "a vicious kicking little brute"! I rode on many of them afterwards, and collectively they did not much improve with further acquaintance. In 1951, when the Controlled Road System was being applied to locomotives tested at Rugby as well as Swindon, the Railway Executive began publishing the reports of the sub-committee for locomotive testing, and it was then that I had the pleasure and privilege of commenting on those reports for *The Engineer*, and on certain occasions writing leading articles on some of the findings. The Bulletin covering the tests of the B1 4-6-0 was the first to be issued from Rugby and was dated August 1951.

It was a massive document mainly concerned with exhaustive tests on the stationary plant which amply confirmed the very good impression the B1 had made in the Interchange Trials of 1948. No. 61353, of the latest batch to be built, was transferred to Durran Hill shed, Carlisle, for the Controlled Road Tests southwards to Skipton and back. The Bulletin includes detailed references to two of such runs, though while the test loads were varied from day to day, according to what particular feature of the locomotive performance was to be examined, one gathered that in some cases the trains were made up to considerably greater tare tonnages than engines of Class 5 would have been expected to convey in express passenger service without a pilot. The maximum I believe was a train of fourteen bogie coaches plus the Horwich dynamometer car; 436 tons, without the staff. In the Bulletin two examples of actual running are shown, both between Appleby and Rise Hill Tunnel. The first was with a load of 343 tons, to demonstrate working under conditions to give a minimum rate of consumption, and the second, with a load of 405 tons, at a high steaming rate. On leaving Durran Hill sidings the engine and crew were given about 30 minutes to settle down to the steaming rates prescribed for the test, and then just after passing Appleby the first weighed bag of coal was given to the fireman under the 'summation of increments' technique. The feed water from the tender was at a constant rate of 16,250 lb per hour, and thus the test began, and continued thus for roughly half an hour, until indeed the main bank from Ormside to Ais Gill had been climbed, and the train was running freely at more than 60 mph beyond Garsdale water-troughs.

The diagrams on pages 155–6 give details from the dynamometer car record, of speed, drawbar pull and the cut-offs used, and shows that the tender feed was maintained at a remarkably constant value throughout. The chart also shows by the 'summation of increments' procedure the coal and water consumption throughout the test. The regulator was kept fully open, and from the passing times recorded it will be seen that the average speed with this fourteen-coach train of 343 tons from Appleby to Dent, just before and just after the actual period of the test, was 42.3 mph for the distance of 23.8 miles. The short downhill run from Appleby enabled the main climb to be entered upon at nearly 70 mph, and

the minimum speed on both the long stretches of 1 in 100 ascent was 33 mph. The maximum cut off used was 36 per cent, on the approach to, and passage through Birkett Tunnel, while on the mile of 1 in 302 gradient past Mallerstang box the speed rose to 40 mph. As against the constant tender feed of 16,250 lb per hour the coal consumption averaged 2,160 lb per hour, an excellent result in view of the hard work involved. The chart should be studied with intense interest.

On the following day, with an increased load of 405 tons, a run was made over the same stretch of line at what was described as a high steaming rate. The average rate of feed from the tender was 18,020 lb per hour, but from the chart which is also reproduced herewith, there seemed to be no visible variation from the mean rate. The coal rate was 2,537 lb per hour, comfortably within the maximum that a single fireman could manage. The speed was much the same as on the previous day as the log of the passing times, and their associated average speeds shows in the accompanying table.

*The up "Thames–Clyde Express" nearing Ais Gill Summit with 'Jubilee' class 4-6-0 No. 45573 Newfoundland. (Millbrook House Ltd — Bishop Eric Treacy)*

Controlled Test Runs with Engine No. 61353, Class B1

| Date | | | 15.8.51 | | 16.8.51 | |
| Load, tons | | | 343 | | 405 | |
| Distance | | Time from passing Appleby | Average speed | Time from passing Appleby | | Average speed |
| Miles | | m s | mph | m s | | mph |
| 0.0 | Appleby | 0 00 | — | 0 00 | | — |
| 2.5 | Ormside | 3 25 | 43.6 | 2 30 | | 60.0 |
| 7.5 | Crosby Garrett | 10 30 | 42.3 | 9 10 | | 45.0 |
| 10.7 | Kirkby Stephen | 15 00 | 42.7 | 13 55 | | 40.5 |
| 17.5 | Ais Gill Box | 26 30 | 35.4 | 26 10 | | 33.3 |
| 20.6 | Garsdale | 30 10 | 50.7 | 29 40 | | 53.1 |
| 23.8 | Dent | 33 35 | 56.1 | 33 25 | | 53.1 |

It is evident from the above table that the first run had been checked at Appleby. On the heaviest of the ascents it is interesting to note from the chart of the second of the two runs, that the cut-offs were between 35 and 40 per cent continuously from Kirkby Stephen to Ais Gill.

The performance with the 405-ton load makes an interesting comparison with what was undoubtedly my own finest run with an LMS 4-6-0 locomotive as told in the previous chapter. On the wartime 10 am up from Glasgow St Enoch the stop at Appleby made the first part of the comparison irrelevant, and as with the 'Jubilee' class engine Victoria, we had reached a maximum of no more than $52\frac{1}{2}$ mph, and it was not until the driver opened out beyond Helm Tunnel that the comparison became so striking. The tare weight of my own train was 364 tons, but it was so packed with both sitting and standing passengers that I had no hesitation in giving the total load behind the tender as 410 tons, roughly the same as that hauled by the B1 on 16th August 1951. As on that day also, the speed reached 50 mph over Crosby Garrett Viaduct and as cut-off advanced to 37 per cent we had settled down to a steady 38 mph above Kirkby Stephen again closely similar work to that on the second test run. But by the time we passed Mallerstang box it was clear that we were drawing well ahead of the wartime schedule, and as I have told in the previous chapter, we passed Ais Gill $4\frac{1}{2}$ minutes early.

At the time the B1 was being put through her paces between Durran Hill and Skipton one of the new British Railways Standard 7MT Pacifics of the 'Britannia' class had also been tried out over the route. Indeed, engine No. 70005 John Milton, had been prepared for testing before even she left the erecting shop at Crewe when brand

*Eastern Region B1 class 4-6-0 No. 61353 with dynamometer car on a test train leaving Skipton for Carlisle.*
(British Railways)

*The prototype* Deltic *on test with the ex-LMS dynamometer car and two mobile test units, with which a heavy load can be simulated, here seen near Armathwaite.* (GEC Traction Ltd)

new, and there is a photograph of her at Skipton ready to leave for Carlisle on a return dynamometer car run in early June of 1951. But as is well known the early history of the 'Britannias' was punctuated with mishaps, none fortunately involving death or injury to staff or passengers.

Therefore it is not surprising that the Bulletin covering the tests at Rugby and on the Settle and Carlisle line was not published until two years later, by which time a second engine of the class had contributed to the massive bank of data contained in the Bulletin.

# 16
# Indigenous Traffic — Control

I should imagine that to many railway enthusiasts the Settle and Carlisle line exists as a fast express route passing for much of its mileage, "what dreary country", as the stout lady in the unbecoming striped costume said in one of Hamilton Ellis's books, making for the first time after leaving St Pancras a comment on the passing scene. This pronouncement came apparently as the train was approaching Ribblehead, and I can quite imagine some days when the prospect there can be bleak in the extreme. But having spent five very formative years of my life in those

*Ex-LMS 8F class 2-8-0 No. 48090 leaving Shotlock Hill Tunnel with anhydrite train from Long Meg to Widnes, November 1967. (G. W. Morrison)*

*A southbound military special passing Stainforth sidings, hauled by 'Jubilee' class 4-6-0 No. 45730* Ocean. (Derek Cross)

mighty dales I know that there were days, indeed weeks, when the prospect was far otherwise and now, for a whole chapter or thereabouts, I am switching off from main line express passenger trains and test runs loaded to gargantuan tonnages, and intend to gossip about some of the more localised activities, both passenger and freight.

The prime object of the Midland Railway in constructing the line was to provide a through and independent route to the Scottish Border,

and so to establish direct connection with the two Scottish railways that were most inclined to provide rival and alternative ways to England than by the West Coast route. On the other hand it is evident from the excellent accommodation for passengers, at even the most remote of wayside stations, and the comprehensive arrangements made for dealing with freight and livestock traffic, it was ensured that local business was not to be neglected. In his mainly statistical book, with the faintly inappropriate title of *Rails in the*

*A southbound load of permanent way materials passing Kirkby Stephen, hauled by a grimy BR Standard 9F class 2-10-0.* (Ivo Peters)

*A Long Meg–Widnes anhydrite train approaching Ais Gill Summit in May 1967, with 9F class BR Standard 2-10-0 No. 92017.* (Derek Cross)

*Fells*, David Jenkinson gives a scholarly analysis of traffic of all kinds from the first opening of the railway until the immediate post-war period after 1918, and then, in the rather depressing age when the threat of closure of the whole line was more than a vague unsettling rumour. The data from 1923 to 1953, on which Mr Jenkinson would have applied his tireless industry, as he has done so thoroughly overall the other periods, were apparently missing. This is unfortunate because they would have covered the period when other methods of transport began to make such serious inroads upon the business that the railway had built up during the first forty years of its operation.

Dealing first with passenger traffic, for which Mr Jenkinson has provided charts for every station on the line showing in each case severally the number of passenger journeys begun there and the revenue collected from each. In this analysis Settle itself easily tops the bill, though from recollections of my own school days in the neighbourhood I would imagine that most passenger journeys booked at Settle would have been for stations south and east of Settle Junction, rather than into the fell country. In years between the two world wars none of the Scotch Expresses called at Settle at all. Of two close school friends of mine, brothers, who came from the ancient Scottish Border town of

Hawick, I never thought to ask them how they came to school, whether continuing in a Waverley Route express to Hellifield and getting a local back to Settle or Giggleswick, or changing at Carlisle and taking the first 'parliamentary' onwards. Incidently, for journeys east of Settle Junction I fancy more residents used Giggleswick station than Settle, because there were many more trains that stopped there! Appleby came second to Settle in pre-Grouping days for passenger business, but even with several of the Scotch Expresses regularly calling there, its takings rarely reached two thirds that of Settle. Appleby blossomed forth as a passenger station in British Railways days, with its takings far exceeding Settle at that time.

In pre-Grouping days of the stations in the real fell country, Garsdale, or Hawes Junction as it then was, was consistently the best, closely followed by Hawes Joint, at the end of the Midland branch where it made an end-on junction with the North Eastern Railway branch up Wensleydale. On the south of Blea Moor, Horton showed a steady climb to prosperity, almost equalling that of Hawes Junction before and during the First World War. In the High Pennines, Ribblehead and Dent could hardly have been expected to generate much traffic of their own, but in the pre-Grouping period, their showings were roughly equal to some of those in

*Another anhydrite train from Long Meg passing Blea Moor, hauled by 9F class 2-10-0 No. 92076 on 29th April 1967. (Derek Cross)*

the relatively lush countryside of the Eden Valley north of Appleby, like New Biggin, Culgaith and Little Salkeld, not to mention two stations higher up the valley, in Crosby Garrett and Ormside. The five last mentioned stations have all now been closed, but Ribblehead and Dent are still open as unmanned halts to deal with Dales Rail activity, to be mentioned.

Langwathby is the only station between Appleby and Lazonby to be retained, albeit only in the guise of an unstaffed halt, but in pre-Grouping days it was one of the busier country stations in the middle reaches of the Eden Valley. Writing of that period it is perhaps too much to say that it, and the adjoining Little Salkeld, had a tourist attraction nearby in the pre-historic monument known as 'Long Meg and her Daughters'. Even so, it was the London & North Western, and not the Midland which cashed in on this association and in 1878 named one of their express engines *Lang Meg*.

Of the five remaining intermediate stations on the Settle and Carlisle line, those lying north of the river crossing at Eden Lacy Viaduct, were immediately busy from the first opening of the railway. Indeed for a time Armathwaite and Cumwhinton surpassed Lazonby in coming third in passenger bookings after Settle and Appleby. North of Armathwaite the relative nearness of Carlisle undoubtedly acted as a magnet to attract

passenger business before the days of public and private road transport. One could guess that the solid block of 'black' in Jenkinson's chart, referring to stations like Cumwhinton and Scotby, included a proportion of season ticket holders who worked in Carlisle and who chose to live in the outlying villages. There is no information from the charts as to what happened between the two world wars, only that when publication of records was taken up again, as shown in the charts, the passenger stations at Cotehill, Cumwhinton and Scotby had been closed. As to the intervening period, although I was in Carlisle fairly frequently between 1929 and 1939, I have to confess that I was never on a regular passenger train that stopped at any of the five stations, much less, calling at the other five between Lazonby and Appleby. I did once venture into the north of this delightful region by the 'back door' as it were, by taking a North Eastern local from Carlisle to Wetherall to see and photograph the beautiful viaduct by which the line to Newcastle crossed the River Eden a short distance down stream from Armathwaite.

Turning to freight, apart from heavy minerals, at the height of its activity among the chief sources of revenue were the transport of cattle, sheep and milk. Although the farming business of the area, particularly the region north of Kirkby

*An up fast goods approaching Ais Gill Summit,*
*hauled by ex-LMS 2-6-0 No. 42864.*
(Millbrook House Ltd — Bishop Eric Treacy)

Stephen, would have made the transport of livestock somewhat intermittent, there were weekly
stock auctions at towns like Settle and Appleby
that would always generate a useful traffic in
the days before road transport took over. It is
difficult for a present-day student of railway
working to imagine the scene in one of the larger
goods yards on the line when cattle were being
loaded or unloaded en-mass, and driven through
the streets to some market place. Modelling
enthusiasts may have faithfully captured in their
lovingly constructed replicas the characteristic
look of those wagons, but the real thing, the
noise, animal and human, the turmoil and the
aroma (!) needed to be experienced at 'full size' to
be thoroughly appreciated. At the busiest times,
long lines of cattle wagons would form trains of
their own, conveyed as a separate entity from one
centre to another, but on a line like the Settle
and Carlisle, the frequency of loading docks at
most of the intermediate stations enabled cattle
wagons in ones or twos at a time to be attached
to the ordinary pick-up goods trains as required,
or perhaps added to a slow passenger train. It
was the same for sheep.

On page one of the July 1905 issue of *The
Railway Magazine*, there was reproduced one
of the earlier of F. E. Mackay's famous train
photographs with the caption 'Milk for London's
Millions'! It actually showed the 10.15 am train of
milk van empties for the West Country passing
the junctions at Old Oak Common and hauled by
the queerly rebuilt 'Badminton' class 4-4-0 *Earl
Cawdor*. This picture came to mind when I was
looking up my references to the construction of

the Express Dairy Company's depot beside the
Settle and Carlisle line a short distance south
of Appleby. This, believe it or not, was another
case of 'Milk for London's Millions', the productivity of the Cumbrian cows was apparently
such, that in 1930 the Express Dairy Company
decided to build a special depot where supplies
from a large area in the Eden Valley could be
concentrated, and conveyed to Cricklewood in
express night trains. While the Great Western
milk trains were made up of long six-wheeled
vehicles "like a prison on wheels" as E. L. Ahrons
picturesquely described them, the LMS for its
Appleby–Cricklewood run used special glass-
lined containers in which the milk was inserted at
the depot, instead of loading churns directly as
they came from the farms. The entrance to the
Express Dairy depot at Appleby was controlled
by a 5-lever ground frame, and this was released
when required from Appleby West signal box.
The milk depot was closed in 1970.

Passing to freight activities at the southern end
of the line, as a boy whose early life had been
spent in the green shires south of the Thames,
I had been thrilled at my first sight of real
mountains in the Lake District and I found the
tremendous gash in the side of the Giggleswick
Scar, man-created by quarrying, awesome indeed.
But there was an even greater operation rather
higher up Ribblesdale at Stainforth. This was
beside the main line, but the quarry in the
Giggleswick Scar had no railway connection.
The Craven Lime Company did not wait for the
Settle and Carlisle line to be completed before
beginning quarrying operations at Stainforth.
In 1873, as soon as the railway was built up from
Settle, the enterprising company established their
first kiln for burning the lime. By arrangement
with the Midland Railway it is believed that
large quantities of lime and limestone were
sent away before the railway was opened for
regular business three years later. The site of the
original kiln, a little to the north of the far-more
extensive plant that followed, was shown on a
railway survey of 1913. The same survey shows
the extensive track layout, the workshop and
cottages, but a mere survey plan could not show
the immense effect of the quarrying into the
hillside, and even an aerial photograph taken
in 1938 did not represent the ultimate result.
Stainforth was an intermediate block post on the
main line from the opening of the railway, and it

*An ex-LMS Stanier 8F class 2-8-0 No. 48708, enters the curve through Dent, with a Long Meg–Widnes anhydrite train, May 1961. Rise Hill Tunnel can be seen in the distance. (G. W. Morrison)*

remained so until the cessation of work on the quarries virtually signalled the end of its usefulness, and it was closed in September 1963.

The block section was then extended from Settle to Helwith Bridge, a distance of some $4\frac{1}{2}$ miles. I remember the bridge itself and the tiny village as one of the staging points on some of our push-cycle runs in the last few terms I was at Giggleswick, but the important siding connections controlled by the signal box were not readily apparent from the highway bridge over the line and the river in the village. This bridge, on which we sometimes paused in our rides to watch for an oncoming up Scotch Express, was the subject of a dispute with the county authorities when the line was being built. A picturesque old bridge had served adequately to carry such traffic as there was and the Midland Railway proposed that the line should be intersected by a level crossing. The county authorities would not hear of this, and so a new bridge had to be constructed to span both the railway and the river. Looking southwards from that bridge there grew up an activity that was not there when I was at school, the granite sidings, serving the works of the Helwith Bridge Granite Company. In his monumental book on the history of the Midland Railway, F. S. Williams tells how the people at Helwith were chiefly engaged in working a slaty kind of stone which, he says, had the remarkable peculiarity of standing perpendicular, whether this was an ingredient of the rock the Granite Company set out to quarry in 1926, I cannot say.

The Granite siding was controlled by a 3-lever

ground frame associated with the signalling at Helwith Bridge. The home signal at the siding was 930 yards from the main signal box, and on its post was mounted the distant signal for the main interlocking. The signal at the siding, and its own associated distant, 450 yards in the rear, were normally in the clear position, and put to danger when authority was given from Helwith Bridge signal box for reversal of the points of the crossover road by electrical release. The stone for transport was carried to the siding by a belt conveyor from a quarry on the right bank of the river. There was no railway connection to the up main line, and the signals associated with the Granite siding were all upper quadrant semaphores, at the time the siding was taken out of use in 1969.

The original function of the signal box at Helwith Bridge, about half a mile north of the village and the road crossing, was to provide signalling for the triangular system of junctions that led to the Ribblesdale Lime Works which lay some distance west of the railway at the foot of the hills, opposite to the fine mountain Peny Ghent, which can be seen to great advantage from a passing train hereabouts. The Helwith Bridge signal box was brought into use in 1896, with a 12-lever frame. This was enlarged by one lever to provide releasing facilities when the ground frame for the Granite siding was installed in 1926. The last quarrying activity south of Blea Moor Tunnel was at Horton, where sight of the name Delaney on a Midland Railway plan of 1913 on a line leading to some more quarries to the west of the line awakened memories of an

*An up heavy goods passing Appleby on 29th June 1961, hauled by 9F class 2-10-0 No. 92167.*
(Derek Cross)

upset of more than 65 years ago. During the last years I was at Giggleswick my sister was at a small private school in Settle, of which the premises were owned by the Delaneys, who were large landowners in the district as well as being industrial magnates. Then the lease for the girls' school property came up for renewing, and the Head Mistress and owner apparently got at such loggerheads with the Delaneys over the revised terms that they gave her notice to quit. She and all the pupils and staff found seclusion at Oakamoor, in the Churnet Valley, in North Staffordshire. In the meantime Delaneys became part of Settle Limes Ltd.

The last item of industrial activity to be referred to in this chapter was sited on the right bank of the River Eden, a short distance downstream from Eden Lacy Viaduct. Access to the works of the Long Meg Plaster & Mineral Company had been provided by the installation of a main line signal box, with regular block working between Little Salkeld to the south and Lazonby to the north. This was put into operation in 1898, but as told in Chapter 4 it was closed in 1915. Such traffic as there was from the plaster works provided for by ground frame control from Little Salkeld, in the same way as with the Granite siding at Helwith Bridge. At the time of the closure of the original signal box the crossover road on the main line was removed, and the only connection was to the up main line. The vast anhydrite development of the 1950s, which needed extra facilities and a new signal box at Long Meg, had only just begun when,

in collaboration with my great friend, the late Bishop Eric Treacy, I wrote the first edition of *Main Lines across the Border*. The new Long Meg box had only been opened in 1955, yet Eric secured a fine picture of a train of empty hopper wagons toiling up to Blea Moor, behind an "Austerity" 2-8-0, returning from Widnes.

The new signal box titled Long Meg Sidings was of the modern, rather unprepossessing flat-roofed type. It was built on the down side of the line to provide the best possible outlook towards the nest of sidings reaching to the quarries. There were three of these where empty trains could be berthed, and two for loaded trains. In addition there was a so-called siding for 'cripples', but in photographs of these sidings this particular line always seemed to be full of loaded wagons, sheeted up ready for dispatch. When the anhydrite traffic first began in 1955, LMS and "Austerity" 2-8-0 locomotives were used, but after the introduction of the 9F class 2-10-0s an allocation of a batch of these to the Settle and Carlisle line was very welcome. They were put on to the anhydrite trains and did very well. What the manning arrangements were I do not know, but I can hardly think that one crew handled them throughout. From Hellifield they used the former LYR, then over the joint LYR and LNWR line to Chorley; next a short section of pure LYR to Adlington, another three miles of 'Joint' to Boars Head, where the West Coast Mainline was entered upon. All unknowingly, I had a trip over this route in the reverse direction when the Birmingham-Glasgow sleeper was for some reason diverted this way north of Wigan. After a long day's work I slept soon after I got into bed, and early next morning in the half-light of a cloudless summer dawn I was surprised to find we were speeding down, not from Shap but from Ais Gill!

Now turning from traffics to control and signalling from Midland Railway days, the line has always been worked on the manual block system, though some important refinements were added after the grevious accident at Hawes Junction on 24th December 1910. At its busiest days, just after the First World War, the block posts northward from Settle Junction were Settle, Stainforth, Helwith Bridge, Horton, Selside, Ribblehead, Blea Moor, Denthead, Dent, Hawes Junction (later renamed Garsdale), Ais Gill, Mallerstang, Kirkby Stephen, Crosby Garrett,

Griseburn Ballast Sidings, Ormside, Appleby, Appleby North Junction, Long Marton, New Biggin, Culgaith, Langwathby, Little Salkeld, Long Meg Sidings (closed 1915, new box in 1955), Lazonby, Armathwaite, Low House Crossing, Cotehill, Howe & Co's Sidings, Cumwhinton, Scotby, Durran Hill Junction and finally Petterill Bridge Junction, the last named being under the control of the North Eastern Railway, later the LNER. Although using conventional lower quadrant semaphore signals the Midland Railway had designed their own distinctive pattern of arm and spectacle using a white circle instead of the conventional white band on the facing side of the red painted arm. In pre-Grouping days also the distant arms were red with the same white circle. Sometimes, as between Ribblehead and Blea Moor, where the block posts were fairly close together, the signal department economised by mounting two distant arms on the same post. The up line distant for Ribblehead was below the down line distant for Blea Moor, and providing an exposition of the back and front of the arms — red with the circle facing, and white with a horizontal black band extending from end to end of the blade.

When the Paget system of Train Control was first introduced, primarily to expedite the working of the vast coal traffic southwards from the Yorkshire collieries, the working of passenger trains was not included. But during the later years of the war, when the ordinary passenger service was much restricted, the opportunity was taken to include all the traffic in the control system. Reporting eventually to the Control Office at Derby there were a number of District Controls, and those governing the working of the Settle and Carlisle line were at Leeds and Carlisle. By means of the private telephone network installed throughout the railway, signal boxes and stations could speak to Control, and Control could speak with any of them individually. Control did not interfere unnecessarily in traffic, it being assumed that it was the duty of the men along the line to keep in contact with the trains only a few chosen signal boxes sent regular routine reports to Control, by telephone announcing the arrival, departure, or passing of trains. On the Settle and Carlisle line the reporting boxes were Blea Moor, Ais Gill, Appleby station, Appleby North Junction and Durran Hill Junction. The five boxes did not necessarily report all train move-

ments. Blea Moor, where there were watering facilities, was required to report the arrival, departure and passing of all freight trains and their engines. Ais Gill, the division point between the Leeds and Carlisle Control areas, was required to report all train movements, particularly the detaching of bank engines. Appleby North was concerned ordinarily only with down line traffic, passenger and freight.

Now to conclude this chapter I am stepping a little outside the realm of indigenous traffics to describe a run I made just before the Second World War on one of the night freight trains using the route. The train in question carried a through and unchanged load from Manchester to Glasgow, and I rode right through, not on the footplate this time but in the guard's brake van. The origin of this unusual trip needs some explaining. One of the monthly magazines to which I was contributing an occasional article on railway subjects, had published two of mine describing footplate runs on fast freight trains, and after the second one of these appeared the editor wrote to me suggesting a trip at the back end of one of these freight trains. My professional work was keeping me very busy at that time, and I put the suggestion on one side; but meeting a friend in the Operating Department of the LMS soon after I put the suggestion to him. He said at once, why not the 8.40 pm from Manchester Ancoats to Glasgow? Although he promised me a rather grisly night he could fix it up any time I

*Another Long Meg–Widnes anhydrite train, here seen passing Dent in April 1967, with 9F class 2-10-0 No. 92009 in charge. (Derek Cross)*

*An unnamed 'Britannia' class 4-6-2 No. 70029 (formerly Shooting Star), on a down freight consisting mainly of empties from Widnes to Long Meg, seen here near Stainforth on 18th April 1967.*
(G. W. Morrison)

wanted to go. This was easier said than done. That train, I gathered, did not run at weekends and it was not until the end of May 1939 that I was able to go. The air was then full of 'wars and rumours of wars' and it was not until some eighteen months later that my account of the trip, in a somewhat censored form, was printed.

This reference to the Midland Scotch goods service is not so irrelevant as it might at first appear. The company had running powers over the Lancashire & Yorkshire lines from Hellifield southwards, and from 1888 they began working the Scotch Expresses with their own engines through to Manchester. At the same time the Carlisle express goods drivers from Durran Hill began running through to the Midland goods station in Manchester, Ancoats, by the same route I was to follow on my trip in May 1939. So far as northbound traffic for the Settle and Carlisle route to Scotland, Ancoats is in really the most inconvenient place in the Manchester perimeter one could possibly imagine. The rail exit from the station faces south-east and we had to be drawn out by a pilot engine, with the brake van leading for nearly a mile, to Ancoats

Junction, where the main line engine was waiting to couple up at the opposite end of the train. We had a load only one short of the maximum scheduled for this service, 31 covered vans vacuum fitted, and with a 20-ton brake van I estimated that the full load behind was about 390 tons. The engine was a "Black Five", No. 5266, working to Carlisle.

Although we were now pointing more or less in the right direction we still had to make a $3\frac{1}{2}$ mile circumlocutionary way round the north-eastern suburbs of Manchester, passing Philips Park, and Miles Platting before joining the east to west main line of the Lancashire & Yorkshire system, to pass through Victoria station, and so to Salford. And from Ancoats goods terminal it had taken nearly three-quarters of an hour before we were properly on our way, and keeping our booked working time exactly. But we were now getting into our real stride at last, and riding on the open rear platform of the van the increased speed was most exhilarating. It was a warm fine night, and even at 9.30 pm dusk was only just coming. Our three tail lamps were lit, and the side ones shone forward too, like great yellow eyes, on each side of the platform. On the gradual rise towards Bolton speed rose to 29 mph the van riding very smoothly, as it did also when we were slowing down to take the sharp curve at Bolton West Junction. The couplings were all screwed tight, every vehicle was fitted with the vacuum brake.

We were now on a bank as steep as Beattock. For $6\frac{1}{2}$ miles from Bolton the gradient is 1 in 72, and up this we went at a steady 20 mph — good going with a 390-ton load. Heavy grades such as this are characteristic of the railways of north-east Lancashire, and after breasting the summit at Walton Siding we entered upon an equally abrupt descent towards Blackburn. The guard and I went inside the van for Walton Tunnel, "a dirty hole", as Bailey put it, full of swirling smoke clouds, and the dim light from one oil lamp showed the vacuum gauge needle dropping back; signals were against us at Spring Vale, and the driver was braking. Nevertheless we were through Blackburn, $24\frac{1}{2}$ miles from Manchester Victoria in $55\frac{1}{2}$ minutes.

But a more severe check came just as we were going down the bank past Langho at 53 mph; permanent way work was in progress at Whalley, and we had to slow down to 15 mph. This put us two minutes behind time, but No. 5266 and her crew were equal to the occasion and brought us into Hellifield exactly on time. It was now 11.5 pm. Five minutes were spent taking water and then we got away on the non-stop run to Carlisle. After a welcome downhill start there comes the gruelling ascent to Blea Moor — a solid 14 miles at 1 in 100. The driver made the most of the favourable start, working No. 5266 up to 52 mph in $3\frac{1}{4}$ miles, but after passing Settle Junction speed quickly fell off, while for half an hour we forged our way up among the giants of the Pennines. It was a fascinating ride — fascinating in its quiet novelty. The moon shining fitfully through banks of cloud revealed a surprisingly

great expanse of wild country. Out on the back platform, out of the beam of the lamps, it was almost light enough to read my watches; on ahead, a splash of bright yellow fire-glow showed the whereabouts of the engine, but at the rear end there was none of the noisy glamour that characterises travel on the footplate. We were getting up in great style, and came past the lonely signal box at Blea Moor exactly four minutes early; the 17.2 miles from Hellifield had taken 38 minutes, and throughout the 14 mile climb we had averaged 26 mph.

At Blea Moor the hardest climbing ends. Getting along on a track on a steep mountainside, where the line is protected by snow fences, we quickly gathered speed; Garsdale was passed at 53 mph and we took the final short rise up to Ais Gill Summit fairly flying, without speed falling below $44\frac{3}{4}$ mph. Some fast downhill running now followed, with several miles at 57 to 58 mph, nearing Kirkby Stephen, but then unfortunately there came delays; a slower freight train was ahead, and we were stopped before she was shunted out of our way. So instead of averaging well over 50 mph we took 30 minutes for the 13.6 miles from Kirkby Stephen through Appleby to Long Marton. Once past the latter station we got a clear road and No. 5266 put on a fine spurt down the lower Eden Valley; 22 miles were reeled off at an average of $52\frac{1}{2}$ mph and we went through Armathwaite at a full 60 mph.

As at Manchester the timing through the crowded purlieus of the passenger station at Carlisle was very liberal, and although we were twice stopped by signals we were able to keep the 18 minutes allowance for the 4.6 miles from Scotby to Kingmoor Yard. Our net time over the 78.5 miles from Hellifield was 115 min a very good average of 41 mph; but our actual time was 142 min. At Kingmoor, No. 5266 came off, and was relieved by another engine of the same class for the continuation running in Scotland.

# 17
# A Test Arena for the Colossi

The Midland Railway always bearing in mind the need for improving the efficiency of its locomotives, had tended to run trials when they were needed on the heavily-graded route nearest to headquarters, that from Derby to Manchester. It was only when the first two Johnson compounds were built, specially for the Scotch Express traffic north of Leeds, that tests, later to be publicised in the technical press, were run on the Settle and Carlisle route. But after the Grouping, with the desire to prove that the compounds were superior to all others, and now possessed of two dynamometer cars, it was the logical thing to base the new trials at Carlisle, where the rival North Western and Caledonian engines were on hand. Because the Operating Department then were planning to re-organise the LMS passenger service on Midland lines they considered that no larger engines than Class 4 compounds would be needed to do the job. The fact that a Class 5 LNWR 4-6-0 of the 'Claughton' class was tested in 1924 was just to show, as Derby was concerned, how much superior a Midland Class 4 engine was to an LNWR Class 5. Although later tests in the interwar years had different objects, dynamometer car trials on the Settle and Carlisle line, with the sole exception of the *Rooke* exploit of 1937, were made with none larger than Class 5 engines.

From 1948 the mechanical and electrical engineers of The Railway Executive knew that they had a test ground par excellence to which the largest and most powerful locomotives could be

sent. In all the 72 miles between Settle Junction and Petteril Bridge Junction outside Carlisle, there was not a single speed restriction and on the falling gradients speeds up to a maximum of 90 mph, sometimes more, could be attained in perfect safety. The only drawback with these steep gradients was they could not be used in continuation of the high output performance required by the test on the uphill sections. The Settle and Carlisle line was thus at a disadvantage compared to the test routes worked over by locomotives undergoing scientific examination by the Controlled Road Testing procedure, after a spell on the Stationary Plant in Swindon Works. There the moderate gradients of the Bristol main line, and of the Badminton line towards South Wales, enabled full speed at maximum steaming rates to be continued, whereas on the Settle and Carlisle line, tests at high or maximum steaming rates had to be ended when the summits were reached in both directions of running. In some cases on southbound runs when engines were being worked very hard the tests were concluded in the neighbourhood of Kirkby Stephen to avoid the risk of getting a heavy slip in Birkett Tunnel.

Over the Settle and Carlisle line, between 1951 and 1958 tests were made on a 'Britannia', a 'Merchant Navy' class 4-6-2 from the Southern, a new BR5 Standard mixed traffic 4-6-0, an ex-LMS 'Duchess' class Pacific, and one of the Class 9F Standard 2-10-0s. The test results, which covered work on the Rugby Testing Station as well as the Controlled Road Test runs out on the

*A test train with 'Britannia' class 4-6-2 No. 70005* John Milton, *standing in Durran Hill sidings, prior to a run to Skipton on 7th June 1951.* (A. Rimmer)

line, were published in the Bulletins issued by British Railways from time to time except, unfortunately, one for the ex-LMS 'Duchess'. However by the kindness of the then-Chief Mechanical Engineer of the London Midland Region I was supplied with some highly significant data of these tests. But one of the most remarkable and annoying features of the road tests of these large locomotives is the paucity of photographic evidence. A few shots, often little better than 'snaps', were taken by engineers in between their regular duties on the test trains in the dynamometer car, but that unfortunately was all. Of course the tests were all made at mid-week, and with the trains of empty stock starting from the sidings at Durran Hill, and at the southern end not going into the passenger station at Skipton, they were more or less occult from public gaze. At Carlisle, while the former Midland running sheds had been closed for a long time, there was a freight line from the LNW to the North Eastern line whereby engines shedded at Upperby Bridge could reach Durran Hill without being seen by any lynx-eyed observer from Citadel station. All the same, it seems odd that the grape-vine had not reached such an experienced and more or less officially credited a photographer as Bishop Eric Treacy.

The first of the really big engines to be tested over the route was the 'Britannia', No. 70005 *John Milton*. As briefly mentioned in Chapter 15, this engine was prepared for testing before leav-

ing the erecting shop at Crewe, and there is little doubt of the intention to issue a Bulletin on the test results as soon as possible, underlining the generally favourable impression created when the locomotives first took the road. Then unbeknown to the general public, and to many non-technical but interested and sympathetic observers, the men most concerned with the running of these engines began to feel that there was something 'not quite right'. Drivers had reported cases of unexplained slipping, and then came the occurrence that could well have been a tragedy, of engine No. 70004 *William Shakespeare* on the inward bound "Golden Arrow" slipping so badly, at high speed west of Ashford, that one of the side rods was buckled and fractured. Fortunately no derailment took place, but the incident was so serious that Riddles took the step of withdrawing the whole class from traffic, pending urgent examinations. From some of those near to the heart of the enquiry I learned that several other engines of the class had become suspect, and one at least had loose wheels.

At the time of the accident to No. 70004, the sister engine, working on the Settle and Carlisle line and being steamed up to rates unheard of in previous British locomotives, had not shown the slightest signs of the coupled wheels moving on their axles. All the same, No. 70005 was sent back to Crewe to await attention with the rest of the class. The 'Britannias', like the Stanier LMS

*Freezing wintry conditions on another test run with No. 70005* John Milton: *taking water at Blea Moor after a maximum output run up to Ais Gill.* (W. H. King)

Pacifics had hollow driving axles, as had the largest Great Western express locomotives, but it was only on the 'Britannias' that the trouble with moving wheels occurred. It was cured by plugging the hollow axles for the length of the wheel fit. Thus modified No. 70005 went back to Carlisle to finish the tests, which from the scanty photographic evidence that has been preserved took place when there was deep snow in the High Pennines. There is no doubt that the boffins at 222 Marylebone Road were determined to make the 'Britannia' outperform every other British steam locomotive in existence, and on a test run made on 15th February 1952 they successfully steamed No. 70005 at a constant feed water rate from the tender at 36,150 lb per hour. The drawbar horsepower frequently rose to well over 2,300, and during the period of the Controlled Road Tests cut-off was never less than 40 per cent, with full regulator, and sometimes nearly 60 per cent.

On a test in conditions giving approximately the most economical coal consumption the feed rate from the tender, during the 30-minutes that the Controlled Road Test lasted, was 22,400 lb per hour. The first weighed bag of coal was delivered on to the footplate soon after passing Armathwaite, and the test was concluded on passing Crosby Garrett. The load behind the tender was 468 tons, but this included two of the mobile testing units, and the electrical load they supplied as a supplement brought the total equivalent to 540 tons. This run was made on 4th

February 1952 and an appreciable fall in speed took place after Culgaith until after Long Marton. This was necessary to observe a temporary speed restriction for civil engineering work, and in order to maintain the constant steaming conditions, the brakes were applied and cut-off in the cylinders increased to nearly 40 per cent. Otherwise the speeds were much the same as one would expect with an ordinary express passenger train over this route, though the equivalent load of 540 tons involved a coal rate of 3,360 lb per hour, and thus needed the provision of two firemen on the footplate. The test train was running in a path not too far ahead of the ordinary express trains leaving Carlisle around noon, the "Thames-Clyde Express" and the "Waverley", and the test train was put into the goods loop at Blea Moor to let them pass. There water was taken and some snaps secured by the testing staff, despite the snow.

Ten days later came the herculean effort at high steaming rate, when the equivalent load, boosted very considerably by the electrical effect from the two mobile testing units, was no less than 850 tons. The dead weight of the actual vehicles was actually less than that of the previous journey. The same speed restrictions applied from Culgaith to Long Marton, and to maintain the constant steam rate, when the brakes were applied to reduce speed to the required limit, involved working the engine up to 59 per cent cut-off. It will be seen there were two bouts of slipping, but it should be added however, that while the test to give the most economic coal consumption was made with Blidworth coal, the testing staff took care to have allocated to them the best used in testing locomotives at Rugby, from South Kirkby Colliery. Comparing the details of the two runs it is also interesting to note the running times made over the 22.8 miles from Lazonby to Crosby Garrett. On 4th February, with an equivalent load of 540 tons, the time was 28 minutes 10 seconds, and on the second day, with the equivalent load of 850 tons, the time was $29\frac{3}{4}$ minutes. These times give average speeds of 48.4 and 46 mph, including the speed restricted length between Culgaith and Long Marton. The coal rate on 15th February was the somewhat staggering one of 5,600 lb per hour, definitely needing two firemen!

However carefully I studied the Bulletin subsequently issued by British Railways, and when writing a commentary upon it for *The Engineer*, and a leading article to tie in with it, I could not help letting my imagination stray back to that snowy 14th February 1952 when such a mighty effort was made for half an hour along the middle reaches of the Eden Valley. One thinks of where a photographer, if he had known what was afoot, would have positioned himself. Beautiful as is the

river scenery above Armathwaite it is rather too confined for such a stupendous spectacle. I would have chosen the line immediately above Griseburn Viaduct where the speed was just under 40 mph and the engine was working in 53 per cent cut-off with full regulator. What a sight that train would have made with the exhaust shooting almost vertically upwards, with a vista across the Eden Valley from the viaduct to snow-clad Crossfell, monarch of this range of the Pennines. And what of the noise. One would have needed the sound-track, stock-in-trade of most locomotive enthusiasts of today, when riding in steam-hauled special trains. One feature of test equipment was missing on these trials — the engine was not indicated, and no shelter was fitted to the front-end. The indicating for these trials had all been done on the stationary plant at Rugby.

Next to go into the arena was one of the new 'BR5' mixed traffic 4-6-0s, No. 73008. This was a design based almost entirely on the famous "Black Five" 4-6-0 of the LMS with certain modifications introduced by British Railways. In the Interchange Trials of 1948 the "Black Fives" were matched against the ex-LNER B1 4-6-0s and the Great Western 'Halls', though for reasons not to be discussed in the present book,

*A later 'Britannia' 4-6-2, No. 70039, then unnamed, but formerly* Sir Christopher Wren, *pounding up past Ais Gill Summit with a heavy special train on 5th February 1967; note the pile of coal on the tender!*
(G. W. Morrison)

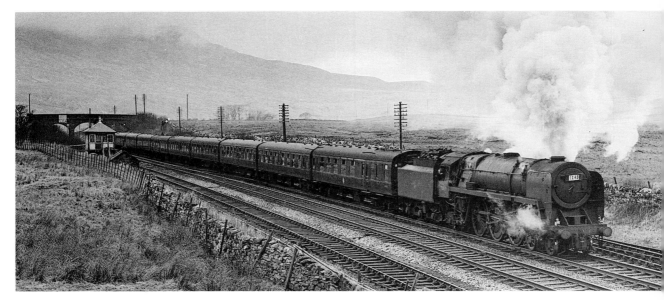

they did not come out as well as the ex-LMS people thought they ought to have done. Once they had got engine No. 73008 on test at Rugby and then on the Settle and Carlisle line it seemed they were determined to show the true colours of the neo-Stanier 4-6-0. As with the 'Britannia' class, No. 73008 was selected for the trials and was prepared for testing during construction of the class at Derby. In the Bulletin subsequently published by British Railways it was stated that the engine had not run more than 880 miles in ordinary traffic before being sent to Rugby for tests on the Stationary Plant. She then ran an equivalent of 9,120 miles on the plant before she was sent up to Carlisle, for another 2,800 miles of running between Durran Hill and Skipton. As with the 'Britannia', all the time with special trains made up of ordinary coaching stock with the Horwich dynamometer car. During the tests on the Settle and Carlisle line the engine was not subjected to indicator trials. Indicating had been very comprehensively carried out at Rugby.

The published Bulletin contains only one chart of an actual test run, described as one at high steaming rate. The mean rate of feed from the tender was 23,100 lb per hour, as against the highest registered with the B1 class 4-6-0 of 18,020 lb per hour. On the trip with the BR5 4-6-0 made on 6th March 1952, the test train included two mobile units behind the dynamometer car, and while the dead weight of the vehicles was 433 tons, the approximate equivalent load was 560 tons. The coal rate was 3,360 lb per hour, thus needing two firemen. As with the B1 trials, the first weighed bag of coal, thereby initiating the 'summation of increments' procedure, was supplied to the footplate near Appleby. Before then of course care had been taken to establish the firing and steaming to the stipulated rate, and then the Controlled Road Test continued up to Ais Gill Summit, and the level gradients almost until passing Dent. The performance of the engine, fired with Grade 1a South Kirkby coal, was excellent. The actual drawbar horsepower never went below 1,000, even on the heaviest gradients above Kirkby Stephen and approaching Ais Gill, when the speed was a little over 30 mph, and it rose to about 1,400 on some of the fast stretches.

Referring to the published Bulletin, it can be seen that in comparable steaming conditions when fired with South Kirkby coal, the drawbar horsepower of the locomotive related to running on level track was 1,300 at 30 mph, tapering off to 1,250 at 60 mph, and the indicated horsepower rose from 1,440 at 30 mph to 1,600 at 60 mph. The test of 6th March 1952 needed some pretty hard pounding of the engine, although of course the machinery must have become used to it by this time, if one can apply a human touch to the bits and pieces of a locomotive. Throughout the Controlled Road Test the cut-off, with full regulator all the time, was never less than 34 per cent,

*The new dynamometer car of 1949, No. 3 (No. M45049) used on certain of the maximum power tests.*
(British Railways)

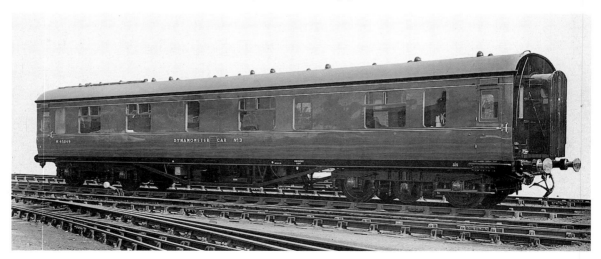

and on the steepest parts of the ascent from Ormside to Ais Gill it was 42 per cent Griseburn Box, 48 per cent at the south end of Birkett Tunnel, and 52 per cent over the last hundred yards or so to Ais Gill. With cut-off quickly reduced after the summit speed rose to 65 mph at Garsdale and then with cut-off increased from 34 to 37 per cent to carry the train through Rise Hill Tunnel the drawbar horsepower rose to 1,400 before the test was concluded.

There is no doubt that Riddles and his staff must have felt highly gratified by the results of the tests on the BR5. While the Bulletin is careful to explain, not all the results when using the somewhat lower graded Blidworth coal showed the consistency of steaming as on the best runs. There is no mention of running with this coal on the Settle and Carlisle line, though many tests were actually made with it. So far as the maximum performance with engine No. 73008 was concerned, the results showed that a locomotive nominally of Class 5 capacity could exceed the maximum efforts of designs, such as the Great Western 'Castles'. In the much publicised trials of No. 4074 *Caldicot Castle* in 1924, the maximum drawbar horsepower was about 1,200 and the indicated horsepower a little over 1,400 on the ascent from Taunton to Whiteball Tunnel. This is not to say that these figures were the maximum any 'Castle' could attain, particularly in carefully regulated test plant conditions. But the diagrams

published in the technical press of 1924 show also that boiler pressure was tending to fall during the ascent to Whiteball, and that water level in the boiler was falling rapidly. This apart, congratulations to all who worked on the BR5 4-6-0 No. 73008 on that splendid test trip of 6th March 1952.

After the BR5 came 4-6-2 No. 35022 *Holland America Line* from the Southern Region, early in 1952. It is sometimes said that certain locomotive designs reflect the personalities of their creators. If this be so there has never been a more vivid example than that of the 'Merchant Navy' class, and equally of their smaller counterparts, the 'West Country' 'Battle of Britain' class. When the London & North Eastern Railway was formed in 1923, and H. N. Gresley was appointed as its Chief Mechanical Engineer, he chose O. V. S. Bulleid as his personal assistant. It was not by any means a choice that gave wholehearted satisfaction among the rest of the widely spread department, but Bulleid's volatile and mercurial ways were largely covered by Gresley's massive calm, and the locomotive work of the LNER went from strength to strength — more or less. The high pressure compound 4-6-4 No. 10000 was one of the failures, despite the efforts of Bulleid to run the engine in regular service. Then, when R. E. L. Maunsell was on the point of retiring from Chief Mechanical Engineer of the Southern Railway and the post was offered to Bulleid he took it with

*Inspection before a maximum power run to Carlisle on Stanier Pacific No. 46225* Duchess of Gloucester.
(W. H. King)

great enthusiasm. In most British railway circles however the post was then regarded as no more than a mechanical caretaker, until the time when the entire Southern Railway system was electrified, at any rate as far west as Salisbury, and Weymouth, but how Bulleid reacted is now a matter of locomotive history.

When he took over at Waterloo the war clouds were already gathering fast, but he was quickly making plans for a super-locomotive to cope with the increasing loads on the boat trains and the principal West of England services. The night ferry trains were often double-headed and that, as a devoted admirer of Sir Nigel Gresley he could not stand. War or no war he went ahead with his great new Pacific, and sensing that the wartime Railway Executive Committee would veto its construction if they had realised it was primarily for express passenger service he successfully 'pulled the wool over their eyes', as the saying goes, by describing them as 'mixed traffic' engines. The publicity department of the Southern Railway loyally backed him up by issuing to the press, photographs of the first engines of the class working goods trains. Mixed traffic engines my foot. They were no more mixed traffic than Sir Nigel Gresley's streamlined A4 Pacifics on the LNER, with which incidently Bulleid himself had had some part in the design. The mixed-traffic myth was perpetuated in the introductory remarks in the British Railways Bulletin on the test results obtained with engine No. 35022, published in January 1954. Bulleid had retired from railway service in Great Britain in 1949, and was then in Dublin, firmly ensconced as CME of the Irish railways. He was not consulted at any time during the tests, and if he ever read the ensuing report he might have been amused at the 'song and dance' engine No. 35022 led the testing staff thus:

"This design of locomotive proved to be difficult to test owing to its inconsistent performance, especially with regard to power output. Not only was it often found impossible to obtain reasonable accuracy of repetition on different occasions but the performance would sometimes change appreciably over quite short periods of time. The changes were usually not of such magnitude as would have affected the locomotive's ability to carry out its normal duties quite effectively, but were such as to make accurate measurement exceptionally difficult, especially on the stationary test plant.

The valve gear, which was a special feature of the design, gave some peculiar difficulties in testing. It was found that the actual cut-off bore no definite or consistent relationship to the setting of the reversing gear, not only for the locomotive as a whole but especially for the individual cylinder ends. In the shorter cut-offs particularly, there was a general tendency for the actual mean cut-off to lengthen with increasing speed but not in a smooth or regular manner. The power output in the short nominal cut-offs in the upper part of the speed range was found to be greater than that of other locomotives, size for size, and was in some cases more than would theoretically be possible at an actual cut-off equal to the nominal cut-off, even assuming that the cylinders were completely filled up to the point of cut-off with steam at full steam chest pressure and that no early release occurred. The true cut-off must have been longer than the nominal. At times quite random changes occurred that appeared to be caused by minute changes of speed or boiler pressure. Some of these random changes were relatively small, though enough to upset the test conditions, but others were of relatively large amount. Whilst changes that occurred over a period of weeks or months might be ascribed to wear of the motion, however small, this could hardly be the case with changes from one day to the next or which occurred, sometimes more than once, in a single test period."

The Bulleid Pacifics in their original form, as engine No. 35022 was during the tests, were always prone to slipping. This was ascribed to the fact that it cannot be run for an appreciable time without lubricating oil reaching the wheel treads and, on the Test Plant, the rollers. Thorough cleaning before every test and wiping of the Test Plant rollers at frequent intervals were necessary to enable any high powered tests to be completed. Whereas usually a severe slip can be tolerated on the line, on the plant it results only in the need to repeat the test in progress. With this locomotive it was also liable to lead to buckling of coupling rods, which occurred on a number of occasions during the tests on the plant and on the line.

It may or may not be significant that no photographic record, or test chart was included in the Bulletin. So far as the Controlled Road Tests were concerned, it was stated that the ranges of speed, nominal cut-off and steaming rate were all appreciably less than on the stationary plant. The maximum steaming rate was limited to about 29,000 lb/hr which sufficed to work a train of 20 bogie coaches, 594 tons, at the scheduled speeds involved, this being the largest number of bogie coaches that have ever been operated over this route. This was over 40% above the rostered tare load, on limited load schedules, for a Class 7 4-6-0, this being the most powerful locomotive normally permitted. Some 3,840 miles were run on these Controlled Road Tests, but how the engine, and more particularly the testing staff, fared has not been made public, except that the engine buckled her coupling rods several times.

The next visitor to the Settle and Carlisle line for testing was also a Pacific, but of a very different kind, and in my opinion the finest express passenger design that has ever run the rails in Great Britain, the 'Duchess' class. Sir William Stanier could never be called an ace-engine designer but he was a superlative workshop man and had the rare gift of selecting the men for posts that came within his large department. In no case was he more successful in choosing T. F. Coleman to succeed to the post of Chief Draughtsman at Derby, after the veteran H. Chambers had relinquished the job. Once the broad outlines of the design had been settled by Stanier himself Coleman virtually did all the detailed designing. In fact, most of the work was done while Stanier was away in India, as a member of the Committee of Enquiry set up after the terrible derailment at Bihta, which caused such a grievous loss of life. At about the same time as engine No. 46225 *Duchess of Gloucester* arrived at Rugby for testing, the prototype BR8 Pacific, No. 71000, was sent to Swindon. The fact that this latter engine was named *Duke of Gloucester* aroused some humorous comments as to which would come off best in this 'husband versus wife' encounter! In the event the Lady had very much the best of it, so much so that presumably to avoid embarrassing the prototype BR8 Pacific the full results from the 'Duchess' trials were never published.

In the meantime, on Mr Smeddle's invitation, I went to Swindon to see No. 71000 running on the stationary plant and later to accompany one of the Controlled Road Tests, in this particular case between Swindon and Westbury via Reading West and the Berks and Hants line. Almost the first words Sam Ell said to me when I arrived at

*Look-out ahead from a 'Britannia' approaching Ribblehead Viaduct, with Whernside as a misty background.* (Millbrook House Ltd — Bishop Eric Treacy)

the plant were "She's a coal scoffer." As always, of course, the tests were carried out with the utmost care and integrity and the published report went further than any others of the series, including a section on Cost of Energy and Performance Diagrams for a series of main line services typical of the locomotive's normal duties, in fact from Euston to Carlisle. At the same time Ell and his men felt that they would like to try certain modifications to the design of the locomotive to try to reduce its inordinately high coal consumption. But on referring it to Derby they would not hear of any change and the engine was returned to Crewe. It was somewhat significant however that it never took its place in the prestigious Euston-Glasgow link, but remained at Crewe North shed working principally to Euston, and not the double-home turns to Perth, which were a feature of the Crewe North duties for Pacifics.

So matters rested for several years until I came to write my book on Sir William Stanier's work.

I felt that the information that had leaked through the grape vine about the trials of the *Duchess of Gloucester* in 1956 was not really adequate. Knowing that some of those who had been smarting over the relatively unimpressive show put up by No. 71000 at Swindon had passed to other scenes, I wrote to Derby and was rewarded, not by any of the full charts of the Controlled Road Tests made on the Settle and Carlisle line, but of the dynamometer car record of a remarkable hill-climbing performance between Settle Junction and Blea Moor. On this occasion the engine was being steamed at the rate of 38,500 lb per hour, the highest ever to be recorded on a Controlled Road Test with a British locomotive, although at Rugby a rate of 40,000 lb per hour was sustained on several prolonged tests. The actual tonnage of the test train worked up to Blea Moor was 442, but the electrical load provided by the two mobile test units was such as to boost the equivalent load to be hauled by the locomotive to no less than 900 tons.

Between Horton and Blea Moor, to which the section of the dynamometer car chart sent to me relates, the engine was working with full regulator, cut-offs between 45 and 50 per cent, and the boiler pressure maintained steadily between 240 and the full 250 lb per sq in. The steam temperature was between 722 and 730 deg Fah. and the exhaust pressure at 6.9 deg. This magnificently sustained effort produced a steady speed of 30 mph on the 1 in 100 gradient, which needed an output of 2,000 drawbar horsepower, though related to level track one has to include the power needed to lift the engine and tender at that speed on a gradient of 1 in 100, in this case an extra 350 horsepower, making the total 2,350. While this superb performance gave ample evidence of the ability of these locomotives to climb the heaviest

gradients of their own West Coast Main Line north of Lancaster, one could feel that with high speed express passenger locomotives the running would have been even more convincing over a less heavily graded route, as that over which the Great Western 'King' class were tested, between Reading and Stoke Gifford. There is however no such stretch in the Settle and Carlisle terrain, so one must be content with the data provided.

The last of the big engines to be subjected to the Controlled Road System of testing was the BR 9F class 2-10-0. This was regarded purely as a freight locomotive and many of the trials were conducted over the former Glasgow & South Western line between Carlisle and Hurlford, some of them at constant speed. The only reference in the published Bulletin to running on the Settle and Carlisle line relates to a test at no more than a moderate rate of steaming, for one of these engines, of 20,050 lb per hour (feed from tender) on a mixed load of 641 tons. This included a number of fitted mineral wagons, taken over the usual course for Controlled Road Testing from Appleby until a little past Ais Gill. Care was apparently taken that the speed should not exceed 55 mph, though in ordinary passenger service, when these engines had been requisitioned in emergency, speeds in excess of 85 mph have been authenticated with them. On the Controlled Road Test graphed in the Bulletin the principal maximum and minimum were 54 mph at Ormside, 28 mph at Griseburn, 40 mph at Crosby Garrett, 26 mph south of Birkett Tunnel, 33 mph at Mallerstang, and 23 mph at Ais Gill. The average speed over the $16\frac{1}{2}$ miles of the test was 33 mph and the coal consumed during this period was 1,454 lbs, thus 88 lb per mile, and nothing to speak of compared with the performances of other engines in this chapter.

# 18
# Last Years of Regular Steam Haulage

During the 1950s, while the strangers were making their surreptitious ways between Durran Hill and Skipton, albeit usually making a great deal of noise about it for the farming community along the line, the "Converted Scots" were continuing on the double-home turns between Leeds and Glasgow St Enoch. The Edinburgh trains were worked to Carlisle by any common user "Black Five" that Whitehall Junction shed happened to have on hand, or so it often seemed. In collecting data for one of my earlier books on locomotive running I made a number of foot-plate journeys on Midland line trains, and one throughout from St Pancras to Carlisle on the "Thames–Forth Express", as it was then named. When we got to Leeds I was interested to see that we were to be taken forward by a Class 5 4-6-0 with Caprotti valve gear, one of a small group built in 1948 with Timken roller bearings throughout, No. 44754. We had an easily manageable load of nine coaches, 300 tons loaded, and this was before the post-war accelerations, so no pilot. The train was then booked to call at Skipton, Hellifield and Appleby. Unfortunately the machinery of the engine seemed at fault. She steamed freely, and

*A Glasgow–Leeds express approaching Settle Junction, June 1962, hauled by 'Britannia' 4-6-2 No. 70054* Dornoch Firth: *note the cone of Pen-y-Ghent on the skyline.* (Derek Cross)

*A 'Britannia' originally in East Anglia, No. 70010* Owen Glendower, *working an Edinburgh–Cardiff Rugby supporters' special, at Kirkby Stephen, 5th February 1967.* (G. W. Morrison)

ran freely when there was any help from the gradients, but as to power there seemed no 'go' in her at all. On the Settle and Carlisle line the result was rather pitiful.

We lost a small amount of time to Hellifield, and then, despite an initial dash up to 68 mph at Settle Junction we came down to a paltry 23 mph at Ribblehead before we were stopped by signal at Blea Moor. The effect of this check added to our poor ascent from Settle Junction made us $10\frac{1}{2}$ minutes down on schedule from Hellifield to Ais Gill. But with a generous 18 minutes for the 17.6 miles down to the Appleby stop we picked up $1\frac{3}{4}$ minutes, running freely, entirely without steam, but not exceeding a maximum of 72 mph. My last run on the train in the autumn of 1957, when it had been renamed "The Waverley", was very different, in lowering stormy weather, when to my disappointment we had to take a pilot for a load of 309 tons tare. My disappointment was short lived however for although we had a distinctly scruffy "Black Five" as train engine and an equally unkempt Midland 7 ft superheater re-build as pilot, the two pairs of men immediately set out to recover the ten minutes or so at which we had started and the result was one of the most exciting, if not the most comfortable, rides I have ever had over this route. The engines were 4-4-0 No. 40552 leading, and 4-6-0 No. 44853. The

pilot went through to Carlisle.

The first stage, to Shipley (Leeds Junction) is sharply timed and we did not re-gain any time here, but once we got beyond Keighley they began to pile it on, and with speeds of 66 to 68 mph we stopped at Skipton in 32 minutes. Another minute was regained to Hellifield, and then we were away indeed into the teeth of the storm. The driver on No. 44853 was working in 25 per cent cut-off at first, but passing Stainforth Quarries he advanced to 40 per cent and soon after Horton he opened out the main regulator to full open. The pilot was going hard also, and in the cold air there was much smoke and not a sign of the high mountains we were now amidst. Before the final opening out on the "Black Five" speed had briefly dropped to 36 mph, but it picked up quickly and we crossed Ribblehead Viaduct at 43 mph, and entered Blea Moor Tunnel at $39\frac{1}{2}$ mph. No more than $24\frac{3}{4}$ minutes from Hellifield to Blea Moor box, another $2\frac{1}{4}$ minutes gained, despite the stormy weather and when we emerged from the long tunnel and were racing over the high tableland, with the mountains only vaguely seen amid the flying clouds, the men on No. 40552 had a thrill of their own to provide us with. At Garsdale water-troughs the tank on their tender had more water than they thought. It quickly overflowed and to the elemen-

*Two 'Jubilee' 4-6-0s, Nos. 45593* Kolhapur *and 45596* Bahamas *on an LGCB excursion, southbound near Armathwaite on 4th June 1966 — both locomotives subsequently preserved.* (Derek Cross)

tal turmoil of the weather in those high regions, we on the train engine, had suddenly to withstand a cascade of water from the front! We were running at 67 mph soon, and topped Ais Gill at exactly 60 mph. A permanent way check at Crosby Garrett, to 15 mph, rather spoiled our fast run downhill from Ais Gill and cost us about two minutes, but we nevertheless stopped at Appleby in 55 minutes from Hellifield, three minutes under schedule despite the check.

From Appleby the Caprotti engine, No. 44754, having got down to more equable gradients had begun to display more of her true form, and being worked continuously in 15 per cent cut-off with the regulator practically full open, made some reasonable speed down to Carlisle. The double-headed train, timings of which are also included in the accompanying table, made some faster times until the immediate approach to Carlisle. Then it appeared that Citadel station was in its often-usual late afternoon muddle, because we were first of all stopped for six minutes, then signalled forward to be stopped a second time, and then graciously allowed to enter the station, 12½ minutes after we had passed Petteril Bridge Junction! I was proceeding to Edinburgh, also on the footplate on this occasion, and it was a great change from the murky rough-and-tumble "Black Five" to climb aboard an immaculately

clean A3 Gresley Pacific for the rest of the journey. In another way it was the prelude to the use of these engines on the Midland Scotch Expresses from Leeds northwards, and that was to come three years later.

By that time the regional boundaries had been changed somewhat. When Nationalisation came in 1948, the boundaries of the Eastern, London Midland and North Eastern Regions had remained those formerly of the LNER, Southern Area, the LMS, Midland Division and the LNER North Eastern Area respectively. In

"The Waverley": Appleby–Carlisle

| Engine No. | | 44754 | | 44853 | |
|---|---|---|---|---|---|
| Pilot Engine | | — | | 40552 | |
| Load, tons E/F | | 285/300 | | 309/325 | |
| Distance | | Actual | Speed | Actual | Speed |
| Miles | | m  s | mph | m  s | mph |
| 0.0 | Appleby | 0  00 | — | 0  00 | — |
| 2.9 | Long Marton | 4  43 | 61 | 4  17 | — |
| 11.0 | Langwathby | 12  15 | 65 | 11  56 | 71 |
| 15.3 | Lazonby | 15  55 | 74½ | 15  29 | 75 |
| 17.7 | Milepost 295 | 17  55 | 61½ | 17  35 | 64 |
| 20.8 | Armathwaite | 20  54 | 70 | 20  12 | 77 |
| 22.7 | Milepost 300 | 22  42 | 60½ | 21  43 | 71 |
| 26.9 | Cumwhinton | 26  17 | 76 | 25  00 | 79 |
| 28.1 | Scotby | 27  15 | 74 | 25  57 | 69 |
| 29.9 | Petteril Bridge Jc | 29  11 | — | 28  00 | — |
| | | — | | sigs sev | |
| 30.8 | Carlisle | 31  45 | | 40  27 | |

*The up "Waverley" nearing Ais Gill Summit hauled by 'Britannia' 4-6-2 No. 70053* Moray Firth, *June 1961. (G. W. Morrison)*

the new arrangement the North Eastern of British Railways was extended from the West Riding complex on the Midland line almost as far as Skipton. The new boundary point was Snaygill signal box, about a mile east of Skipton and covered by booked passing times in the working timetables. The operating arrangements, as well as the civil engineering boundaries were covered also, and this put all the Leeds running sheds concerned with long distance express traffic under the motive power superintendent of the North Eastern Region, with his headquarters still at York. The Leeds sheds coming under his wing were Whitehall Junction, Copley Hill and Farnley, in addition to the previous North Eastern shed at Neville Hill.

At that time the Motive Power Superintendent was F. H. Petty. Whether from ancestry or inclination I don't know, but in spirit he was a thoroughgoing 'Geordie', and I found when I was doing my book on the history of North Eastern Railway locomotives his enthusiasm was infectious. He not only looked out interesting workings where I could see the older NER freight engines at work, but was insistent that I sampled the few remaining duties of the celebrated R class 4-4-0s (LNER Class D20). And this was the man into whose charge the Whitehall Junction engines working on the Midland Scotch Express double-home turns to Glasgow St Enoch now came. In the Motive Power Department of the London Midland Region the "Converted Scots" had somehow descended from the pinnacle of fame which they had earned when first introduced.

To avoid the intermediate power classification '5X', applied to the "Baby Scots" and the 'Jubilees' these had been designated Class 6, and the "Converted Scots" like the 'Britannias', Class 7. From certain areas in the LM operating department there arose complaints that the "Converted Scots" were not Class 7 at all. The complaints were so insistent that BR Headquarters had to arrange for one of these engines to be put on to the Rugby Testing Plant to find out what, if anything was the matter with it. It seemed strange to me after Harrison, when CME of the London Midland Region, had previously confided in me personally that he thought the "Converted Scots" were the best engines the LM had. I suppose it was no more than natural that a former LNER man would have no time for Pacifics except for those designed by Sir Nigel Gresley!

Hardly had the fuss over the "Converted Scots" died down, which certain operating men on the LM Region regarded as no more than a storm in a tea cup, than the North Eastern Region was taking delivery of new English Electric Type 4 diesels for the East Coast Main Line express services. This would make some of the Gresley A3 Pacifics at Heaton and Gateshead sheds surplus to requirements, but while as one former LNER man termed them "those old things" might in any other circumstances been consigned to the scrap heap, the oldest of them being more than thirty years old, Petty had a very different use for them.

When K. J. Cook from Swindon, arrived at

*The up "Thames–Clyde Express", just after crossing Dent Head Viaduct, with a "Black Five" No. 44668 piloting a converted 'Royal Scot' No. 46109* Royal Engineer. *(G. W. Morrison)*

Doncaster to take up his dual appointment as Chief Mechanical Engineer of both the Eastern and the North Eastern Regions of British Railways he was well aware of the generous clearances that had been built into the Gresley Pacifics ever since their first construction and of the characteristic 'ring' that their motion had. As he once put it to me: "We scrap", naturally referring to his work at Swindon, "at the clearances they provided when new". Once having taken the measure of things he made arrangements for the system of optical lining up of frames and motion parts to be installed at Doncaster. Erection of repaired Gresley Pacifics was in future to the standards that had been set up in the 1930s at Swindon, as I experienced to my delight when I rode the A3 that took over haulage of the "Waverley" on the trip previously referred to in this chapter. And then Petty had sent some of these rejuvenated A3s to Whitehall Junction to take over the double-home turns to and from Glasgow St Enoch.

As soon as I knew what was going on I made application for a footplate pass to ride the "Thames–Clyde Express", and thereby I first met a man who was to be a very good friend, Locomotive Inspector A. H. Pullan, of Whitehall Junction. In LMS days no more than one person was permitted on the footplate other than the driver and fireman, and this tradition had been continued on the Midland Division of the LM Region at first, and all the earlier footplate journeys of mine described in this book had been made solo. Now I found Inspector Pullan

a tremendous enthusiast. He had grown up on the Midland, in its early transitional days to the LMS, and he was far from one of those men who were exclusively for the products of Derby, right or wrong. On the LMS he had graduated through North Western engines to the neo-Derby of the "Baby Scots", and to the neo-Swindon of the Stanier 4-6-0s, and I was interested to find him one of the few Midland men who had a good word to say for the 'Claughtons'. Out of my natural partiality for the products of Crewe I quizzed him on their reputation, in some quarters, for being indifferent steamers. "Steam", he exclaimed "they would steam on bricks, if they were properly fired!" As a fireman, incidentally, he had been on the "Baby Scot" No. 5538 when she was christened *Giggleswick* with full scholastic honours at Settle station in the late autumn of 1938.

It was a day in early August 1960 when I first rode on the A3 Pacifics on the "Thames–Clyde Express". I had travelled down from St Pancras that same morning on the "Waverley", so as to have plenty of time for the changeover at Leeds and for the subsequent Glasgow train, the A3 No. 60077 *The White Knight* came backing down. In her earlier days as A1 class No. 2576 the engine had been experimentally fitted with the A.C.F.I. feed-water heater, but that apparatus had been removed before the 220 lb per sq in boiler had been fitted. On the "Thames–Clyde Express" we had a good load of eleven bogies, 390 tons tare, nearly up to the maximum allowed for an A3 over this route, 405 tons, and at first we did well.

*The up "Thames–Clyde Express" nearing Ais Gill Summit behind ex-LNER Class A3 4-6-2 No. 60082* Neil Gow. (Bishop Eric Treacy)

Leaving Leeds just over one minute late, and observing a permanent way 'caution' which cost us another two minutes, we were on time at Settle Junction and also at Blea Moor, despite running into some very unseasonable August weather on the 'Long Drag', with drizzling rain and mist above Settle, which caused some slipping near Ribblehead.

But soon after we emerged from Blea Moor Tunnel we were in dead trouble. One of the injectors had been 'playing silly', as the saying goes on the 'Long Drag', and at Dent the second one went completely. With no more water entering the boiler the regulator had perforce to be shut, and from $62\frac{1}{2}$ mph at Garsdale we drifted over Ais Gill Summit while every effort was being made to get one injector to pick up again. Pullan had decided that the engine was in no state to continue from Carlisle to Glasgow and so we stopped at Kirkby Stephen for him to 'phone to have a fresh engine ready to take over. In the meantime the driver and fireman had got one injector working and by use of the first valve of the regulator and 15 per cent cut-off we made quite a brilliant run down the Eden Valley. We had plenty of steam, but the water supply was at a premium. Despite a short permanent slowing to 30 mph after Long Marton we averaged $66\frac{1}{2}$ mph over the 28.1 miles from Appleby to Scotby, or 69 mph net and would have regained two minutes, but for the inevitable delays outside Carlisle.

When he heard what had happened Petty at once offered to arrange another trip, but because of other commitments it was towards the end of October before I could go, and by that time the load of the train was unfortunately two coaches lighter. I was however rewarded by a superb run, and the details of this and the previous one are shown in the adjoining table. On the first run the driver of *The White Knight* had evidently been well-schooled in the best way to handle an A3 for he at once opened to full regulator and set the cut-off at 25 per cent. Although there was a permanent way 'caution' on the first stage to Shipley the engine was steaming freely, and cut-off was shortened from 25 per cent to 17 at Bingley, and to 12 per cent at Keighley. This gave us no more than a maximum of 58 mph before Snaygill, but full regulator and 17 per cent took us up the rising gradients to Milepost 230 in excellent style, and despite the hindrance of the permanent way check before Apperley Bridge we had regained the one minute of arrears with which we had started from Leeds on passing Hellifield. Because of the permanent speed restrictions on the line between there and Settle Junction the engine was worked on the first valve of the regulator so as not to exceed the limit of 60 mph past Long Preston, but as soon as Settle Junction came into sight the regulator was opened to the full, and we began the 'Long Drag' at 70 mph, now one minute early.

By this time the weather had soured-up on us and we went up through Settle and North Ribblesdale in drizzling rain. The driver continued his use of 17 per cent cut-off at first, but at Horton he advanced to 25 though this did not arrest a further fall in the speed, through slipping, before Ribblehead. By tradition, I discovered the firing was eased then and we entered Blea Moor Tunnel with only 180 lb per sq in, showing on the gauge. It was at Dent Head that the troubles with the injectors started, resulting in the stop at Kirkby Stephen, previously mentioned. The fast running shown in the table after the permanent way check at Long Marton was made with the engine working in 15 per cent cut-off with no more than the first valve of the regulator open. There was a slight opening out to take the train over the undulating gradients from Lazonby, but the regulator was shut altogether at the last summit point, at Milepost 300. But for the concluding checks from Durran Hill inwards we should have regained two minutes from Appleby to Carlisle, but against our total loss of twelve minutes on schedule, only eight minutes could be set against signal and permanent way checks; the remaining four minutes must go against the engine.

The repeat trip, with No. 60036 *Colombo*, with which I had previously enjoyed a good trip from Newcastle to Edinburgh with the "North Briton", when the engine was stationed at Gateshead, was exhilarating. This driver did not work below 20 per cent cut-off, and with the regulator not fully open for the faster stretches. The steam chest pressure gauge was not working on this engine, and as far as Hellifield the fireman kept the boiler pressure around 180 to 190 lb per sq in. The speed was excellent from the outset, and from Settle Junction, where the regulator was opened to the full and cut-off advanced at once to 25 per cent. We fairly stormed up the 'Long Drag', never falling below 43 mph until the firing was eased after Ribblehead, and we fell to 38 mph when entering Blea Moor Tunnel. Pressure had been kept at between 195 and 205 lb per sq in throughout the ascent with the cut-off unchanged at 25 per cent. We went easily over the tableland

on 15 per cent cut-off and half regulator, and when we passed Ais Gill, having left Leeds six minutes late, two minutes early, the rest of the run was a mere 'doddle' in comparison. The net time was 124 minutes, and on this occasion we got a clear run into Carlisle.

Nearly two years before I made my trips on the "Thames–Clyde Express" I had been approached by *The Railway Magazine* to take over authorship of the monthly feature "British Locomotive Practice and Performance", from Cecil J. Allen, who was retiring after having been in "the hot seat" since 1911! It was going to be no light task, because recently my professional work at Westinghouse had advanced to something of a climax with my being appointed Chief Mechanical Engineer of the Signal and Mining Division. Fortunately the directors with whom I was mainly concerned were enthusiastic about my extra-mural activities, and regarded the papers I gave to literary and technical societies, articles in the press, and the then occasional book, as accolades in the public relations sphere of the Company. Then in the early summer of 1963,

*The "Thames–Clyde Express" passing Ais Gill box with "Black Five" No. 44886 piloting an A3 Class Pacific No. 60038* Firdaussi, *16th July 1960. (G. W. Morrison)*

## Leeds–Carlisle: The "Thames–Clyde Express"

| Run No. | | | 1 | | 2 | |
|---|---|---|---|---|---|---|
| Date | | | 4.8.60 | | 21.10.60 | |
| Engine No. | | | 60077 | | 60036 | |
| Engine Name | | | *The White Knight* | | *Colombo* | |
| Loads, tons E/F | | | 390/410 | | 317/335 | |
| Start mins late | | | $1\frac{1}{4}$ | | 6 | |
| Distance Miles | | Sch min | Actual m s | Speed mph | Actual m s | Speed mph |
| 0.0 | Leeds | 0 | 0 00 | — | 0 00 | — |
| 0.6 | Whitehall Jc | | 2 05 | — | 2 35 | — |
| 3.3 | Kirkstall | | 6 18 | 54 | 6 57 | 52 |
| 4.6 | Newlay | | 7 49 | 56 | 8 30 | 56 |
| — | | — | p.w.s. | 30 | — | 53 |
| 7.6 | Apperley Br | | 12 07 | 50 | 11 49 | $54\frac{1}{2}$ |
| 10.9 | Shipley Br | 15 | 16 30 | 25* | 16 00 | — |
| 13.8 | Bingley | | 20 33 | 56 | 20 15 | 55 |
| 17.9 | Keighley | 23 | 24 05 | 48 | 23 52 | 50 |
| 23.1 | Cononley | | 29 22 | $55\frac{1}{2}$ | 28 35 | 66 |
| — | Snaygill Box | 31 | — | 58 | — | 70 |
| 26.2 | Skipton | 33 | 34 05 | 40* | 32 35 | — |
| 29.9 | Gargrave | | 38 25 | 54 | 36 43 | 57 |
| — | | — | — | 46 | p.w.s. | 20 |
| 32.8 | Bell Busk | | 41 56 | 50 | 40 50 | $51\frac{1}{2}$ |
| 34.9 | Milepost 230 | | 45 42 | 45 | 43 21 | $50\frac{1}{2}$ |
| 36.2 | Hellifield | 47 | 46 06 | 58 | 45 38 | 60 |
| 39.5 | Settle Junc | 51 | 49 09 | 70 | 47 42 | $64\frac{1}{2}$ |
| 41.4 | Settle | | 50 59 | 58 | 49 41 | 57 |
| 43.2 | Stainforth Box | | 53 00 | 49 | 51 38 | 52 |
| 45.8 | Helwith Br Box | | 57 26 | $33\frac{1}{2}$ | 55 03 | 44 |
| 47.5 | Horton | | 60 01 | 37 | 57 17 | 47 |
| 49.8 | Selside Box | | 64 22 | $33\frac{1}{2}$ | 60 11 | 46 |
| 52.2 | Ribblehead | | 69 05 | 29/33 | 63 27 | 43/44 |
| 53.5 | Blea Moor Box | 73 | 71 35 | $26\frac{1}{2}$ | 65 14 | 38 |
| 56.4 | Dent Head Box | | 77 17 | 43 | 69 23 | 54 |
| 58.4 | Dent | | 79 30 | 53 | 71 35 | 53 |
| 61.6 | Garsdale | | 82 55 | $62\frac{1}{2}$ | 75 05 | 58 |
| 64.7 | Ais Gill Box | 86 | 87 26 | — | 78 12 | 54 |
| 68.2 | Mallerstang Box | | 90 28 | — | 81 35 | 70/73 |
| 71.5 | Kirkby Stephen | | 95 12 | — | 84 33 | $62\frac{1}{2}$ |
| — | | | 101 45 | — | — | — |
| 74.7 | Crosby Garrett | | 106 49 | 58 | 87 40 | — |
| 76.7 | Griseburn Box | | 108 52 | 68 | 89 40 | 66 |
| 79.8 | Ormside | | 111 35 | 76 | 92 13 | 75 |
| 82.2 | Appleby | 103 | 113 34 | 69 | 94 15 | 63 |
| 85.1 | Long Marton | | 116 21 | — | 96 42 | 75 |
| — | | | p.w.s. | 30 | p.w.s. | 30 |
| 89.6 | Culgaith | | 120 55 | 66 | 101 27 | 75 |
| 93.3 | Langwathby | | 123 55 | 74 | 104 30 | eased |
| 94.7 | Little Salkeld | | 125 02 | 82 | 105 55 | 60 |
| 97.5 | Lazonby | | 127 15 | 75 | 108 57 | 58 |
| 99.9 | Milepost 295 | | 129 13 | 65 | 111 28 | 52 |
| 103.0 | Armathwaite | | 131 48 | 76 | 114 24 | 69 |
| 104.9 | Milepost 300 | | 133 23 | 67 | 116 20 | 54 |
| 106.2 | Cotehill | | 134 35 | 72 | 118 06 | 69 |
| 109.1 | Cumwhinton | | 136 58 | 65 | 120 11 | — |
| 110.3 | Scotby | | 138 04 | 68 | 121 19 | 65 |
| — | | | sigs | | — | 65 |
| 112.1 | Petterill Br Jc | | 140 52 | | 123 40 | |
| — | | | sig stop | | — | |
| 113.0 | Carlisle | 136 | 148 07 | | 126 28 | |

when the Yorkshire Branch of the Railway Correspondence and Travel Society were organising a "Three Summits Tour" from Leeds, covering Ais Gill, Beattock, and Shap, in that order, my wife and I were invited to be guests of the Society,

with me giving a lecture to the members in Leeds on the eve of the actual run. With plenty of advance notice we decided to make the occasion the prelude to a few days holiday in the North Country, and drove up to Bolton Abbey to a favourite hostelry, whence we travelled to Leeds for the evening meeting.

In the course of the very pleasant gathering I learned the engine for the following day, at any rate from Leeds to Carlisle, and back over Shap and down the Ingleton line was to be the A4 Pacific *Golden Eagle*, then numbered 60023. That engine, when carrying her original number, 4482, recalled two previous encounters, each of a totally different kind. When I was at Westinghouse head office at York Way, King's Cross, I used frequently to have a quick lunch at the Georgian Tea Room on No. 10 Platform prior to doing a little loco spotting, and one day early in January 1936 I saw that there was something of a gathering at the outer end of the platform. It proved to be the first express train run of the latest A4 Pacific, No. 4482 *Golden Eagle*. Only four engines of the class had previously been built, and they had been painted silver, to match the "Silver Jubilee" train. The new engine was painted standard LNER green. The Locomotive Inspector who was in charge recognised me and invited me on to the footplate. But out of the corner of my eye I saw a tall, gaunt, instantly recognisable figure elbowing his way through the crowd. Gresley himself — he had not then been knighted — and so I jumped off, and left the Inspector to do the explaining. A press photographer had climbed one of the signal gantries and got a good shot of *Golden Eagle* leaving with the 1.20 pm "Scotsman". In the picture Gresley himself is standing six-foot to the right of the engine, while I can be discerned on the platform beside the departing train.

My second encounter with *Golden Eagle* was even more intimidating. I was making some footplate trips in the summer of 1945 when running conditions and locomotive maintenance were at their worst. On the Saturday in question I was engaged on a marathon ride from Colchester to Edinburgh (!) via Ipswich, March, Lincoln and Doncaster before joining the engine of the down "Flying Scotsman" at York. The engines I had ridden so far that day were reasonably good, except for a shockingly rough B1 from Ipswich to March, but when the "Scotsman"

*The down "Thames–Clyde Express" passes Holbeck yard, hauled by A3 Class 4-6-2 No. 60088* Book Law. (Millbrook House Ltd — Bishop Eric Treacy)

came into York my heart sank, seventeen coaches, more than 600 tons behind the tender and a black, scruffy *Golden Eagle*, of which the Peterborough men booking off cheered us with the words "the bloody thing won't steam"! Hubert Foster was there to photograph our departure, and when I had climbed into the cab, and I looked out to bid him farewell he pointed his camera at me, and the resulting picture was not one of the happiest of portraits! Actually the relieving crew put up a very good show, by the standards of running then prevalent.

Several times in the enlivening discussions that characterised that very pleasant meeting of the RCTS in Leeds I was asked if there was any hope of *Golden Eagle* equalling, or perhaps even surpassing, the superb performance of the Stanier Pacific *City of Liverpool* on a previous RCTS excursion two years previously. I had not been a passenger myself, but by the kindness of two different correspondents I was furnished with the necessary data, and wrote up the occasion in one of my regular articles in *The Railway Magazine*. On this particular Sunday 'wrong-line working' was in force between Dent and Garsdale and it was to offset the effects of this delay that the tremendous uphill effort between Settle Junction and Blea Moor was made, no less than an average speed of 59 mph between these two points — *fifty*

*nine miles per hour* — with a load of 360 tons! I estimated that the equivalent drawbar horse-power on that occasion was 2,200, not far short of the gargantuan effort of the *Duchess of Gloucester* referred to in the previous chapter, which was the combined efforts of two firemen.

With this in mind I drove, with my wife, to Skipton on the Sunday morning, but when *Golden Eagle* turned up there were some portentously long faces on the footplate. The left-hand injector had failed. While many passengers entrained the usual routine to make a reluctant injector pick up proved of no avail, and in the meantime Inspector Pullan had been busy on the telephone. We drew out abreast of Skipton sheds; fitters emerged and repairs "while you wait" were commenced. It was an anxious half-hour. While an A4, in an emergency, could have got through on one injector, this was not enough to sustain the vigour with which it was intended to attack the 'Long Drag'; and there was the return journey, over Shap, to remember, which the same engine had to do the same evening. Steam was being hurriedly raised on a Stanier "Black Five" that was on Skipton shed; but everyone hoped that such a resort as double-heading the A4, or, even worse, taking her off altogether, would be avoided. With repairs completed, to everyone's relief the injector picked up, and some 45 minutes

London Midland Region: Hellifield–Carlisle
RCTS Special: 30th June 1963
Load: 10 coaches, 329 tons tare 360 tons full
Engine: Class A4 4-6-2 No. 60023 *Golden Eagle*

| Distance Miles | | Sch min | Actual m s | Speed mph |
|---|---|---|---|---|
| 0.0 | HELLIFIELD | 0 | 0 00 | — |
| 1.2 | Long Preston | | 2 44 | — |
| 3.3 | Settle Jc | 4 | 4 50 | 70½ |
| 5.2 | Settle | | 6 39 | 57 |
| 7.0 | Stainforth Box | | 8 41 | 47 |
| 9.6 | Helwith Bridge | | 12 46 | 33½/37½ |
| 11.3 | Horton | | 15 33 | 33 |
| 16.0 | Ribblehead | | 23 52 | 35 |
| 17.3 | Blea Moor | 26 | 26 00 | 38/35 |
| 20.1 | Dent Head | | 30 58 | 52/49 |
| 25.4 | Garsdale | | 36 55 | 62 |
| 28.5 | Ais Gill | 39 | 40 18 | eased |
| 32.0 | Mallerstang | | 44 26 | 62 |
| 35.3 | Kirkby Stephen | | 47 30 | 68 |
| 38.5 | Crosby Garrett | | 50 13 | 76 |
| 43.6 | Ormside | | 53 43 | 90 |
| 46.0 | APPLEBY | 56 | 55 23 | 82 |
| 48.9 | Long Marton | | 57 30 | 86/82 |
| 53.4 | Culgaith | | 60 41 | 88 |
| 57.1 | Langwathby | | 63 13 | 82 |
| 58.5 | Little Salkeld | | 64 12 | 88 |
| 61.6 | LAZONBY | | 66 22 | 82 |
| | | | — | 69 |
| 66.8 | Armathwaite | | 70 51 | 75 |
| | Low House Box | | 72 56 | 69 |
| 72.9 | Cumwhinton | | 75 43 | 81 |
| 75.9 | Petteril Bridge Jc | | 78 44 | — |
| | | | sigs | — |
| 76.8 | CARLISLE | 90 | 82 30 | — |

after our advertised time we started away. Permanent way work near Bell Busk involved some wrong-line working, and the log detailed in the table herewith begins with our passing Hellifield South box, at walking pace, to set down the pilotman. The times can be reckoned equivalent to those from a normal start from the station.

Although we got away in good style it was soon evident that nothing in the way of a record ascent was being attempted. From the initial 70½ mph over Settle Junction speed fell away to 33½ mph at the top of the 1 in 100 through Stainforth Gorge; the recovery on the brief level past Helwith Bridge was to no more than 37½ mph and we were down to 33 by Horton. A 'thumbs down' signal from the footplate indicated that they were in trouble again. Actually, that injector had failed again before Hellifield, and the whole run to

Carlisle was performed with only one injector in action. In such circumstances the times, as detailed in the table, were the results of highly skilful enginemanship. There was some recovery above Horton, but they were desperately short of water between Blea Moor and Ais Gill, and after Garsdale, when the level in the glass was almost on the point of disappearing altogether, steam had to be shut off. It was notable in such conditions that no more than a minute should have been lost between Hellifield and Ais Gill.

Downhill, at first, we ran some considerable distance, without steam; but the right-hand injector was working satisfactorily, and after Kirkby Stephen, with the water rising in the gauges, the regulator was opened again. No reader of those articles needed to be told that an A4 required little encouragement to "fly", especially on so favourable a road, and from Crosby Garrett *Golden Eagle* certainly spread her wings. I would not be so dogmatic as to assert that Sunday, 30th June, witnessed the absolute record for the Ais Gill-Carlisle descent, but it must be very near it. After Kirkby Stephen the pace was increased to a full 90 mph at Ormside Viaduct, and the hump on which Appleby station stands was cleared at a minimum of 82 mph. There was no speed restrictions between Long Marton and Culgaith on this trip, and the average speed from Ormside to Lazonby was exactly 85 mph. A slight restriction was in force over the beautiful stretch between Lazonby and Armathwaite but we attained 81 mph on the final descent and finished into Carlisle in 82½ minutes from Hellifield. We said farewell to *Golden Eagle* while we continued on the round trip in Scotland. But when we got back there was the engine with her crew all smiles to take us back over Shap. The magnificent hill climbing that followed is another story, except that we were running over the route that might have been the Midland main route to Carlisle. Down the Ingleton line we went cautiously, and it was only after we had slacked to 25 mph through the moorland Clapham Junction that we got a final burst of speed, touching 73 mph below Giggleswick and the 40 mph required from this direction over Settle Junction.

It is sad to recall that the last years of regular steam haulage on the Settle and Carlisle line included a bad accident. The train concerned was the now-defunct 9.5 pm sleeping car express from Glasgow to London via the Glasgow & South

Western and Midland route, on which one locomotive and crew worked through from Glasgow
to Leeds. On the night of 20-21st January 1960
the engine was 'Britannia' 4-6-2 No. 70052 *Firth
of Tay*, with no more than a moderate load of
eight coaches. The train left Carlisle at 12.3 am,
two minutes late, but despite extremely bad
weather, of gale force winds and driving snow,
that small lateness was made up by covering the
48 miles up to Ais Gill Summit in 67 minutes. It
was when the steaming was eased after climbing
the gradient that the driver, H. Waites of Leeds,
sensed that there was something wrong with the
engine, with what appeared to be a severe knock
on the right-hand side. It got worse when he shut
off steam altogether, so he applied steam again,
steadied the speed with the brake and stopped at
Garsdale for examination.

The conditions there at 1.16 am could not have
been worse. In darkness and blinding snow he
went round the engine, with the aid of a small
pocket torch; but the right-hand big-end which he
suspected as being the problem was quite cool,
and after a stop of no more than four minutes he
decided to go on, at moderate speed, to Hellifield,
where a more detailed examination of the engine
could be made. The knocking continued, but by
keeping steam on lightly and controlling the train
on the long descent from Blea Moor by the brake
it did not appear to get any worse. In hindsight,
knowing what was really amiss with the engine,
it is astonishing that it was able to continue as
long as it did, because near Milepost 268, 31 miles
north of where the accident occurred, the bottom
inner slide bar on the right-hand side had fallen
off, followed nine miles later by the outer bottom
slide bar. From Milepost $259\frac{1}{4}$ the crosshead had
no support from the underside, and had been
kept approximately in position by the guiding
effect of the piston rod in the gland. It might be
thought surprising that Driver Waites did not
notice this when he stopped to examine the engine
at Garsdale, but the Inspecting Officer of the
Ministry of Transport, Brig C. A. Langley, did
not criticise him for this, having regard for the
appalling weather conditions prevailing at the
time. The crosshead and piston rod came completely adrift about three-quarters of a mile north
of Settle station, and with the assembly still
attached to the driving wheel through the connecting rod it drove deep into the formation,
over-turned into the trailing position, and the

*The "Thames–Clyde Express" passing the site of
the old low-level station at Holbeck, Leeds, hauled
by 'Britannia' 4-6-2 No. 70044* Earl Haig.
(Millbrook House Ltd — Bishop Eric Treacy)

crosshead pulled the nearest rail of the down line
completely out of gauge. The express locomotive
stayed on the rails, but as ill-luck would have it
a down freight was approaching. Its engine was
derailed on the damaged track, heeled over
towards the express, collided and tore the sides of
the coaches out. Five passengers in the express
were killed and eight injured.

In the subsequent inquiry, nearly everything
centred upon how the express locomotive came to
be in such a condition that the right-hand bottom
slide bars fell out. The design of the 'Britannia'
class locomotives was a synthesis of the best
practice on the former privately owned railways,
and the crosshead and slide bars were pure
Gresley. Its reliability had been proved without
question during the long history and sterling
performance of the Gresley Pacifics, K3 class
Moguls and 'Green Arrow' 2-6-2s; yet on the
'Britannias' it proved a troublesome detail. The
three-bar slide bar assembly was built up from a
single, wide top bar, and two bottom bars spaced
so as to allow the dependent part of the crosshead
to work between. At each end there were packing
pieces between the top and bottom bars. One bolt
at each end held the bottom bars to the top bar.
It was a sound and well-proven design, but in
applying it to the 'Britannias' there was a difference from the previous Doncaster practice. The
actual build-up of the assembly was the same,

with the nuts of the securing bolts uppermost; but whereas on the Gresley engines this fastening was well clear and readily accessible, on the 'Britannias' it was tucked underneath the very large rearward steam chest, which extended some distance beyond the rear cylinder cover. Those nuts, particularly for the inner bottom slide bar, were somewhat inaccessible.

As Brig. Langley emphasised in his report "... difficulty in reaching such parts can lead to slack maintenance..." and although the record of engine No. 70052 since its last general overhaul was perhaps exceptional in this respect, the standard of maintenance of the motion of engines of that class had not been satisfactory in a number of depots, and failure to tighten the bolts properly had not been confined to the depots under reference. On engine No. 70052 the bolts had been reported loose on nine occasions since its previous general repair at Crewe, from which it had been released to traffic on 26th September 1959. Its record, immediately prior to the accident, was thus:

18th January 1960 Daily examination at home shed (Polmadie): right-hand front slide bar bolts found loose and tightened. Engine worked 7 am train Glasgow to Carlisle.

19th January 1960 Returned Carlisle to Glasgow (St Enoch), examined at Corkerhill; 4 pm Glasgow (St Enoch) to Leeds: bolts reported loose; tightened at Holbeck shed.

20th January 1960 10.35 am Leeds to Glasgow (St Enoch) with Corkerhill men. No defects reported 9.5 pm Glasgow (St Enoch) to Leeds, with Leeds men. Accident occurred 1.48 am next morning.

After the accident, when it was found that the bottom slide bars had completely disappeared, an intensive search was made for the missing parts, with the following remarkable results:

| Mileage | Part Found |
|---|---|
| 270 miles 1,640 yd | One nut, one bolt with the split pin bent up. |
| 270 miles 15 yd | One nut. |
| 267 miles 1,560 yd | Right-hand bottom inner slide bar with the rear bolt jammed in the bolt hole. |
| $264\frac{1}{2}$ miles (Birkett Tunnel) | Right-hand front packing piece. |
| $259\frac{1}{4}$ miles | Right-hand bottom outer slide bar, one nut, one bolt with the split pin sheared off, right-hand rear packing piece. |
| 237 miles | Scene of accident. |

The final collapse of the slide bar assembly took place about half a mile after the train had breasted Ais Gill Summit, and undoubtedly gave rise to the severe knocking noticed by the driver.

By way of explanation as to why the engine could continue to be worked at all after this failure, when running in fore gear with the regulator open, the thrust normally exerted by the crosshead on the slide bars, neglecting the effects of friction, was vertically upwards throughout the revolution, but downwards when coasting. Thus so long as steam was kept on, the crosshead was working against the broad upper slide bar, which remained in position. Naturally the detail of the bottom bar fastenings came in for severe criticism, and the design was subsequently changed by British Railways, to have the head of the bolt at the top and the nut and split pin fastening at the bottom, where it was readily accessible. As Brig. Langley commented: "The difficulty of keeping bolts tight on railway engines arises from the vibration produced by steel wheels running on steel rails and this is accentuated by wheelslip which often occurs on starting and sometimes on rising gradients when extra power is applied. The constant reversal of stresses in motion slide bars presents an even greater problem in keeping these bolts tight. The connections should, therefore, be designed to resist these vibrations and to be easily accessible for examination and tightening".

*The up "Thames–Clyde Express" on Ais Gill Viaduct hauled by Class A3 4-6-2 No. 60092* Fairway *in 1960.* (Millbrook House Ltd — Bishop Eric Treacy)

# 19
# The Diesels Move In

Even while I was making my footplate journeys on the Class A3 Gresley Pacifics British Railways were already taking delivery of a new design of Type 4 diesel-electric locomotive, the Derby-built 'Peak' class, with the Sulzer engine. The first ten, and eventually the only ones to be named after English and Welsh mountains, had engines imported from Sulzer's works in Switzerland. All the remainder of this large class had a slightly larger engine of the same design, built under an agreement with Sulzers, by Vickers Armstrong Ltd at the Shipyard Works at Barrow in-Furness. These latter engines had

a nominal bhp of 2,500 at an engine speed of 750 rpm.

It was stated that the first ten locomotives, Nos D1–D10, were being allocated to Crewe North shed, but otherwise it seemed that the entire stud was being sent to the Midland Division to take over the entire passenger train working. Furthermore the availability of diesels generally was being put to use by extending the rosters of locomotives to trains running far beyond the confines of the LM Region, from York to Newcastle for example, and in some cases from Bristol to Plymouth. The locomotives

*Settle Junction in 1964, before the configuration of the track was modified to later BR standards. A local train from Hellifield to Carlisle, hauled by a Type 2 diesel No. 7582, 15th August 1964. (Derek Cross)*

of the 'Peak' class were delivered very rapidly from Derby, too rapidly for the motive power depots to be ready to receive them, and unfortunately they did not at first get the specialised maintenance service they needed, and failures were frequent.

I do not know if any of the original ten ever worked on the Settle and Carlisle line. Certainly their names included four, *Cross Fell*, *Whernside*, *Ingleborough* and *Penyghent*, that would be familiar to travellers by its trains; but I feel that the shades of the immortal Jeanie Deans would not have approved of her beloved "muckle blue hill they ca' Ingleboro'" being included in the 'Peak' class. I had my first footplate over the route on one of the new locomotives in November 1961. The numbering of them had begun at D1 *Scafell Pike*, and the one I rode was No. D103. The intensive rosters worked out for these engines was very evident in this case. On the previous day it had left Derby for Manchester and then worked an afternoon express from Manchester to St Pancras. After spending the night in London it had next worked down on the "Waverley Express", and it was only the geography of Leeds Wellington station that prevented its going on to Carlisle with that train. As it was, it backed out from the buffer stops, was remanned, and ready to take the "Thames–Clyde Express" to Glasgow St Enoch. The driver proved to be an old friend, A. Othick of Leeds, Whitehall Junction, with whom I had ridden on the "Black

Five" 4-6-0 that gave one such a boisterous and exhilarating run on the "Waverley" four years earlier. Inspector Pullan came as well, and so we were a happy party on the footplate.

As an express locomotive assignment it was the merest 'push over' of a job. The time schedule had not yet been accelerated from steam days, and we had the usual nine coach train of the winter service. Suffice it be said, we left Leeds $7\frac{3}{4}$ minutes late and passed Blea Moor $5\frac{1}{4}$ minutes early, after two checks. I have not tabulated the log of our running in any detail except from Settle Junction up to Blea Moor, where the locomotive was being driven at full power except for a brief intermission at Horton, where the distant signal was not fully in the clear position, and the driver eased up to make sure we were 'right away'. From Settle Junction we were sustaining a steady 60 mph on the 1 in 100 through to Helwith Bridge, where the brief easing of the gradient brought an acceleration to $62\frac{1}{2}$ mph until we sighted the faulty distant signal of Horton. I have estimated that the equivalent drawbar horsepower on this stage was 2,070, and impressive as it was however, it did not surpass the mighty effort of the Stanier Pacific *City of Liverpool* on the RCTS tour train earlier in that same year, on which the estimated output was 2,200 edhp. On my diesel run, again with full power on, we accelerated from 35 mph at Horton to 50 at Ribblehead, $54\frac{1}{2}$ mph over the viaduct and 53 mph at Blea Moor Tunnel, by which time

*An up freight train approaches Settle Junction in wintry weather on 7th February 1983, with the front of the Type 4, diesel Class 40 No. 40022 having snow encrusted on it. No sign of Pen-y-Ghent on this day!* (Brian Morrison)

Leeds–Carlisle: The "Thames–Clyde Express"
Load: 9 coaches, 315 tons tare, 330 tons full
Engine: 'Peak' class diesel-electric No. D103

| Distance Miles | | Sch min | Actual m s | Speed mph |
|---|---|---|---|---|
| 0.0 | Leeds | 0 | 0 00 | — |
| 3.3 | Kirkstall | | 4 21 | 65 |
| 4.6 | Newlay | | 5 48 | 58 |
| 7.6 | Apperley Bridge | | 8 36 | 66 |
| 10.9 | Skipley B Jc | 16 | 12 35 | 20* |
| — | | | p.w.s. | — |
| 17.0 | Keighley | 24 | 21 57 | — |
| 26.2 | Skipton | 36 | 32 40 | — |
| 29.9 | Gargrave | | 36 46 | $64\frac{1}{2}$/54 |
| 34.9 | Milepost 230 | | 42 02 | 58 |
| 36.2 | Hellifield | 50 | 43 32 | $51\frac{1}{2}$ |
| 39.5 | Settle Jc | 54 | 47 18 | 60 |
| 41.4 | Settle | | 49 13 | 60 |
| 43.2 | Stainforth Box | | 50 58 | 60 |
| 45.8 | Helwith Bridge Box | | 53 39 | 60 |
| — | | | sigs | $62\frac{1}{2}$ |
| 47.5 | Horton | | 55 27 | 35 |
| 49.8 | Selside Box | | 58 50 | $47\frac{1}{2}$ |
| 52.2 | Ribblehead | | 61 39 | 50/$54\frac{1}{2}$ |
| 53.5 | Blea Moor Box | 76 | 63 02 | 53 |
| 64.7 | Ais Gill Box | 89 | 75 25 | — |
| 82.2 | Appleby | 104 | 93 00 | |
| 97.5 | Lazonby | | 108 26 | $72\frac{1}{2}$ (max) |
| 112.1 | Petteril Bridge Jc | | 123 26 | |
| — | | | sigs | |
| 113.0 | Carlisle | 139 | 127 30 | |

easing had started. In any case by then we were more than five minutes early. The log of the run, abbreviated from Blea Moor onwards, shows how easily we needed to run downhill.

Before the 'Peak' class diesels came to the Settle and Carlisle line, before even the Controlled Road Tests with major steam locomotives had been concluded, there had come the prototype English Electric *Deltic*, now resting in honourable retirement in the Science Museum at South Kensington. This remarkable locomotive, built in 1955, was then the most powerful diesel-electric power plant that had ever been mounted on a single locomotive chassis. Its designed total output of 3,300 horsepower was to provide a maximum rail tractive effort of 52,500 lb and a continuous effort of 29,000 lb at 35 mph. This latter would provide a drawbar horsepower of about 2,400 at the speed of 35 mph, but connoisseurs of locomotive performance history will recall that in favourable conditions, admittedly at higher speeds, locomotives of Sir William Stanier's 'Duchess' class 4-6-2s have been recorded as achieving outputs of more than 2,600 equivalent drawbar horsepower. The difference between such feats and the designed maximum output of the 'Deltic', is that with the steam locomotives, they were mostly brief efforts for immediate needs, whereas the 'Deltic' could be relied on to give that effort merely by 'turning

*Settle Junction, February 1983, with the track altered, as a Skipton to Ribblehead Quarry empties passes, hauled by Class 25/2 No. 25247 (Brian Morrison)*

on the taps', as the saying goes. The only times a Stanier Pacific was pounded to this extent for any length of time were in the Controlled Road Trials of the *Duchess of Gloucester* described in Chapter 17, when two firemen were needed to take alternate shares of the coal heaving that was involved.

With a negligible amount of teething troubles the prototype 'Deltic' went into top class express passenger service between Liverpool and Euston. It did so well that at an early stage full dynamometer car trials were arranged on the Settle and Carlisle line. These, while conducted between Durran Hill Junction and Skipton, as with steam locomotives, were not of the Controlled Road Test nature. Some of the 'Deltic' tests were made using no more than the No. 3 dynamometer car and the two mobile test units. These latter, as I experienced myself on the Southern when one of the 'Merchant Navy' 4-6-2s was on test between Clapham Junction and Salisbury, could provide a heavy electrically applied load, if required. The British Railways Board issued a comprehensive Bulletin on the tests of the prototype 'Deltic', and in it was the chart of a run from Durran Hill Junction up to Ais Gill, not with a simulated heavy load, but with 20 bogie coaches making up a total actual tonnage of 642 tons. There was, of course no need for any preliminary warming up in this case and the test started in earnest

the moment the right-away had been given at Durran Hill. Even so, from the apparently very slow start to Scotby it would seem that the long train took some manoeuvering to get out of the sidings. The accompanying log, which it must be admitted is not in the precise form usually expected in my books, has been compiled from the data shown on the chart of the run published in the Bulletin covering the tests of this locomotive, with comparison on the 'elapsed time' scale with the passage of the various stations and signal boxes en route. The maximum and minimum speeds have been read from the speed graph on the chart.

The power output from the locomotive was in three distinct stages, from Scotby to the approach to the Lazonby speed restriction, from the clearance point from this to the permanent speed restriction near Long Marton, and from there to the conclusion of the test just after Ais Gill Summit. During these three spells when full power was being applied the drawbar horsepower was consistently above 2,000, mostly around 2,200. There was one noticable intermission, near Armathwaite, when running at well over 70 mph, and a severe wheel slip needed the shutting off of power briefly but resulting in little reduction of speed. The principal ascent from Ormside to Ais Gill was a notable performance with a load of 645 tons. This 15.1 miles of steep

*Another snowy scene near Settle Junction, as the four-coach 10.00 Carlisle to Leeds train approaches with Class 45 No. 45070 on 8th February 1983. (Brian Morrison)*

climbing was accomplished in 15 min 40 sec, at an average speed of 58 mph, with a minimum speed of 50 mph on the final length of 1 in 100 gradient.

The Bulletin includes some interesting statistics of the complete round trip from Carlisle to Skipton and back made the same day, as follows:

Carlisle (Durran Hill Junction)–Ais Gill
Dynamometer Car Test Run
Load: 642 tons tare, 645 tons loaded
Locomotive: The English Electric Prototype *Deltic*

| Distance Miles | | Actual m s | Average speeds mph | Max and min speed mph |
|---|---|---|---|---|
| 0.0 | Durran Hill Jc | 0 00 | — | — |
| 1.1 | Scotby | 4 55 | 13.4 | — |
| 2.3 | Cumwhinton | 6 50 | 37.4 | 47 |
| 6.8 | Low House Box | 11 35 | 56.7 | 57 |
| 8.6 | Armathwaite | 13 00 | 75.0 | 75 |
| — | | p.w.s. | — | 18 |
| 13.6 | Lazonby | 19 10 | 48.6 | — |
| 16.7 | Little Salkeld | 23 25 | 43.6 | 55 |
| 18.1 | Langwathby | 25 40 | — | 55 |
| 21.8 | Culgaith | 29 05 | 64.5 | 70 |
| — | | p.w.s. | | 24 |
| 26.3 | Long Marton | 34 40 | 49.5 | 40 |
| 29.2 | Appleby | 38 10 | 49.7 | 60 |
| 31.6 | Ormside | 40 30 | 61.7 | 73 |
| 34.5 | Griseburn Box | 43 05 | 67.5 | 57 |
| 36.7 | Crosby Garrett | 45 25 | 56.0 | 63 |
| 39.9 | Kirkby Stephen | 49 35 | 60.6 | 56 |
| 43.2 | Mallerstang Box | 52 28 | 52.0 | 52/57 |
| 46.7 | Ais Gill Box | 56 10 | 54.5 | 50 |

| | Carlisle to Skipton | Skipton to Carlisle |
|---|---|---|
| Distance on test, actual (miles) | 82.9 | 82.9 |
| Distance under power (miles) | 57.9 | 47.9 |
| Time | | |
| Actual running (min) | 91 | 86 |
| Actual under power (min) | 64 | 50 |
| Actual drifting and braking (min) | 27 | 36 |
| Average speed | | |
| on running time (mph) | 54.6 | 57.9 |
| under power (mph) | 54.3 | 57.5 |
| Average actual drawbar horsepower | 1943 | 1743 |
| Average actual drawbar tractive effort (tons) | 5.99 | 5.08 |

Now reverting to the 'Peak' class the introduction of these on the Settle and Carlisle line for the double-home turns between Leeds and Glasgow St Enoch prompted the timetable people to make some notable accelerations of the service. When I was the author of the monthly "Locomotive Practice and Performance" feature in *The Railway Magazine* a pen-friend, who I never had the pleasure of meeting personally, Mr H. G. Ellison, sent me a series of carefully compiled logs, in both directions on the "Thames–Clyde Express", then running non-stop in both directions between Leeds and Carlisle except on

*The down "Royal Scot" diverted to the Settle and Carlisle line on 3rd June 1967, leaving Cat Clint Tunnel near Armathwaite, and hauled by Class 47 No. D1625* (Derek Cross)

summer Saturdays. The working time for the down train was cut to $120\frac{1}{2}$ minutes for the 113 mile run, but I wonder how many drivers, or inspectors paid any attention to that rather absurd half-minute. The southbound train was allowed 126 minutes, thus preserving the discrepancy between the down and up working times that had existed from the first post-war schedules of 1920, which were very evident in the celebrated locomotive exchange running of 1923–4 with the non-stop trains between Carlisle and Leeds, and return.

Mr Ellison is an experienced recorder and I was glad to use his data exactly as he submitted it to me. I thought this should be mentioned because some of his timing points are not the same as I have used in this book so far, and the trains themselves were routed from the platforms in the City station at Leeds, whereas all the earlier runs originated or terminated at the one-time Wellington station of the former Midland Railway. Four of Mr Ellison's runs on the down train are tabulated herewith. The first two are with the usual nine-coach train, and the third was with two extras, on New Year's Day 1964. The fourth run was on a summer Saturday, with intermediate stops at Skipton, Hellifield, Settle and Appleby, and a very much heavier load. It is interesting to compare the accelerated schedule with that being worked when I made my footplate journeys on the A3 Pacifics.

It is interesting to see that after a sharp initial

|  | 1960 (min) | 1963 (min) |
|---|---|---|
| Leeds | 0 | 0 |
| Shipley | 15 | $13\frac{1}{2}$ |
| Keighley | 23 | $20\frac{1}{2}$ |
| Skipton | 33 | 31 |
| Hellifield | 47 | 42 |
| Settle Junc | 51 | 45 |
| Blea Moor | 73 | $67\frac{1}{2}$ |
| Ais Gill | 86 | 78 |
| Appleby | 103 | $93\frac{1}{2}$ |
| Carlisle | 136 | $120\frac{1}{2}$ |

booking to Keighley half a minute extra was allowed to Skipton to be followed by no more than eleven minutes from Skipton to Hellifield. But the most surprising timing of all was the $22\frac{1}{2}$ minutes booked from Settle Junction to Blea Moor, an average of not more than 37.4 mph, and slower than the former timing with steam traction. My own first footplate run with a diesel, as tabulated earlier in this chapter, was made on a still slower overall timing though the allowance from Settle Junction to Blea Moor remained at 22 minutes. The remarkable feature of the 1963 schedule is of the speeds booked downhill, with no more than 27 minutes for the final 30.8 miles from Appleby into Carlisle!

Although there was no mention of it made in the comprehensive data supplied by Mr Ellison, now more than 25 years ago, I should imagine

*Another diversion: a Glasgow–Liverpool express, on the curve below Wild Boar Fell 1st August 1965, worked by Class 47 No. D1968. (Derek Cross)*

*An empty mineral wagon special, Carlisle to Sheffield near Cotehill, hauled by Class 40 No. 40182 on Sunday 9th March 1975. (M. Bryce)*

something of the 'recovery time' philosophy must have been incorporated in the formulating of the 1963 schedules over this route. The practice of the so-called 'scientific train timing' stemmed from the experience of the Great Western Railway when they had come to analyse the intermediate working times of some their more exacting schedules in respect of the power output of the locomotives. They had found that in general the best drivers worked their engines at an approximately uniform rate of steaming, dropping a minute or so on certain sectional timings, knowing that the arrears could easily be recovered later. Subsequently, particularly into post-war schedules, small amounts of recovery time came to be inserted, to provide a margin against time lost in observing temporary speed restrictions for permanent way work. A senior locomotive inspector with whom I rode many thousands of miles on the footplate always emphasised that the recovery time in crack train schedules "did not belong to the driver", and if there were no incidental delays, on a train like the up "Bristolian", which had two instances of a 4-minute recovery allowance, the train could be expected to arrive in Paddington eight minutes early, which it did on many occasions, to my knowledge.

In the 1963 schedule of the down "Thames–Clyde Express" one would have imagined the bulk of the recovery time allowance to be put in between Settle Junction and Blea Moor, because on the first of Mr Ellison's runs tabulated herewith, the gain on booked time was almost eight minutes with lower speeds than those of my

footplate run of 1961 on the slower timing. On the second run the average from Settle Junction to Blea Moor was a full 60 mph. Starting from Leeds however, the first run did not keep the exacting time to Keighley, but with the aid of some minutes of recovery time, was on schedule passing Skipton, and the almost entirely adverse length to Hellifield was covered at speeds of between 64 and 68 mph. Careful attention was paid to the prescribed slack through Hellifield station and the 'Long Drag' was entered upon at 70 mph. The second run was brought almost to a stand at Shipley by adverse signals, and following a fine spurt over the easy road beyond Keighley and a maximum of 77 mph at Snaygill box the train was brought to a dead stop in Skipton station. Despite this, and the hindrance of a permanent way check to 25 mph after Gargrave, the loss in time from Leeds passing Hellifield was only $1\frac{3}{4}$ minutes.

The third run, opening the New Year of 1964, began with a start 21 minutes late from Leeds and with a gross load of 370 tons behind the locomotive, the going was very fine at first. The sharp initial timing to Keighley was kept, and despite a long permanent way caution near Gargrave, the booked passing time at Hellifield was no more than fractionally exceeded. With the heavier load the 'Long Drag', even with the use of full power, could not be expected to be climbed as rapidly and the average speed from Settle Junction to Blea Moor was 54 mph. But the working time from Leeds had been cut from $67\frac{1}{2}$ minutes booked to 59 min 50 sec despite the check near Gargrave. The working times over the tableland section were always optimistic from early Midland Railway days, but with the 'Peaks' a time of $10\frac{1}{2}$ minutes from Blea Moor to Ais Gill gave no problems. As will be seen from the table the times ranged from 10 min 6 sec, 11 min 5 sec, to 10 min 48 sec, the longer time on the second being caused by a slowing to 43 mph at the entrance to Blea Moor Tunnel.

Continuing to comment on the running of the three trains making non-stop runs from Leeds to Carlisle the first one, having passed Ais Gill ten minutes inside booked time, could hardly have expected to gain more on the sharp allowance of $43\frac{1}{2}$ minutes for the 48.3 miles, including the slowing over the length north of Long Marton which was subject to repair. The speeds shown in the table, with three separate maxima of more than 80 mph, are enough to illustrate what was expected in the early days of the diesel age on this route. The second run, from passing Ais Gill at the high minimum speed of 67 mph, began similarly, but then checks hindered the running between Appleby and Lazonby. But then a fine concluding spurt was put on through the Eden Gorge with a maximum speed of 80 mph near Armathwaite, all to no avail, because this was

evidently one of those occasions when complete chaos used to reign in Citadel station at Carlisle, and the train was kept a long time waiting for signals outside. On the third run Mr Ellison expressed his disappointment to me that harder running was not made down from the Summit, though to be sure a time of 43 min 42 sec from Ais Gill to the stop in Carlisle would have been reckoned pretty rapid by former standards.

Now comes the interesting run on a summer Saturday morning when a load of 445 tons was taken. The driver made excellent use of the power of the 'Peak' class locomotive on this occasion, aided by an almost complete absence of incidental delays. To Skipton he ran at the same speed as that of the ordinary weekday train, and between Skipton and Hellifield full power must have been used throughout. From the stop right on the 1 in 100 gradient at Settle the uphill performance was most impressive and I calculate that the equivalent drawbar horsepower from Helwith Bridge to Blea Moor must have been around 2,450. To crown all Ais Gill Summit was topped at the highest minimum speed of any in the table, 70 mph. Some fast running was also made down, especially after Appleby. Even so,

*The diverted 07.20 Euston to Glasgow InterCity express between Rise Hill Tunnel and Garsdale, hauled by Class 47/4 No. 47406 in early style InterCity livery, 25th March 1989.* (Brian Morrison)

*The 10.45 Leeds–Carlisle train nearing Garsdale, 25th March 1989 hauled by two Class 31/4 diesel locomotives; No. 31407 leading No. 31446.* (Brian Morrison)

four separate maxima of over 80 mph were not enough to keep the optimistic schedule of 29 minutes for the 30.8 miles from Appleby to Carlisle, when two permanent way 'cautions' were operating. With a clear road into Citadel station, I think time would have been kept, but for the second check.

In the southbound direction it has always seemed to be traditional for the overall times to be slower and that was the case with the accelerated diesel timings introduced in 1962. Yet even though the working allowance between Hellifield and Leeds was the same as for the northbound run, 42 minutes, it appears that Mr Ellison considered the running over that part of the line of so little interest that in the logs he sent to me he included no times, or other details between Hellifield and Leeds. But certainly the performance on the four runs in the table, between Carlisle and Hellifield is striking enough.

The first run, with the minimum basic load, was checked at the start and took 14 min 44 sec to get through Armathwaite, but from there the going was brilliant, with the unusual maximum speed of 78 mph after Culgaith, and an ascent from Ormside to Ais Gill at an average speed of 63 mph. The second run was unchecked at first, and made very good time to Culgaith, but the engineering slack before Long Marton was this time severe, and although improving on his booked allowance was not so energetic on the main of the ascent, from Ormside up to Ais Gill. The third run started in tremendous style, with a

390 ton load, and the speeds of 77 mph below Low House box, and 77 again at Lazonby took the train through the latter station a full minute ahead of all the others in the table. Then came checks, and time was not kept to Appleby. The fourth run, while starting well from Carlisle was also severely checked before Appleby.

On runs three and four the climbing to Ais Gill with 390 and 410 ton trains was really splendid. Both drivers made full use of the descent from Appleby to Ormside Viaduct, attaining speeds of 76 and 78mph after which the 15.1 miles up to Ais Gill were climbed at average speeds of more than 60 mph in both cases. Indeed the net times on both these runs showed averages of more than 60 mph from the start at Carlisle, as of course did run No. 1, with the lighter load. There was some fast running over the tableland to Blea Moor on some of these runs particularly on No. 1, with a speed of 81 mph at Blea Moor itself. On the third run, after a maximum of 79 mph at Garsdale, and running at more moderate speed to Blea Moor, this driver allowed his locomotive to attain a maximum of 89 mph near Horton. For the most part however, as Mr Ellison emphasises by the paucity of detail in the logs, there was really little of interest in the running of these trains from Blea Moor southwards.

In 1967 there was a sequel to the spectacular running of the prototype 'Deltic' diesel-electric locomotive. In that year Mr Alan Pegler, who had purchased the *Flying Scotsman* locomotive had, with the backing of *The Railway Magazine* organised a round trip from King's Cross to

Leeds–Carlisle: The "Thames–Clyde Express"

| Run No. | | | 1 | | 2 | | 3 | | 4 | | |
|---|---|---|---|---|---|---|---|---|---|---|---|
| Engine: 'Peak' class | | | D49 | | D81 | | D90 | | D12 | | |
| Load, tons E/F | | | 314/325 | | 310/330 | | 356/370 | | 421/445 | | |
| Distance Miles | | Sch. min | Actual m s | Speeds mph | Actual m s | Speeds mph | Actual m s | Speeds mph | | Actual m s | Speeds mph |
| 0.0 | Leeds City | | 0 00 | — | 0 00 | — | 0 00 | — | 0 | 0 00 | — |
| 3.2 | Kirkstall | | 5 53 | 66 | 6 00 | 61/53 | 5 37 | 62 | | 6 11 | 65/58 |
| 7.6 | Apperley Bridge | | 10 02 | 62 | 10 29 | 68 | 9 44 | 66 | | 10 31 | 64 |
| — | | | — | — | sigs | | — | — | | — | |
| 10.7 | Shipley | | | | | | | | 15½ | 14 07 | 20 |
| | (Leeds Jc) | 13½ | 13 40 | 20 | 14 51 | 5 | 13 42 | 23 | | 18 16 | 67 |
| 13.8 | Bingley | | 17 42 | 63 | 18 31 | 71 | 17 29 | 70 | 22½ | 21 26 | 50 |
| 17.0 | Keighley | 20½ | 21 07 | 50 | 21 36 | 45 | 20 47 | 55 | | 24 15 | 75 |
| 20.0 | Steeton | | 23 50 | 68 | 24 22 | 77 | 23 23 | 67 | | — | — |
| — | | | p.w.s. | | 30 50 | — | — | | 33½ | 30 11 | — |
| 26.2 | Skipton | 31 | 30 24 | 25 | 31 23 | — | 29 30 | 40 | | 3 42 | 58 |
| 28.6 | Delaneys Sdg | | 33 07 | 64 | 35 03 | 67 | 52 50 | | | — | |
| — | | | — | — | p.w.s. | | p.w.s. | 30 | | 7 52 | 63 |
| 32.8 | Bell Busk | | 36 57 | 68 | 39 27 | 25 | 39 01 | 59 | | 9 44 | 59 |
| 34.7 | Milepost | | | | | | | | 12 | 11 52 | — |
| | 229¾ | | 38 42 | 64 | 42 17 | 52 | 40 57 | 60 | | | |
| 36.2 | Hellifield | 42 | 40 11 | 60 | 43 56 | 66 | 42 21 | 66 | 4 | 4 13 | 66 |
| 39.4 | Settle Jc | 45 | 43 10 | 73 | 46 42 | 69/64 | 45 17 | 68 | 9 | 6 38 | — |
| 41.4 | Settle | | 44 58 | 63 | 48 37 | 60 | 47 12 | 60 | | — | — |
| 45.8 | Helwith Br | | 49 27 | 56/60 | 53 06 | 58/63 | 51 51 | 56/60 | | 7 19 | 45/51 |
| 47.5 | Horton | | 51 07 | 58 | 54 41 | 61 | 53 31 | 57 | | 9 18 | 49 |
| 52.2 | Ribblehead | | 56 13 | 53/56 | 59 23 | 59/61 | 58 30 | 55/57 | | 15 09 | 47/51 |
| 53.4 | Blea Moor | 67½ | 57 36 | 54 | 60 38 | 43 | 59 50 | 55 | 19 | 16 42 | 46 |
| 61.6 | Garsdale | | 65 03 | 78 | 69 12 | 80 | 67 46 | 70 | | 24 33 | 73 |
| 64.6 | Ais Gill | 78 | 67 43 | 58 | 71 43 | 67 | 70 38 | 57 | | 27 08 | 70 |
| 71.5 | Kirkby Stephen | | 73 23 | 81 | 77 06 | 81 | 76 32 | 76 | | 32 35 | 85 |
| 74.7 | Crosby Garrett | | 75 52 | 73 | 79 39 | 75 | 79 11 | 68 | | 35 18 | 65 |
| 79.7 | Ormside | | 79 48 | 84 | 83 26 | 84 | — | 82 | | 39 20 | 78 |
| 82.2 | Appleby | 93½ | 81 45 | 62 | 85 25 | 65 | 85 22 | 63 | 46 | 42 35 | |
| 85.2 | Long Marton | | p.w.s. | 55 | p.w.s. | 65 | p.w.s. | 68 | | p.w.s. | 71/35 |
| — | | | | | sigs | | — | — | | — | |
| 93.2 | Langwathby | | 91 14 | 77 | 95 25 | 71 | — | 70 | | 11 28 | 82 |
| — | | | — | 84 | p.w.s. | 30 | — | — | | — | |
| 97.5 | Lazonby | | 94 28 | 78 | 100 23 | 71 | 98 14 | 76 | | 14 43 | 78/83 |
| 99.9 | Milepost 295 | | 96 23 | 70 | 102 32 | 67 | — | 63 | | 16 32 | 76 |
| | | | | | | | | | | 18 58 | 82 |
| 103.0 | Armathwaite | | 98 51 | 78/71 | 104 59 | 80/73 | 102 48 | 77 | | 20 24 | 60/84 |
| 104.6 | Low House | | 100 08 | 78/68 | 106 15 | 78/63 | | 55 | | p.w.s. | 55 |
| 109.1 | Cumwhinton | | 103 47 | 78 | 110 06 | 76 | 108 12 | 75 | | — | — |
| — | | | — | | sig stop | | — | | | — | |
| 113.0 | Carlisle | | 109 00 | | 132 26 | | 114 20 | | 29 | 30 01 | |
| | Net time | | 108 | | 108 | | | | | 112 | |

Newcastle and Carlisle, primarily to celebrate the fiftieth anniversary of non-stop running between London and Newcastle. On reaching Tyneside, the special train, named the "Hadrian Flyer" was to be taken across to Carlisle by one of the latest 'Deltics', and worked thereby southwards over the Settle and Carlisle line, to where high speed running could be resumed for the rest of the journey back to King's Cross. I was not able to go on the trip personally, but one of my

| Run No. | | | 1 | | 2 | | 3 | | 4 | |
| Engine: 'Peak' class | | | D110 | | D99 | | D97 | | D129 | |
| Load, tons E/F | | | 310/330 | | 346/360 | | 361/390 | | 369/410 | |
| Distance Miles | | Sch. min | Actual m s | Speeds mph | Actual m s | Speeds mph | Actual m s | Speeds mph | Actual m s | Speeds mph |
|---|---|---|---|---|---|---|---|---|---|---|
| 0.0 | Carlisle | 0 | 0 00 | — | 0 00 | — | 0 00 | — | 0 00 | |
| — | | | sigs | | | | | | | |
| 0.9 | Petteril Br Jc | | 3 24 | 27 | 2 37 | | 2 10 | 30 | 2 57 | 25 |
| 3.9 | Cumwhinton | | 7 25 | 55 | 6 56 | $48\frac{1}{2}$ | 6 14 | 53 | 7 15 | 52 |
| — | | | p.w.s. | | — | — | — | | | |
| 5.1 | Howes Siding | | 9 19 | 30 | — | | 7 31 | 62 | 8 32 | 61 |
| 6.8 | Cotehill | | 11 43 | 53 | 10 14 | $56\frac{1}{2}$ | 9 14 | 60 | 10 17 | 60 |
| 8.3 | Low House | | 13 21 | 75 | 11 50 | $59\frac{1}{2}$ | 10 44 | 77 | 11 48 | 72 |
| 9.9 | Armathwaite | | 14 41 | 69/76 | 13 14 | $72\frac{1}{2}$ | 12 04 | 67/72 | 13 10 | 63/72 |
| 13.0 | Milepost 295 | | 17 43 | 66 | 15 56 | $69\frac{1}{2}$ | 14 48 | 66 | 15 55 | 67 |
| 15.4 | Lazonby | | 19 21 | 76 | 17 49 | $78\frac{1}{2}$ | 16 47 | 77 | 17 52 | 76 |
| — | | | — | 63 | — | $63\frac{1}{2}$ | p.w.s. | 20 | — | 63 |
| 23.3 | Culgaith | | 26 11 | 78 | 24 33 | $74\frac{1}{2}$ | 25 29 | 73 | 24 42 | 73 |
| — | | | p.w.s. | 55 | p.w.s. | $37\frac{1}{2}$ | p.w.s. | 35 | p.w.s. | 30 |
| 27.8 | Long Marton | | 30 21 | 63 | 28 59 | — | 30 17 | — | p.w.s. | 25 |
| 30.8 | Appleby | 33 | 33 10 | 69 | 33 20 | 50 | 33 41 | 62 | 34 05 | 58 |
| 33.2 | Ormside | | 35 13 | 78 | 35 48 | $66\frac{1}{2}$ | 35 52 | 76 | 36 16 | 78 |
| 36.1 | Griseburn Box | | 37 43 | 65 | 38 59 | 49 | 38 27 | 60 | 38 47 | 61 |
| 38.2 | Crosby Garrett | | 39 37 | 61 | 41 33 | $54\frac{1}{2}$ | 40 30 | 70 | 40 50 | 69 |
| 41.5 | Kirkby Stephen | | 42 52 | 59 | 45 15 | 49 | 43 28 | 61 | 43 48 | 60 |
| 44.8 | Mallerstang | | 46 10 | 59/66 | 49 32 | 46/47 | 46 52 | 56/61 | 47 16 | 56/61 |
| 48.3 | Ais Gill | 56 | 49 30 | 61 | 54 15 | $47\frac{1}{2}$ | 50 34 | 54 | 50 57 | 55 |
| 51.4 | Garsdale | | 52 03 | 78 | 57 15 | 70 | 53 14 | 79 | 53 42 | 70 |
| 54.6 | Dent | | 54 51 | 69 | 60 12 | 65 | 56 08 | 59 | 56 36 | 72/59 |
| 59.5 | Blea Moor | $66\frac{1}{2}$ | 58 44 | 81 | 64 46 | $63\frac{1}{2}$ | 60 39 | 72 | 60 54 | 70 |
| 65.5 | Horton | | 63 26 | 70/80 | 69 50 | 76 | 65 01 | 89 | 65 57 | 77 |
| — | | | p.w.s. | 30 | — | | p.w.s. | 35 | p.w.s. | 30 |
| 71.5 | Settle | | 69 35 | 60 | 74 54 | — | 70 58 | 73 | 72 43 | 66 |
| 73.5 | Settle Jc | $80\frac{1}{2}$ | 74 22 | 68 | 76 43 | — | 72 44 | 65 | 74 37 | 60 |
| — | | | — | — | p.w.s. | 10 | — | — | — | — |
| 76.8 | Hellifield | 84 | 78 30 | — | 83 44 | — | 76 19 | 48 | 78 11 | 50 |
| — | | | checks | — | — | — | checks | | — | |
| 112.9 | Leeds City | 126 | 124 07 | — | 125 34 | — | 141 11 | | 121 25 | |
| | Net time to Hellifield | | $70\frac{1}{2}$ | | 80 | | $72\frac{1}{2}$ | | 74 | |

regular correspondents sent me detailed logs of all the day's running and the performance of the 'Deltic', southbound from Carlisle, makes an exciting tailpiece to this chapter. Never previously, and I should imagine never since with all the restrictions subsequently imposed, has such running ever been made over the Settle and Carlisle line. The log compiled by Mr Winkworth is tabulated herewith, and in presenting it in my own book I can say that the recorder was among the most experienced of my correspondents during my authorship the 'Locomotive Practice and Performance' in *The Railway*

*Magazine*, and the details may be taken as fully authentic. I mention this because some of the more critical of my readers might perhaps think that I had 'fallen' for a tall story!

The going from the Summit near Low House Crossing was terrific with its average of all but 88 mph from Armathwaite to Culgaith, while from Ormside, until the speed restriction above Kirkby Stephen supervened, looked like taking the train over Ais Gill Summit at a minimum of about 70 mph! No time, also, was wasted in the descent of the 'Long Drag', with the twelve miles from Blea Moor to Settle station covered at an

Carlisle–Skipton: The "Hadrian Flyer"
Locomotive: 'Deltic' No. D9005
*The Prince of Wales's Own Regiment of Yorkshire*
Load: 10 coaches, 348 tons tare, 365 tons full

| Distance Miles | | Sch min | Actual m s | Speeds mph |
|---|---|---|---|---|
| 0.0 | Carlisle | 0 | 0 00 | — |
| 0.9 | Petteril Bridge Jc | | 3 05 | 30/58 |
| 3.9 | Cumwhinton | | 6 18 | 55 |
| 9.9 | Armathwaite | | 12 07 | 86 |
| 13.0 | Milepost 295 | | 14 19 | 84 |
| 15.4 | Lazonby | | 15 56 | 91 |
| 19.7 | Langwathby | | 18 51 | 88/92 |
| 23.3 | Culgaith | | 21 17 | 88 |
| — | | | p.w.s. | 56 |
| 27.8 | Long Marton | | 25 17 | — |
| 30.8 | Appleby | 30 | 28 01 | 71 |
| 33.2 | Ormside | | 29 52 | 84 |
| 36.1 | Griseburn Box | | 32 00 | 76 |
| 38.2 | Crosby Garret | | 33 42 | 75 |
| 41.5 | Kirkby Stephen | | 36 12 | 73 |
| — | | | p.w.s. | 53 |
| 44.8 | Mallerstang Box | | 39 22 | 60 |
| 48.2 | Ais Gill Box | | 42 50 | 63 |
| 51.4 | Garsdale | | 45 15 | 78/70 |
| 59.5 | Blea Moor Box | | 51 47 | 79/90 |
| 71.5 | Settle | | 60 07 | 91 |
| 73.5 | Settle Jc | 67 | 61 35 | 80 |
| 76.8 | Hellifield | 71 | 64 10 | 66 |
| 80.2 | Bell Busk | | 66 57 | 82 |
| 86.8 | Skipton | 81 | 72 47 | |

Net time $71\frac{1}{2}$ minutes

average of 87 mph. After such an experience I can well imagine that the continuation of the run from Doncaster to King's Cross, even though it included some spells of 100 mph running, seemed like an anti-climax!

*The 09.09 diverted Glasgow-Central to Brighton express, between Garsdale and Rise Hill Tunnel, hauled by Class 47/4 diesel No. 47452, March 1989.* (Brian Morrison)

# 20
# Reliefs, Specials and the Embargo on Steam

While the 'Peak' class diesel-electrics had taken over the principal Scotch Express services from the end of 1961, there were many times in the years before the fateful autumn of 1968 when steam locomotives continued to be used for fast express running over the Settle and Carlisle line, mainly to provide power for relief trains at times of heavy holiday traffic. I was busy with other affairs in those years and had no opportunities of travelling on the line myself, but correspondents to my articles in *The Railway Magazine* kept me well informed, and because of their kindness the script of the present chapter of this book has been prepared. It has a sad climax, not only in respect of the embargo on the use of preserved steam locomotives on any routes owned by British Railways, but also in the total closure of the far-famed Waverley Route from Carlisle to Edinburgh, as from January 1969. The embargo on steam fortunately did not last too long, though its effects profoundly influenced the events to be recalled in Chapter 21. Much will also be written later about the closing of the Waverley Route.

Coming now to steam locomotives on relief Scotch Expresses, Mr Ellison secured an excellent example of the running of an advanced section of the up "Thames–Clyde Express", which was all the more interesting in that the engine was of one of the Caprotti Class 5 4-6-0s, No. 44857,

*A northbound mixed freight at Horton, hauled by 'Britannia' class 4-6-2 No. 70029 (formerly* Shooting Star*) on 18th April 1967. (G. W. Morrison)*

*A panoramic shot of the full length of the southbound "Cumbrian Mountain Express" crossing Arten Gill Viaduct with preserved 'Merchant Navy' class 4-6-2 No. 35028* Clan Line, *8th April 1989.*
(David Eatwell)

not only so, but of the variety having a twin-orifice blast pipe and double chimney. In my own experience the Caprotti Class 5 4-6-0s did not seem the most successful of the breed, but this was certainly a stimulating occasion, well worth Mr Ellison's venture in being 'lured' into the relief section of the train instead of waiting for the 'Peak' hauled main train to arrive at Carlisle, from Glasgow. The schedule of this relief section was not quite as fast as that of the regular train, being allowed 132 minutes non-stop against 126 minutes. But this was very considerably faster than the best times observed in the days of purely steam haulage. Although my correspondent does not comment on this, one could imagine that after diesel working of the Leeds–Carlisle non-stop runs, the water-troughs near Garsdale were out of commission, because the relief train on which Mr Ellison travelled had to stop at Skipton to take water. Despite this however the train passed Wortley Junction in plenty of time to finish the run from Carlisle within the diesel schedule of 126 minutes had it not been for the signal stops outside.

The load was not very heavy for a Class 5 locomotive and no more than moderate progress was made as far as Lazonby, indeed more than $1\frac{1}{2}$ minutes were dropped on the smart schedule time for this section. But despite the permanent way slowing before Long Marton the train was comfortably on the right side of time at Appleby and the main ascent to Ais Gill was quite first class. From Ormside Viaduct, crossed at 68 mph, the speed had not once gone below 50 mph until Kirkby Stephen had been passed, and then from a minimum of 43 mph at the south end of

Birkett Tunnel it rose smartly to 50 mph past Mallerstang. The final minimum of 44 mph at Ais Gill was also excellent. The tableland section was covered briskly, and then the 'Long Drag' was descended in positively hurricane style, with an average of 84 mph throughout from Horton to Settle Junction and a final and sustained maximum of 88 mph past Settle Junction itself. So, despite a signal check at Bell Busk the train stopped for water at Skipton in ten minutes less than the working time allowed to pass that station.

Because of the stop the train was no more than five minutes ahead of booked time at Snaygill, and with the restrictions subsequently enforced, there could be little chance of gaining more until after Shipley had been passed. But I should imagine there was some recovery time included in the schedule over the last stage, because the time to passing Wortley Junction, 112 miles from Carlisle was only 120 min 11 sec, and this would have permitted a finishing time into Leeds of a little under 123 minutes if the road had been clear. At the foot of the log I have quoted Mr Ellison's estimated net time for the journey, $115\frac{1}{2}$ minutes. This assumes a normal passage through Skipton, and maintenance of the working time of two minutes between that station and Snaygill signal box. This is a reasonable reckoning, because had the water-troughs at Garsdale been functioning, no stop at Skipton would have been necessary.

The next 'relief' run was recorded by a Canadian friend, who like Mr Ellison, was 'lured' into a steam hauled relief to the southbound "Waverley" in Edinburgh, and at first wished

Carlisle–Leeds: Relief to
The "Thames–Clyde Express"
Load: 7 coaches 230 tons tare, 240 tons full
Engine: Caprotti valve gear
class 5 4-6-0 No. 44857

| Distance Miles | | Sch min | Actual m s | Speeds mph |
|---|---|---|---|---|
| 0.0 | Carlisle | 0 | 0 00 | — |
| 2.7 | Scotby | | 5 52 | 37 |
| 5.1 | Howes Siding | | 9 23 | 48 |
| 6.8 | Cotehill | | 11 40 | 44 |
| 8.3 | Low House Box | | 13 43 | 61 |
| 9.9 | Armathwaite | | 15 20 | 55/64 |
| 13.0 | Milepost 295 | | 18 27 | 57 |
| 15.4 | Lazonby | 19 | 20 37 | 72 |
| 19.7 | Langwathby | | 24 26 | 62 |
| 23.3 | Culgaith | | 27 40 | 68 |
| — | | | p.w.s. | 55 |
| 27.8 | Long Marton | | 31 53 | 61 |
| 30.8 | Appleby | 36 | 35 02 | 50 |
| 33.2 | Ormside | | 37 35 | 68 |
| 36.1 | Griseburn Box | | 40 35 | 51 |
| 38.2 | Crosby Garrett | | 42 58 | 57/62 |
| 41.4 | Kirkby Stephen | | 46 23 | 50 |
| 44.8 | Mallerstang Box | | 50 38 | 43/50 |
| 48.3 | Ais Gill Box | 59 | 55 12 | 44 |
| 51.4 | Garsdale | | 58 12 | 70/61 |
| 54.6 | Dent | | 61 21 | 72/62 |
| 59.6 | Blea Moor Box | 70 | 65 41 | 68 |
| 65.5 | Horton | | 70 16 | 83 |
| 71.5 | Settle | | 74 34 | 86 |
| 73.5 | Settle Jc | 84 | 75 58 | 88 |
| 76.8 | Helliefield | 87 | 78 28 | 68 |
| — | | | sigs | |
| 80.2 | Bell Busk | | 81 38 | 30 |
| 84.3 | Delaney's Siding | | 86 03 | 70 |
| 86.8 | Skipton | 99 | 89 05 | — |
| — | | | 93 09 | — |
| 88.1 | Snaygill Box | 101 | 96 02 | 48 |
| 93.0 | Steeton | | 100 51 | 67 |
| 95.9 | Keighley | 109 | 103 38 | 60 |
| 99.2 | Bingley | | 106 33 | 70 |
| 102.3 | Shipley Leeds Jc | 116 | 109 47 | 30 |
| 105.3 | Apperley Bridge | | 113 27 | 70 |
| 109.8 | Kirkstall | | 117 30 | 60 |
| — | | | sig stop | |
| 113.0 | Leeds City | 132 | 130 00 | |

Net time 115½ minutes

he had not been so tempted. The first engine failed and had to be taken off at Hawick, and the substitute was steaming so badly as to take three quarters of an hour to struggle up the 10½ miles to Whitrope. Reading my friend's letter reminded me of my first footplate journey after the war on

the regular 10.5 am from Edinburgh Waverley, which had not then been dignified by restoration of its pre-war name. We had a V2 class 2-6-2 in spanking external condition, but the coal was a load of such dross that a kitchen maid of that era might well have despaired of getting it lit at all! We staggered up to Falahill, just managing to keep the wheels turning over the Summit, and we took a bank engine from Hawick up to Whitrope. Thus assisted we were not too late on arrival in Carlisle. On my Canadian friend's trip, fortunately a "Black Five" in good condition, was waiting to take over. Because of the adventures in Scotland the train had arrived very late in Carlisle and a freight had been allowed to precede it from Durran Hill Yard. It was not until after the stop at Appleby that the express got a really clear road and then, as the accompanying log shows, the results were spectacular.

Starting from Appleby the maximum speed at Ormside Viaduct did not exceed 56½ mph, but thereafter the climbing was superb. My Canadian friend took very full and expert detail, and from the average speed of 50.8 mph over the 15 miles from Ormside to Ais Gill Summit one can deduce some very interesting particulars about the engine performance. I have calculated that the equivalent drawbar horsepower, that is the power that the engine would be exerting on level track, was 1,160. Comparing this with the output exerted by the BR5 4-6-0 on the Rugby Stationary Testing Plant when going all-out on Blidworth coal it seems that the Stanier "Black Five", No. 45028, was equally being extended to her utmost during the 17 min 40 sec of this analysis. On the test plant the BR5 was being worked with a fully opened regulator and 32 per cent cut-off, but from my own experience on the footplate of many "Black Fives" I should imagine that the driver was working with a considerably longer cut-off, and with the regulator not fully open. In any case it was a grand effort, nobly sustained over the tableland to Blea Moor. I am however not altogether surprised that the downhill timing of no more than eleven minutes for the 14 miles from Blea Moor to Settle Junction was not kept, with its average of 76.3 mph! It is extraordinary to reflect on how the working times on the descending gradients of this line were modified after the introduction of the 'Peak' class locomotives.

It would seem however that the steam

Appleby–Hellifield
Load: 7 coaches, 229 tons tare 235 tons full
Engine: Stanier Class 5 4-6-0 No. 45028

| Distance Miles | | Sch min | Actual m | s | Speed mph |
|---|---|---|---|---|---|
| 0.0 | Appleby | 0 | 0 | 00 | — |
| 2.5 | Ormside | | 4 | 10 | $56\frac{1}{2}$ |
| 5.3 | Griseburn Box | | 7 | 44 | 44 |
| 7.5 | Crosby Garrett | | 10 | 31 | 53/59 |
| 10.7 | Kirkby Stephen | | 14 | 00 | 51 |
| 14.0 | Mallerstang Box | | 17 | 59 | 47/54 |
| 15.3 | Milepost 262 | | 19 | 23 | 56 |
| 16.3 | Milepost 261 | | 20 | 29 | 54 |
| 17.5 | Ais Gill Box | 24 | 21 | 51 | $52\frac{1}{2}$ |
| 20.6 | Garsdale | | 24 | 45 | 72 |
| 23.8 | Dent | | 27 | 35 | 64 |
| 25.9 | Dent Head Box | | 29 | 25 | 72 |
| 28.7 | Blea Moor Box | 36 | 31 | 57 | 63 |
| 30.0 | Ribblehead | | 33 | 05 | 72 |
| 34.8 | Horton | | 37 | 00 | 75 |
| 36.4 | Helwith Bridge Box | | 38 | 30 | 70 |
| 40.8 | Settle | | 41 | 56 | 75 |
| 42.7 | Settle Junction | 47 | 43 | 31 | 76 |
| 44.8 | Long Preston | | 45 | 19 | $62\frac{1}{2}$ |
| 46.0 | Hellifield | 51 | 47 | 04 | — |

locomotives often called upon to work relief trains at busy holiday times, or rather the crews diagrammed to work them, frequently became caught up in the acceleration euphoria. It certainly seemed the case when another of my *Railway Magazine* correspondents, Mr B. J.

Mullaky, travelled by the 10.15 am relief to the regular 10.25 am from Leeds to Glasgow. The former train was the Saturdays-only 6.40 am from Birmingham and my friend's carefully compiled log, which it was a great pleasure to study, begins at Hellifield. For an eight-coach train of 285 tons, a 'Jubilee' class 4-6-0 was provided, one of those now happily preserved, No. 45593, *Kolhapur*. After the usual brisk start from Hellifield speed fell away in what might be called the usual steam style to an interim minimum at Helwith Bridge, but after the slight recovery normally experienced, there was a remarkable uphill acceleration, to no less than 39 mph sustained on the long 1 in 100 above Horton, to 41 mph over Ribblehead Viaduct, and nothing less than 39 mph again before entering Blea Moor Tunnel. This was good work, completely belying any thought that the engine put on to this relief was a 'down-at-heel' unit almost fit for the scrap heap. And emerging from Blea Moor Tunnel she proceeded like a 'bat out of hell' across the tableland, reaching no less than $79\frac{1}{2}$ mph at Dandry Mire Viaduct and clearing Ais Gill Summit at 68 mph!

The descent to Ormside was fast, but not more than ordinarily so, with a driver who was in a hurry, but it was after the stop at Appleby that the real record breaking began. In Chapter 18 I wrote of the fast descent from Ais Gill with the Gresley streamlined A4 Pacific *Golden Eagle*,

*A Birmingham–Glasgow express approaching Blea Moor box 8th August 1964, hauled by 'Britannia' 4-6-2 No. 70049 Solway Firth. (G. W. Morrison)*

*'Jubilee' class 4-6-0 No. 45729* Furious *passing Stainforth sidings in June 1961, with an excursion from Huddersfield to Helensburgh.* (Derek Cross)

and also of one made in the early 1900s by a Johnson "Belpaire" 4-4-0, after having detached its pilot at the Summit. But these two runs, records indeed as they were, were surpassed completely by the performance of *Kolhapur* on the 10.15 am from Leeds in August 1966, at any rate north of Appleby. Over the 20.7 miles from Culgaith to Scotby the three runs made the following times, the earlier ones not being comparable through not stopping at Appleby.

MR No. 2607: load 320 tons, 17 min 2 sec, average 72.8 mph.

A4 No. 60023: load 360 tons, 15 min 59 sec, average 77.9 mph.

Jubilee No. 45593: load 285 tons, 14 min 56 sec, average 82.8 mph.

It was between Long Marton and Lazonby that *Kolhapur* made the most amazing running, though equally the speed on the undulating stretch towards Armathwaite and beyond, beats any records that have ever come to my notice. With a clear road into Carlisle the time from Appleby would not have been more than 28 minutes, giving a start to stop average of 66 mph! My correspondent did not include details of the working times of the train, and in my transcription of his notes I did not think to ask my friends in the Operating Department of the London Midland Region for them to enrich the account of a magnificent performance. But

as shown in the table of logs on the diesel-hauled "Thames–Clyde Express" in Chapter 19 the working time from passing Appleby to the stop in Carlisle was only 27 minutes.

The 'Jubilee' *Kolhapur* was an ordinary traffic department engine at the time, but the next one to be featured in this chapter is a very special preserved unit, the ex-LNER A4 Pacific No. 4498 *Sir Nigel Gresley*, restored to pre-war livery and numbering, and owned by the A4 Locomotive Society. This celebrated engine was booked for its first public run on Sunday 1st April 1967 from Crewe to Carlisle and back, outward by the West Coast Main Line and returning via the Settle and Carlisle line, and thence via Manchester. I was honoured to be invited as a guest of the Society on this notable occasion, but unfortunately, because of other commitments I had to cry off at the last minute, and another good friend and fellow enthusiast of the stop-watch took my place, Mr F. G. Cockman. The notable running that he recorded duly appeared in one of my monthly articles in *The Railway Magazine*. Some spectacular speed was run on certain stages of the northbound journey, though of course it was the return that concerns this book. The load was no mere featherweight, twelve corridor coaches, having a tare weight of 423 tons, and with practically every seat taken, at least 450 tons full. During their spell on the Leeds-Glasgow

10.15 am Leeds–Carlisle, as from Hellifield
Load: 8 coaches, 264 tons tare, 285 tons full
Engine: "Jubilee" class 4-6-0 No. 45593 *Kolhapur*

| Distance Miles | | Actual m | s | Speed mph |
|---|---|---|---|---|
| 0.0 | Hellifield | 0 | 00 | — |
| 3.3 | Settle Junction | 4 | 28 | 65 |
| 5.2 | Settle | 6 | 27 | 53½ |
| 9.6 | Helwith Bridge Box | 14 | 00 | 30 |
| 11.3 | Horton | 16 | 58 | 34½ |
| 13.7 | Milepost 245 | 20 | 58 | 39 |
| 16.0 | Ribblehead | 24 | 27 | 41 |
| 17.3 | Blea Moor Box | 26 | 20 | 39 |
| 22.2 | Dent | 32 | 05 | 65 |
| 25.4 | Garsdale | 34 | 54 | 79½ |
| 28.4 | Ais Gill Box | 37 | 19 | 68 |
| 32.0 | Mallerstang Box | 40 | 12 | 76 |
| 35.3 | Kirkby Stephen | 42 | 48 | 77½ |
| 38.5 | Crosby Garrett | 45 | 10 | 86 |
| 40.7 | Milepost 272 | 46 | 52 | 72 |
| 43.6 | Ormside | 48 | 56 | 83½ |
| 46.0 | Appleby | 52 | 37 | — |
| 2.9 | Long Marton | 4 | 17 | 65 |
| 7.4 | Culgaith | 7 | 47 | 83½ |
| 11.0 | Langwathby | 10 | 23 | 83½ |
| 12.4 | Little Salkeld | 11 | 20 | 93 |
| 15.3 | Lazonby | 13 | 13 | 92 |
| 17.7 | Milepost 295 | 14 | 58 | 76 |
| 20.8 | Armathwaite | 17 | 17 | 85 |
| 22.7 | Milepost 300 | 18 | 44 | 73 |
| 24.0 | Cotehill | 19 | 43 | 80 |
| 26.9 | Cumwhinton | 21 | 50 | 85 |
| 28.1 | Scotby | 22 | 43 | — |
| — | | sig stop | | — |
| 30.8 | Carlisle | 31 | 10 | — |

double home turns the A3 Pacifics were limited to a maximum tare load of 405 tons, so that 423 tons for an A4 appears as though it was also a maximum. Sunny April weather favoured most of the northbound journey, but by afternoon conditions had turned distinctly sour and train running enthusiasts were already beginning to wonder how the engine would cope with such a heavy load.

The schedule of this train allowed 40 minutes from Carlisle to passing Appleby and 68 minutes to Ais Gill. This was similar to that of the test trains in the 1923-4 locomotive exchanges, when Class 4 engines of both Midland and LNWR designs were loaded up to maximum tare tonnages of 350. *Sir Nigel Gresley* began well with that heavy train attaining 37 mph on the initial 1 in 132 past Scotby, and passing Lazonby, 15.4 miles in 22 min 8 sec. But signal checks at Long Marton and Appleby, the latter down to 25 mph, somewhat nullified the first advantage, even though Appleby itself was passed in 37 min 50 sec, 2¼ minutes inside scheduled time. By that time it was snowing, and the rail conditions were bad. I can recall only too well a footplate experience on another of the A4s, with a very heavy train and how, even with a dry rail, we slipped repeatedly when climbing the bank out of Berwick-on-Tweed up to Burnmouth, and I can quite imagine how things developed from Ormside up to Ais Gill on that April day of 1967. There was much slipping, and speed fell to

*The down "Thames–Clyde Express" near Horton with Gresley A3 Pacific No. 60082* Neil Gow, *3rd June 1961. (G. W. Morrison)*

*Southbound enthusiasts' special near Armathwaite, 26th April 1980, hauled by preserved and beautifully turned out 'Jubilee' No. 5690 Leander. (John Titlow)*

26 mph at the southern end of Birkett Tunnel. There was a recovery to 32 mph on the brief easing of the gradient past Mallerstang box, and then nine successive quarter-miles were run at $31\frac{1}{2}$, 28, $27\frac{1}{2}$, 26, 27, 26, 27 and 31 mph, the last mentioned being the speed at which the Summit had been passed.

The time over the 17.5 miles from Appleby to Ais Gill had taken 32 min 59 sec, instead of the 28 minutes booked, and because of the previous gain the train was no more than $2\frac{3}{4}$ minutes down from Carlisle, but the running over the tableland section to Blea Moor was so slow as to suggest that the engine was short of steam after the toilsome uphill grind from Ormside. No time was regained on the subsequent downhill section, and the train drew in at Hellifield 100 min 52 sec from Carlisle, 76.8 miles. Without any information of the conditions on the footplate on that snowy afternoon it is not possible to give any reliable assessment of the locomotive performance, except to emphasise the extent to which weather conditions can influence train running in these often unhospitable regions.

In the meanwhile time marched inexorably on to Sunday 11th August 1968, which had been fixed as the last day British Railways would run a steam-hauled train. In retrospect the event seems the crowning feat of an executive, or at least of certain members of it, determined to crush without sentiment the last symbols of an industry which had made a massive contribution to the rise and prosperity of Great Britain, as one of the foremost industrial nations of the world. The very poster advertising the trip, under banner headlines, *British Rail runs out of steam*, in its mixture of naïveté and nonsense, left many of us speechless at the time, but now appears no more than silly, in view of what has happened since. The route chosen for the running of "British Railways' last Steam Train" was over familiar ground to readers of this book, because the Settle and Carlisle line was to be traversed in both directions. The shades of George Stephenson and his intrepid band of pioneer railway builders was also invoked because this "last train" also traversed the full length of the Liverpool & Manchester Railway in both directions, and photographic stops were made at Rainhill and Parkside. For a ten-coach train a "Black Five" 4-6-0, No. 45110 was used from Liverpool to Manchester.

Long before the actual start the enthusiast coverage of the event was phenomenal. Rarely one imagines have the platforms of Lime Street station been pounded by such an eager throng, not only on the platform from which the special was about to depart but everywhere else as well, including massed photographers lined up perilously near to the track on which the other 9.10 am from Lime Street, the electric express to Euston, was already raring to go. One could understand that British Rail, having lost their way, did not want to give much advertisement to the actual train, and throughout the day the smokebox fronts of the engines involved bore nothing more than the reporting number of the train, 1157. I have not seen any photographs of how the train was greeted when it stopped first at Rainhill and then at Parkside. I should imagine that the crowds there included many motoring enthusiasts who followed the train on its travels. At Manchester, where the crowds were almost as great as in Liverpool, the "Black Five" was replaced by a 'Britannia' which was to take the train forward to Carlisle. This was No. 70013 *Oliver Cromwell* which had spent most of its early years in East Anglia, and to which it was returning after the trip on 11th August was completed. From Manchester the special, with the 'Britannia' carrying the same non-commital appelation, 1157, followed the route of the former Midland Scotch Expresses from Manchester, stopping at Blackburn to the delight of hundreds

*'Jubilee' 4-6-0 No. 45562* Alberta *on a Hunslet-Carlisle freight train near Horton, 30th September 1967.*
(G. W. Morrison)

of local enthusiasts, and so on to Hellifield.

None of my train-timing friends seemed to have made the journey, presumably because the frequency of stops for photographic or other purposes would have made any development of a sustained locomotive effort unlikely. But looking through the railway press of the day one can be surprised at the brief coverage of the event. Were the organs of the Press not invited, or were there enough fare paying passengers as to leave no room for any reporters? The photographic coverage as far north as Ais Gill, was tremendous. Well before the train was expected the small station yard at Dent, of all places, was becoming congested with cars, and the early arrivals had a

bonus in the form of a pair of smartly turned "Black Fives" coupled together, Nos 44871 and 44781, speeding north, light engine. It transpired that these two engines had been sent north to provide haulage for the southbound run of "The Last Train", or as someone rather unkindly expressed some time afterwards, in case the 'Britannia' had failed, and was not able to return south! By the time the special was due the little station yard at Dent was positively congested with cars, and both platforms and the convenient overbridge provided grandstands for the numerous spectators of all ages and both sexes, who had gathered to watch the train go slowly through. Doubtless most of these then leapt into their cars

*A second shot of the Hunslet–Carlisle freight hauled by No. 45562* Alberta, *approaching Ribblehead, involving some fast motoring by the photographer!* (G. W. Morrison)

*No. 45562* Alberta, *the last engine of the 'Jubilee' class to be withdrawn (November 1967), pounds up to Ais Gill Summit in lowering weather with a chartered excursion, "The South Yorkshireman" on 7th October 1967.* (G. W. Morrison)

and drove as fast as they could for the road beside Ais Gill Summit, where the train was scheduled to make a photographic stop.

The scene here, as pictured by a fine photograph in *The Railway Magazine*, is to me a faint reminder of the pitch at Twickenham, after 'no side' has been blown after a hard fought Rugby international, and enthusiastic supporters are streaming on to the field in droves. At Ais Gill on 11th August 1968, not only were the cutting sides lined with spectators, but men, women and children were down on the actual line, in the six foot, and the *four-foot* of the up main line! It was of course a Sunday and there would not be many trains about anyway; but if at that particular juncture Mallerstang had rung and offered any kind of train on the up main line, it is fairly certain that the signalman at Ais Gill would have had to refuse it, until the special had left for Carlisle and the crowds had more or less dispersed. No mention is made in the literature that came my way of any similar assemblies at Appleby, or indeed at Carlisle. But there for the return journey the two "Black Fives" previously noted replaced *Oliver Cromwell*. It was significant of the 'belt and braces' tactics employed in providing motive power this "Last Train", that it should be double-headed. A load of no more

than ten coaches would have been a mere nothing to *one* "Black Five" in good form.

The photographers gathered in the High Pennines to see them come back on that fine sunny afternoon, and with two engines, the special was pictured climbing the last miles to Ais Gill in excellent style. Not only were both engines very clean but both were evidently in good condition with not a wisp of steam escaping past the pistons or glands of either engine. Although No. 44871 was to be saved for preservation, being purchased privately, the other was destined for the scrap yard! More spectators gathered to photograph the train as it crossed Dent Head Viaduct before plunging into Blea Moor, while some others, forsaking their cars for a time 'took to the heather' as the Scots would express it, and climbing high above the portal of the tunnel got a bird's eye view. The day was not ended for these enthusiasts with the passage of engines 44871 and 44781, for after a discrete interval the signals were lowered again, and far away to the north, as it came round the curve through Dent station, was the 'Britannia', No. 70012 *Oliver Cromwell* running light, on the first stage to its eventual home in Norfolk.

As it turned out of course the "Last Steam Train on British Railways" proved eventually to be anything but the last, but that same autumn season was to preface the death-knell of another facet of the British Rail system, none other then the closure, as from January 1969, of the much loved Waverley Route, from Carlisle to Edinburgh. It is not too much to say that the existence of this trunk line, tapping the important Border towns of Hawick and Galashiels, and serving the potentially profitable tourist region of what became known as the 'Scott country', proved as much of an incentive, perhaps even more so than the potential traffic of the Glasgow & South Western towards the enterprising of the Midland Railway's independent route to Carlisle. The immediate objective of course was Edinburgh, and through carriages from St Pancras were run immediately the Settle and Carlisle line was opened for through traffic. But the Midland management was watching points in Scotland very closely, and particularly the project of the Forth Bridge Company, which in 1873, was authorised to build a railway some 15 miles long from the Queensferry branch of the North, round the Firth of Forth to link up with existing lines near Inverkeithing. The firth itself was to be crossed at the point where it narrows to no more than a wide river, where the present highway bridge at Kincardine now is.

However, when by Act of July 1882 the Forth Bridge Company were empowered, in substitution for the railway originally authorised, to build a railway no more than $4\frac{1}{4}$ miles long spanning the firth on a great viaduct, the Midland Railway was one of the foremost guarantors in fact the largest, so far as financial backing was concerned. The four railway companies involved were the North British, the North Eastern, the Great Northern and the Midland, and the Act provided for an absolute and perpetual guarantee of a dividend of 4 per cent per annum and the four companies were made liable for the following proportions; Midland $32\frac{1}{2}$ per cent; NBR 30 per cent, and the NER and GNR, $18\frac{3}{4}$ per cent each. The famous bridge was completed in 1890, and almost at once the Midland began to organise through services beyond Edinburgh over the tracks of its Scottish partner. So far as Aberdeen and Perth were concerned through carriages from St Pancras, and sometimes even from Bristol, were welcomed on the North British but it was another matter when the 'High Command' at Derby began enterprising through sleeping cars over the Highland to Inverness. Northward from Perth at that time every effort

was made to keep train loads at a minimum, and the Highland management grudged the effort of running sleeping cars.

The Highland people, noted with some concern that by the time they reached Perth from the South some of these through carriages and sleepers were sparsely filled, particularly those from the Midland route. There were indeed times when they refused to take the through carriages forward when there was vacant accommodation in the local part of the trains from Perth. To change at 5.30 am in the morning was bad enough for ordinary passengers, but to empty sleeping cars at that time caused some furious remonstrancy from both passengers and the English railways. In the reverse direction there were many occasions when Inverness refused to run the St Pancras sleeper because there was not a paying load, and in 1897 the Highland advised Derby that they would not convey the Midland car at all. The same cavalier treatment was also meted out to both the East and West Coast companies on occasions, but with the dawn of the new century a more conciliatory attitude was fostered at Inverness, and sleeping cars from all three routes worked in regularly. The development of tourist traffic on the West Highland Railway attracted the Midland management, and of course the North British were ready enough to cooperate, with the running of through carriages

*Preserved Stanier 'Pacific', No. 46229* Duchess of Hamilton, *on shed at Carlisle Upperby ready to work the "Cumbrian Mountain Express" on 8th November 1980.* (David Eatwell)

*'Castle' class 4-6-0 No. 7029* Clun Castle *passes Durran Hill Junction with a special for Leeds and the South.* (Derek Cross)

between St Pancras and Fort William. The climax of pre-1914 developments so far as traffic over the Settle and Carlisle line was concerned was the introduction of a Highland express in 1901 leaving St Pancras at 7.20 pm and reaching Carlisle at 1.30 am. This conveyed through carriages and sleeping cars for Inverness and Fort William.

Regular through carriage and sleeping car services from the Midland line to Inverness and Fort William were not revived after the First World War, but the 9.15 pm Waverley sleeper still conveyed through carriages for Aberdeen, which were attached to the "Night Scotsman" in

Edinburgh to make up a gargantuan load, which always needed double-heading. I saw it often when I was on holiday at Stonehaven in 1929 and 1930. Sometimes it had to be divided, and I have a photograph of the first portion, consisting only of the Midland coaches, near Muchalls, hauled by an old Holmes rebuilt 4-4-0. Now this once-fascinating outlet for the Midland north of Carlisle is no more, and a great tract of the Border Country, southwards from the Firth of Forth to the Tyne, and extending between the East Coast and West Coast main lines, is entirely devoid of railways. *Eheu fugaces, laburtur anni,* as the classicists might say!

# 21
# The Centenary

In 1965 Beeching retired from the Chairmanship of the British Railways Board. Philip Shirley, the archiconoclast had gone earlier and Beeching's successor, though personally selected and nurtured by him, proved a more fiery personality than even the dynamic lady who Lord Wilson had installed as Minister of Transport could deal with, and she had sacked him. Then at last we had a Chairman who had been a life-long professional railwayman, in Bill Johnson. Early in the 1970s the total ban on steam locomotives running anywhere on British Railways had been partially lifted, and when the time came for preparations to begin in earnest for the celebration of the Settle and Carlisle Centenary in the winter of 1974–5, everyone concerned, and not only those intimately connected but railway enthusiasts the world over, were deeply gratified that the threat of closure had receded, for a time anyway. It would have been ironic if the Centenary had been marked by the closing of the line to all through traffic. To celebrate the event the Settle and District Civic Society had set up a Railway Centenary Sub-Committee of which the Hon. Secretary, N. J. Mussett, is a master at Giggleswick School, and a close family friend. He has sent me copies of the newsletters the Society published from time to time, and in February 1975 this newsletter had an important tailpiece, thus:

"What a stroke of good fortune that the Settle–Carlisle line did not fall victim to the threat of closure after all! Apart from the social and tourist potential of the line, it still provides a significant alternative route between Scotland and England. For example, the wild weather of last December brought down the wires on the newly-electrified West Coast line at Hest Bank and Tebay; all traffic had to be re-routed over the Long Drag for two days or so whilst the

*Preliminary reconnaissance: the Author with Alex Murray, PRO of the LM Region at Ais Gill signal box.* (British Railways)

damage was repaired. And now in January, we notice that Anglo-Scottish traffic roars up and down Ribblesdale on Sundays while track maintenance is carried out on the West Coast route. The adaptability and continuing usefulness of the S & C perhaps needs as much publicising as the 'Electric Scots' themselves!"

As an old boy of Giggleswick School I was coopted as a part-time honorary member of the Centenary Committee, and I am delighted to be able to quote from two snippets in their second newsletter. The first is from my good friend, Pat Koppel, whose family lived at Stainforth, and who for some years was a Governor of Giggleswick School. One of his family anecdotes concerns Thomas Foster Knowles who frequently travelled north on a night express, arriving at Hellifield between 2 and 3 in the morning. He kept a hammock in the stationmaster's office. The hammock was slung from rings set in the walls of the waiting room and he then settled down to several hours of comfortable sleep before catching the train on to Settle or Giggleswick!

"Thomas Knowles also used to buy his whisky from Ainslie and Heilbronn's distillery near Turnberry, and it came down in 11-gallon casks, ovenproof. On its arrival at Settle station, the stationmaster alerted Mr Knowles and he arrived by horse (though in later days, by motor car) with a tap and spigot, together with a set of Sykes' hydrometers. In the stationmaster's office he would let out half a jug of whisky, test its specific gravity (which was usually correct) and then drink it with the stationmaster. If there was any adverse variation he put in a claim immediately on the spot."

The same newsletter contained a quotation from Wildman's Household Almanack, dated Settle 1875. "At the Settle Junction, which is about $2\frac{1}{2}$ miles below the town, towards Leeds, the Turnpike Road has been diverted and improved. Two bridges are nearly finished, the one under and the other over, both the Leeds and Lancaster and the Settle and Carlisle Railways, for the convenience of the landowners.

A signal box has been erected at the south end of the station yard, and a station will shortly be commenced here for the interchange of traffic,

*On 1st May 1976, the Settle and Carlisle Centenary special from Carnforth, near High Bentham, hauled by No. 790* Hardwicke *and No. 4472* Flying Scotsman. *(David Eatwell)*

the necessary excavations having been made, and some permanent way laid.

The double line is laid from the Junction to Batty Green, and a goods engine makes regular journeys, with materials, to the tunnel about four times a day.

At Settle the station building is being roofed in, the Station Master's House foundations and those of the other buildings are ready for the superstructure and the platforms and other walls are finished.

Near the Settle station a row of six cottages (is) being constructed, and, after the same pattern eight are being built at Selside, and six more at Salt Lane, which latter place is one mile south from Batty Green. They are of a pretty order of architecture, and from the various arrangements and the substantial manner in which they are being executed should be appreciated by the servants of the Company for whose convenience they are being put up. The erection of such structures shows a wise policy, as unless the men are comfortably housed, it will be a difficult task to keep them at their various posts, in the solitary and dreary places through which the line runs."

The 'close-it-down' faction at the British Railways Board, having been apparently out-voted in 1974, more enterprising local interests, headed by the Yorkshire Dales National Park Committee, initiated the Dales Rail experiment in the spring of 1975. By this the stations of Horton, Ribblehead, Dent, Garsdale and Kirkby Stephen, which had previously been closed, were being reopened for three weekends that summer. On the Saturdays special trains ran from Leeds at 08.03 and 17.03 and on the Sundays one train only departed at 08.38. Each train ran no further than Appleby, but passengers, who it was emphasised could only book through the National Park Offices (Dales Rail Project) could join the special trains at Bradford (Forster Square), Shipley, Bingley, Keighley and Skipton. In the case of the first named station of course the train had to take the branch from Shipley, and reverse at Bradford. The project met with immediate success, and was repeated on a more ambitious scale in the following year, though not to the extent of going into Bradford and reversing. In 1975 the regular passenger train services had shrunk from one daytime and one night

service between St Pancras and Glasgow, and one day service between Leeds and Glasgow. In the summer service there was a Saturday's only train between Sheffield and Glasgow, and in Scotland these trains took the Caledonian route. Details of the actual timings are shown as an addendum to the chapter.

While the Dales Rail Project was being developed in the spring of 1975 in quite another connection I became aware of a family named Sharland, living on the eastern side of Bristol. Being aware of the Railway Centenary Sub-Committee's efforts to trace something more of the young engineer whose association with the railway was so dramatic, albeit all too brief, I made contact with the Bristol family of the same name with the interesting result told in Chapter 2. Unfortunately I was not able to accompany the New Zealand uncle and aunt of my new friends in Bristol when they went to Settle in the summer of that same year, and met the members of the Railway Sub-Committee. I was very fully involved at that time with another great anniversary, none other than the sesquicentenary of the opening of the Stockton & Darlington Railway; in connection with which I had been greatly honoured to receive an invitation from the Institution of Mechanical Engineers to collaborate with my good friend, the late Roland C. Bond, in the presentation of the James Clayton Memorial Lecture, of which the title was to be '150 years of Uninterrupted Progress in Railway Engineering'. In addition to its first presentation, to an audience of more than 800 at Imperial College in London, there were occasions at Bath, Manchester, Newcastle, Glasgow, Hull and Liverpool during the winter of 1975-6. In between which I had to give much thought to the lectures I was to present on behalf of the Railway Sub-Committee of the Settle and District Society.

In the midst of my other activities I was delighted when I received Newsletter No. 5 from Settle to read how very fully the New Zealand family Sharland had been briefed up, as to what was planned for the following year. Also, how interested I was to see reproduced a photograph of the young engineer, who unhappily did not live to see the line he surveyed completed, let alone in full operation. The claims on my time, meanwhile, were as enjoyable as they were pressing. The Railway Centenary Sub-Committee had organised three Inaugural Meetings, on Saturday

*The engines of the steam special having been on exhibition at Settle station for most of the day, returning 'light-engine' to Hellifield to collect the special train that had been worked south from Carlisle. It had journeyed thence via the West Coast route.* (David Eatwell)

afternoons, on 10th January in Carlisle, on 17th January in Appleby, and on 24th January in Ingleton. At each meeting the film 'The Long Drag' was to be shown. I was to be the guest speaker in Carlisle. David Jenkinson, then of the National Railway Museum at York, at Appleby, and my good friend and collaborator Eric Treacy, Lord Bishop of Wakefield, at Ingleton. But at the last minute he was prevented from coming, and as I was to be there in any case I stepped into the breach.

In the meantime the Dales Rail Project had met with such success that in the same newsletter it was reported that it was being extended to certain stations north of Appleby in 1976. Early in the New Year the Yorkshire Dales National Park

Hardwicke *and* Flying Scotsman *again near Giggleswick on the return special bound for Euston, via Carnforth, 1st May 1976.* (David Eatwell)

Committee issued a leaflet outlining the extended programme, from which the following paragraphs may be quoted. "Although the line, which in 1976 celebrates its Centenary for passenger traffic, remains open for express and freight traffic, services were withdrawn from local stations in 1970, leaving hillfarming communities virtually without public transport service, and making a magnificent part of the National Park almost totally inaccessible to people without their own transport."

The aim of the Dales Rail experiment is to achieve a partial restoration of local passenger trains on the line. Stations have been restored to an adequate standard for 'occasional' use in co-operation with British Rail, by means of financial support provided by the National Park Committee, Cumbria County and Eden District Councils, and the Countryside Commission. The service, which operates between Spring and Autumn on selected weekends, is based on a close partnership between British Rail, the National Bus Company and the Yorkshire Dales National Park Committee to provide trains and linking bus services in the National Park.

The purpose of the service is threefold; to provide access to the National Park for people without their own transport, to provide an attractive alternative park-and-ride service from urban areas for people who would normally have used their cars on the National Park's crowded road system, and to provide a service for the local community in the Yorkshire Dales National Park and in Cumbria to enjoy a day's shopping in West Yorkshire or Carlisle.

In addition, the remarkable beauty of the rail journey provides a tourist feature in its own right, both for the ordinary tourist and the rail enthusiast, and this additional tourist traffic helps support the service. The guided walks which are arranged on Sundays provide the visitor with a valuable way of discovering the National Park."

In the extended programme the hitherto closed stations at Armathwaite, Lazonby and Langwathby were re-opened as unstaffed halts, and the Dales Rail trains stopped additionally to provide connection from the former LYR line as far south as Blackburn. The direct connection with Bradford was not included however, neither was the stop at Shipley. Connection with the Dales Rail trains, which in 1976 made their first call out of Leeds at Bingley, had to be made by ordinary service trains. An innovation in 1976 was the extension of the Dales Rail service to Carlisle on Saturdays, the up morning train leaving at 8.5 am. On Sundays, when no Dales Rail trains ran north of Appleby, the National Park organisation announced a series of Guided

*An earlier gala occasion at Settle station, in 1938: the naming ceremony of the engine No. 5538 Giggleswick, 'Patriot' class 4-6-0. (Author's collection)*

*At the top table at the S&C Centenary Banquet: left to right, Bishop Eric Treacy, the Chairman, Alan Bennett, Mrs Treacy, and the Author, O. S. Nock. (K. & J. Jelley)*

Walks, led by experienced guides, some of them fairly strenuous! The Dales Rail timetable for the Centenary Year is shown in a second addendum to this chapter.

When plans were being formulated for the running of the Centenary Special, on 1st May, the million-dollar question remained "Would British Railway relax the prevailing ban, just for one day, and allow the centenary special train to be hauled by steam?" To try to help the committee I pulled all the strings that I could think of at Euston, and elsewhere. The obstacle was the business of turning the engines at Carlisle, and avoiding their passing under the overhead electric wires. There were suggestions that steam working should terminate at the old Durran Hill shed location and that the train should be hauled thence into Citadel station by diesel; but the only concession eventually made was that the engine which had worked the special across from Carnforth in the morning should be allowed to proceed up the Carlisle line afterwards, as far as Settle, and be on exhibition during part of the afternoon.

I shall never forget that weekend. On Friday, 30th April, using the M4, M5 and M6 motorways in succession we drove up to Giggleswick, and on arrival we were horrified to learn that *both* engines booked to haul the centenary special from Carnforth to Hellifield on the following morning had failed! We were to have had the Midland compound No. 1000, and a "Black Five" 4-6-0 which had spent much of its active life on the Settle and Carlisle road. Nigel Mussett, one of the Giggleswick masters involved, and the

secretary of the Railway Centenary Committee, told us that arrangements were being made to get *Flying Scotsman* across from the National Railway Museum at York, to provide the main haulage for the special, while at Carnforth the historic LNWR 2-4-0 No. 790 *Hardwicke*, was in good trim, and would act as pilot to the big Pacific. While feeling relieved to hear that there would be steam locomotives available to haul the special, it was ironic that, on so predominantly a Midland occasion, recourse had to be made to London & North Western, and LNER engines to help out. Steam or not for the 'Long Drag' we were a light-hearted little party gathered at Giggleswick station on the Saturday morning, to travel to Carnforth to join the Centenary Special: Pat Koppel, and James Colyer-Ferguson, W. R. Mitchell, who had written entertainingly about the shanty life at Ribblehead, and of course Nigel Mussett, the Hon. Sec. of the Railway Centenary Sub-Committee. Eric Treacy and his wife joined us at Carnforth.

Olivia and I had the privilege of riding in the VIP saloon, next to the engines on the steam run across from Carnforth. On that occasion I must admit that on many moments of that journey my thoughts went back, not to the Settle and Carlisle as I knew it in my early stop-watching days, but to the times when perforce I had to alight from the train at Giggleswick, and felt often like Shakespeare's 'Whining school-boy, with his satchel, and shining morning face, creeping like snail unwillingly to school'! On May Day 1976, with *Hardwicke* and *Flying Scotsman* in partnership we were photographed a hundred and more times between Carnforth and Hellifield, where the diesel to take us on to Carlisle was waiting, but once arrived at Hellifield the enthusiasts virtually 'took over' photographing the two steam engines from every conceivable angle, irrespective of the fact that as far as the Settle and Carlisle line was concerned they were a pair of hastily procured interlopers.

For the northbound run to Carlisle we were now at the tail end of the train, though the backward view through the rear windows of the VIP saloon was tempered somewhat by the increasing heavy clouds, which above Horton settled into pouring rain. At Dent we stopped to exchange greetings with the other Centenary Special, which had left Euston at 08.50, travelled by the West Coast Main Line through to Carlisle, and then, at 13.00 hours exchanged electric for diesel traction for the southbound run to Settle. Passengers on the Euston train were allowed to alight here to see the elegant vintage stock that was included in our own train. A correspondent writing in *The Railway Magazine*, summed up the conditions vividly, "Leaving the luxury of our Mk III air-conditioned coaches" he wrote, "we stepped out on to the platform to be numbed by driving rain which sheeted down from the mist-clad hills in cold drenching torrents. The navvies of a hundred years ago must have toiled to build the line in conditions exactly like this. To reach the vintage stock one had to negotiate an almost impossible route akin to scaling a mountain; there was just time to have a quick look round before the locomotive gave a blast on its siren and the train moved off into the mist. No sooner had it done so than a whistle blew on the far side of the line and everyone started the long trek back to the up platform, along the road; over the bridge; through the gate; down the bank; across the stream; up the other side; round behind the snow fence and 'mind how you go down the slippery wooden steps' to the platform. With hordes of people scrambling desperately across Monkey Beck in the driving rain as wardens blew their whistles to hurry everybody, I felt that we ought to be chained together, carrying boulders and wearing suits with broad arrows printed on them."

On their eventual arrival in Settle, with the rain easing off somewhat, these passengers had a sight of *Hardwicke* and *Flying Scotsman* parked in the station sidings. Since we left earlier in the day they had been to Shipley to turn on the triangle

*Presenting the old signal box name board from Ais Gill, to Alan Bennett. Standing on left; Bobby Howes and Alex Murray, seated below, Mrs Olivia Nock, Bishop Treacy and Alan Bennett.* (Yorkshire Life)

New BR Timetable

| | | | Mondays to Saturdays | | | Sundays | |
| --- | --- | --- | --- | --- | --- | --- | --- |
| | | A | | B | C | D | E |
| Leeds | dep | 0232 | 0901 | 1040 | 1236 | 0305 | 1533 |
| Settle | dep | — | 0958 | — | 1335 | — | — |
| Appleby | dep | 0421 | 1044 | 1219 | 1423 | 0502 | 1727 |
| Carlisle | arr | 0501 | 1124 | 1259 | 1503 | 0551 | 1824 |
| Carlisle | dep | 0513 | 1136 | 1302 | 1516 | 0603 | 1830 |
| Glasgow Central | arr | 0747 | 1353 | 1526 | 1643 | 0855 | 2052 |

| | | | Mondays to Saturdays | | | Sundays | |
| --- | --- | --- | --- | --- | --- | --- | --- |
| | | F | G | H | | I | J |
| Glasgow Central | dep | 2250K | 0930 | 1045 | 1610 | 2130N | 1100 |
| Carlisle | arr | 0123 | 1152 | 1213 | 1824 | 0004 | 1348 |
| Carlisle | dep | 0138L | 1155 | 1227 | 1826 | 0014 | 1353 |
| Appleby | dep | — | — | 1306 | 1904 | — | 1438 |
| Settle | dep | — | — | 1359 | 1955 | — | — |
| Leeds | arr | 0401M | 1428 | 1452 | 2046 | 0308 | 1700 |

A  Dep St Pancras 2130; sleeper from Nottingham
B  Dep Sheffield 0942; Saturdays 7 June–30 August only
C  Dep St Pancras 0800
D  Dep St Pancras 2130; sleeper from Nottingham
E  Dep St Pancras 1005
F  Sleeper to Nottingham arr 0639 (0626 on Mondays)
G  Saturdays only, 7 June–30 August
H  To St Pancras, arr 1917
I  Sleeper to Nottingham, arr 0547
J  To St Pancras arr 2147
K  Sundays to Fridays
L  0128 on Mondays
M  0347 on Mondays
N  Saturdays

Dales Rail Timetable

West Yorkshire and Cumbria Service
Saturdays April 3rd, May 1st, June 5th, July 3rd, August 7th, September 4th, October 2nd

Train times shown in column headed A apply *only* to Saturdays, April 3rd and May 1st. Train times shown in column headed B apply to remaining Saturdays.

| | A | B | | | |
| --- | --- | --- | --- | --- | --- |
| Carlisle | 0805d | 1309a | 1350a | 2049a | 1845d |
| Armathwaite | 0825 | 1253 | 1334 | 2035 | 1904 |
| Lazonby | 0834 | 1242 | 1323 | 2024 | 1914 |
| Langwathby | 0842 | 1229 | 1310 | 2013 | 1929 |
| Appleby | 0900 | 1205 | 1246 | 1957 | 1949 |
| Kirkby Stephen | 9019 | 1152 | 1233 | 1944 | 2008 |
| Hawes | 0905d | 1200a | 1245a | 1955a | 1955d |
| Sedbergh | 0905d | 1200a | 1245a | 1955a | 1955d |
| Garsdale | 0936 | 1138 | 1219 | 1930 | 2026 |
| Hawes | 1000a | 1110d | 1150d | 1900d | 2045a |
| Sedbergh | 1000a | 1110d | 1150d | 1900d | 2045a |
| Dent | 0946 | 1130 | 1211 | 1922 | 2034 |
| Ribblehead | 0954 | | | | 2044 |
| Horton | 1003 | 1108 | 1149 | 1900 | 2053 |
| Settle | 1017 | 1054 | 1135 | 1847 | 2102 |
| Hellifield | 1028 | 1041 | 1122 | 1838 | 2115 |

| | | | | | |
|---|---|---|---|---|---|
| Skipton | 1043 | 1022 | 1103 | 1820 | 2134 |
| Keighley | 1055 | 1008 | 1049 | 1754 | 2146 |
| Bingley | 1103 | 1001 | 1043 | 1747 | 2152 |
| Leeds | 1128a | 0938d | 1021d | 1724d | 2213a |

Connecting BR services at Bingley for Shipley, Bradford (NB Dales Rail tickets NOT valid on these trains).

Worth Valley Railway steam trains at Keighley for Haworth, details from General Manager, Worth Valley Railway, Haworth, Keighley, West Yorkshire.

Sundays April 4th, May 2nd, June 6th, July 4th, August 8th, September 5th, October 3rd.

| | | |
|---|---|---|
| Appleby | 11.25a | 18.30d |
| Kirkby Stephen | 11.12 | 18.49 |
| Keld | 12.15a | 18.00d |
| Hawes | 11.25a | 18.35d |
| Dent Village | 12.05a | 18.10d |
| Sedbergh | 11.25a | 18.30d |
| Garsdale | 10.58 | 19.07 |
| Hawes | 10.35d | 19.30a |
| Sedbergh | 10.35d | 19.30a |
| Dent | 10.50 | 19.14 |
| Ribblehead* | | 19.25 |
| Horton | 10.28 | 19.33 |
| Settle | 10.14 | 19.43 |
| Hellifield | 10.01 | 19.56 |
| Skipton | 09.43 | 20.15 |
| Keighley | 09.28 | 20.36 |
| Bingley | 09.22 | 20.45 |
| Shipley | 09.16 | 20.51 |
| Bradford FS | 09.09 | 21.04 |
| Leeds | 08.40d | 21.27a |

On Sundays April 4th and May 2nd ONLY the departure times on the outward journey only will be 15 minutes later.

* Ribblehead station is only open for southbound (Leeds) trains. Passengers wishing to return to Ribblehead from Leeds on Saturday evenings may do so by changing trains at Dent.

Connecting bus services shown in italics. Buses depart from the usual Ribble/United bus-stops as shown in the Company's timetables and meet all trains at Garsdale station.

d = departure time        a = arrival time

there. In the meantime my good friend, 'Bobby' Howes and his wife had joined us at Carlisle. He, as Assistant General Manager of the London Midland Region, was to be one of the speakers at the banquet to be held at Settle station on our return, and he was appropriately dressed. Eric Treacy and I, and our wives, were dressed for a day in the country. We had been assured beforehand that although official proceedings would begin as soon as we arrived at Settle there would be plenty of time to change, and that rooms had been set aside in the station house at Ribblehead for us to do so during a scheduled photographic stop of 30 minutes or so on the journey back. But the day had turned very wet, and from one cause or another the diesel-hauled special became

very late. When we eventually got to Ribblehead, not only were the conditions pretty hopeless for photography, but the organisers decided to cut the stop to less than ten minutes, to make up as much time as possible. There was no question of the four of us going to the station house to change; it had to be done in the saloon, with only eleven miles of fast downhill running to go before our arrival in Settle. May Treacy and Olivia were one after the other accorded the seclusion of the 'loo', while Eric and I shielded from public gaze by a ring of fellow guests changed our trousers in the open saloon!

For the Banquet a large marquee had been erected in the station yard at Settle. It was fortunate that it was completely water tight, and more or less draught proof as well, for while it had been raining off and on during the whole day in this district, the deluge that had greeted us earlier at Ribblehead, had moved to Settle by evening and it was now teeming with rain, though not enough to drown the high spirits of what proved a memorable occasion. At the top table Alan Bennett, already well known in the North as a writer and radio commentator, was in the Chair, and beside him to right and left were Eric and May Treacy, Olivia was next to Eric, and beside her Bobby Howes.

On the left side, I was beside May. All too soon the ground inside the marquee behind the top table was rapidly becoming little less than a quagmire. The caterers and their staff, however, were magnificent, and the motherly old Yorkshire waitress who was looking after us, excused herself for a moment to go and put on a pair of 'Wellies', in which she afterwards padded up and down on the sodden ground. Olivia was sitting next to Eric Treacy, and she often recalled the running commentary that accompanied her very efficient serving of the meal. It began in earnest after she had changed into gum boots. In broadest Yorkshire dialect she told Eric and Olivia how all that week she had prayed for fine weather, but she was disappointed that the Good Lord had not answered her prayers. Then, without seeing his 'front' she continued, patting Eric affectionately, and commenting upon what a fine pair of shoulders he had. (Shades of our Rugger days!). Then he turned to speak to Olivia. He was, of course, in full clerical regalia, and she saw! When she had recovered her breath she gasped: "Oh, my God, oh my Lord: oh your Grace. . . ." But he put the old dear completely at her ease, with the charm and spontaneity that was so characteristic of his whole life. Towards the close of the evening Bobby Howes, assisted by Alex Murray, Public Relations Officer of the LM Region, presented Alan Bennett with a nameboard from Ais Gill signal box.

# 22
# Into the New Age

In the spring of 1976, when I was still in full-flood in my 22-year stint as regular author of the 'Locomotive Practice and Performance' feature in *The Railway Magazine*, I wrote two articles, the first was subtitled 'Midland days', but the second was 'Into the New Age'. Beginning the latter article I wrote:

After the Grouping, in 1923, it was perhaps inevitable that the Settle and Carlisle would become the poor relation among Anglo-Scottish express routes despite the predominating Midland influence in the first few years of the LMS. For one thing, it is very doubtful if it ever brought much more than prestige to the Midland coffers, if a section-by-section costing of revenue against operating, maintenance, and fixed charges had been revealed. It might seem graceless to write in somewhat deprecating terms of such a truly magnificent piece of railway, for which I personally have always a special and quite unshakeable affection; but it is important to emphasise the economic side, so that its vicissitudes since 1923 may be better appreciated.

After the brief honeymoon of the nationalised British Railways, and the joyous assumption by some in quite high authority that all would be well with railway finances "once we had got rid of steam", the economic blizzard set in, and the shadows began to close in over the Settle and Carlisle. The threat of closure became a very real one, despite its obvious value as a diversion route, and the artery it provided from the North Midlands and the West Riding of Yorkshire to Carlisle. In railway circles the imminence of closure became an even greater reality when the British Railways Board was having much difficulty in providing overwhelming financial evidence to justify

the cost of electrifying the West Coast Main Line. There was much scheme-making to route as much as possible of all Anglo-Scottish traffic 'under the wires', and by closing the other lines thus denuded of their traffic.

The complete abandonment of the Settle and

*Coming up the 'little' North Western line to Settle Junction is an oil-tank train hauled by Class 40 No. 40080 on 8th February 1983.*
(Brian Morrison)

*The 07.09 Glasgow–Penzance express diverted via the Settle and Carlisle line, on 25th March 1989, seen here just after passing Garsdale, with two Class 47s, Nos 47218 and 47454.* (Brian Morrison)

Carlisle line between Horton and Long Meg Sidings was one of the projects that figures largely in these proposals, but fortunately things did not work out that way. After the West Coast Main Line electrification had been authorised the working out of the traffic pattern, and particularly the planning over the freight services, resulted in the decision to run only fully-braked trains over Shap. This in turn allowed for a simplification of the signalling arrangements, by the omission of all catch points on the steep gradients. It also had an important reaction on the Settle and Carlisle which henceforth became the only route to Carlisle and Scotland from Lancashire and the Midlands over which partially-fitted freight trains could be run, unless they were to go from Hellifield to Carnforth and thence round the Cumberland coast. Of course one can appreciate that the ultimate aim of British Railways will be to eliminate all partially-fitted freight trains; but the present role of the Settle and Carlisle does not depend on the brake equipment of freight rolling stock.

By the year 1976 it was becoming evident that the Settle and Carlisle was no longer a 'poor relation' with the present situation over line occupation on the West Coast Main Line north of Preston during the night hours, which I shall be discussing in some detail, with examples of actual freight train working, in a future article of this series, the Settle and Carlisle is no longer a 'poor relation', but a vital artery, and one which could become even more important with still further passenger train acceleration under the wires. All this, of course, is traffic and business policy rather than locomotive practice in its more specialised sense; but it arises from the enhanced capacity of modern motive power, and the potentialities it has for still further development. At the present time the Settle and

Carlisle line is subject to a speed limit of 60 mph throughout, though this does not prevent some very smart start-to-stop runs being made, as I shall show later.

It is with the freights rather than with passenger trains that the principal role of this famous line then lay, and it is interesting to examine the present utilis-ation, so far as through trains are concerned. In Table 1 are set out details of the regularly scheduled down freight trains. The important point to note is the number of trains that do not originate in Midland territory and which, but for the heavy occupation of the line over Shap, and the absence of catch points on the steep gradients, would take the West Coast route. These are all important trains, in many cases providing the Registered Wagon Service. They have a uniform booked speed of $25\frac{1}{2}$ mph up the 'Long Drag' from Settle Junction to Blea Moor, so timed that the heaviest scheduled loads can be handled by a single diesel-electric locomotive of classes 45, 46 or 47. The overall average speed of 35 mph from Settle Junction to Petteril Bridge Junction, Carlisle, provides for the moderate downhill speeds necessary on such steep gradients with partially-fitted trains.

On the up road freights, mostly with a standard timing of 125 min for the $72\frac{3}{4}$ miles from Petteril Bridge Junction to Settle Junction, pass the former place at 01.48, 02.43, 03.08, 03.33, 04.22, 06.14, 07.10, 07.48, 08.18, 08.48, 09.45, 14.54, 18.58 and 21.43. The work-ing times laid down for these trains are as shown in Table II and in this case I have quoted the distances as given in the current working timetable, rather than those usually employed in logs of passenger train running.

From this it will be seen that the line is being quite extensively utilised by regularly scheduled trains, while it is of course invaluable as a diversion route, when occupation by the civil engineer or other circumstances make the line over Shap unavailable. In the case of West Coast expresses normally worked by one electric locomotive throughout, it is now common practice to couple the diesel required for the diversion route ahead of the electric locomotive, and haul the latter 'dead'. Normal working can then be resumed as soon as the train comes under the wires once again, with the electric locomotive taking up its rostered diagram again.

So far as present day passenger services are concerned I have details of two runs that show the effect of the maximum speed limit of 60 mph. With the normal loads and use of the powerful diesel-electric locomotives it cannot be said to be very severe. The run set out in Table III on the morning Leeds–Glasgow express was recorded by Mr D. S. M. Barrie. It began with a very smart run from Keighley over a section to which the 60 mph limit does not apply, and although my friend did not actually register it, 'even time' from the dead start must surely have been attained soon after Cononley. Then, if the speed limit is to be strictly observed, the allowance of only $17\frac{1}{2}$ min for the 15.2 miles from Skipton to Settle is very sharp, and was not precisely kept. Over a route of such fluctuating and relatively steep gradients, with a powerful locomotive and a moderate train load, it is not always easy to keep the speed between such narrow limits, and this driver was clearly exercising skill.

*The 09.33 Leeds–Morecambe train passing Settle Junction, showing clearly the modified track layout. Swindon-built Class 123 DMBS No. E52089 leads a class 123/124 dmu combination on 7th February 1983.* (Brian Morrison)

At the end of the year 1977 came the welcome news that steam traction would again be permitted over the line, and the first runs were made over the Easter weekend of 1978 by a

## Table I: Settle and Carlisle Line: Down Through Freights

| Time passing Settle Junction | | Time passing Petteril Bridge Junction | Av Speed mph | Av Speed Settle Junction to Blea Moor |
|---|---|---|---|---|
| 00.14 | 15.18 ThO Empties West Thurrock–Corkicle | 02.22 | 35 | 25.5 |
| 01.19 | 22.18 RWS from Brewery sidings | 03.24 | 35 | 25.5 |
| 04.46 | 23.33 RWS from Nottingham | 06.51 | 35 | 25.5 |
| 06.15 | 03.05 from Healey Mills (Wakefield) | 08.42 | 29.5 | 23.5 |
| 10.07 | 04.24 RWS from Bescot | 12.12 | 35 | 25.5 |
| 10.34 | 05.05 Parcels, Crewe South Yard to Carlisle Yard | 12.39 | 35 | 25.5 |
| 11.43 | 03.15 RWS from Cardiff | 13.48 | 35 | 25.5 |
| 11.54 | 07.10 from Tinsley | 14.35 | * | * |
| 13.51 | 03.15 SO RWS from Cardiff | 15.56 | 35 | 25.5 |
| 14.15 | 05.10 SO from Willesden | 16.20 | 35 | 25.5 |
| 14.39 | 22.05 from St Blazey | 16.42 | 35.5 | 25.5 |
| 16.02 | 12.03 from Healey Mills | 18.29 | 29.5 | 23.5 |
| 19.29 | 11.00 MO RWS from Cardiff | 12.40 | 33.5 | 25.5 |
| 22.26 | 18.15 from Stoke Yard | 00.31 | 35 | 25.5 |
| 22.45 | 20.08 RWS from Ribble Yard | 00.50 | 35 | 25.5 |
| 23.07 | 20.33 RWS from Walton Old Junction Warrington | 00.50 | 35 | 25.5 |
| 23.37 | 20.10 RWS Tinsley to Glasgow | 01.31 | 38 | 35 |

ThO Thursdays only; SO Saturdays only; MO Mondays only; RWS Registered Wagon Service; * Picks up water cans at Blea Moor, and sets them down at Appleby.

Table II: LM Region: Carlisle–Settle Junction
Freight Train Timings: Pass to Pass

| Distance | | | Time | Av speed |
| m | ch | | min | mph |
| 0 | 00 | Petteril Bridge Jc | 0 | — |
| 16 | 28 | Long Meg Sidings | 29 | 33.8 |
| 29 | 74 | Appleby | 51 | 36.9 |
| 40 | 52 | Kirkby Stephen | 72 | 30.7 |
| 47 | 35 | Ais Gill | 88 | 24.8 |
| 58 | 52 | Blea Moor | 104 | 34.5 |
| 72 | 50 | Settle Jc | 125 | 40.0 |
| 75 | 77 | Hellifield | 131 | 33.0 |

Table III: LM Region: Keighley–Appleby
Load: 7 cars, 249 tons tare, 260 tons full
Locomotive: Class 45 diesel No. 45035

| Distance | | Sch | Actual | | Speeds |
| Miles | | min | m | s | mph |
| 0.0 | KEIGHLEY | 0 | 0 | 00 | — |
| 3.0 | Steeton | | 4 | 02 | 75 |
| 6.1 | Cononley | | 6 | 39 | 72 |
| — | | | sigs | | |
| 9.2 | SKIPTON | 12½ | 10 | 37 | — |
| 3.7 | Gargrave | | 5 | 05 | 60/58 |
| 6.6 | Bell Busk | | 8 | 00 | 62 |
| 10.0 | HELLIFIELD | 11½ | 11 | 30 | 63/57 |
| 13.3 | Settle Jc | | 14 | 49 | 60/55 |
| 15.2 | SETTLE | 17½ | 17 | 41 | 60* |
| 1.8 | Stainforth Sdgs | | 3 | 53 | 52 |
| 4.4 | Helwith Bridge | | 6 | 56 | 56/54 |
| 6.1 | Horton | | 8 | 33 | 61 |
| 8.4 | Selside | | 10 | 53 | 59/61 |
| 10.8 | Ribblehead | | 13 | 18 | 56/60 |
| 12.1 | Blea Moor | 15½ | 14 | 36 | 58½ |
| 17.0 | Dent | | 18 | 45 | 66/57 |
| — | | | p.w.s. | | 23 |
| 20.2 | Garsdale | | 24 | 12 | — |
| 23.3 | Ais Gill | 27 | 28 | 29 | 50 |
| — | | | p.w.s. | | — |
| 40.8 | APPLEBY | 45 | 48 | 25 | — |

* Speed before stop

charter train named the "Norfolkman". This was hauled over the Settle and Carlisle line by the LNER V2 class 2-6-2 No. 4771 *Green Arrow*. The name of the train was a tribute to my good friend Bill Harvey, who has consummated a lifelong career in the Locomotive Department of the LNER and BR, by tending preserved units, and *Green Arrow* was immaculately restored to full running condition under his care at Norwich. The charter trains on 25th and 27th March both started from Euston, being electrically hauled to Stockport, and diesel hauled to Leeds where *Green Arrow* took over. The Steam Locomotive Operators Association had very kindly invited me, as representing *The Railway Magazine*, to travel on the first train. But unfortunately, because of other commitments, I was unable to go,

*A train of empty stone hopper wagons from Carlisle to Ribblehead, hauled by Class 25 diesel No. 25054 in February 1983.* (Brian Morrison)

and one of my regular correspondents, an expert stop-watcher in the person of Mr C. M. Napper was able to take my place, and his record of the running appears later in this chapter.

As I then wrote, and what I said then applies with redoubled force more than a dozen years later, steam locomotives on tour trains have to be handled very gently. Spare engines generally do not exist, and a failure on the road could not only cause great inconvenience to the ordinary traffic of British Railways, but would almost certainly result in a diesel having to be sent to the rescue to haul the cripple ignominiously out of harm's way. While those locomotives accepted for hauling specials are constantly subjected to the most stringent examination it is always advisable to take things easily when out on the road. Furthermore there is the question of manning. The number of enginemen with experience of firing a large locomotive, and still physically fit to do so, is growing ever less, although I know that among those who do come within this category there are still some keen and expert hands. All this was brought very much home to me as I

*Stone for Healey Mills leaving the quarry at Ribblehead hauled by Class 40 No. 40152 in February 1983.*
(Brian Morrison)

studied the log that Mr Napper compiled, and I compared the engine performance with some of the runs I have logged with V2 engines in the past, and particularly one with *Green Arrow* herself, when she was brand new, and regularly on the 3.35 pm Scotch Express goods from King's Cross to Peterborough.

On the run over the Settle and Carlisle line on 25th March the special train left Leeds $10\frac{1}{4}$ min early, and with so easy a schedule as 42 min for the 26.2 miles to Skipton nothing very special was

to be expected. In fact four minutes were lost, but even after the stop to change engine crews Skipton was left four minutes early. Details of the run forward from Hellifield are set out in the accompanying table. There were lengthy stops at Dent for photographs, Garsdale for water, and Armathwaite, and despite extremely bad weather, with falling snow at the higher levels, the locomotive seemed completely master of the modest task set to her. Mr Napper tells me that even in climbing the 'Long Drag' a relatively

*The stone train for Healey Mills had to proceed north from Ribblehead to Blea Moor to allow the locomotive, No. 40152, to change to the opposite end of the train to continue the journey southwards.*
(Brian Morrison)

*A West Coast route diversion, the 08.52 Euston to Inverness, hauled by Class 47 No. 47439, nearing Garsdale on 25th March 1989. (Brian Morrison)*

short cut-off was used, with very little noise. Speeds down to 20 mph on a 1 in 100 gradient, with a 470-ton load, can be compared with the same engine's 32 mph up to Potters Bar, on 1 in 200, with a 500-ton fitted freight. I should imagine that the cut-off on 25th March was well inside 20 per cent.

There was some pleasantly brisk running downhill from Ais Gill, though of course it must be borne in mind that there was a line maximum speed of 60 mph, throughout over this route at that time. As will be seen from the log there were some slight excesses on the steeply falling section

*A Sundays-only diversion: the 10.00 Glasgow–Liverpool express near Cotehill, hauled by Class 47 No. 47454 on 9th March 1975. (M. Bryce)*

down to Crosby Garrett. But though the actual running, as a piece of locomotive performance, was of little interest, in view of past achievements over this route, and of the record of the V2 class in particular, the great thing was to witness the opening of this superb line to steam once again, and to appreciate the immense amount of enjoyment that the occasion gave, not only to those travelling in the train but to the intrepid enthusiasts, who, in their hundreds, braved the appalling weather and thronged the bleak countryside to see the train go by. The engine itself appeared to be in excellent form, steaming freely, and even at the relatively low minimum speeds on the 'Long Drag' showing no tendency to slip.

The very next charter trip over the line, on 13th May, was however saddened by a personal tragedy, none other than by the death of the Rt Rev. Eric Treacy, formerly Bishop of Wakefield. On this day he had motored across from his retirement home in the Lake District to see and photograph the celebrated BR 9F class 2-10-0 No. 92220 *Evening Star* at Appleby, and when mingling with the enthusiastic crowd around the train he had a sudden heart-attack and died on the station platform. *The Railway Magazine*, knowing of my long personal association with him asked me to append a memoir to the next 'Locomotive Practice and Performance' I was writing, and July 1978 I wrote: "It is more than fifty years since I first met Eric Treacy — beside a main-line railway it is true, but with neither of us taking any notice of the passing trains. We were playing Rugby Football and so intent were we on the business in hand that neither of us was aware of the other's interest in railways. It was

British Rail: LM Region
Special Train: Hellifield–Carlisle
The "Norfolkman"
Load: 12 coaches, 434 tons tare, 470 tons gross
Locomotive: Class V2 2-6-2
No. 4771, *Green Arrow*

| Distance Miles | | Sch min | Actual m s | Speed mph |
|---|---|---|---|---|
| 0.0 | HELLIFIELD | 0 | 0 00 | — |
| 1.25 | Long Preston | | 2 59 | 43 |
| 3.25 | Settle Jc | 7 | 5 12 | 65 |
| 5.25 | SETTLE | | 7 22 | 50 |
| 9.65 | Helwith Bridge | | 16 54 | 19/30 |
| 11.30 | Horton | | 21 27 | 28 |
| 16.00 | Ribblehead | | 33 19 | 20/25 |
| 17.25 | Blea Moor Box | 35 | 36 28 | 23 |
| 18.10 | Blea Moor Tunnel South | | 38 43 | 20 |
| 19.60 | Blea Moor Tunnel North | | 41 54 | 49 |
| 22.15 | Dent | 47 | 47 33 | — |
| 3.25 | Garsdale | 9 | 8 16 | — |
| 3.05 | Ais Gill | 7 | 5 51 | 38 |
| 9.95 | Kirkby Stephen | | 13 36 | 63 (max) |
| 13.10 | Crosby Garrett | | 16 44 | 64 (max) |
| 16.50 | Helm Tunnel South | | 20 07 | 53/61 |
| 18.15 | Ormside | | 21 45 | 59 |
| 20.60 | APPLEBY | 28 | 24 16 | 54 (min) |
| | | | p.w.s. | 26 |
| 23.55 | Long Marton | | 27 32 | — |
| 28.10 | Culgaith | | 34 38 | 61 |
| 31.65 | Langwathby | | 38 32 | 47 |
| 35.95 | LAZONBY | | 43 47 | 55 |
| 38.85 | Baron Wood S. Tun. S | | 47 04 | 53/57 |
| 41.45 | Armathwaite | 56 | 51 18 | — |
| 1.60 | Low House Box | | 3 11 | — |
| 6.05 | Cumwhinton | | 8 41 | 55 (max) |
| 7.25 | Scotby | | 10 12 | — |
| 10.00 | CARLISLE | 18 | 18 05 | — |

after Eric was ordained and took up his ministry in Liverpool that the latter part of our mutual interest drew closer together, and his work as a devout and vigorous churchman, and his skill as a railway photographer, became more ingeniously and happily interlinked.

At Edge Hill running shed he let it be known that when out on the line he would be wearing a white armband. It was railway spotting in reverse, because if the engine crew he had photographed gave him the date, engine number and train on which they had spotted him he would send them copies of the photograph. His activities became very popular. He was not only Vicar of Edge Hill, but honorary padre of Edge Hill shed!

My own contacts with him have remained continuous and strong, and never more so than when we jointly produced *Main Lines across the Border* in 1960, and more recently in the centenary celebrations of the Settle and Carlisle Railway. As a great churchman he will be long remembered, but equally he will be remembered for the great pleasure he has given to countless railway enthusiasts by his magnificent photographs, and by all for the warm humanity and rich sense of humour that made him so completely at home in any gathering".

In that same issue of *The Railway Magazine* it was announced that a memorial train, the "Lord Bishop" would be run by the Steam Locomotive Operators Association as a tribute. This again was started from Euston, on 30th September, and having travelled up to Giggleswick the previous day, I was ready to join the special when it called at Hellifield next morning, to exchange the diesel for *Flying Scotsman*. A few weeks earlier I had enjoyed the privilege of an engine pass for the "Cumbrian Coast Express", between Carnforth and Sellafield, and in the yard at Steamtown I met the young lady cleaner who was responsible for the immaculate condition in which engine No. 4472 always took the road. Imagine getting up at the crack of dawn, driving over thirty miles from her home beside Ullswater, and then getting under an engine to make sure that the rods, axles, and all else between the frames was as spotless as the external paintwork! On 30th September there she was at Hellifield busy cleaning off the blemishes that this lowering autumnal morning had made to *Flying Scotsman's toillette* on the run across from Carnforth.

After joining the special train, in the course of the climb to Blea Moor and afterwards, I was asked several times how the performance of the engine with that heavy train compared with any of my previous recordings. The heaviest loads that I have personally noted taken up this famous incline were one of 450 tons, with a converted 'Royal Scot' on the wartime "Thames–Clyde Express" and one of 470 tons on the morning Leeds–Glasgow express in 1931, just before a

*The Eric Treacy memorial plaque on Appleby Station.* (Brian Morrison)

Bank Holiday. I have set out the times made on these two runs alongside those of *Flying Scotsman* on the "Lord Bishop" train. To help in the makings of the inevitable comparison I have added certain ratios at the foot of the table. The comparison is not entirely fair, because although the 'Scot' was making up time comfortably on a wartime schedule the 'Claughton' and its pilot were working to a much faster one, and dashed away from Hellifield in appropriate style.

I have subjoined to the table the average speeds over the upper ten miles of the ascent, when they had settled to a fairly steady figure, and have added estimates of the actual and the equivalent drawbar horsepower involved. Below these I have worked out the values of equivalent drawbar horsepower in relation to the nominal tractive effort of the locomotive concerned. This shows, as might be expected, that the 'Claughton' and its pilot were doing relatively the hardest work, while we could tell from the sound of the exhaust that *Flying Scotsman* was not being unduly exerted. While it is one thing to work these preserved engines hard for brief periods, as in the climbs to Lindal Moor on the "Cumbrian Coast Express", it would be quite another to flog them hard for half an hour on end to make a spectacular ascent from Settle Junction to Blea Moor. We can only rejoice that they are being main-

*The "Cumbrian Mountain Express" approaches Ais Gill Summit, hauled by No. 4472* Flying Scotsman *on 5th April 1980.* (David Eatwell)

tained in such splendid condition, and out on the road, handled with such discretion.

Since then a variety of preserved locomotives have been used on the charter trains over the route, and when *Granada* publishers asked me to write a book on reminiscences of the last days of steam, to be titled *From the Footplate*, my final chapter dealt with the Settle and Carlisle line. I was able to include some beautiful photographs taken by David Eatwell and, by special request of the publishers, my dear friend Derek Cross came down from his farmlands in Ayrshire to photograph me in full footplate regalia beside *Flying Scotsman* at Carnforth for the dust jacket of the new book. But in 1984, just before the book was published, he died. It seemed with his passing the shades were once again closing in on the Settle and Carlisle line itself. British Rail's management appeared dead set on its closure, and despite the most authoritative pleas and petitions, in the anxious years from 1985 onwards, none could save it. Salvation eventually came from the most unlikely quarter, the Government itself, having taken heed of all the arguments advanced in its favour, and early in 1989 British Railways were ordered to keep it open!

*The Author with other passengers on the southbound "Cumbrian Mountain Express" at Garsdale in freezing weather, 22nd March 1980.*
(Author's Collection)

## Climbing the 'Long Drag'
### (Hellifield–Blea Moor)

| Run No. | | 1 | 2 | 3 |
|---|---|---|---|---|
| Year | | 1945 | 1931 | 1978 |
| Engine No. | | 6117 | 5932* | 4472 |
| Engine Name | | *Welsh Guardsman* | *Sir Thomas Williams* | *Flying Scotsman* |
| Load, tons, gross | | 450 | 470 | 485 |
| Distance | | Actual | Actual | Actual |
| Miles | | m    s | m    s | m    s |
| 0.0 | HELLIFIELD | 0    00 | 0    00 | 0    00 |
| 3.3 | Settle Jc | 5    15 | 4    45 | 5    51 |
| 7.3 | Milepost 238½ | 11    12 | 9    55 | 12    43 |
| 11.3 | Horton | 18    49 | 16    05 | 21    52 |
| 16.0 | Ribblehead | 26    53 | 23    45 | 33    34 |
| 17.3 | Blea Moor (pass) | 28    57 | 25    50 | 36    53 |
| Average speed (mph) | | | | |
| Post 238½ Blea Moor | | 32.8 | 37.1 | 25.5 |
| Actual dhp | | 1,065 | 1,281 | 864 |
| Equivalent dhp | | 1,332 | 1,761 | 1,099 |
| Edhp per ton of nominal TE | | 89.2 | 94.6 | 67.8 |

* Piloted by ex-MR 7 ft Class 2 superheater 4-4-0 No. 458, No. 5932 — was original small-boilered type.

# 23
# Epilogue — a Gala of Steam

Amid the relief felt by all railway enthusiasts at the countermanding by the Government of the decision by the British Railways Board finally to close the line, this final chapter of mine could well have been imagined as a euphoria of future hopes and plans for new development. But I have written

*No. 4498* Sir Nigel Gresley, *on an excursion from York to Carlisle crossing the lower Sherrif Brow bridge in the gorge of the Ribble between Stainforth and Helwith Bridge, 7th May 1988.*
(David Eatwell)

of this line for upwards of 120 years in this book, and I feel it is now for younger scribes to continue the story, and instead, with the adornment of a magnificent collection of photographs taken by various friends within the last few years, I am presenting a final gala of steam traction over this historic route. All the same, it seems to have gained publicity of an unwelcome kind during the autumn season of 1991, from the slipping of various classes of motive power because of an accumulation of leaves on the track. The experience of two friends of mine travelling in one of the prestigious weekend luxury tour trains, returning from Mallaig to St Pancras by this route, was interesting in that their train was stopped at Kirkby Stephen because of the inability of the diesel-hauled service passenger train ahead to climb the final miles to Ais Gill. Then, on getting the right away, the Class 47 diesel on the tour train could not get away because of leaves on the track and they had to wait about two hours at Kirkby Stephen until a second diesel arrived from Carlisle to give some help!

In some cases, not so serious, any opportunity for regaining lost time afterwards was more or less precluded by the existence of the overall speed restriction of 60 mph over the entire route. Slipping with the engines of express trains was no new thing even in the heyday of regular steam traction. In one of my pre-war notebooks I have a detailed log of the 2.42 pm up Scotch Express from Carlisle in November 1931, with a

*The RCTS — SLS "North Eastern Tour" train approaching Dent, with Arten Gill Viaduct in the far distance, in 1963. The locomotive is the Stanier 'Pacific' No. 46238 City of Carlisle. (G. W. Morrison)*

load of 330 tons hauled by one of the unrebuilt 'Claughton' class 4-6-0s that had then been transferred to the Midland Division. It was a dismal afternoon of drizzling rain mixed with sleet, but on the first stage booked to stop at Appleby in 40 minutes from Carlisle, we just managed to keep time. Then on the mountain section with the east wind freshening to flurries of snow mixed with the rain I could tell from the occasional jerkiness of the travelling that the engine was slipping, and although we did not fall below $24\frac{3}{4}$ mph at any point, this incidentally near Griseburn signal box, we lost $3\frac{3}{4}$ minutes on the scheduled 29 minutes from Appleby up to Ais Gill Summit. Then, with no overall speed limits to bother about we went like the wind, reaching

*The northbound "Cumbrian Mountain Express" passing Horton, hauled by ex-Southern Railway 4-6-0 No. 850 Lord Nelson on 24th January 1981. (Brian Morrison)*

*In winter sunshine the "Cumbrian Mountain Express" crosses bridge No. 27, often referred to as Sherrif Brow bridge, with the preserved "Black Five" 4-6-0 No. 5407 at the head, with a class 25 'Ethel', train heating locomotive behind, 25th November 1989.* (David Eatwell)

a maximum of 88 mph between Blea Moor and Settle Junction, and clocking into Hellifield no more than a minute late.

But it is on the severe mountain gradients that many of the preserved locomotives used occasionally over this route have been distinguishing themselves so brilliantly. My own disability has unfortunately prevented my travelling up there to see for myself, but by the kindness of Mr Douglas Landau I have been furnished with an invaluable collection of data from a number of different enthusiasts, whose recording ability puts anything I could do in the prime of my stop-watching days completely in the

shade! I am only sorry that space, at the conclusion of a long book, does not permit more extensive coverage of the fascinating information so kindly made available to me. I have been particularly interested in the performance of the re-constructed Class 8 Pacific No. 71000 *Duke of Gloucester*, because in its original form it appears to have been a disappointing engine. Certainly in my own experience there were some far from satisfactory features in the performance. I was intrigued when, for its full dress trials on a stationary testing plant, and subsequently with a dynamometer car out on the line, that BR sent it to Swindon rather than Rugby. This

*Southbound with the "Cumbrian Mountain Express" the rebuilt Bulleid Pacific No. 35028* Clan Line *is approaching Crosby Garrett on a raw April day in 1989, when there were still some slivers of snow on the Pennines in the distance.* (David Eatwell)

was fortunate for me because I was then in constant association with the Chief Mechanical Engineer's department of the Western Region, and was invited to see some of the tests on engine No. 71000 in progress. There was no doubt about the power capacity, but as the test engineer, the inimitable Sam Ell, expressed to me, as mentioned earlier, "She's a coal scoffer!"

This was certainly borne out in the test Bulletin later published by British Railways, which I had the task of reviewing for *The Engineer*. In the meantime I had gathered that before the engine left Swindon an approach was made to BR headquarters for permission to experiment with some changes in the draughting, which it was thought was contributing to the inordinate coal consumption. But after, I learned, of some acrimonious verbal exchanges between Swindon and Derby the engine was returned to the LM Region and stationed at Crewe North shed. There it quickly became the most unpopular engine in the top link, restricted, because its inordinately high coal consumption, to runs between Crewe and Euston, single-home, and Crewe and Carlisle. I had only one run with the engine in regular service on the up "Midday Scot" when it came on at Crewe for the run to Euston. It was a dreary performance, far below the average of the 'Princess Royal' class Pacifics, let alone the 'Duchesses'.

When I learned that the once-condemned engine was being restored I was very interested to see, in due course, if the recommendations that Swindon made about the re-drafting had been incorporated. This aside, the magnificent hill climbing performances of No. 71000 on the Settle and Carlisle line bear the stamp of efficient working, though I have not seen any coal consumption figures so far. In any case, with the continuing existence of the 60 mph limit on maximum speed any comparison of past with present working would not be fair. From Mr Landau and his friends I have received such a wealth of running data, that I am proposing to deal only with the section between Appleby and Garsdale in the up direction and in addition to the work of Pacifics Nos 46229, 71000 and 60009, with their recent records, I am able to include logs with the LMS Pacifics *Princess Elizabeth*, and the Southern 4-6-0s No. 777 *Sir Lamiel* and No. 850 *Lord Nelson*.

I have first of all included in a separate table the runs with the ten-wheeled engines. So far as the 'King Arthur' and the LMS "Black Five" No. 4767 are concerned it ought to be added that in the heyday of steam haulage on this route that the maximum tare load for an unpiloted Class 5 engine, until the introduction of the fastest pre-war schedules just before the Second World War, was 340 tons. That covered non-stop running between Carlisle and Leeds at an average speed of 49 mph, with all the restricted lengths of line south of Skipton. The pass-to-pass time between Appleby and Ais Gill was 29 minutes, and on my best run in these conditions, with a load of 335 tons, this time was improved to 27 minutes. The engine, incidentally, was none other than *Sir Gilbert Claughton* immaculately clean in Midland red. Of course there is a world of difference between the fixing of load limits for

*While making a round trip from York, the Settle and Carlisle line and thence to Newcastle, No. 4468* Mallard, *takes the train between Long Meg and Lazonby on 17th July 1988. (The ancient monument of Long Meg cannot be seen from the railway.)* (David Eatwell)

*The northbound "Cumbrian Mountain Express" emerging from Blea Moor Tunnel, with the preserved Class V2 2-6-2 No. 4771* Green Arrow, *6th May 1989.* (David Eatwell)

a complete link of engines, some of which might be in pristine condition and others so run down as to be barely capable of work, that the timetable demanded. The preserved engines on the other hand are necessarily taken care of, in special ways. The 'King Arthur' that is preserved, No. 777 *Sir Lamiel*, was in ordinary working the maker of the record run with the up "Atlantic Coast Express" from Salisbury to Waterloo, when the 83.8 miles were covered in $72\frac{3}{4}$ minutes, an average of 69 mph, with a load of 345 tons. On hearing of this exploit, made well before the Second World War, some of those who had technical responsibility for Southern Locomotives were incredulous, and returned a verdict that the run must have been made with a strong following wind to assist!

On the run tabulated, made in December 1982, engine No. 777 did some excellent work with a gross load of 440 tons behind the tender, not falling below $31\frac{1}{2}$ mph anywhere on the ascent. That minimum speed was registered at the southern end of Birkett Tunnel, near to another site associated with the Arthurian legend, Pendragon Castle. So far as locomotive working is concerned, the time of the 'King Arthur' tied to within a few seconds with my own best run in ordinary operating conditions, between Ormside Viaduct and Ais Gill, and with a load of 440 against 335 tons.

*With Pen-y-Ghent partially hidden in mist the famous Stanier 'Pacific' No, 6201* Princess Elizabeth *climbs the 'Long Drag' with the "Cumbrian Mountain Express" on 24th August 1991.* (David Eatwell)

Now on to *Lord Nelson*, on a run made in September 1983, the load was one coach heavier, and as the tabulated details show there was some pretty level pegging as far as Crosby Garrett station. I shall always remember a personal acquaintance I had with this engine, now nearly forty years ago. I had a footplate pass one morning to ride one of the Ocean Specials from Southampton Docks to Waterloo carrying passengers newly arrived from the USA by the RMS *Queen Elizabeth*. Three trains were provided, and the second of the three was to be worked by *Lord Nelson*. The other two were to be worked by Bulleid Pacifics, and as I had a free choice, I naturally plumped for the second of the three trains. I shall always remember how we backed down to the Ocean Quay and how the huge lofty bows of the great Cunarder seemed almost on top of us. Reminiscences aside, on the tabulated journey *Lord Nelson* did well on the upper stages of the ascent to Ais Gill not falling below $35\frac{1}{2}$ mph at the southern end of Birkett Tunnel and after a fine recovery past Mallerstang, registering the notable minimum speed, with a 465-ton load, of 39 mph at Ais Gill.

Now comes the one and only LMS "Black Five" 4-6-0 fitted with the Stephenson link motion, No. 4767, later to be named *George Stephenson* and now based on the North Yorkshire Moors Railway. The engine was built in 1947 when H. G. Ivatt was Chief Mechanical Engineer, and a number of new "Black Fives" were constructed with variations from the ordi-

nary Walschearts gear standard on the great majority of the class. I fancy that there must have been some Great Western influence in the equipment of this engine. On the GWR, while the 4-cylinder 4-6-0s with their own setting of the Walschearts gear were the acknowledged greyhounds of the fleet, the 2-cylinder engines from the 'Saints' downward were revered for their hard work on severe gradients. A top link driver who had ample experience of both varieties of 4-6-0 once said that the 4-cylinder 'Stars' always needed some finesse in driving, whereas you could "punch a Saint" as hard as you liked. Certainly in my own experience of running on the heavily graded West to North route from Bristol via the Severn Tunnel to Shrewsbury, the uphill performance of the 'Saints' in maximum loading conditions were superior to not only the 'Stars' but also to the 'Castles'. On the run tabulated engine No. 4767 got away from Appleby in fine style, and level pegging with the 'King Arthur' as far as Kirkby Stephen. But, then presumably because they were getting ahead of the workings laid down for this particular duty, the engine was eased down.

The fourth log tabulated brings in another of my footplate friends, indeed I had a pass to ride *Green Arrow* when she was almost brand new and regularly working the afternoon Scotch Goods between King's Cross and Peterborough in August 1937. At that time only four engines of the Class V2 had been built, and I have always been glad that the pioneer of the class was one of

*A magnificent picture of No. 4498* Sir Nigel Gresley *on the down "Cumbrian Mountain Express" near Armathwaite on 7th May 1988, showing the beautiful river scenery and distant view of the village of Kirkoswald.* (David Eatwell)

those selected for preservation. The log tabulated was made in February 1991, almost 54 years after the construction of the original engine, and the recorder of the train, Mr D. Bradbury commented that it was "a notable thrash up to Ais Gill, though little could be heard of it from the milepost side of the train in the 10th coach". It was indeed giving considerably the fastest climb of the four runs. This particular train was not scheduled to stop at Garsdale and that station was passed through at 55 mph. On the descent from Ribblehead dense fog was encountered, and the general speed was indeed somewhat lower than on the "notable thrash" from Ormside Viaduct to Ais Gill.

Now turning to the Pacifics, Mr Landau has furnished me with a beautifully compiled collection of data relating to the ascent from Ormside Viaduct up to Ais Gill, from which I have extracted the details included in the accompany-ing table. Mr Landau has also worked out, by computer, the average values of the equivalent drawbar horsepower sustained during the $15\frac{1}{4}$ miles of ascent on an average gradient of 1 in 121. In my table I am pleased to be able to append the names of the dedicated enthusiasts who recorded the details in such precision. My thanks are gratefully acknowledged to them all. As one who had, until recent years, a constant and well nigh life-long acquaintance with the line, I am astonished by the tremendous loads taken on some of these journeys, though the hazard of leaves accumulating on the sparsely used tracks led to the reduction in the train make-up, down to no more than eight coaches on one notable journey.

Runs Nos 1 and 3 were made in the summer season of 1980, before the orgy of record-breaking attempts began. Even so, the "Lizzie" on No. 1 run made a mighty good ascent,

Appleby–Garsdale — 10-Wheeled Engines

| Run No. | | 1 | | | 2 | | | 3 | | | 4 | | |
|---|---|---|---|---|---|---|---|---|---|---|---|---|---|
| Engine No. | | 777 | | | 850 | | | 4767 | | | 4771 | | |
| Engine Name | | *Sir Lamiel* | | | *Lord Nelson* | | | *George Stephenson* | | | *Green Arrow* | | |
| Class | | NI5 'King Arthur' | | | LN | | | 5MP | | | V2 | | |
| Railway Co. | | Southern | | | Southern | | | LMS | | | LNE | | |
| Load tons E/F | | 415/440 | | | 434/465 | | | 395/420 | | | 416/440 | | |
| **Distance** | | | | | | | | | | | | | |
| Miles | | m | s | mph | m | s | mph | m | s | mph | m | s | mph |
| 0.0 | Appleby | 0 | 00 | — | 0 | 00 | — | 0 | 00 | — | 0 | 00 | — |
| 1.3 | MP 276 | | — | | | — | | | — | | 3 | 39 | 44 |
| 2.0 | MP $275\frac{1}{4}$ | 4 | 26 | $52\frac{1}{2}$ | 4 | 29 | 52 | 4 | 19 | 50 | | — | 53 |
| 2.3 | MP 275 | | — | | | | | | — | | 4 | 51 | — |
| 3.8 | MP $273\frac{1}{2}$ | 6 | 44 | $41\frac{1}{2}$ | 6 | 43 | 43 | 6 | 42 | 39 | | — | |
| 5.3 | Griseburn | 9 | 10 | $34\frac{1}{2}$ | 9 | 04 | $36\frac{1}{2}$ | 9 | 20 | 33 | 8 | 54 | 39 |
| 6.8 | MP $270\frac{1}{2}$ | 11 | 32 | 40 | 11 | 21 | $39\frac{1}{2}$ | 11 | 46 | $38\frac{1}{2}$ | | — | |
| 7.5 | Crosby Garrett | 12 | 34 | $42\frac{1}{2}$ | 12 | 26 | 43 | 12 | 50 | $42\frac{1}{2}$ | | — | |
| 8.5 | MP $268\frac{3}{4}$ | 13 | 35 | $47\frac{1}{2}$ | 13 | 44 | $49\frac{1}{2}$ | 14 | 11 | 49 | | — | $51\frac{3}{4}$ |
| 10.7 | Kirkby Stephen | 17 | 08 | 35 | 16 | 43 | 38 | 17 | 08 | $37\frac{1}{2}$ | 16 | $03\frac{1}{2}$ | $43\frac{1}{2}$ |
| 11.3 | MP 266 | 18 | 07 | 38 | 17 | 37 | 40 | 18 | 07 | eased | | — | 46 |
| 12.3 | MP 265 | 19 | 45 | $35\frac{1}{2}$ | 19 | 10 | $37\frac{1}{2}$ | 20 | 03 | 29 | | — | |
| 13.3 | MP 264 | 21 | 32 | $31\frac{1}{2}$ | 20 | 49 | $35\frac{1}{2}$ | 22 | 26 | $23\frac{1}{2}$ | 19 | $39\frac{1}{2}$ | 40 |
| 14.3 | MP 263 | 23 | 15 | 40 | 22 | 24 | $42\frac{1}{2}$ | 24 | 41 | $33\frac{1}{2}$ | 21 | $04\frac{1}{2}$ | 45 |
| 15.3 | MP 262 | 24 | 48 | $37\frac{1}{2}$ | 23 | 49 | 41 | 26 | 34 | $30\frac{1}{2}$ | 22 | $27\frac{1}{2}$ | 42 |
| 16.3 | MP 261 | 26 | 27 | 36 | 25 | 18 | 40 | 28 | 42 | $27\frac{1}{2}$ | | — | |
| 17.3 | MP 260 | 28 | 09 | 34 | 26 | 49 | 39 | 31 | 04 | $23\frac{1}{2}$ | 25 | 27 | 39 |
| 17.5 | Ais Gill | 28 | 35 | — | 27 | 12 | — | 31 | 42 | — | 25 | $49\frac{1}{2}$ | — |
| 19.3 | MP 258 | 30 | 57 | 54 | 29 | 33 | $48\frac{1}{2}$ | 34 | 34 | 45 | | — | |
| 20.6 | Garsdale | 34 | 09 | | 32 | 06 | | 38 | 11 | | 29 | 23 | 55 |
| Recorder | | B. Basterfield | | | B. Basterfield | | | — | | | D. Bradbury | | |

*No. 46203* Princess Margaret Rose *going hard with the southbound "Cumbrian Mountain Express" past Birkett Common on 24th August 1991.* (David Eatwell)

although not so vigorous as that of her sister engine on the second run. *Princess Elizabeth* with a gross trailing load of 455 tons did not fall below 38 mph at any part of the accent, and registered the notable minimum speed of 42 mph at the southern end of Birkett Tunnel. No. 46203 *Princess Margaret Rose* was in magnificent form in the early autumn of 1991 and with a load of 480 tons made an average speed of 48½ mph throughout, and maintaining 1,825 equivalent drawbar horsepower. It is always a pleasure to learn of further exploits of this engine, recalling the memorable run she gave me from Crewe to

Euston on the "Red Rose" in the last days of steam on the West Coast route, as described in the final chapter of my book *Great Locomotives of the LMS*.

Then coming to the Gresley A4s, engine No. 4498, in July 1980, gave a sound performance with a 445-ton load, but four years later No. 60009 *Union of South Africa*, did some notable work with a heavier train of 495 tons, although subject to some delay en route. Then, fired by the record-breaking efforts of *Duchess of Hamilton*, and the rejuvenated BR No. 71000 *Duke of Gloucester*, an attempt was made to

*A down special express crossing Moorcock Viaduct just after leaving Garsdale, hauled by 'Jubilee' class 4-6-0 No. 5593* Kolhapur *on 21st March 1987.* (Millbrook House Ltd — John Shuttleworth)

*A fine broadside shot of No. 6201* Princess Elizabeth *just after leaving Shotlock Hill Tunnel with the "Cumbrian Mountain Express", 24th August 1991.* (David Eatwell)

see what an A4 could do. In late autumnal weather in 1991, with the wet-leaves hazard still prevalent, the load was reduced to eight coaches only, 311 tons tare, and with a very vigorous start from Carlisle the treacherous woodland stretch past Scotby was successfully passed, and from the restart from Appleby a truly record time was made up to Ais Gill Summit. Even so, the power output as shown by Mr Landau's calculations in the fourth column of the table was considerably below those of certain of the other engines in the table, notably Nos 46229 and 71000, naturally because of the much reduced load.

The two runs with *Duke of Gloucester*, Nos 6 and 7 in the table, were both magnificent performances. Referring to the official test Bulletin issued by BR in 1957, I find it was only by the use of first grade Class 1a coal that a maximum output of 2,100 equivalent drawbar horsepower was achieved, and that when using Blidworth coal, the standard for general locomotive testing with the British Transport Commission, the maximum sustained output was less than 1,800 ebhp, Mr Landau's calculations show averages around 2,100. It is natural that many readers

would wish to make close comparisons between the work of this engine and that of the Stanier 4-6-2 *Duchess of Hamilton*, on which the details in the table show them to be roughly equal. On the other hand the published test Bulletin relating to No. 71000 shows that the maximum sustained power output, with the highest quality coal was 2,100 edhp, almost the same as what Mr Landau has calculated for the recent runs over the Settle and Carlisle line with this engine. But with regard to the 'Duchess' class, I must refer to the monumental trials made with the sister engine, No. 46225 *Duchess of Gloucester*. Unfortunately, as mentioned, no Bulletin was issued to cover this work, but I was supplied with copies of the dynamometer car record on one particularly memorable journey when an equivalent load of 900 tons was taken up the 'Long Drag' between Settle Junction and Blea Moor at a sustained minimum speed of 30 mph.

On that occasion the dynamometer registered a constant pull of 2,000 horsepower between Helwith Bridge and Ribblehead. This was the actual pull, whereas the usual form of expression for comparative purposes relates the pull for

Summary of Notable Pacific Ascents: Mileposts 275 to $259\frac{1}{4}$ (Ormside–Ais Gill)
Average rate of ascent 1 in 121

| Railway | Engine | Load | Time m s | Speed mph | Average | Recorder |
|---------|--------|------|----------|-----------|---------|----------|
| 1. LMS | 6201* *Princess Elizabeth* | 12,423 1/2/455 | 20 36 | 44.5 | 1600 | S. Leyland |
| 2. LMS | 46203 *Princess Margaret Rose* | 12,454/480 | 18 51 | 48.5 | 1825 | S. Leyland |
| 3. LNE | 4498 *Sir Nigel Gresley* | 12,418/445 | 21 15 | 43.2 | 1525 | — |
| 4. LNE | 60009 *Union of South Africa* | 13,456/495 | 20 43* | 44.2 | 1675 | G. A. M. Wood |
| 5. LNE | 60009 *Union of South Africa* | 8,311/325 | 15 42 | 58.3 | 1815 | G. A. M. Wood |
| 6. BR | 71000 *Duke of Gloucester* | 12,443/465 | 17 00 | 53.8 | 2100 | D. J. Veltom |
| 7. BR | 71000 *Duke of Gloucester* | 13,482/512 | 18 23 | 49.8 | 2025 | D. J. Veltom |
| 8. LMS | 46229 *Duchess of Hamilton* | 13,455/482 | 17 57 | 51.0 | 2150 | D. J. Veltom |
| 9. LMS | 46229 *Duchess of Hamilton* | 14,533/560 | 19 25 | 47.1 | 2075 | G. A. M. Wood |
| 10. LMS | 46229 *Duchess of Hamilton* | 14,535/560 | 19 31 | 46.9 | 2000 | G. A. M. Wood |

level track, thus needing to take into account the power needed to propel the weight of the engine and tender up the gradient, in the case of the 'Long Drag', 1 in 100. Thus the equivalent drawbar horsepower of the *Duchess of Gloucester* on the test run was around 2,300. Continuing upwards with the same rate of evaporation in the boiler the edhp at about 50 mph would have been about 2,500, as against 2,100 with engine No. 71000. Mr Landau has made many calculations concerning the maximum efforts of engine No. 46229 on her great runs of 1984 and 1985, and considers that the maximum was around 2,800, as against the sustained 2,300, at 30 mph, on the test trip with No. 46225. The maxima estimated for the two 'Princesses', two A4s and No. 71000 are 2,100, 2,250 and 2,600 edbhp respectively.

In conclusion it is perhaps appropriate that

*On the occasion of a record climb to Ais Gill, on 20th July 1991, the BR Class 8 Pacific No. 71000* Duke of Gloucester *approaches Birkett Tunnel with the "Cumbrian Mountain Express". (David Eatwell)*

my own book on the Settle and Carlisle railway should end with a further reference to performance on the 'Long Drag'. From the autumn of 1916, when I first went to Giggleswick School as a boarder, I became conscious of the Midland Scotch Expresses pounding up the bank towards Blea Moor, and now as a final offering I have tabulated a fine run made by one of the most revered of all preserved LMS locomotives, the 4-6-2 No. 46201 *Princess Elizabeth*. I have been supplied with a log compiled by Mr D. J. Veltom, when travelling one day by the "Cumbrian Mountain Express" when it started from Blackburn. His log from Hellifield onwards is a model of precise recording, noting the passing of every *quarter* milepost except when an occasional obstruction blocked the view. My own log herewith is a necessarily abbreviated version. Mr Veltom has noted that during the period when the speed was well above 40 mph the cut-off was mostly around 35 per cent, far below the continuous 49 to 50 per cent used on engine No. 46225 during that terrific dynamometer car test run. On Mr Veltom's run No. 46201 was eased after Milepost 246 and passed Ribblehead with steam blowing off. And so, with the train disappearing into the blackness of Blea Moor Tunnel I also bring down the final curtain.

---

Not quite, after all! Hardly had the final proof corrections been completed, the index drafted and typed, and the parcel packed up and ready to send to the publishers before two bulky letters arrived, by the same post, one from South East London and one from Cork (!), sending me some important data relating to the running of the latest Pacific engine to be used on the line, the ex-BR(ER) Class A2 Peppercorn 4-6-2 No. 60532 *Blue Peter*. Mr Brian J. Mullally on one of his visits to England managed to get a run on the "Cumbrian Mountain Express" northbound and he logged it in the fullest detail, at almost every milepost from Lostock Hall to Carlisle. He is a fully experienced recorder and I am glad to be able to include details of the fine running from Hellifield to Garsdale on this occasion. They were slowed to walking pace to pick up some railway personnel through the former station, and stopped at Garsdale instead of the advertised stop at Appleby. The downhill running from Ais Gill was of no interest because of the speed limit imposed throughout. With a gross trailing load of about 465 tons the uphill running from Settle Junction to Blea Moor was very good seeing that it was made in pouring rain throughout. The average speed between mileposts $236\frac{1}{2}$ (Settle) and $246\frac{3}{4}$, before the speed restriction over Ribblehead Viaduct was 44.1 mph. An abridged log between Hellifield and Garsdale is included herewith.

Then from Mr Douglas Laundau I have received a most scholarly analysis of the four southbound runs made by the engine between March and August 1992, from which it seems clear that *Blue Peter* has joined the two engines previously recorded as being able to average 2,000 equivalent drawbar horsepower, or more, for about 18 minutes on end, between Ormside up towards Ais Gill. The two others were, of course, the Stanier Pacific No. 46229 *Duchess of Hamilton*, and the BR No. 71000 *Duke of Gloucester*. The records of the three engines were stated to be:

|       |               |
|-------|---------------|
| 46229 | 2,150 EDBHP   |
| 71000 | 2,100 EDBHP   |
| 60532 | 2,050 EDBHP   |

The Cumbrian Mountain Express (as from Blackburn)
Load: 12 coaches, 446 tons tare, 465 tons full
Engine: 4-6-2 No. 46201 *Princess Elizabeth*

| Distance Miles |                  | Time m  s | Speed mph |
|----------------|------------------|-----------|-----------|
| 0.0            | Hellifield (pass) | 0  00    | 25        |
| 0.7            | MP 232           | 1  10     | 40        |
| 1.7            | MP 233           | 2  25     | 53        |
| 2.7            | MP 234           | 4  23     | 62        |
| —              | *Settle Junction* | —        |           |
| 3.7            | MP 235           | 5  22     | 61        |
| 4.7            | MP 236           | 6  27     | 52        |
| —              | Settle           | —         | 50        |
| 5.7            | MP 237           | —         | —         |
| 6.7            | MP 238           | 7  50     | 46        |
| —              | *Stainforth*     | —         |           |
| 7.7            | MP 239           | 9  10     | 45        |
| 8.7            | MP 240           | 10  38    | 43        |
| —              | *Helwith Bridge* |           | 44        |
| 9.7            | MP 241           | 11  54    | 47        |
| 10.7           | MP 242           | 13  11    | 46        |
| —              | *Horton*         |           |           |
| 11.7           | MP 243           | 14  29    | 45        |
| 12.7           | MP 244           | 15  48    | 46        |
| 13.7           | MP 245           | 17  08    | 44        |
| 14.7           | MP 246           | 18  32    | 41        |
| 15.7           | MP 247           | 19  59    | 41        |
| —              | *Ribblehead*     |           |           |
| 16.7           | MP 248           | 21  38    | 34        |

On the first run with No. 60532 on 21st March a tremendous start was made, but the engine had to be eased after Milepost 268 because the injectors could not keep pace. This was put right by the next run, and this and a subsequent one, in August are summarised in the following table.

| Date | Load E/F Tons | Time MP 275–259 min | sec | Speed mph | EDBHP Average | Max |
|---|---|---|---|---|---|---|
| 21.3.92 | 12-437/473 | 17 | 33 | 52.1 | 1,920 | 2,350 |
| 18.4.92 | 11-404/430 | 16 | 47 | 54.5 | 2,050 | 2,350 |
| 15.8.92 | 12-440/470 | 17 | 43 | 51.6 | 2,000 | 2,850 |

I must add that the recording from the train on which these most important assessments have been made were made by Mr D. J. Velton of Harpenden.

The "Cumbrian Mountain Express"
from Hellifield (passed dead slow) to GARSDALE
Load: 12 coaches, 441 tons tare, 465 tons gross
Engine: Class A2 4-6-2 No. 60532 *Blue Peter*

| Distance Miles | Timing Points | Time m | s | Speed mph |
|---|---|---|---|---|
| 0 | Hellifield Post 231 | 0 | 00 | — |
| $3\frac{1}{4}$ | Settle Junction Post $234\frac{1}{4}$ | 4 | 29 | 67 |
| $5\frac{1}{2}$ | Settle Post $236\frac{1}{2}$ | 6 | 39 | 51 |
| — | Helwith Bridge | — | | 40/44 |
| $11\frac{1}{2}$ | Horton Post $242\frac{1}{2}$ | 14 | 52 | $40\frac{1}{2}$ |
| 15 | Horton Post 246 | 19 | 35 | 46 |
| 18 | Blea Moor Post 249 | 25 | 27 | slow |
| 20 | Northend of Tunnel Post 251 | 28 | 19 | 52 |
| $22\frac{1}{4}$ | Dent Post $253\frac{1}{4}$ | 30 | 26 | 70 |
| $25\frac{3}{4}$ | Garsdale Post $256\frac{3}{4}$ | 35 | 24 | — |

# Appendix

Experimental Results of working of 3-cylinder compound, No. 2631 in 1902, originally published in *Engineering* in 1903.

EXPERIMENTS ON THREE-CYLINDER COMPOUND LOCOMOTIVE; MIDLAND RAILWAY.

TABLE I.—PARTICULARS OF WORKING OF COMPOUND ENGINE "No. 2631."

| DATE | VEHICLES | | WEIGHT: Mean of Coaches, Passengers, and Luggage (tons) | WEIGHT: Engine and Mean of Tender (tons) | WEIGHT: Mean of Train, Total (tons) | SECTION OF LINE AND LENGTH | Length (miles) | Number of Intermediate Stops and Starts | RUNNING TIMES Booked (min.) | RUNNING TIMES Actual, Included (min.) | RUNNING TIMES Actual, Deducted (min.) | RUNNING TIMES Delays by Signals and Special Stops (min.) | RUNNING SPEEDS Booked (miles per hour) | RUNNING SPEEDS Actual, Included (miles per hour) | RUNNING SPEEDS Actual, Deducted (miles per hour) | RUNNING SPEEDS Delays by Signals and Special Stops (miles per hour) | COAL CONSUMED Per Mile (lb.) | COAL CONSUMED Per Mile per Ton Weight of Train (lb.) | COAL CONSUMED Total (gals.) | WATER EVAPORATED Per Pound of Coal (lb.) | WATER EVAPORATED Per Pound of Coal from and at 212 deg. Fahr. (lb.) | Re COAL | REMARKS — GENERAL |
|---|---|---|---|---|---|---|---|---|---|---|---|---|---|---|---|---|---|---|---|---|---|---|---|
| | | | | | | **10.6 A.M., LEEDS TO CARLISLE.** | | | | | | | | | | | | | | | | | |
| Oct. 17 | Leeds to Skipton | 9=12½ | 207 | 110.9 | 317.9 | Leeds to Ais Gill | 64.65 | 3 | 93 | 88 | 86 | 41.7 | 41.7 | 44.1 | 45.1 | 31.8 | .123 | 3320 | 9.2 | 11.2 | Manvers Main | Stopped at Lazonby and Armathwaite. Light side wind. |
| | Hellifield to Carlisle | 6=8 | 141 | 106 | 247 | Ais Gill to Carlisle | 48.387 | 2 | 57 | 56 | 48 | 50.9 | 51.8 | 60.5 | | | | | | | | |
| | Leeds to Carlisle | | 192.6 | 105.4 | 298 | Leeds to Carlisle | 113.037 | 5 | 150 | 144 | 134 | 45.2 | 47.1 | 50.6 | | | | | | | | |
| Oct. 18 | Leeds to Skipton | 9=12½ | 212.5 | 111 | 323.5 | Leeds to Ais Gill | 64.65 | 3 | 93 | 90.25 | 88.25 | 41.7 | 43 | 43 | 44 | 37 | .14 | 3290 | 7.7 | 9.39 | Ditto. | Special stop at Armathwaite. |
| | Hellifield to Carlisle | 6=8 | 148 | 106.5 | 254.5 | Ais Gill to Carlisle | 48.387 | 1 | 57 | 57 | 53 | 50.9 | 50.9 | 54.7 | 48 | | | | | | | |
| | Leeds to Carlisle | | 158.5 | 105.5 | 264 | Leeds to Carlisle | 113.037 | 4 | 150 | 147.25 | 141.25 | 45.2 | 46 | 48 | | | | | | | | |
| Oct. 27 | Leeds to Skipton | 11=14 | 221 | 110.7 | 331.7 | Leeds to Ais Gill | 64.65 | 3 | 93 | 90 | 89 | 41.7 | 43 | 43 | 43.6 | 32.1 | .118 | 3290 | 9 | 10.93 | Ditto | Light side wind. |
| | Hellifield to Carlisle | 7=9 | 150.5 | 106.4 | 256.9 | Ais Gill to Carlisle | 48.387 | 1 | 57 | 57 | 51 | 50.9 | 50.9 | 56.8 | 48.4 | | | | | | | |
| | Leeds to Carlisle | | 164.5 | 105.5 | 270 | Leeds to Carlisle | 113.037 | 4 | 150 | 147 | 140 | 45.2 | 46.1 | 48.4 | | | | | | | | |
| Oct. 29 | Leeds to Skipton | 11=14½ | 236 | 110.8 | 346.8 | Leeds to Ais Gill | 64.65 | 3 | 93 | 93 | 90 | 41.7 | 43 | 43 | 43 | 37 | .135 | 3350 | 8 | 9.76 | Ditto | Foggy, and rails greasy. |
| | Hellifield to Carlisle | 7=9 | 223 | 106 | 329 | Ais Gill to Carlisle | 48.387 | 3 | 57 | 54 | 52 | 50.9 | 53.7 | 56.8 | 47.7 | | | | | | | |
| | Leeds to Carlisle | | 168.3 | 105.2 | 274 | Leeds to Carlisle | 113.037 | 3 | 150 | 147 | 142 | 45.2 | 46.1 | 47.7 | | | | | | | | |
| Oct. 30 | Leeds to Skipton | 9=12½ | 207.5 | 111.1 | 318.6 | Leeds to Ais Gill | 64.65 | 3 | 93 | 92 | 90 | 41.7 | 42.1 | 43 | 43 | 33.1 | .129 | 3150 | 8.4 | 10.24 | Ditto | Stopped at Lazonby and Armathwaite. Fine; light side wind. |
| | Hellifield to Carlisle | 6=8 | 141.9 | 106 | 247.9 | Ais Gill to Carlisle | 48.387 | 2 | 57 | 57 | 51 | 50.9 | 50.9 | 56.8 | 48.1 | | | | | | | |
| | Leeds to Carlisle | | 150.2 | 105.8 | 256 | Leeds to Carlisle | 113.037 | 5 | 150 | 149 | 141 | 45.2 | 45.5 | 48.1 | | | | | | | | |
| Nov. 7 | Leeds to Skipton | 9=12½ | 207.5 | 110.9 | 318.4 | Leeds to Ais Gill | 64.65 | 4 | 93 | 93 | 90 | 41.7 | 41.7 | 43 | 43 | 32.6 | .127 | 3200 | 8.6 | 10.5 | Ditto | Stopped at Blea Moor and Lazonby. Heavy side wind. |
| | Hellifield to Carlisle | 6=8 | 141.9 | 106.3 | 248.2 | Ais Gill to Carlisle | 48.387 | 1 | 57 | 57 | 51 | 50.9 | 52.7 | 56.8 | 45.1 | | | | | | | |
| | Leeds to Carlisle | | 149.6 | 105.7 | 255.3 | Leeds to Carlisle | 113.037 | 5 | 150 | 147 | 141 | 45.2 | 46.1 | 45.1 | | | | | | | | |
| | | | 157.37 | 105.51 | 262.83 | Leeds to Carlisle | 113.037 | | 150 | 146.87 | 139.87 | 45.2 | 46.1 | 48.4 | | 33.9 | .125 | 3250 | 8.48 | 10.34 | | Mean for above six trips. |
| | | | | | | **1.28 P.M., LEEDS TO CARLISLE.** | | | | | | | | | | | | | | | | | |
| Oct. 22 | Leeds to Carlisle | 10=15½ | 259.3 | 104.5 | 363.8 | Leeds to Ais Gill | 64.65 | 1 | 86 | 84.25 | 82.25 | 45.1 | 46 | 47.1 | 47.1 | 43.3 | .110 | 3630 | 7.4 | 9.02 | Manvers Main | Light wind. |
| | | | | | | Ais Gill to Carlisle | 48.387 | 1 | 48 | 45 | 45 | 60.5 | 64.5 | 64.5 | 64.5 | | | | | | | |
| | | | | | | Leeds to Carlisle | 113.037 | 1 | 134 | 129.25 | 127.25 | 50.5 | 52.4 | 53.2 | | | | | | | | |
| Oct. 24 | Leeds to Carlisle | 10=15½ | 258.7 | 104.1 | 362.8 | Leeds to Ais Gill | 64.65 | 1 | 86 | 86 | 85 | 45.1 | 45.1 | 45.6 | 45.6 | 46.7 | .129 | 3770 | 7.14 | 8.7 | Ditto | Heavy side wind. |
| | | | | | | Ais Gill to Carlisle | 48.387 | 1 | 43 | 43 | 43 | 60.5 | 67.4 | 67.4 | 67.4 | | | | | | | |
| | | | | | | Leeds to Carlisle | 113.037 | 1 | 129 | 129 | 128 | 50.5 | 52.5 | 52.9 | | | | | | | | |
| Nov. 1 | Leeds to Carlisle | 9=14½ | 245 | 103.6 | 348.6 | Leeds to Ais Gill | 64.65 | 1 | 86 | 34 | 34 | 45.1 | 46.1 | 46.1 | | 44.8 | .128 | 3990 | 7.87 | 9.6 | Ditto | Heavy side and head wind. |
| | | | | | | Ais Gill to Carlisle | 48.387 | 1 | 48 | 47 | ... | 60.5 | 61.6 | 51.7 | | | | | | | | |
| | | | | | | Leeds to Carlisle | 113.037 | 1 | 134 | 131 | ... | 50.5 | 51.7 | | | | | | | | | |
| Nov. 3 | Leeds to Carlisle | 9=14½ | 245.6 | 104 | 349.6 | Leeds to Ais Gill | 64.65 | 1 | 98 | 85 | ... | 45.1 | 45.6 | 45.6 | | 46.7 | .133 | 3790 | 7.17 | 8.74 | Ditto | Light side wind. |
| | | | | | | Ais Gill to Carlisle | 48.387 | 1 | 44 | 44 | ... | 60.5 | 66 | 60 | | | | | | | | |
| | | | | | | Leeds to Carlisle | 113.037 | 1 | 134 | 129 | ... | 50.5 | 52.5 | | | | | | | | | |
| Nov. 8 | Leeds to Carlisle | 9=14½ | 244.6 | 104.6 | 349.2 | Leeds to Ais Gill | 64.65 | 1 | 84 | 84 | 82 | 45.1 | 46.1 | 47.2 | 47.3 | 46.2 | .132 | 3710 | 7.1 | 8.66 | Ditto | Heavy rain; light wind. |
| | | | | | | Ais Gill to Carlisle | 48.387 | 1 | 48 | 48 | 48 | 60.5 | 60.5 | 60.5 | 52.1 | | | | | | | |
| | | | | | | Leeds to Carlisle | 113.037 | 1 | 132 | 130 | 130 | 50.5 | 51.3 | 52.1 | | | | | | | | |
| | | | 250.64 | 104.16 | 354.8 | Leeds to Carlisle | 113.037 | | 134 | 130.53 | 129.05 | 50.5 | 52.08 | 52.48 | | 45.5 | .128 | 3778 | 7.33 | 8.94 | | Mean for above five trips. |

# EXPERIMENTS ON THREE-CYLINDER COMPOUND LOCOMOTIVE; MIDLAND RAILWAY.

## TABLE I. (continued).—PARTICULARS OF WORKING OF COMPOUND ENGINE "No. 2631."

**3.55 P.M., CARLISLE TO LEEDS.**

| DATE | VEHICLES | Mean of Coaches, Passengers, and Luggage (tons) | Engine and Mean of Tender (tons) | Mean of Train, Total (tons) | SECTION OF LINE AND LENGTH | miles | No. of Intermediate Stops and Starts | Booked time (min) | Actual Included (min) | Actual Deducted (min) | Booked speed (m.p.h.) | Actual Included (m.p.h.) | Actual Deducted (m.p.h.) | Coal per Mile (lb) | Coal per Mile per Ton of Mean Total Weight (lb) | Water Total (gals) | Water per lb of Coal (lb) | Water per lb of Coal from and at 212 deg. Fahr. (lb) | Re COAL | GENERAL |
|---|---|---|---|---|---|---|---|---|---|---|---|---|---|---|---|---|---|---|---|---|
| Sept. 16 | Carlisle to Leeds  6=10½ | 173.00 | 107.12 | 290.39 | Carlisle to Blea Moor / Blea Moor to Leeds / Carlisle to Leeds | 59.55 / 53.487 / 113.037 | 5 | 79 / 61 / 140 | 83 / 67 / 135 | 68 / 49 / 117 | 45.2 / 52.6 / 48.4 | 52.5 / 47.6 / 52.5 | 52.5 / 65.4 / 68 | … | … | … | … | … | Particulars of coal and water consumption not taken on this date | Stopped by signals five times between Hellifield and Leeds. |
| Oct. 17 | Carlisle to Leeds  5=9 | 145.9 | 108.3 | 254.2 | Carlisle to Blea Moor / Blea Moor to Leeds / Carlisle to Leeds | 59.55 / 53.487 / 113.037 | … | 79 / 61 / 140 | 75 / 64 / 139 | 75 / 61 / 136 | 45.2 / 52.6 / 48.4 | 47.6 / 50.1 / 47.6 | 47.6 / 52.6 / 50.1 | 28.2 | .111 | 2550 | 8 | 9.76 | Manvers, 40 per cent.; Featherstone, 60 per cent. | Fine. Light wind. Checked by signals between Hellifield and Leeds. |
| Oct. 18 | Carlisle to Leeds  5=9 | 145.9 | 107.1 | 253 | Carlisle to Blea Moor / Blea Moor to Leeds / Carlisle to Leeds | 59.55 / 53.487 / 113.037 | … | 79 / 61 / 140 | 74 / 63 / 137 | 74 / 61 / 135 | 45.2 / 52.6 / 48.4 | 48.8 / 50.9 / 48.8 | 48.2 / 52.6 / 50.1 | 27.3 | .108 | 2685 | 9.35 | 11.4 | Manvers, 35½ per cent.; Featherstone, 64½ per cent. | Fine. Light side wind. Checked by signals between Hellifield and Leeds. |
| Oct. 27 | Carlisle to Leeds  6=10½ | 178.3 | 108.4 | 287.2 | Carlisle to Blea Moor / Blea Moor to Leeds / Carlisle to Leeds | 59.55 / 53.487 / 113.037 | … | 79 / 61 / 140 | 77 / 63 / 140 | 77 / 61 / 138 | 45.2 / 52.6 / 48.4 | 46.4 / 50.9 / 48.4 | 46.4 / 52.6 / 49.1 | 23.4 | .08 | 2750 | 10.4 | 12.6 | Manvers, 30 per cent.; Featherstone, 70 per cent. | Fine. Checked by signals between Hellifield and Leeds. |
| Oct. 29 | Carlisle to Leeds  5=9 | 150.8 | 108 | 258.8 | Carlisle to Blea Moor / Blea Moor to Leeds / Carlisle to Leeds | 59.55 / 53.487 / 113.037 | … | 79 / 61 / 140 | 75 / 63 / 138 | 75 / 60 / 135 | 45.2 / 52.6 / 48.4 | 47.6 / 50.9 / 47.6 | 47.6 / 53.4 / 50.1 | 22.3 | .08 | 2650 | 10.5 | 12.8 | Manvers, 15½ per cent.; Featherstone, 84½ per cent. | Rain. Medium side wind. Checked by signals between Hellifield and Leeds. |
| Oct. 30 | Carlisle to Leeds  5=9 | 145.9 | 108.3 | 254.2 | Carlisle to Blea Moor / Blea Moor to Leeds / Carlisle to Leeds | 59.55 / 53.487 / 113.037 | … | 79 / 61 / 140 | 73 / 65 / 138 | 73 / 61 / 134 | 45.2 / 52.6 / 48.4 | 48.9 / 49.3 / 48.9 | 48.9 / 52.6 / 50.6 | 24.82 | .09 | 2470 | 8.8 | 10.7 | Manvers, 19 per cent.; Featherstone, 81 per cent. | Fine. Checked by signals between Hellifield and Leeds. |
| Nov. 7 | Carlisle to Leeds  5=9 | 148.6 | 106.4 | 255 | Carlisle to Blea Moor / Blea Moor to Leeds / Carlisle to Leeds | 59.55 / 53.487 / 113.037 | … | 79 / 61 / 140 | 75 / 64 / 139 | 75 / 61 / 134 | 45.2 / 52.6 / 48.4 | 47.6 / 50.1 / 48.7 | 47.6 / 52.6 / 50.6 | 26.5 | .104 | 2920 | 9.7 | 11.8 | Manvers, 18 per cent.; Featherstone, 82 per cent. | Heavy side and head wind. Checked by signals between Hellifield and Leeds. |
| … | … | 152.65 | 107.75 | 290.4 | Carlisle to Leeds | 113.037 | … | 140 | 138 | 132.7 | 48.4 | 49.08 | 51.2 | 25.42 | .095 | 2705 | 9.45 | 11.5 | Mean of all above trips for times and speeds, and of six trips for coal and water. | |

## TABLE II.—PARTICULARS OF RUNS.—TRAIN, SPEED, LINE, AND DATE.

| | Leeds to Skipton. | Skipton to Hellifield. | Hellifield to Ais Gill. | Ais Gill to Appleby. | Appleby to Carlisle. | Totals. |
|---|---|---|---|---|---|---|
| **10.6 a.m. Aug. 21, 1902** Miles | 26.187 | 10.013 | 28.45 | 17.187 | 30.8 | 113.037 |
| Coaches, passengers & luggage (Weight) | 390.3 tons | 111.6 tons | … | 239.85 tons | … | … |
| Total | 410.2 " | 230.28 " | … | 344.05 " | … | … |
| Length of train | 271.5 ft. | 518.3 ft. | … | … | … | … |
| Number of axles | 24 | 43 | … | 43 | … | … |
| Time | 44 min. | 17 min. | 38 min. 75 sec. | 38 min. 25 sec.* | 38 min. 38 sec. | 2 hrs. 38 min. |
| Speed | 35.7 | 35.3 | 44 | 49.8 | 42.9 | … |
| Miles | 26.187 | 10.013 | 28.45 | 17.587 | 30.8 | 113.037 |
| **5.33 p.m. Sept. 5, 1902** Coaches, passengers & luggage (Weight) | 592.72 tons | … | 329 tons | 229.2 tons | … | 58.28 |
| Total | 392.22 " | … | 334 " | 485.1 " | … | 113.037 |
| Length of train | … | … | 485.1 ft. | … | 27 min. | 248 tons |
| Number of axles | 45 | … | 43 | 43 | 46.1 | 352 " |
| Time | … | … | 15 min. | 15 min. | 28.45 | 614.8 ft. |
| Speed | … | … | 70.3 | 70.3 | 70.3 | 52 |
| Miles | 26.187 | 10.013 | 28.45 | 17.587 | 30.8 | 113.037 |
| **10 a.m. Oct. 12, 1902** Coaches, passengers & luggage (Weight) | … | … | … | … | … | 248 tons |
| Total | … | … | 37 min. | 15 min. 10 sec. | 26 min. 17 sec.* | 352 " |
| Length of train | … | … | 28.45 | 70.3 | 70.3 | 614.8 ft. |
| Number of axles | 33 min. 15 sec.† | 12 m. 35 sec. | 42 m. 43 sec. | … | … | 52 |
| Time | 47.2 | 48 | 40 | 69.6 | … | 2 hrs. 10 min. 52.15 |
| Speed | … | … | … | … | … | … |

\* Including signal delays and special stop at Lazonby.
† Including 3½ minutes delay running slow, taking on and putting down pilot man at Lees.

## TABLE III.—PARTICULARS OF RUNS.—TRAIN, SPEED, LINE, AND DATE.

| | Carlisle to Ormside. | Ormside to Ais Gill. | Ais Gill to Blea Moor. | Blea Moor to Hellifield. | Hellifield to Skipton. | Skipton to Leeds. | Totals. |
|---|---|---|---|---|---|---|---|
| **3.55 p.m. Aug. 21, 1902** Miles | 33.257 | 15.1 | 11.163 | 7.287 | 10.013 | 26.157 | 113.037 |
| Coaches, passengers & luggage (Weight) | … | … | … | … | … | … | 173.69 tons |
| Total | … | … | … | … | … | … | 280.59 " |
| Length of train | … | … | … | … | … | … | 378.8 ft. |
| Number of axles | … | … | … | … | … | … | 35 |
| Time | 37 min. | 24 min. | 19 min. | 17 min. | 12 min. | 31 min. | 2 hrs. 11 min. |
| Speed | 54 | 37.8 | 60.9 | 60.9 | 50 | 50.6 | 51.7 |
| Miles | 33.257 | 15.1 | 11.163 | 7.287 | 10.013 | 26.157 | 113.037 |
| **3.55 p.m. Sept. 16, 1902** Coaches, passengers & luggage (Weight) | … | … | … | … | … | … | 173.69 tons |
| Total | … | … | … | … | … | … | 280.59 " |
| Length of train | … | … | … | … | … | … | 378.8 ft. |
| Number of axles | … | … | … | … | … | … | 35 |
| Time | 39 min. | 21 min. | 11 min. | 13 min. † | 11 min. | 31 min. | (Carlisle to Hellifield, 81 min.) (Average speed, 56.9) |
| Speed | 55.4 | 43.1 | 60.8 | 79.7 | 60.8 | 26.157 | |
| Miles | 33.257 | 15.1 | 11.163 | 7.287 | 10.013 | 26.157 | 113.037 |
| **4 p.m. Oct. 12, 1902** Coaches, passengers & luggage (Weight) | … | … | … | … | … | … | 248 tons |
| Total | … | … | … | … | … | … | 353.5 " |
| Length of train | … | … | … | … | … | … | 614.8 ft. |
| Number of axles | … | … | … | … | … | … | 52 |
| Time | 41 m. 40 sec. | 23 m. 6 sec. | 12 min. | 14 m. 34 sec. | 9 m. 49 sec. | 29 m. 33 sec. | 2h. 10m. 47s. |
| Speed | 48.3 | 39.2 | 55.8 | 71.2 | 60.9 | 53.02 | 51.87 |

\* Including 3 minutes' delay by signals, running slow from Armley † to Leeds.
† Including time coming to standstill at Hellifield.

# Bibliography

**Journals**

*The Engineer*
*Engineering*
*The Railway Engineer*
*The Railway Gazette*
*The Railway Magazine*
*The Locomotive*
*Railways*
*Institution of Mechanical Engineers*, Proceedings
*Institution of Locomotive Engineers*, Proceedings

**Books**

*Williams's Midland Railway 1876, New Edition 1968*, David & Charles, Newton Abbot
*The Story of the Settle–Carlisle Line*, by Frederick W. Houghton and W. Hubert Foster, Norman Arch Publications, Bradford 1948
*British Locomotives from the Footplate*, O. S. Nock, Ian Allan Ltd 1950
*4000 miles on the Footplate*, O. S. Nock, Ian Allan Ltd 1952
*Main Lines Across the Border*, O. S. Nock and Eric Treacy, Thomas Nelson & Sons, Edinburgh, 1960. New Edition, with all new photographs by Derek Cross, Ian Allan Ltd 1982
*Rails in the Fells*, David Jenkinson, Peco Publications & Publicity Ltd, Beer, Seaton, Devon 1973
*Stations and Structures of the Settle and Carlisle Railway*, V. R. Anderson & G. K. Fox, Oxford Publishing Co., Poole, Dorset 1986.

# Index